Research Methods in
Critical Security Studies

This new textbook surveys new and emergent methods for conducting research in critical security studies, thereby filling a large gap in the literature of this emerging field.

New or critical security studies is growing as a field, but still lacks a clear methodology; the diverse range of the main foci of study (culture, practices, language, or bodies) means that there is little coherence or conversation between these four schools or approaches.

In this ground-breaking collection of fresh and emergent voices, new methods in critical security studies are explored from multiple perspectives, providing practical examples of successful research, design and methodologies. Drawing upon their own experiences and projects, thirty-two authors address the following turns over the course of six comprehensive sections:

- Part I: Research design
- Part II: The ethnographic turn
- Part III: The practice turn
- Part IV: The discursive turn
- Part V: The corporeal turn
- Part VI: The material turn

This book will be essential reading for upper-level students and researchers in the field of critical security studies, and of much interest to students of sociology, ethnography and international relations (IR).

Mark B. Salter is Professor at the School of Political Studies, University of Ottawa, Canada. He is editor of *Mapping Transatlantic Security Relations* (Routledge 2010), and author of *Rights of Passage: The Passport in International Relations* (2003) and *Barbarians and Civilization in International Relations* (2002).

Can E. Mutlu is a PhD candidate (ABD) at the School of Political Studies, University of Ottawa, Canada. He is the Communications Director of the International Political Sociology Section of the International Studies Association (IPS-ISA).

Research Methods in Critical Security Studies

An introduction

**Edited by Mark B. Salter
and Can E. Mutlu**

Routledge
Taylor & Francis Group

LONDON AND NEW YORK

First published 2013
by Routledge
2 Park Square, Milton Park, Abingdon, Oxon, OX14 4RN

Simultaneously published in the USA and Canada
by Routledge
711 Third Avenue, New York, NY 10017

Routledge is an imprint of the Taylor & Francis Group, an informa business

British Library Cataloguing in Publication Data
A catalogue record for this book is available from the British Library.

Library of Congress Cataloging-in-Publication Data
Research methods in critical security studies : an introduction /
edited by Mark B. Salter and Can E. Mutlu.
p. cm.
Includes bibliographical references and index.
1. International relations–Social aspects–Research–Methodology.
2. Security, International–Social aspects–Research–Methodology.
I. Salter, Mark B. II. Mutlu, Can E., 1984–
JZ1251.R48 2012
355'.0330072–dc23
2012018335

ISBN: 978–0–415–53539–7 (hbk)
ISBN: 978–0–415–53540–3 (pbk)
ISBN: 978–0–203–10711–9 (ebk)

Typeset in Times
by Keystroke, Station Road, Codsall, Wolverhampton

MIX
Paper from
responsible sources
FSC
www.fsc.org   FSC® C004839

Printed and bound in Great Britain by
TJ International Ltd, Padstow, Cornwall

Contents

List of illustrations   ix
List of contributors   xi
Acknowledgements   xvii

1 Introduction   1
   MARK B. SALTER

PART I
Research design   **15**

   Introduction   15
   MARK B. SALTER

2 Wondering as research attitude   25
   LUIS LOBO-GUERRERO

3 Criticality   29
   XAVIER GUILLAUME

4 Do you have what it takes? Accounting for emotional and material
   capacities   33
   ANNE-MARIE D'AOUST

5 Attuning to *mess*   37
   VICKI SQUIRE

6 Empiricism without positivism: King Lear and critical security
   studies   42
   ANDREW W. NEAL

7 Engaging collaborative writing critically   46
   MIGUEL DE LARRINAGA AND MARC G. DOUCET

PART II
The ethnographic turn   **51**

   Introduction   51
   MARK B. SALTER

 8 Travelling with ethnography   59
   WANDA VRASTI

 9 Reflexive inquiry   63
   RAHEL KUNZ

10 Listening to migrant stories   67
   HEATHER L. JOHNSON

11 Learning by feeling   72
   JESSE PAUL CRANE-SEEBER

12 How participant observation contributes to the study of (in)security
    practices in conflict zones   76
   JEAN-FRANÇOIS RATELLE

13 Dissident sexualities and the state   80
   MEGAN DAIGLE

PART III
The practice turn   **85**

   Introduction   85
   MARK B. SALTER

14 The practice of writing   93
   HANNAH R. HUGHES

15 Researching anti-deportation: socialization as method   97
   PETER NYERS

16 Act different, think *dispositif*   101
   PHILIPPE BONDITTI

17 Expertise in the aviation security field   105
   MARK B. SALTER

18 Testifying while critical: notes on being an effective gadfly   109
   BENJAMIN J. MULLER

PART IV
The discursive turn   **113**

Introduction   113
CAN E. MUTLU AND MARK B. SALTER

19 Archives   121
LUIS LOBO-GUERRERO

20 Legislative practices   125
ANDREW W. NEAL

21 Medicine and the psy disciplines   129
ALISON HOWELL

22 Speech act theory   133
JUHA A. VUORI

PART V
The corporeal turn   **139**

Introduction   139
CAN E. MUTLU

23 Affect at the airport   149
PHILIPPE M. FROWD AND CHRISTOPHER C. LEITE

24 Emotional optics   154
CAN E. MUTLU

25 Affective terrain: approaching the field in Aamjiwnaang   158
SARAH MARIE WIEBE

26 Theorizing the body in IR   162
ROSEMARY E. SHINKO

27 Reading the maternal body as political event   165
TINA MANAGHAN

28 Corporeal migration   169
TARJA VÄYRYNEN

PART VI
The material turn   **173**

Introduction   173
CAN E. MUTLU

29 Infrastructure   181
CLAUDIA ARADAU

30 The Internet as evocative infrastructure 186
NISHA SHAH

31 The study of drones as objects of security: targeted killing as military
strategy 191
DAVID GRONDIN

32 Objects of security/objects of research: analyzing non-lethal weapons 195
SEANTEL ANAÏS

33 Pictoral texts 199
JUHA A. VUORI

34 Tracing human security assemblages 203
NADINE VOELKNER

Bibliography 207
Index 236

Illustrations

Tables

PI.1   Research design in critical security studies   19
PII.1   Research design in ethnography   51
PII.2   Examples of ethnographic research design   54
PIII.1   Research design in field analysis   85
PIII.2   Examples of research design in field analysis   88
PIV.1   Research design in discourse analysis   113
PIV.2   Examples of discursive research design   117
PV.1   Research design in corporeal approaches   139
PV.2   Emotions and affective reactions   140
PV.3   Examples of corporeal research design   144
PVI.1   Research design in material cultures   173
PVI.2   Examples of material cultures research design   177

Boxes

Bourdieu and the practice turn   4
Foucault and the specific   5
Butler and performativity   7
Latour and the Actor Network Theory   8

Contributors

Seantel Anaïs is an Assistant Professor in the Department of Sociology at the University of Victoria. Her current research program focuses on two areas: critical security studies and critical socio-legal studies. Two of her ongoing research projects address these concerns: the first involves an analysis of the materialities of sites of security by focusing on Cold War nuclear test and training ranges and their post-9/11 transformations; the second focuses on official fatality inquiries and the connection between police use-of-force and emergent psychiatric and medical conditions such as "excited delirium" and "intermittent explosive disorder".

Claudia Aradau is Senior Lecturer in International Relations in the Department of War Studies, King's College London, UK. Her research interrogates the effects of security practices for political subjectivity and emancipation. Most recently, her work has focused on materialities of (in)security, and the role of anticipation for security governance. She is the author of *Rethinking Trafficking in Women: Politics out of Security* (Palgrave 2008) and co-author, with Rens van Munster, of *Politics of Catastrophe: Genealogies of the Unknown* (Routledge 2011).

Philippe Bonditti is Assistant Professor at the Instituto de Relações Internacionais, PUC-Rio (IRI/PUC-Rio, Brazil) and Associate Researcher to the CERI-Sciences Po (Paris, France). He holds a PhD in Political Science (International Relations) from Sciences Po Paris. His research explores the contemporary mutations of political modernity, interrogating the transformation of the practices associated with the modern state sovereignty especially those developed in the scope of "counterterrorism". He is a member of the editorial board of the *Journal Contexto Internacional*.

Jesse Paul Crane-Seeber has a BA in a self-designed major "Resisting Hegemony" from Ithaca College, USA. His dissertation for a PhD in International Relations from American University analyzes the occupation of Iraq in terms of soldiers' embodied interaction and identity negotiation. He did a two-year post-doctorate at Bremen International School of Social Sciences and is now a Teaching Postdoc at North Carolina State University. He has written about US military operations, gender relations and pop-cultural representations of contemporary war. Jesse is currently researching the politics of manhood in the military and writing a book on the occupation of Iraq.

Megan Daigle has recently completed her PhD in the Department of International Politics at Aberystwyth University, UK. She has previously studied at the University of Ottawa, the Institut d'Études Politiques de Grenoble and the Universidad de la Habana. She is currently turning her thesis, for which she did six months' fieldwork in Cuba, into a book with the provisional title, *From Cuba with Love: Sexuality, the Discourse of "Prostitution", and Governance of Bodies in the Post-Soviet Era*.

Anne-Marie D'Aoust is an Assistant Professor at the Université du Québec à Montréal, Canada. Her current research focuses on the problematization of marriage migration by various states, and theoretically reflects on the ways in which love, as an emotion, is being used as a complex technology of control, risk management, and empowerment of migrants. In collaboration with William Walters, she is also working on a long-term research project entitled "Security and Its Publics", which explores the dynamics of the legitimation and contestation of security programs and policies in diverse fields, as well as the cultural, legal, and political practices of making things public.

Marc G. Doucet is Associate Professor at Saint Mary's University, Canada, where he has been teaching in the Department of Political Science since 2000. His areas of research have included international relations theory, radical democracy, and the alter-globalization movement. His current research draws from recent literature on biopower and sovereign power in order to examine contemporary forms of international intervention. He is the co-editor of *Security and Global Governmentality: Globalization, Governance and the State* and has published articles in *Review of Constitutional Studies, Security Dialogue, Theory & Event, Contemporary Political Theory, Millennium: Journal of International Studies, Alternatives: Global, Local, Political*, and *Global Society: Journal of Interdisciplinary International Relations*.

Philippe M. Frowd is a doctoral student in International Relations in the Department of Political Science at McMaster University, Canada. His dissertation research centres on the growing adoption of biometric identification systems in the context of security and surveillance practices in the global south. His work specifically examines how identity management practices in sub-Saharan Africa are framed through the discourse of development, and how transnational security cooperation shapes identification and border control policies. More generally, his research interests include international relations theory, surveillance studies, the regulation of mobility, and citizenship.

David Grondin is Professor at the School of Political Studies of the University of Ottawa, Canada. He recently edited a special issue in *Geopolitics* and is the Associate editor of *War Beyond the Battlefield* (Routledge 2012). His current research focuses on the impact of the "revolution in military affairs" on imagining the US ways of war. This led him to sift through militainment (the synergy of the entertainment industry with the military) to explore the close links between science fiction, the entertainment industry (video games and Hollywood cinema), robotics and the defence industries (drones and supersoldiers), and the Pentagon (especially the crucial role of DARPA).

Xavier Guillaume is Lecturer in International Relations at the University of Edinburgh. He specializes in international political and social theory, with a focus on problématiques pertaining to the identity/alterity and citizenship/security nexuses. His most recent publications include his first monograph, *International Relations and Identity* (Routledge 2011), "From Process to Politics" (*International Political Sociology* 2009), "Travelogues of Difference: IR Theory and Travel Literature" (*Alternatives: Global, Local, Political* 2011), and "Resistance and the International: The Challenge of the Everyday" (*International Political Sociology* 2011).

Alison Howell is a Post-Doctoral Research Fellow at the Humanitarian and Conflict Response Institute (HCRI) at the University of Manchester, UK, where she is also Director of External Relations. She previously held a Social Sciences and Humanities Research Council of Canada Post-Doctoral Fellowship in Politics at Manchester, and a Fulbright Scholar and Distinguished Chair at Brown and SUNY. Her book, *Madness in International Relations: Psychology, Security and the Global Governance of Mental Health*, was published by Routledge in 2011. Her research spans the fields of critical security studies, the political sociology of health and medicine, war and military studies, and humanitarianism.

Hannah R. Hughes is a PhD student in the International Politics Department at Aberystwyth University, UK and Researcher for the Centre of Health and International Relations (CHAIR), Aberystwyth University, UK. The central focus of her research is the conceptualization of climate change as a social and political issue, which she has explored through a study of the Intergovernmental Panel on Climate Change (IPCC). Her interest in climate change and the sociological approach of Pierre Bourdieu has forced her to continually re-evaluate the methodological tools she employs as she grapples to understand and interrogate this complex issue.

Heather L. Johnson holds the post of Lecturer in the School of Politics, International Studies and Philosophy at Queen's University Belfast, UK, having received her PhD from McMaster University in 2011. Her dissertation, entitled *Borders, Migration, Agency: Re-Imagining Global Non-Citizenship in Irregularity* is based upon field work in 2007–2008 and investigates the politics of political agency and non-citizenship for refugees and asylum seekers as they encounter border control regimes in Tanzania, Spain, Morocco, and Australia. She examines how mobile individuals both participate in, and challenge, the shaping of the global refugee regime. Recent work appears in *Third World Quarterly*.

Rahel Kunz is Lecturer at the Institute of Political and International Studies, University of Lausanne, Switzerland. Her main research interests are the governance of international migration, gender issues in migration and development, gender and security sector reform, and feminist and post-structuralist theories. She has published articles in the *Journal of European Integration*, the *Review of International Political Economy*, and *Third World Quarterly*, is the author of *The Political Economy of Global Remittances: Gender, Governmentality and Neoliberalism* (Routledge 2011) and co-editor of *Multilayered Migration Governance: The Promise of Partnership* (Routledge 2011) with S. Lavenex and M. Panizzon.

Miguel de Larrinaga is Assistant Professor at the University of Ottawa, Canada. His research focuses on the deployment of discourses and practices of security broadly understood. He has worked on human security issues, the weaponization of space and security, and global governmentality. Presently, he is working on projects related to the political sociology of security studies, non-lethal weapons and international intervention in relation to sovereign power, biopower, and disciplinary power. He is co-editor of *Security and Global Governmentality: Globalization, Governance and the State* and has published articles in *Canadian Foreign Policy, Security Dialogue, International Journal, Alternatives: Global, Local, Political, Geopolitics* along with a variety of chapters in edited volumes.

Christopher C. Leite is a doctoral student in International Relations and Modern Political Thought in the School of Political Studies at the University of Ottawa, Canada. His dissertation research focuses on the links between the use of "Rapid Reaction" rhetoric by institutions of the European Union (EU), practices of risk management, and processes of legitimization of public authority. More specifically, his work looks at the foreign, military, immigration, and crisis management policies of the EU. His more general research interests include international relations theory, social and political theory, critical security studies, and European politics.

Luis Lobo-Guerrero is Senior Lecturer in International Relations at Royal Holloway, University of London, UK. He has been Visiting Professor at the University of Hamburg and Visiting Research Fellow at King's College London. His work is a problematization of the political economy of security which he has explored by focusing on technologies of risk such as insurance. He is the author of *Insuring Security: Biopolitics, Security and Risk* (Routledge 2011) and *Insuring War: Sovereignty, Security and Risk* (Routledge 2012). He is currently completing the third volume of the trilogy entitled *Insuring Life: Value, Security and Risk*.

Tina Managhan is a Senior Lecturer in International Relations at Oxford Brookes University, UK. She completed her PhD at York University, Canada and specializes in the areas of critical security studies, gender, international relations, identity politics, and US foreign policy. Her recent publications include *Gender, Agency, War: The Maternalized Body in U.S. Foreign Policy* (Routledge 2012) and articles in *Review of International Studies* and *Geopolitics*.

Benjamin J. Muller is Associate Professor of Political Science at King's University College, Canada, and a member of the Centre for American Studies at Western University, Canada. Muller has taught at Queen's University Belfast, the University of Victoria, Simon Fraser University, and held a visiting research fellowship at the Border Policy Research Institute at Western Washington University. He has provided expert testimony to the Canadian Parliament and provided research for NATO and the EU. In addition to his monograph, *Risk, Security, and the Biometric State: Governing Borders and Bodies* (Routledge 2010), he has contributed chapters in a number of edited collections and published in various academic journals including *Security Dialogue, Citizenship Studies, Geopolitics,* and *Studies in Social Justice*.

Can E. Mutlu is a PhD candidate at the School of Political Studies at the University of Ottawa, Canada, specializing in International Relations. He is the Communications Director of the International Political Sociology Section of International Studies Association (IPS-ISA), member of the visuality cluster of the ESRC funded International Collaboratory on Critical Methods in Security Studies (ICCM), a member of the editorial and communications team for the journal *International Political Sociology*, and a founding member of the *Canadian Critical Security Studies Network*. His recent research appears in *Comparative European Politics, European Journal of Social Theory* and *Environment and Planning D: Society and Space*.

Andrew W. Neal is Lecturer in Politics and International Relations at the University of Edinburgh. He is author of *Exceptionalism and the Politics of Counter-Terrorism: Liberty, Security and the War on Terror* (Routledge 2010) and co-editor (with Michael Dillon) of *Foucault on Politics, Security and War* (Palgrave 2008). He is a founding executive member of the International Studies Association Theory Section and was co-investigator in the ESRC training network "An International Collaboratory on Critical Methods in Security Studies". He served on the *International Political Sociology* editorial team from 2006 to 2011 and is currently on the editorial board of *Security Dialogue*.

Peter Nyers is Associate Professor of the Politics of Citizenship and Intercultural Relations with the Department of Political Science at McMaster University, Canada. His research focuses on the social movements of non-status refugees and migrants, in particular their campaigns against deportation and detention and for regularization and global mobility rights. He is the author of *Rethinking Refugees: Beyond States of Emergency* (Routledge 2006), co-editor of *Citizenship between Past and Future* (Routledge 2008) and *Citizenship, Migrant Activism and the Politics of Movement* (Routledge 2012), and editor of *Securitizations of Citizenship* (Routledge 2009). He serves as the associate editor of *Citizenship Studies*.

Jean-François Ratelle is a PhD candidate in Political Science at the University of Ottawa, Canada. His dissertation deals with Islamic radicalization, political violence and (in)security practices in the North Caucasus. He conducted thirteen months of ethnographical research in Russia including six months in the North Caucasus (Dagestan, Chechnya, and Kabardino-Balkaria). His main research interests include the micro-dynamics of political violence, Islamic radicalization, civil wars, terrorism, and the North Caucasus.

Mark B. Salter is Professor at the School of Political Studies, University of Ottawa, Canada. He is editor of *Politics at the Airport* and *Mapping Transatlantic Security Relations* and the sole author of *Rights of Passage: The Passport in International Relations* and *Barbarians and Civilization in International Relations*. Recent research appears in *Geopolitics*, *Political Geography*, *International Political Sociology*, *Security Dialogue*, and *The European Journal of Social Theory*. Salter is associate editor for *International Political Sociology* and *Security Dialogue*.

Nisha Shah is Assistant Professor in the School of Political Studies at the University of Ottawa, Canada. Her research explores the role of material objects and artefacts in world politics, which she examines by considering how and why things such as technological instruments and physical geographies become important political and ethical components in the historical evolution of frameworks of governance and war. She has published articles in *Security Dialogue*, *International Political Sociology*, *Political Geography*, *Globalizations*, and *International Journal of Media and Cultural Politics*, and is co-editor of *Metaphors of Globalization: Mirrors, Magicians and Mutinies* (Palgrave 2008).

Rosemary E. Shinko is Professorial Lecturer at American University, USA. She received her PhD from the University of Connecticut, USA and her doctoral research focused on deconstructive approaches to the study of sovereignty. Professor Shinko is a postmodern International Relations theorist and has published articles in the *Columbia Journal of International Affairs*, *International Studies Perspectives*, *International Studies Association Encyclopedia*, and *Millennium, Journal of International Studies*. She has also authored several book chapters and is at work on a co-authored book on International Relations Theory and her own book on postmodern approaches to the study of International Relations.

Vicki Squire is currently Associate Professor in International Security at University of Warwick, UK, having been an RCUK research fellow at the Department of Politics and

International Studies and at the Centre of Citizenship Identities and Governance, Open University. Her research crosses the fields of critical citizenship, migration, and security studies, reflecting her interest in the materialization, development, and transformation of socio-political formations and subjectivities under conditions of intensified mobility. Squire is author of *The Exclusionary Politics of Asylum* (Palgrave 2009), editor of *The Contested Politics of Mobility* (Routledge 2011), and assistant editor of the journal *Citizenship Studies*.

Tarja Väyrynen is Academy Research Fellow at the University of Tampere, Finland. Her current research deals with post-conflict trauma politics, hegemonic history-writing, and silence. She is leading a research group on corporeality, movement and politics (COMPORE) and has recently published in *Body & Society*, *European Journal of Women's Studies* and *Millennium: Journal of International Studies*.

Nadine Voelkner is a DPhil candidate in International Relations at the University of Sussex, UK. Her research revolves around understanding the political in the governance of global health and migration for which she has drawn on Foucault and Deleuze. She has a particular theoretical and methodological interest in the role of materiality in (global) governance systems. She has recently published on these themes including in the form of "managing pathogenic circulation" as well as the securitization of disease. She is a co-investigator to the International Collaboratory on Critical Methods in Security Studies (ICCM).

Wanda Vrasti is Humboldt post-doctoral fellow at Humboldt University, Berlin. Her work broadly covers governmentality studies, autonomist Marxist and anarchist critiques of capital, and the politics of everyday life as it pertains to issues of labour and leisure. Her ethnographic investigation of *Volunteer Tourism in the Global South: Giving Back in Neoliberal Times* was published by Routledge in 2012. Previous works have been published in *Millennium: Journal of International Studies, Review of International Studies*, and *Theory & Event*.

Juha A. Vuori is a University Lecturer at the Department of Political Science and Contemporary History at the University of Turku, Finland. His main research focus has been on the critical development of securitization theory through illocutionary logic, semiotics, and the application of approach to the People's Republic of China. He has edited a number of books and published in journals such as *European Journal of International Relations, Security Dialogue, Asian Journal of Political Science, Issues & Studies*, and *Politologiske Studier*. He is the president of the Finnish International Studies Association and former editor in chief of *Kosmopolis*.

Sarah Marie Wiebe is a PhD Candidate in the School of Political Studies, University of Ottawa, Canada. Her areas of expertise include Canadian Politics and Public Administration. She has published on the politics of reproduction and reproductive justice, biopolitics, security, and body theory. Her dissertation, entitled: *Anatomy of Place: Ecological Citizenship in Canada's Chemical Valley* employs interpretive research methods and political ethnography. Her ongoing research with citizens of the Aamjiwnaang First Nation examines the contested nature of a perceived pollution problem and the impact on the well-being of this community.

Acknowledgements

The Editors would like to acknowledge the support of the Social Sciences and Research Council of Canada, the Faculty of Social Science and the Research Development Program (Vice-President Research) at the University of Ottawa. With their support, the University of Ottawa hosted a workshop, "New Methodologies in Critical Security Studies", 14–15 March 2011, which became the core of this book and provided editorial support for its publication.

We would like to acknowledge the intellectual and professional support of our colleagues: Miguel de Larrinaga and David Grondin were co-organizers of the initial workshop and have provided constant intellectual support. J. Peter Burgess was encouraging from the earliest stages of this project. In Europe, a similar project was led by Jef Huysmans, Claudia Aradau, Andrew Neal, and Nadine Voelkner, the International Collaboratory on Critical Methodologies (ICCM) in Security Studies, an ESRC funded project (RES-810-021-0072). While a number of scholars are involved in both projects, the ICCM tackles the epistemology question head-on rather than the design of the methods themselves, and our aim was to talk more specifically about research design. We appreciate that both of these projects run in the same direction, and appreciate the generous view of the academy that fosters the kind of dialogue we have had between the two projects. The anonymous reviewers were also very generous with their time and critical view, which made the project much stronger and for which we are grateful.

The book was also made possible by the close and sympathetic friendship and intellectual partnership between the Editors, and the interest, support and hard work of the contributing authors. We would like to thank Christopher Leite for editorial support. Adam Sandor also provided logistical support for the initial workshop. Andrew Humphrys and the team at Routledge have been extremely enthusiastic about this project, and we appreciate their advocacy.

1 Introduction

Mark B. Salter

Our core motivation behind this project was a desire to champion clear research design and rigorous method in critical security studies. As a reflexive field, engaging with security practices and mainstream academic accounts of these practices, critical security studies have placed more emphasis on being critical of the established paradigms and practices and less emphasis on clarity and method. With this book, we wanted to start seriously thinking about two questions: "How do we do the kind of research we do?" and "How can others produce similar research projects?" To answer these questions, as editors, we pushed the contributors to focus on four general areas of designing critical inquiry: The *object of research*, *research question*, *research design*, and *results and challenges of conducting of research*.

The result was thirty-four short chapters by thirty-two authors from around the world, structured around six sections. Each of these methodological turns – ethnographic, practice, discursive, corporeal, and material – has a concise overview written by the editors, and multiple examples for how this tool has been used in particular research designs. The authors demonstrate the varied ways that these tools can be used through different projects and set out some of the advantages and pitfalls for their use. We asked each contributor to present a different case study, a different perspective, to one of these approaches that they are known for. We have brought together some more established scholars of the field with promising young scholars who will shape the direction of critical security studies in the years to come. More importantly, we hope that this book will also inspire other students of the field to pay attention to these questions of clarity and rigour surrounding methodology and research design. This introduction sets the groundwork by interrogating the two key terms: critique and inquiry.

Being critical

Within the critical community, there is a vigorous debate about both the content and the politics of the term *critical*. As political scientists, sociologists of the international, or theorists, we cannot feign ignorance of the workings of power and exclusion inherent in the identification of an *us* and a *them*. Part of the common consensus about criticality is that there are not six principles that one can sign up for to separate true criticality from some deviation from the norm (as there was with Morgenthau's program for realism). The objects of research vary greatly: the change in particular policies or strategies of government, the overt politicization of individuals and groups, the functioning of bureaucracies and non-state organizations, linguistic and ideational formations, the agency of non-human actants, and the technologization of emotions into global governance. By focusing on research design and critique, we are highlighting methodological questions over ontological abstraction: how we do what we do, rather than the nature of doing. We can identify some similar postures, the ways that researchers position themselves in respect to their object of study.

Four postures of critical inquiry

1   Social and political life is messy: our analyses must reflect our belief that we cannot identify any single unifying principle in social and political life; methodological pluralism is a hallmark of this belief.
2   Agency – the capacity to act – is everywhere: it can be found in individuals, groups, states, ideational structures, and non-human actants.
3   Causality is emergent, rather than efficient: analyses set out the conditions of possibility for a set of politics, identities, or policies, rather than a single or complex source.
4   Research, writing, and public engagement are inherently political: we understand politics in its broadest sense to mean questions concerning justice, power, and authority; critical scholarship means an active engagement with the world.

Openness to the world is a characteristic of all social scientific inquiry, but what is unique about these four critical postures is a tendency towards self-undermining. This Socratic irony is a familiar rhetorical device in the Platonic Dialogues: Socrates feigns ignorance or more specifically accepts the argument of his interlocutors in order to expose its inherent contradictions; Socrates is constantly undoing the authority of his own assertions. Contemporary critical scholars are also fond of Socratic irony, in particular, emphasizing the openness or serendipitous nature of their methods, which may appear as weakness to more traditional scholars. The expression of self-doubt comes from a reluctance to be programmatic, schematic, or prescriptive, which many critics of liberal thought have accused as being ideological, imperialism, or at the very least exclusionary. This description of the limits of one's own tools is understood amongst the community to be its greatest strength, avoiding the moral sin of hubris or the political sin of exclusion. "We have no research program", critical scholars often aver, but the intended meaning is: to have a research program is to endorse a political position and close off innovation, emancipation, critique, or discovery.

Inquiry

We do not cede rigour, and wish to retain an openness to the empirical field. One persistent question which arises in our research practice is: if we are open to the complexity of the object of our research, how do we know when we are finished? Within an interpretivist frame, what counts as sufficiency, coherence, or criticality? Let us take three examples of dominant methodologies and the problems of inquiry. Separate from the philosophical questions about the unknownability or unpredictability of experience, interpretivism does not have the pat answers to the questions of sufficiency, coherence, and proof that scientism offers. What is a defensible amount of data? How is the internal argument defended? What counts as corroboration? Positivistic social science can offer internal and external tests: logic, evidence, and modelling alternative explanations. Interpretivist methods, such as ethnography, field analysis, genealogy, or somatic enquiry marshal these tests in radically different ways. With this collection, we argue that there is over twenty years of solid work that demonstrates the utility, efficacy, and political relevance of these methods, and we might move forward without reinventing critical inquiry in each intervention.

We offer a new set of tools, or rather tools that are relatively new to IR: discourse, field analysis, ethnography, the study of affect and the somatic, and neomaterialist object analysis. Starting from the reflexivist position, we argue that the world is given through our methods of studying it, but that it is not all language, that is, to say that everything is discursive does not mean to imply that the world is reducible to language. The collaborators within this book demonstrate through their own research design how material, discursive, and somatic practices interpolate our professional and political practices.

Our research is driven by an emergent notion of causality. Connolly argues that we can "challenge the sufficiency of both efficient models of causality in social science and acausal images of mutual constitution in interpretive theory" (Connolly 2004: 342). The careful genealogies of sovereign power or the field analyses of security practices have shown clearly that the model of efficient causality cannot explain or understand change in these social and political practices. Nor are we content to describe change or structure as if there were no power inequalities, or that all linguistic events or practices are equally effective. Both of these models underplay resistance and recursion, and indeed the contingent notion of politics, which is at the heart of change. Connolly's understanding of emergent causality then allows for the dispositions of discourses, institutions, structures, and agents to render some paths possible. Empirically, we would argue that this model better approximates what we can know about social and political fields, without attempting a general theory of all discourses, institutions, structures, or agents.

The ethnographic turn

Inspired by Geertz, ethnography can be defined as "thick description" (1973: 5) of a personal encounter between the researcher and another culture. More emphatically, it represents both a research method of immersion and encounter, and a writing style that specifically puts the researcher in the text. Fundamentally self-reflexive, the question of criticality is embedded within the genre of ethnographic writing. The answers to the questions of sufficiency and coherence, however, are less clear: what is a sufficient description of this encounter? If the subject of the ethnography is the encounter, what is a sufficient amount of material, data, experience, affect that is understood as authoritative? We distinguish our scholarly work as different from investigative journalists or documentarians – but is that simply in the style of writing, the discipline with which we write or organize our field notes, our interactions with the studied culture? What is a coherent account of the encounter?

The practice turn

Articulated by Bourdieu, the meanings of discourses and practices are assumed to come from their use within specific fields. The field is a social space in which actors compete, struggle, cooperate, and interact, according to particular "rules of the game". Certain underlying laws or principles, given meaning by the habitus, govern the field: "a system of cognitive and motivating structures" (Bourdieu 1990a: 53). Understood as a "generative grammar able to produce an infinite number of new sentences according to determinate patterns and within determinate limits", the habitus as a "structured structure" nevertheless can encounter objective structures, such as space or economic system (Bourdieu 2005: 30–31). To make visible the habitus and particular relations of struggle, competition, and dominance, analysts point to informal knowledge, social positions, and networks, the analysis of which is led by the agents engaged in the social field. The question of coherence, then, is more easily answered: the field is constituted by the boundaries of self-identification, evidenced by professional practices. But the questions of sufficiency and criticality persist. In practical terms, the research strategy involves identifying a professional field, understanding the "rules of the game" through language, practices, and informal knowledge, and identifying the struggles for different kinds of economic, symbolic, and political capital. Sufficiency of data is also easier to demonstrate, because one can identify the rules of the game and the dominant struggles in a way that is more easily replicated by other scholars, although this is limited because the habitus is always in flux, always relating to objective structures. However, gaining access to a new field, and coming to understand the language, politics, and bureaucratic games, has the effect of potentially compromising the criticality of the researcher. When Der Derian goes on manoeuvers with the American military, or Bigo speaks to European policing agencies, they often reaffirm their criticality in their scholarly work – in other words, they need to demonstrate involvement in and loyalty also to the academic field. If the researcher is always already using the language of the professionals, how can one design a critical field analysis?

Bourdieu and the practice turn

Sociology Professor at the Collège de France and Director of the Centre de Sociologie Européenne, Pierre Bourdieu is an important figure in critical security studies through what has been termed the *practice turn*. Bourdieu's key thinking tools (which he opposed to theories), capital, field, and habitus, his commitment to the rigour of sociological analysis, and his self-reflexive public engagement, are all increasingly used in constructivist and critical IR debates. Anti-reductionist, Bourdieu seeks to move beyond a dualist agent-structure explanation of society, and focuses on practices.

Bourdieu first establishes that the scholar can identify many forms of capital: social, cultural, and symbolic. Similar to economic capital that allows for investment or consumption, or political capital that allows for policy or public decisions, social, cultural, and symbolic capital can be accrued and spent, which allows for certain kinds of actions, and plays a role in struggles or contestations for scarce resources or authority claims. Empirically, this can help explain differences in influence or outcome that cannot be explained by economic or political disparities.

Bourdieu uses the term *field* to identify autonomous spheres of society, such as education, journalism, politics, etc. He argues that each field has its own independent rules of the game, which is a kind of generative grammar: the field is not defined simply structurally by institutions, laws, or norms, nor is it constructed simply by the actions of its participants. Rather, the field is defined by a generative grammar, a set of principles by which all possible rules and behaviours are described, often recursively, "that's business/politics/art for you". Fields are characterized by struggle, competition, cooperation, hegemony, and transversal relations.

The everyday practices, and common-sense, of these fields constitute the *habitus* – the feel of a particular field, which gave a sense of what was possible, the internalization of the structure of the field. Bourdieu often wrote about fields in which he was engaged, such as *Homo Academicus* or *The Algerians*, and some degree of immersion is necessary to understand the quotidian, common-sense of the field (also defined as doxa). Bourdieu was also deeply concerned with the body and the way that bodily practices were shaped. Thus, he was interested in the ways that social distinctions were embodied in taste, opinions, and daily practices.

In critical security studies, the practice turn has come from two directions: constructivists seeking ways of operationalizing Wendt's structuration theory (Pouliot 2010, Adler and Pouliot 2011), and scholars driven by empirical changes in security practices (Bigo 1996, Williams 2007). The work of diplomats or security officials, for example, must be understood as conforming to certain rules and incentives, as well as struggles and disequilibria, within the field of diplomacy or particular institutions, that have to do with the distribution of social, cultural, and symbolic capital as much as the distribution of raw economic or political capital. The practice turn is discussed in Section III.

The discursive turn

Inspired by Nietzsche and Foucault, a genealogy "will cultivate the details and accidents that accompany every beginning; it will be scrupulously attentive to their petty malice; it will await their emergence, once unmasked, as the face of the other" (Foucault 1997b: 144). Genealogy is not a search for authorized, originary moments of a particular set of practices or politics; rather there is a focus on the breaks, silences, and disruptions in a discourse, institutions, and practices (Vucetic 2011). Even in their meticulous and encyclopedic details, how, then, do we compare different genealogies? What is sufficient proof for a successful genealogy? Unlike traditional histories, which might be disrupted by the discovery of a new archival cache, what fresh evidence could disrupt the narrative of Der Derian's *On Diplomacy* (1987) or Bartelson's *Genealogy of Sovereignty* (1995)? If they are not replicable in the same experimental sense, how do we grant these new narratives authority? The question of criticality is inherent in the form, in contrast to dominant historical narratives, where genealogy is always reflexive, undermining the very authority that the tests of coherence and sufficiency might grant. From a research design point-of-view, however, this question poses a fundamental challenge: what is a sufficient or coherent genealogy?

Foucault and the specific

Collège de France lecturer Michel Foucault is one of the most important thinkers in the pantheon of critical security studies, who repeatedly engaged with the question of method. He was a public intellectual, and often commented on that role and the milieu of contemporary French society, connecting his academic production to contemporary issues or struggles. At root, Foucault is concerned with the facilitating conditions of possibility for a particular set of power relations. Based on his early work *Archeology of Knowledge*, Foucault privileged a very wide understanding of discourse: "practices that systematically form the objects of which they speak" (1972: 49). Not just the words or the signs about the object (madness, prisons, or sexuality), but the practices that made statements and decisions about those objects possible. For Foucauldian critical security studies, then, the question is: what are the practices that make it possible to speak about a common object called security?

Deeply concerned with the production of knowledge, norms, and power, Foucault argued that political science had over-emphasized the figure of the sovereign, and that power must be understood to be both repressive and positive. In his analyses of the phenomenon of madness and psychiatry, the evolution of the prison system in France, or the discourses about self and sexuality, Foucault continually avoids and criticizes reductionist accounts: his method is "an *ascending* analysis of power, starting, that is, from its infinitesimal mechanisms, which each have their own trajectory, their own techniques and tactics, and then see how these mechanisms of power have been – and continue to be – invested, colonised, utilised, involuted, transformed, displaced, extended, etc., by ever more general mechanisms and by forms of global domination" (1980: 97). Through his analysis of *governmentality*, for example, the rule of a population through statistics, the question of insurance and risk become models of quotidian practices of knowledge/power creation that have definite political, economic, and social effects. Between the concern of the mutual constitution of power/ knowledge, the definition of power as circulatory and networked, and the focus on practices of authorization, subjugation, and subjectivization, Foucauldian analysis often starts with bodily practices – or more specifically, the way that the body is described, inscribed, given meaning, and disciplined to perform particular social, economic, and political functions. He examines through these particular discourses of madness, criminality, and sexuality how "the body is molded by a great many distinct regimes: it is broken down by the rhythms of work, rest, and holidays; it is poisoned by food or values, through eating habits or moral laws; it constructs resistances" (1998: 380).

Foucault often identifies his work as *genealogical*, that is, in the Nietzschean tradition of "gray, patient, meticulous, and patiently documentary" (1998: 369). Rather than a quest for the pure originary moment of origin of a particular discourse, the purpose of genealogy "is to identify the accident, the minute deviations – or conversely, the complete reversals – the errors, the false appraisals, and the faulty calculations that gave birth to those things which continue to exist and have value for us" (1998: 374). As a method, genealogy is precisely a genre of critique ". . .showing that things are not as obvious as people believe, making it so that what is taken for granted is no longer taken for granted. To do criticism is to make harder those acts which are now too easy . . . it is a matter of making conflicts more visible, of making them more essential than clashes of interest or mere institutional blockages" (2000: 456–457). Foucault then often aims to write a non-teleological *history of the present*, which does not presume that the present was the only possible future.

In critical security studies, Foucault has inspired many studies into the daily prac- tices, discourses, and mechanisms of security. In addition to Bartelson's *Genealogy of Sovereignty* (1995) and Campbell's *Writing Security* (1998), we can also point to Isin's *Being Political: Genealogies of Citizenship* (2002) and Lobo-Guerrero's *Insuring Security* (2010). The wider questions of productive power and the analysis of power/knowledge networks have, of course, been widely addressed, as can be seen through this book.

The corporeal turn

Fresh work on the affective and somatic has migrated from social and cultural theory into IR, focusing on the role of the body, emotions, and affect. Indebted to feminist scholarship and poststructuralist work inspired by Foucault, corporeal approaches examine the way that the body is both a site of politics and a site of resistance. Whether derived from Connolly's engagement with neuroscience and the brain/body relationship in *Neuropolitics* (2002) or from Butler's work on sexuality and the corporeal *Gender Trouble* (1999), a growing number of scholars are bringing the question of emotion, affect, and the somatic into political and critical focus, often pinpointing evidence in rhetoric, public discourse, regulations and law, practice, experience, autobiography, and popular culture. Scholars have not come to a consensus on how to do this kind of work; there is no consensus on the best or optimal kind of research design for corporeal study. If one of the primary epistemological foundations of IR, and security studies, has been rationalism, unpacking both the unitary subject and the way of thinking about thinking has a powerful critical potential. There is, however, a gap between the philosophical criticism of the rational modern subject in Butler and Connolly, and methodologically-individualist studies in this field about particular bodies and the construction of national identities. While internal coherence or logical consistency remain clear tests in this emergent literature, it is not clear what counts as sufficient. What is proof of bodily experience, or affect? How do we measure the difference between affective reactions? How do we generalize the insights of neuroscience to politics?

Butler and performativity

Judith Butler is a poststructuralist social theorist who has primarily contributed to the fields of feminism, queer theory, and political philosophy. Butler's work has been widely referenced across numerous branches of social sciences and humanities. Butler, however, is most famously known for her work on the concept of *performativity* in relation to subjectivity, gender, and sexuality. Performativity, in this case, refers to types of expressive action or practice used in performing a type of being or identity. These expressive actions of performativity are an essential part of one's core identity; in fact, performativity is the *practice* of construction of identity. Given Butler's emphasis on repetitive expressive actions as core of one's identity, the concept of performativity presents a direct critique of gender analysis solely based on discursive methods.

While Butler's discussion of performativity focuses on the construction of our gendered and sexualized identities, the concept lends itself to discussing various intersubjectivities such as race, colonialism, or ethnicity among other identity markers. Whereas for Butler gender and sexuality are performative acts, they are involuntary choices that are shaped by "regulative discourses" that disciplines the subject to conform to certain societal norms and expectations associated with a given identity. In this line of argument, Butler relies heavily on Foucault and influential psychoanalysts such as Freud and Lacan.

In particular, with the concept of performativity, Butler challenges the binary biological accounts of gender and sexuality – male/female, masculine/feminine – arguing that these categories are socially constructed and not *natural* or *biological*

givens. In *Gender Trouble* (1999) Butler problematizes these concepts using a combination of discourse analysis, genealogy, and psychoanalytical concepts.

In political science proper, research projects using performativity often focus on the
formation of intersubjectivities. In particular, this approach lends itself to more critical
approaches such as feminisms, post-colonialisms, and psy-approaches. In critical
security studies, performativity is often used in practice-driven research that focuses
on formation of intersubjectivities in instances such as the role of training/formative
periods on socialization of individuals into a certain field or identity marker. In this
book, we see a good example of the kind of research in Crane-Seeber's chapter
(Chapter 11), on his autobiographical account of how he interprets the transformation
of his gendered (inter)subjectivity in relation to enlisted marines. Similarly, Shinko
(Chapter 26) and Managhan's (Chapter 27) chapters use Butler's works as an
inspiration.

In recent years, beyond her work on performativity, Butler's argument on the petty-
sovereign in *Precarious Life* (2004) found a wide audience in critical security studies.
The petty-sovereign presents a direct challenge to the legally deterministic account of
sovereign power in the literature on political exceptionalism. In particular, her point
on the diverse range of identities and performativies, and their significance for
everyday practices of exceptional measures presents a methodological challenge for
scholars relying solely on discourse analysis to study exceptional measures.

The material turn

Object-analysis, or neomaterialism in some versions, examines complex assemblages of
things and humans, refusing to privilege the human. This emergent literature often focuses
on a particular site or a particular problem field: Latour and Woolgar examine the production
of scientific facts *in situ* in *Laboratory Life* (1979), Bennett's *Vibrant Matter* (2010) looks at
the 2003 North American power outage, and de Goede traces the financial-security assemblage (2012). However, unlike field analysis, it is unclear how these kinds of analyses can
ever be finished or compared. What could be a sufficient demonstration of an assemblage?
How can we tell what things count?

Latour and the Actor Network Theory

Bruno Latour and his colleague Michel Callon from the Centre de Sociologie de
l'Innovation (Center for Sociology of Innovation) at the École nationale supérieure
des mines de Paris, along with John Law, are credited for the innovative approach to
the study of material-semiotic networks, also known as the Actor Network Theory
(ANT). Although referred to as a *theory*, the ANT does not so much offer a theory, but
rather a *method* to account for the emergence and continuous transformations of
material-semiotic networks. In particular, ANT focuses on how different actor-
networks – emerging from relations among actants – come together and act as a whole

through anthropological, or practice-driven research that includes a combination of methods such as participant observation, discourse analysis, and mapping. Similarly, ANT has developed, or incorporated from other branches of Science and Technology Studies (STS), a unique set of methods and concepts that include: notions of translation, generalized symmetry, and scientometric tools used to map innovations in science and technology.

While the ANT is often considered to be a part of the practice turn in social sciences and humanities, Latour et al.'s insistency on the agency of non-humans, is both a critique of more established sociological approaches focusing on practice – such as Bourdieusian approaches covered in Chapter 3 of this book – and an attempt to broaden the agency within the broader practice turn to include non-humans as *actants*. While critiques of ANT, have often focused on human intentionality to establish a quantifiable distinction between human and non-human actants, ANT scholars have maintained their position that intentionality does not play a central role in their approach that focuses on relationalities; their use of the term agency does not presuppose intentionality.

ANT does not simply place emphasis on the agency of actants – in terms of their status, or power – but instead focuses on the interaction between actants to arrive at conclusions on the practices of a given actor-network. As such, ANT does not start from a hierarchical, or a traditionally structuralist, departure point. Instead, through mapping of interactions and relationships within a given spatial or conceptual field of analysis, it establishes a map of relations that highlight the inner dynamics of an actor-network.

As part of the ANT, scholars look at explicit strategies for relating different elements – *actants* – together in order to form coherent networks. It is, however, important to note that the ANT does not assume coherency within the network of relations; conflict and discrepancies are natural parts of actor-network relations. According to this approach, actor-network relations are potentially ephemeral or transient, existing within a dynamic of constant making and remaking; actor-network relations require repeated performances to exist. Without habitual practices, or performances, the network will eventually dissolve. In other words, social relations exist only in process and as such, they must be performed repeatedly and continuously to exist.

In critical security studies, the ANT is an emerging method that is proving useful in discussions on the role of objects – non-human actants – such as critical infrastructure, drones, or non-lethal weapons. The final section of this book on "Material Cultures" looks at this material/practical turn in critical security studies.

Each of these methods has significant structural limits in terms of research design. As we articulate in the following chapter, these limits need to be an explicit part of the articulation of interpretivist methods:

- What is a sufficient proof?
- What is the critical position?
- How is this argument coherent?

One of the most interesting and productive aspects of this project has been the frank discussion of research design limits, processes, and failures. The genre of academic writing often makes our research design choices seem inevitable, whereas there is a great deal of limit, failure, and mistakes that largely go unrecorded and silent. Lobo-Guerrero, for example, discusses how his initial archive at Lloyd's of London was destroyed by fire, and how he went about trying to find other sources. Howell is unable to interview key subjects in her research. Daigle discusses openly the difficulties and accommodating practices of researching in Cuba on illegal sexual relationships. Crane-Seeber talks about the dynamics of doing ethnographic work with soldiers, and the dynamics of acceptance and "going native". Grondin sets out how he studies drone technologies that are largely secret. In most cases, none of these stories had found an outlet in the formal knowledge of the discipline, because the publication system of our discipline does not reward explicit failure. Although, the publication system actually requires a production and circulation of failure – quantified in rejection rates that are calculated in impact factors.

Map of the book

Our collaboration comes from a common impulse to assert some common principles that can provide a clear framework for dialogue on methods within our research community. We combine overviews of the chief methods in critical inquiry and then provide a variety of research designs by leading researchers. True to our philosophy, we are guided by the empirical field of actually-existing research in critical IR. We demonstrate our principles through examples, and consequently represent the many voices within our community.

To represent the plurality of methods and perspectives, our contributors have set out their research design in terms of (1) a research question, (2) the method adopted, and (3) preliminary results and challenges. These short pieces are not the definitive conclusion of large research projects, but rather articulations of the work plan. We would enthusiastically encourage our audience to read further into the work of our partners in this collection, who exceed any one subfield or one set of debates.

The first set of contributions engages in the key questions of criticality, inquiry, and the conditions for intellectual production. Each of these authors points to the openness to the subject of inquiry. Lobo-Guerrero (Chapter 2) explores the critical attitude of wonder that accompanies his encounter with the research puzzle, which for him evokes feelings of both curiosity and wonder that impel research, which powers his later chapter on the archive. Guillaume (Chapter 3) unpacks the notion of criticality, and identifies the way in which methodological and ontological postures are both inherently political and deeply embedded in the research design. D'Aoust (Chapter 4) surveys the emotional and material dynamics of research, which are so often underplayed or overlooked in research about research. Squire (Chapter 5) also engages with openness in research and describes her engagement with sanctuary practices, articulating very clearly the politics of creating knowledge in these contested fields. Neal (Chapter 6) identifies a tendency in contemporary critical writing to privilege the theoretical over the empirical, and he argues for a return to empiricism – without the pretenses of science that positivism brings, which he demonstrates in his later chapter on reading legislative practices. De Larrinaga and Doucet (Chapter 7), who have been research partners for a number of years, explore the dynamics of collaborative writing through the epistolary form. Between the attitudes, the strategies, and the tactics, this section provides an introduction to the foundational questions: how do we think about our politics in relation to our methods? The remaining chapters provide a set of answers for how we can actually *do* the research. We have grouped the remaining contributions in terms of their dominant methodology: ethnography, field analysis, discourse analysis, the corporeal, and material culture.

The ethnographic turn in IR came to the fore with Vrasti's (2008) provocation, and she has provided a reflection on ethnographic practices to start off this section (Chapter 8). She concludes that the writing and research practices of ethnography exceed disciplinary introversion and reaffirm a commitment to openness and to "repopulate international politics with human life". Kunz (Chapter 9) illuminates the unintended impact of her research on the communities she studies, by charting the way that her critical analysis of the expansion of neoliberal policies had the perverse effect of spreading those policies. Johnson (Chapter 10) recounts her own research journey studying specific sites of non-status migrants, grappling with the questions of engagement, participation, and dialogue. Crane-Seeber (Chapter 11) shares his changing perception of his own masculinity while doing ethnography on an American military base, connecting ethnography with the critical place of the ethnographer, and the impact that the field can have on the researcher. Ratelle (Chapter 12) places his own mobility in question as he describes an auto-ethnographic project: evaluating his own arrest and detention in Russia, with a view to suggesting the utility of political ethnography to critical security studies. Daigle (Chapter 13) shares a similar research dynamic in examining criminalized personal relations in an authoritarian state, and integrates the difficulties in her research process by putting her experience as a researcher at the heart of her writing practice.

The practice turn is specifically indebted to Bourdieu's thinking tools. Hughes (Chapter 14) demonstrates, with incredible clarity and elegance, the evolution of her research question, using the concepts of habitus, field, and interest. While initially supposing that the International Panel on Climate Change conceptualized climate change in a particular way, and seeking to map out that conceptual map, she comes to realize that the organization does not conceptualize at all, but rather its predominant practice is writing. Nyers (Chapter 15) explains the empirical, political, and institutional conditions for the possibility of his theoretical work, specifically talking about engagement with the field of non-status groups and activists, and the professional associations that support his theoretical innovation. Bonditti (Chapter 16) articulates an engagement with the field by describing the research process involved in using a dispositif as a thinking tool. Salter (Chapter 17) and Muller (Chapter 18) both engage with the question of becoming-expert in fields of professionals, and playing public roles. Salter traces his involvement in aviation security and provides a narrative for his closer and closer involvement in the professional field; Muller, in contrast, details how he resists the pull of the field to maintain a clear distance between his object of study and role as critic.

The discursive turn is understood by our collaborators in the widest possible sense, comprising private and government archives, legislative practices, professional discourses, and popular culture. Lobo-Guerrero (Chapter 19) exemplifies his wondrous methodology through a clear recounting of his archival work: when a key private archive is lost to fire, he recounts how he used other historical documents from government sources to read back to the missing archive, and indeed the serendipitous centrality of one document. Neal (Chapter 20) is also concerned with state archives, but focuses on legislative practices rather than executive or bureaucratic policy. Empirically, this provides a counterpoint to more familiar and univocal narratives concerning exceptionalism and executive power in times of crisis, but also provides a series of methodological challenges. Howell (Chapter 21) faces a similarly heterogeneous set of texts and practices in her overview of critical research into the psychiatry, psychology, and related psy-disciplines, and she explains how she manages her field, in particular when direct access is impossible. Vuori (Chapter 22) examines the political culture of the People's Republic of China, bringing the questions of discourse and translation to bear on discourse analysis.

The corporeal turn has garnered a great deal of recent attention in social and political theory, and increasingly in IR. Frowd and Leite (Chapter 23) combine the affective and somatic with site-specific analysis of technological practices by mapping out security screening policies at airports. Mutlu (Chapter 24) advances the debate about affect by examining not only the link between feeling and the object of securitization, but also through the reactions of disgust related to the September 11th Photo Project. Wiebe (Chapter 25) argues convincingly that her field research with the Aamjiwnaang First Nation is, in essence, an affective research strategy, as she participates herself in the precarious ecology of Canada's "Chemical Valley", and she clearly sets out the ethical and political dynamics of being a researcher in a complex, charged, and sometimes noxious environment. Shinko (Chapter 26) maps out the theoretical directions whence the body comes to IR, highlighting feminist and postcolonial traditions to focus on questions of resistance and autonomy. Managhan (Chapter 27) also engages with the question of embodied resistance, specifically through the maternal body and motherhood as a discursive practice. Väyrynen (Chapter 28) also focuses on the governance of mobility through embodied practices of migration, which yields a rich, multiple methodology.

The material turn represents an emerging method that examines assemblages that involve both human and non-human actants. Aradau (Chapter 29) examines the role of infrastructure as the physical platform that makes certain kinds of community or resistance possible. Shah (Chapter 30) interrogates one of the primary material infrastructures of the global: the Internet. Investigating the professional field that brings protocols to the physical web, she brought a number of tools to bear, discourse analysis, new materialism, and spatial analysis – along with the metaphorical grids on which those competing logics were constructed. Grondin (Chapter 31) sets out the challenges in studying the secret life of military drones, and in particular the agency that is represented through this virtualization of war and killing. Anaïs (Chapter 32) also examines technologies by researching the affective dimension of non-lethal weapons, with a specific and clear strategy for analyzing these objects. Vuori (Chapter 33) examines the Doomsday Clock – as both a sign and an object that has particular effects. Voelkner (Chapter 34) engages in a material analysis by tracing the practices of human security, and in particular the communications between the institutions of global governance and multiple sites of human migration and smuggling in Southeast Asia.

Alternate readings of this book are encouraged. We could arrange the contributors according to subject area, in terms of critical security studies, citizenship and refugee studies, global governance, gender studies, international political sociology, or basic IR theory. A security studies lens could focus on the soldier experience with Crane-Seeber, the human security and development nexus with Voelkner, Ratelle's engagement with the comparative politics literature on political violence, Salter, Muller, and Frowd and Leite's discussions of aviation security, weapons and warfare with Anaïs and Grondin. A gender studies lens would emphasize the question of sex tourism and affect with Daigle, childcare regime research plans and gender norms through D'Aoust, the complex relation of bodies and power through Shinko and Managhan, and gendered scripts of migration with Väyrynen. A global governance view would highlight Hughes' work on the IPCC, Voelkner and Kunz's work on the discourse and practices of development, Johnson's ethnography of migration routes, and Shah's analysis of the administration of the Internet. A citizenship studies take would accent Squire's discussion of sanctuary cities, Johnson and Nyers' work on mobility and deportation, and Väyrynen's analysis of the bodily practices of migrants.

Instead, we have grouped them according to their methods to emphasize the variety of approaches within this community. Regardless, the editors aspire to lead the reader to a much wider field of methods and subjects. The honesty, openness, and self-reflexivity of the contributors to their research projects has allowed us a window into the messy academic kitchen that produces polished publications. Sources of this messiness range from lack of access to data, peoples, and sites, to theoretical and methodological contradictions. One thing is clear: research process is a learning curve; it requires curiosity, vigour, and stamina. We believe reading about these discussions of challenges and failures will provide valuable lessons for other scholars when they begin the research design process. The methods covered in this book represent some of the promising inter-disciplinary approaches to critical security studies today. These contributions demonstrate that clarity in methods and research design is not inherently opposed to theoretical complexity. As such, they combine diversity, reflexivity, and methodological and theoretical openness.

The first and most common issue that we identified in discussion of methods is the confusion with taking theory as method. Given that there is already more than twenty years of solid work in critical security studies that demonstrates the utility, efficacy, and political relevance of the methods we have presented in this book, we can now focus on these questions rather than reinventing critical inquiry at the beginning of each intervention. While theoretical origins are important in shaping the overall research process, in critical inquiry, these explanations of origins and demonstration of the knowledge of these departure points usually end up resembling a ritual rite of passage (separation from the old, moment of transition, invocation of the new). This can detract from the vigour of the research project. While theory is an important pillar of being critical, theory alone does substitute for method. Each theory has a bespoke method, and so the invocation of different theoretical frames has to be done with care as to the actual research design; critical scholars must pay attention to the tensions between Foucauldian power/knowledge genealogy and Bourdieusian field analysis, or Latour-inspired object-analysis and Rabinow's self-reflexive ethnography. That is to say, the slack combination of different theoretical traditions leads to concrete methodological problems: what counts as data, what does that data represent, how are those data related? Theory alone grounds our research in a certain philosophical tradition, but it does not answer questions of clarity, coherence, and reflexivity – three challenges to interpretivist approaches we have identified in the research design chapter. This is not a call to fundamentalism or fragmentation, but rather to include method as an explicit pillar of research that supports the argument as much as theory.

The second question which arises in terms of research design is openness to the field – and in particular, how to plan for fieldwork, archival and genealogical work, field analysis, or corporeal analysis. Research design is substantially underplayed in contemporary critical IR, and when it is engaged it is through the lens of positivistic social science that describes methods as either qualitative or quantitative. The dominance of constructivism in American IR has allowed for a soft sociology to creep into the discipline without any rigorous consideration of method: ideas, culture, and practice have all become operationalized through acts without unpacking the rationalist assumptions of the underlying subject, which sociology and anthropology have long since abandoned. It is not that we should cease to be pirates, but that we must become better pirates.

Part of the challenge of this collection – both in its construction and in its conclusion – is to embody the openness and criticality that is crucial to this community. Rather than provide a prescription for the *right* way to use a particular method, we have surveyed multiple, successful projects that use ethnographic, field, discursive, corporeal, and material culture analyses in different ways. What the diversity of voices demonstrates, however, is that there is a robust community of critical scholars that are doing good work that is mutually comprehensible, cumulative, and productive; with a clearer sense of design and method, this community can be more assertive and engage with mainstream security studies and IR with a full-throated voice.

Suggested reading

Burgess, J.P. (ed.) (2010) *The Routledge Handbook of New Security Studies*, New York: Routledge.

Edkins, J. and Vaughan-Williams, N. (eds) (2009) *Critical Theorists and International Relations*, New York: Routledge.

Fierke, K.M. (2007) *Critical Approaches to International Security*, Malden, MA: Polity.

Jackson, P.T. (2011) *The Conduct of Inquiry in International Relations: Philosophy of Science and Its Implications for the Study of World Politics*, New York: Routledge.

Klotz, A. and Prakash, D. (eds) (2008) *Qualitative Methods in International Relations: A Pluralist Guide*, New York: Palgrave Macmillan.

Law, J. (2004) *After Method: Mess in Social Science Method*, New York: Routledge.

Moses, J.W. and Knutsen, T.L. (2007) *Ways of Knowing: Competing Methodologies in Social and Political Research*, New York: Palgrave Macmillan.

Peoples, C. and Vaughan-Williams, N. (2010) *Critical Security Studies: An Introduction*, New York: Routledge.

Shepherd, L.J. (ed.) (forthcoming) *Critical Approaches to Security: An Introduction to Theory and Methods*, New York: Routledge.

Sil, R. and Katzenstein, P.J. (2010) *Beyond Paradigms: Analytic Eclecticism in the Study of World Politics*, New York: Palgrave Macmillan.

Thrift, N. (2008) *Non-Representational Theory: Space, Politics, Affect*, New York: Routledge.

Part I

Research design

Introduction

Mark B. Salter

A serious engagement with the empirical drives the research community in this collection, even as we recognize that it is crucial to develop and refine our theoretical frameworks. Clean research design has been hobbled by our common critical impulse to undermine, or at least identify and then problematize, the authority of knowledge claims. This reflexive desire to identify the limits of our theoretical frame and methodological instruments has led to jargon-heavy projects that can weaken the effective communication of our results. Clarity in methods and research design, political importance, and theoretical complexity are not inherently opposed, as the collaborators in this book demonstrate. Across the different approaches, there is a consensus that the empirical field should drive the methodological choices and the limits of the empirical field and its conditions of intelligibility must be identified.

In the Introduction, we identified three practical challenges for interpretivist methods:

1 *Sufficiency*: when can we stop our actual data retrieval in interpretivist methods, such as genealogy, ethnography, field, somatic, object, or discourse analysis?
2 *Coherency*: what counts as a compelling argument in the tracing of competing logics, cultures, or meanings?
3 *Criticality*: what is a reasonable articulation of a critical position, if we are seeking engagement and not objectivity?

What counts as good, clean, or clear research design, particularly if we are freed from the yoke of aping hard scientific methods? First, we are concerned with legibility and not replicability. Because we use ethnographic methods, participant observation, or object and field analyses, it may not be possible to precisely replicate our experiments, double-blind our coding, or conduct statistical tests. Research design must be explicit, then, in its choices: the object of analysis, the research question, the method chosen, the data that counts as true, and the way that data is interpreted. We must also be clear about the possibilities for triangulation: because methodology is prioritized over ontology, it is possible to corroborate analysis and conclusions through multiple methodologies. Research projects must emphasize their novelty, either by adding a new case study to an already existing methodological framework or by proposing a new framework.

In creating a clean research design, three principles are clear:

1 Clarity: how much can we remove and still retain the essential research question?
2 Fit: what method is appropriate for the object of study?
3 Reflexivity: what is the role of the researcher in interpretivist methods?

Clarity

If we believe that the social and political world is messy, that agency is everywhere, and that causality is emergent, then our standards for clarity cannot be parsimony or efficiency. Our test for causality has to revert to a claim about clarity: are the conditions of possibility sufficiently clear? How can we help engineer that clarity into an interpretivist research design?

A clean research question identifies the core relations that are under study, but does not seek efficiency or coherence, or even parsimony of explanation of those relations. In the following chapters, we can see that clean research questions do not preclude messy explanations – mess in the best sense. Law argues that social reality and our understandings of it are messy, and as such what is required is not a single technique, but rather "an assemblage [which is] an episteme plus technologies. It is ad hoc, not necessarily very coherent, and it is also active" (Law 2004: 41). Hughes, for example, sets out an incredibly clear question: how does the International Panel on Climate Change conceptualize climate change (Chapter 14). In her chapter, she demonstrates clearly how her investigation of the actual practices that she had previously operationalized as "conceptualizations" were in fact practices of writing, and her research question was revised accordingly. Similarly, Neal has a very clean question "what is security politics like?", but this leads to a complex and rich study into legislative practices concerning counter-terrorism (Chapter 20). Contextualizing the formal and informal norms within the British legislature on exceptional policies requires a deep analysis of the official and supplementary archive of UK politics, which challenges some of the major narratives in critical security studies about exceptionalism. Without sacrificing complexity, simple, clean questions communicate most effectively.

Interpretivist methods tend towards the immersive: it is the foundational claim of ethnography or field analysis that the researcher adopts the life-world or the habitus of the objects of research; similarly corporeally-attuned research should be self-reflexive about the emotional and affective process of immersion. Researchers need tools to identify what is crucial to the key arguments that they are making and the necessarily over-abundance of data. If we are concerned with emergent, rather than efficient causality, then our choices about data collection and retention are not straightforward. We are not simply looking for an operationalization of independent variables, but a more complex web of facilitating conditions, localized spheres of influence, and networks of embodied, feeling actors. In a genealogical method, we cannot say one archive is sufficient: as Bonditti says below, the archive is virtually infinite (Chapter 16). In an ethnographic research project, we could not say two months in the field is sufficient. In a Bourdieusian field analysis, we would not say four professional meetings are enough. In a corporeal analysis, we could not identify one feeling or emotional experience alone that would be compelling. Often, the end of our research period is determined by external or institutional factors, such as funding, the length of degree programs or sabbaticals, or the availability of sources.

An unambiguous research design will clearly set out: the case study or studies under scrutiny, the reason for its selection, and the values at stake in the particular articulation of that relation. There is an inclination towards the specific in interpretivist methods, but that does not mean that more generalizable conclusions cannot be drawn. Case selection must still be defended, either because the case is typical of a larger phenomenon or because it is unique but important in some other articulated way. This leads to the question of fit.

Fit

Not only are different critical methods appropriate for different objects of study, different methods are useful to understand the same messy and complex object of study. Using emergent causality as our touchstone, the methods below are understood as tools for breaking down complex reality into understandable narratives, and different tools are appropriate depending on the empirical field under analysis. Because we do not start from a theoretical position that necessarily privileges one method over another, our analyses face the empirical directly.

In several cases, the objects of study cannot be directly engaged, either because of ethical or pragmatic restrictions. Howell uses the reporting on the liberation of a psychiatric care facility in Baghdad to unpack (if not unravel) the discourses and practices for governing the madness in Iraq, but she could not ethically or pragmatically interview the patients (Chapter 21). Similarly, Daigle gains tremendous access to Cubans who are the object of attempted governance of their sexual and romantic relations with foreigners, but the conditions of research with such a vulnerable populace severely limits her ability to conduct the research project openly (Chapter 13). In the projects of Nyers (Chapter 15) and Johnson (Chapter 10), there is also a great concern for the practices of the representation for vulnerable non-status immigrants.

Methodological flexibility is one of the hallmarks of this critical community, and the vibrant discussion of what actually constitutes good critical research is one of the reasons for this book. There is a clear debate, as indicated by Vrasti, over the practice of ethnography in International Relations (IR). At least two strands of Bourdieusian-inspired field analysis have been promoted by Bigo (1996), Williams (2007), and Pouliot (2010) (although Pouliot himself explains his methodology using ethnographic terms). The key tools for interpretivist discursive analysis – the genealogy and dispositif – are still under debate, even after nearly forty years since their original articulation. Analysis of pop or high culture artifacts stretch back to the early 1990s and the cultural turn in IR theory, but it has yet to find a large audience. Deconstructive and straight readings of novels, film, video games, design, and art borrow their methods from other fields. Corporeal analysis, while informed by feminist and social theory, does not have an established method. Furthermore, these methods bleed together – the source materials are similar: archives, speeches, policy documents, laws, institutions, interviews, and objects. A concern with the corporeal and the bodily is found within Geertz, Bourdieu, Foucault, Massumi, and Scarry – and within each of the originary disciplines (anthropology, sociology, social theory, feminism). Thus, for us, the choice of method is also the assertion of what role the research plays in the narrative, and what literature we intend as our audience.

We do not need to invent methods from new cloth. Indeed, it can be counterproductive to produce an infinite variety of tools or qualifications on a correct, fundamentalist reading of a particular method, which is why this collection and its contributors avoid using neologisms. This methodological pluralism makes it imperative, however, that we set out in our research design what is foregrounded and what is obscured by our particular method. Relations of power are equally evident in espionage novels and arms control treaties, but in each case the operation of power is radically different. We can read novels as statements of values and identity that are as effectual as international agreements, and vice versa. However, we must be clear about the implication of our manner of reading and writing. Lobo-Guerrero discusses how the literal disappearance of his primary archive, from Lloyd's of London, led him to triangulate the same empirical material through other sources (Chapter 19).

Table PI.1 describes the key concepts for each of the methods in this book, allowing for wide variation in their use. We highlight the primary mode of collection, what data is broadly used, and the relations that each tool illuminates. Based on this schema, we can suggest the kinds of objects of analysis that fit each method.

Ethnographic methods are best suited to accessible self-identified groups that are amenable to either participant observation or interviews and life-histories. Access, immersion, and reporting are common challenges for the ethnographer. Gaining access to the target culture, as illustrated by both Johnson and Nyers, may be particularly challenging when the group under study is marginal, vulnerable, or closed – or, as in the case of a security organization, secretive as demonstrated by Salter (Chapter 17), Frowd and Leite (Chapter 23), and Grondin (Chapter 31). Managing immersion in the field – the dynamics of empathy and distance – also becomes a significant challenge, as Crane-Seeber shows, in particular the self-awareness to be conscious and mindful of the effects of the field on the researcher (Chapter 11). Finally, as Vrasti demonstrates, a final challenge for ethnographers is the recording and reporting of their experience: ethnography as a form of writing (Chapter 8). IR has little experience with ethnography *qua* ethnography, but ethnographic tools are often used in organizational ethnographies to understand the workings of particular institutions – and in particular groups or institutions with clearly-defined boundaries.

Field analysis is better suited to a particular set of professional practices that transcend traditional categories of analysis, such as public/private, domestic/international, inside/ outside. For example, European security professionals establish networks, common languages, and best practices, as well as competing across national and institutional boundaries for the capital at stake in governing transnational issues such as organized crime, migration, or terrorism. Focusing less on the individual experience of a studied organizational culture than ethnography, field analysis assumes that the field is an objective structure that can be defined and illustrated through empirical proof, even as the internalized subjective understandings of the norms and rules of that field are informal.

There is an emphasis in all of these methods on discourse analysis, almost always a supplement to other research practices. In ethnographic, field, and somatic methods, however, the purely discursive is supplemented with observational, interviewing, or other kinds of analyses. At some level, this arises from the confusion between the wider and more specific definitions for the term discourse and discourse analysis. Within qualitative methods, discourse analysis can mean the persistence of metaphors connected to a particular object, or it can mean more rigorous content analysis of particular texts. It is certainly not limited to textual analysis, or the transcription of other kinds of events. In some variations of this method, the audience reaction is irrelevant, and for others crucial, particularly those that seek an efficient cause. For this genre of discourse analysis, the selection of text, genre, and precise language formations (metaphors, performative language, specific words) is necessary for clear research. Hansen, for example, identifies different textual sites of analysis: "official discourse, wider public debate, cultural representations, marginal political discourses" (2006: 81). Hansen and others rely on the notion of intertextuality, that is that the particular meaning of key terms can be understood only in relation to the other terms with which they circulate and through which they are defined differentially.

For example, the particular meaning of security has changed radically over the past decades (Chilton 1996), and can only be understood in relation to other key terms, such as state, sovereignty, and stability. In critical scholarship, particularly indebted to Foucault, discourse is defined more broadly as any archive of statements, the institutions and configurations of power/knowledge and truth that condition how they are *sayable*. For Foucault,

Table PI.1 Research design in critical security studies

Method	Ethnography	Field analysis	Discourse analysis	Corporeal	Material culture
Object	Culture of self-defined group (institution, space, ethnic group, family)	Formal and informal practices within a structured, rule-governed social sphere	Set of verbal or written statements	Bodily reactions and their socio-political meanings and interpretations	Objects, assemblage of human and non-human actants
Key concepts	**Norms, identity** (self and group; in-group/ out-group)	**Habitus** (subjective dispositions or understandings about the objective field), **doxa** (unconscious values and beliefs), **capital** (symbolic, cultural)	**Genealogy** (historical production of particular forms of truth), **securitization** (performative linguistic connection between issue and value of security)	**Affect** (an intensity that exists in the body), **emotion** (the mediated form of affect embedded within the socio-linguistic domain), **somatic** (things that are of or relating to the body)	**Actants** (material mediators between actors and systems), **agency** (capacity of a thing/person to impact its surrounding)
Collection	Participant observation, interviews, discourse analysis, autoethnography	Participant observation, interview, discourse analysis	Archival analysis, content analysis, deconstruction	Autoethnography, discourse analysis (textual and visual), practices and policies	Tracing, mapping, discourse analysis, participant observation
Data	Field notes, interviews, material culture	Practices, discourses, norms, institutions, relationships	Archives, speeches, popular and high cultural artifacts	Experiences, references in/to images, objects, practices, speeches	Objects, infrastructures, networks, technologies
Relations	Hierarchy, relationships, structure, resistance, transversality	Competition, cooperation, domination, transversal	Power-knowledge, inclusion/exclusion	Interpretations, perceptions and subjugations	Emergence, continuity, transformation
Fit	Self-identified group to which researcher can gain access	Professional sector united by common meta-identity (security, journalism, academia), which the researcher can observe	Change in meaning of politically-significant terms, tropes and identities, which the researcher can read	Corporeal origins of discourses, policies and practices that aim to control bodies and their relations with security	Networks that include practices and things

discourse is not simply language, but the systems of knowledge that make particular statements possible. Discourse analysis is best suited for archives, literary or artistic products, or series of statements that are accessible. Accessibility must be assessed in terms of both the availability of data, but also, as Neumann insists, the appropriate cultural or tacit knowledge to make sense of that discourse (2008b). Neal demonstrates that the interpretation of the parliamentary archive, for example on counter-terror legislation, requires a great deal of background knowledge about parliamentary procedure as well as the partisan, personal, and political dynamics of the time (Chapter 20). Vuori shows that securitization speech acts in the People's Republic of China rely on a completely different set of genres and forms than do those in democratic societies (Chapter 22). Grondin (Chapter 31) and Anaïs (Chapter 32), on the other hand, must triangulate their objects of study indirectly, because the primary archives are secret or classified.

While ethnographic and field analyses, and even discourse analysis in the Foucauldian or Bourdieusian sense, focus on the incorporation of circuits of power and bodily practices, corporeal analyses take the body as a specific site of politics. Affect in this sense is understood as the bodily or corporeal response to stimuli, and emotion the socially-constructed meaning attached to that affective response. Somatic studies also foreground the way that particular bodies – gendered, sexualized, racialized bodies – are controlled and managed in differential ways. Wiebe (Chapter 25) and Howell (Chapter 21) both examine how illness is governed indirectly, through institutions and governmental programs as well as citizen groups. Frowd and Leite look at the way that bodies are interpellated by technologies, either in space or through screening policies (Chapter 23). Since many of these studies use discursive or ethnographic and field analysis methods, somatic analysis is best suited to studies that foreground the body itself.

Materialist analysis displaces the privilege of human agents and focuses on assemblages of human and non-human actants. Based on the observation that the most abstract or scientific of facts are collected, distributed, and analyzed through material conditions for their production and recording (the cell requires the microscope, the experiment the genetically stable mouse, etc.), this method is best suited to systems that emphasize the mutual constitution of knowledge and power. Anaïs and Grondin, for example, look at how the materiality of weapons systems structures the meanings of violence and war. Shah compares the physical infrastructure of the Internet with its socially-constructed protocols.

Because of the interplay between these methods and common empirical sensitivity towards cultural, professional, discursive, material, and bodily practices, the question of fit is as much about the object of study and accessibility to research material as it is about the disposition of the researcher. The position the research takes in the actual research practice is also a crucial matter of design.

Reflexivity

In all of these methods, the researcher plays a serious role in both the activity of investigation and the narration of results. We can identify at least three ways in which the positionality of the research would change the research design. First is the personal position of the research in wider political and social structures of race, class, gender, sexuality, and nationality. This does not mean that only women can be feminists or only refugees can study irregular citizens, or that one has an ethical obligation to publicize one's identifications or allegiances, but simply that those positions influence both one's unquestioned assumptions, one's access, and the way that others relate. Ratelle's autoethnography of ethnic-racial profiling in the

Caucuses is made possible by his physical similarity to the target population which helps him get arrested or detained at checkpoints, while his Canadian nationality obviates some of the dangers in this strategy (Chapter 12). Crane-Seeber is able to embed with his target population of men in the American military because of his gender (Chapter 11). Vuori is able to conduct discourse analysis on texts in Mandarin because of his language skills (Chapter 22). Dislocation can be equally valuable – as a primary experience of ethnographers by exposing those behaviours and beliefs that we take for granted in terms of our social, political, or personal position. Said was deeply concerned with a problem he termed "travelling theory":

> The first time a human experience is recorded and then given a theoretical formulation, its force comes from being directly connected to and organically provoked by real historical circumstances. Later versions of the theory cannot replicate its original power; because the situation has quieted down and changed, the theory is degraded and subdued, made into a relatively tame academic substitute for the real thing.
>
> (2000: 436)

Second is the institutional position, both as an academic and within the object of research. Interpretivists accept that meaning in the world is socially-constructed, which implies an ethical obligation to be mindful of the political and social conditions for the production of authoritative knowledge, even when that institutional position is unstable. Academic milieu differ radically in terms of preparation, expectation, and structure, which have substantial impacts on the way that funding, research, and publications are incentivized or made possible. The availability of European funding envelopes has made possible a number of different professional relationships and collaborative networks (including the ICCM and the c.a.s.e. collective).[1] European, Canadian, and American academies rank and value different kinds of research and publications, evident in the rankings by the Research Assessment Exercise (and upcoming Research Excellence Framework) in the United Kingdom, or the Social Science Citation Index, as well as how these evaluation tools are used in training, hiring, tenure, and promotion practices. The requirements of granting agencies, like the Economic and Social Research Council (UK), the Social Sciences and Humanities Research Council (Canada), or the Social Science Research Council, Macarthur, Mellon, Carnegie, and Ford Foundations, etc. (US), each have their own priorities and deliverables, which has the effect of changing what research projects are pitched, funded, and publicized. Nyers talks specifically about the way the CitizenLab made access to and engagement with some communities possible and also facilitated some forms of publication (outside of the habitual academic presentation) (Chapter 15). Daigle, on the other hand, must dissemble to the state and academic authorities about the object of research and her method (Chapter 13). Self-identification of these conditions is important to reflexivity.

Again, dislocation can be productive. To take an example from outside of this collection, Foucault talks in particular about the utility of dislocation when writing about his research for *The Birth of the Clinic*. He says,

> ... there was no clear professional status for psychologists in a mental hospital. So, as a student in psychology, I had a very strange status [in the Hôpital Ste. Anne]. I was actually in a position between the staff and the patients ... it was a consequence of this ambiguity in my status which forced me to maintain a distance from the staff. It was only a few years later when I started writing a book on the history of psychiatry that this

malaise, this personal experience, took the form of a historical criticism or a structural analysis.

(1997a: 123)

As we see, access is particularly sensitive in the security field, where access is difficult. Salter faces this dilemma in his field analysis of aviation security (Chapter 17); Kunz is struck by the unintended consequence of her research (Chapter 9), etc. Ethnographers and anthropologists have faced this question directly, as we will see later, because of the complicity of anthropological studies with military, imperial, and colonial projects. Johnson, Nyers, Daigle, and Kunz are all careful to hide the identity of their informants. The degree of difference or complicity with the object of study is a matter of continual negotiation, and must be made explicit in the communication of results if not the research design.

Third is the question of *intellectual* disposition, the self-positioning as an expert, observer, student, etc., separate and distinct from the world. We could derive this concern from any number of sites (Plato, Machiavelli, Gramsci, Fanon, etc.): Foucault and Bourdieu both share this concern about the way the intellectual relates to the world. Foucault talks about the general and the specific intellectual, whereas Bourdieu critiques the scholastic point of view. Foucault argues that in the past the intellectual spoke on behalf of universal values in the name of truth, but that "a new mode of the 'connection between theory and practice' has been established. Intellectuals have become used to working . . . within specific sectors, at the precise points where their own conditions of life or work situate them (housing, the hospital, the asylum, the laboratory, the university, family and sexual relations)" (2000: 126). He points to a danger of this specific intellectual becoming isolated, parochial, or failing to connect that specific struggle to wider circuits of power, as Salter (Chapter 17) and Muller (Chapter 18) illustrate in this book. There is a necessary translation required between the language and the genre of academic and policy worlds, and social, cultural, and symbolic capital changes value in the translation. However, the intellectual also has an opportunity to interact with wider political-economy of truth within a society.

> In societies like ours, the "political economy" of truth is characterized by five important traits. Truth is centred on the form of scientific discourse and the institutions that produce it; it is subject to constant economic and political incitement; it is the object of immense diffusion and consumption; it is produced and transmitted under the control, dominant if not exclusive, of a few great political and economic apparatuses (university, army, writing, media); finally, it is the issue of a whole political debate and social confrontation. . . . The intellectual has a threefold specificity: that of his [sic] class position; that of his conditions of life and work linked to his condition as an intellectual (his field of research, his place in a laboratory, the political and economic demands to which he submits or against which he rebels, in the university, the hospital, and so on); finally, the specific of the politics of truth in our societies. And it's with this last factor that his [sic] local position can take on a general significance, and that his local, specific struggle can have effects and implications that are not simply professional or sectoral.
>
> (Foucault 2000: 131–132)

This question of engagement is at the heart of the ethical drive of the intellectual: not to simply see the world as a thing but to be disposed towards it. Bourdieu argues that without careful attention to the practice of creating academic knowledge, we run the risk of "retiring from the world and from action in the world in order to think that action" (1990b: 382).

Within this broader community of critical scholars, there are a number of postures towards engagement: from scholar-agitator to activist to social critic to policy-advisor. What unites our sense of reflexivity is a sense that one's stance should be clear.

Note

1   COST Action A24, The Social Construction of Threats; FP6 Sixth Framework Research Programme of the DG Research (European Commission), Challenge Program: Liberty and Security; INEX Project: The European internal/external security continuum.

Suggested reading

Bourdieu, P. (1990a) *The Logic of Practice*, Cambridge: Polity.

Butler, J. (1993) *Bodies that Matter: On the Discursive Limits of "Sex"*, New York: Routledge.

Foucault, M. (1998) "Aesthetics, Method, and Epistemology", in J.D. Faubion (ed.) *Essential Works of Michel Foucault, Vol. 2*, New York: The New Press.

Latour, B. (2005) *Reassembling the Social: an Introduction to Actor-Network-Theory*, New York: Oxford University Press.

Law, J. (2004) *After Method: Mess in Social Science Method*, New York: Routledge.

Said, E. (2000) *Reflections on Exile and Other Essays*, Cambridge: Harvard University Press.

Schwartz-Shea, P. and Yanow, D. (2012) *Interpretive Research Design: Concepts and Processes*, New York: Routledge.

Check list

1   Is the research question clean?
   a   Does it connect a case study or multiple case studies to key concepts and set out the relation to be studied?
   b   Is there a clear contribution to the literature?
   c   Is the research process flexible enough to allow for failure and success equally?
2   Does the method fit the object of study and the data available?
   a   What is the impact of the methodological choice? What relations are made visible or prominent?
   b   What elements of the emergent causal environment can be mapped?
   c   Is triangulation possible, can multiple methods be used?
3   What is the impact of the social, class, institutional, and identity positions of the researcher on the object of research?
   a   What is the role of the researcher in this method, and how will that relation be explicitly engaged?
   b   In what genre can this research be published (public, academic, policy), with what different rules and potential impacts?

2 Wondering as research attitude

Luis Lobo-Guerrero

Introduction

Wondering is an attitude to approach research material on the grounds of its very existence. Its starting point is to encourage the researcher to pose questions on why something has been presented or analyzed in a particular way; what needs to be in place for a particular idea, which appears obvious or simple, to be possible, and indeed, thinkable; and what role do those ideas and thought play on the way the world is portrayed? It invites the researcher to focus on the details from which singularities in ways of thinking (Veyne 2010) can be analyzed. As Salter points out in the introduction to Part I, it also pays attention to the inter-textuality of context; not the ready-made one, but that which renders the empirical intelligible.

Wondering as a research attitude liberates itself from frameworks for analysis to make sense of the world (Neal, Chapter 6). It does not take the object of analysis for granted since encountering it is part of the process. It demands instead the sharpening of the researcher's senses to identify difference and ascribe meaning to that which appears to be without logic, as exceptional, miraculous, or magical. Wondering in this respect defies the very idea of research *design* since it entails a departure from carefully measured hypotheses and rationally focused "clean" questions. It leaves the researcher *exposed* to the surprise of thinking . . . in the wild. It becomes a pioneering endeavour since it assumes "the ordinary" as always exceptional (Nancy 2000: 10). When this attitude towards research is radically embraced, it tests the researcher's capacity to depict its newly crafted knowledge to the world in common language. In some cases new words and expressions will be required. Wondering requires courage to relate to the unexpected, resourcefulness to face the unrelated, and restlessness to persist with the adventure of opening up new paths of knowledge.

Wondering, however, does not take place in the abstract. It is not speculative thinking for its own sake. It is instead a way of facilitating the possibility of doing critique, not "as a matter of saying that things are not right as they are", but of "pointing out on what kind of assumptions, what kind of familiar, unchallenged, unconsidered modes of thought the practices we accept rest . . . practicing criticism is a matter of making facile gestures difficult" (Foucault 1988: 154–155, Guillaume, Chapter 3). In this respect, wondering precedes critique. It allows for the singularities of a practice or a discourse to stand out and for the researcher to make them explicit. Once this is done, following Veyne, the "arbitrary and limited nature [of phenomena presented as necessary] becomes apparent" (2010: 37).

Wondering as a critical research attitude is necessary for the crafting of knowledge. It continuously challenges the orthodoxy upon which philosophies are built. This is always an important matter since, as Nietzsche observed, "as soon as any philosophy begins to believe in itself . . . [i]t always creates the world in its own image; it cannot do otherwise" (2000: 206). Wondering allows thought to be otherwise.

My concern with wondering as a research attitude can be illustrated with the process that led to the writing of the book *Insuring War: Sovereignty, Security and Risk* (2012). The book explores a historical relationship between the marine insurance market of London and the capacity of the British state to wage war, drawing on experiences from the Napoleonic wars, the world wars, and the post-Cold War period. In documenting this relationship I began to find historical cases that in principle defied a logic of security, or at least, of national security as we know it since the Second World War. For example, I found that in 1739, in the context of the War of Jenkins' Ear in which trade with Spain was forbidden, Spanish ships were legally insured at Lloyd's of London. It followed that losses inflicted by the Royal Navy and British privateers on Spanish ships were paid for at the London market. Wondering how such a paradoxical mercantilist mentality (O'Brien 2002, Lipson 1934, Morgan 2002) could be reconciled with the idea of the security of the state (Schonhardt-Bailey 2006, Clark 2004), I began researching Parliamentary debates from that decade which detailed the discussion for and against the insurance of enemy ships and labelled them as "King's enemy risks".

Such a label attracted my attention and made me wonder further how a rationality of insurance, operating as a technology of risk (Ewald 1991), and a rationality of national interest were related? I later found out that in 1793, during the American revolutionary unrest, in what can be considered to be a transition between a logic of mercantilism and an incipient liberal political economy, Parliament prohibited the insurance of King's enemy risks. Trying to make sense of that prohibition and while researching the British National Archives in London, I was pleased to find a set of correspondence between the Committee of Lloyd's of London and the Board of Admiralty starting in 1794 and covering the totality of the Napoleonic Wars.

I marvelled at the mere existence of that correspondence. In the process of identifying some of the singularities of the relationship evident in the communications, I came across a phrase that helped me understand a crucial transformation in the political economy of the period. It also helped me make sense of the importance of the relationship between insurance and the national interest in the performance of sovereignty. In a letter sent by the Committee of Lloyd's to the Board of Admiralty in 1806, insurers made reference to Britain as "this Commercial Kingdom". Intrigued by the phrase, I began to research contextual sources to understand the nature of the relationship between these two entities. I could then establish the extent to which the sovereignty of Britain relied on a partnership in risk with the Lloyd's of London insurance market.

At the start of the project all I had was a burning curiosity to know if there could be any relationship between the insurance of ships and the capacity of the British state to wage war. That curiosity was part of a wider concern to understand the emergence and development of technologies of security premised on a rationality of risk (such as insurance), in relation to the unfolding and development of liberal governance in the modern period. To the best of my knowledge, and to my surprise, a problem that I considered central to the understanding of International Relations and Security Studies had not been directly addressed by scholars in the discipline. The paradigms available offered, if any, minimal understanding of the issues at stake. Some knowledge could be rescued from Economic and Legal History, and the History of Ideas. Secondary literature on the subject was very limited. All I had at my disposal was an article by Clark describing some cases of the insurance of enemy ships in time of war (2004) and three books on the history of Lloyd's of London with patchy references to the interaction between Lloyd's, the Admiralty, and the British government since the eighteenth century (Gibb 1957, Wright and Fayle 1928, Martin 1876). The question, then, had to remain vague and formulated in speculative terms. The objective was to wonder about any significant detail that would allow me to venture into what appeared to be uncharted territory. I resorted to exploring what archival material I could find on the matter, in the way I describe in my chapter on archives in this book (Chapter 19).

Only after analyzing the correspondence in detail, that is, highlighting the singularities which signalled the particular features of the Lloyd's–Admiralty relationship at the time, was I in the position to understand the problem at stake: the sovereignty of the British state as a partnership in risk management. This finding implied a change in the nature of the original question and led to an engagement with the political economy of the period, not from a disciplinary perspective but through archaeological and genealogical research (Bonditti, Chapter 16). I could then relate the understanding of the "Commercial Kingdom" to a wider problem of credit in time of war and a more complex and apparently obscure phenomenon of moral economy on which I cannot elaborate here, but that can be read about in the book. I then continued to interrogate the interaction between marine insurance and the state in time of war for the cases of the two world wars and the post-Cold War period.

Allowing myself the possibility to wonder about an apparent relationship (apparent because at the start of the project I was yet to confirm its evidence), I was intrigued by an incredibly rich phenomenon for which I could only formulate a coherent and tightly defined research question in the concluding stages of the writing of the book. That question will now allow me to continue wondering about my wider intellectual concerns in future research.

As is evident by now, wondering as a research attitude implies the need to react to surprises and capitalize on them. Surprises are here understood as unexpected disruptions in the order of knowing about phenomena. They constitute opportunities to challenge established truths by resorting to creative tactics to make sense of meaning that does not seem logical. These tactics inevitably lead to reading beyond disciplines, official narratives and authorized and authoritative texts. They demand from the researcher the capacity to weave networks of knowledge in the process of linking apparently disparate pieces of evidence into a coherent narrative for which an understanding is sought. My particular project focused on making sense of the logics and rationalities underlying the Lloyd's–Admiralty/British State relationship in time of war. This led me to explore several sites that involved a great deal of archival material as a way of developing a form of historical epistemology of this relationship.

By exploring archival material (Chapter 19) I identified a set of singularities that provided clues to how to approach the problem at stake. Using those singularities as constitutive of events I could then approach secondary literatures to learn as much as possible about the contexts under which those events had taken place. This led me to formulate further questions that required further archival and bibliographic explorations as the basis for new questions. I soon realized that the narratives that I began to build through my questioning reflected a particular logic with a clear set of conditions of possibility and operability. In turn, they reflected a wider rationality of thought which was ultimately what I was interested in making explicit in the book. By carefully revealing the premises implicit in the logic of security articulating the insurance–war relationship I was in a position to highlight and analyze some of the principles and values supporting what I detail in the book as a rationality of risk management in time of war.

Conclusion

Wondering as a research attitude resembles the charting of waters without the help of a magnetic pole as a point of reference. It requires continuous strategic self-awareness to understand where the project is going to prevent falling into the depths of ever-seductive epiphenomena. Detailing the existence and development of a relationship demands both attention to the detail to reveal the rules of interaction, and attention to the context which helps understand the wider relations of power that define the interface. Balancing both detail and context was the biggest challenge of the project since it soon became clear that detail did not determine context and context did not contain the detail. Through wondering about the project I was constantly reminded that it was the surprise of the event that ultimately helped me characterize the relationship of insurantial sovereignty.

Methodologically, the greatest challenge of wondering as a research attitude is that it does not provide the researcher with a *telos*. Surprises are always there if our attitude allows them to be. They operate not as a destination of the research enterprise but as a disruption of the rational effort that is usually undertaken as a method of *discovery*. The surprise as a disruption of the rational materializes in the researcher's capacity to perceive that excess that makes the very rational possible, that which does not fit, that which is left outside but whose very exclusion habilitates the rationality that made the technology, idea, or concept possible. The surprise, in this respect, is an opening into the possibility of challenging the rationality that made ideas and systems of thought possible in the first place, a window into an empirical space that is usually shaded by the apparatuses built upon it (Neal, Chapter 6). In this respect, then, wondering as a research attitude is more an *ethos* than a *telos*.[1]

Note

1   I am grateful to Philippe Bonditti for prompting me to clarify this issue.

Suggested reading

Covino, W.A. (1994) *The Art of Wondering: A Revisionist Return to the History of Rhetoric*, Portsmouth: Heinemann.
Daston, L. and Park, K. (2001) *Wonders and the Order of Nature, 1150–1750*, New York: Zone Books.
Foucault, M. (1988) "Practicing Criticism", in L. Kritzman (ed.) *Michel Foucault: Politics, Philosophy, Culture: Interviews and Other Writings 1977–1984*, New York: Routledge.
James, C. (2011) *Philosophy: An Introduction to the Art of Wondering*, Boston: Wadsworth Publishing.
Rubenstein, M.J. (2009) *Strange Wonder: The Closure of Metaphysics and the Opening of Awe*, New York: Columbia University Press.

3 Criticality[1]

Xavier Guillaume

Introduction

Criticality is a self-conscious posture and attention to "the way different kinds of linguistic, social, political and theoretical elements are woven together in the process of knowledge development, during which empirical material is constructed, interpreted and written" (Alvesson and Sköldberg 2000: 5). Yet, it possesses two distinct qualities. First, it recognizes the different dimensions of knowledge production whether in light of the researcher's reflexive objectification of the researched, the researcher's insertion within a scientific field and their relations with other researchers, and, finally, the influence of this scientific field on the construction of the researched (Bourdieu and Wacquant 1992b). Second, it avoids a disengagement (Haraway 1988: 590) from acknowledging and accepting the political posture behind every choice made in the mediation between ontology, epistemology, and methods. Criticality in a research design precisely guides the self-conscious mediation between these different dimensions of the research under the premises that the knowledge originating from, pertaining to, and produced by the researcher will be a politically-situated knowledge (Haraway 1988).

Criticality is especially important in security studies and, more generally international studies, because the concepts and categories that are employed by the researchers are the same as the state's. Being critical is thus to avoid thinking about the state and the international as the state would like to be thought. In Bourdieu's words, criticality helps the researcher avoid the "scholastic illusion" which puts him in a state of idleness (1994: 217). In this state, their "thinking's premises" – its social, historical, gendered, institutional, ideological, and cultural conditions of possibility at the individual and social level – are "in an unthought stage" (1994: 217). The function of criticality in a research design is a rather *negative* moment of attention and cautiousness when the researcher is at this specific stage of their research when the empirical dimension takes the lead. At the research design level, one has to acknowledge that ontological assumptions and empirical choices are political assumptions and choices (Hay 2006). Consequently, critical research design is a self-conscious posture counteracting the potential idleness of empirical research (Alvesson and Sköldberg 2000: 129). Criticality should reinstill a form of wandering between theory and empirics when the research might be on automatic pilot by concentrating primarily on its empirical and technical dimensions, the methods, as ends in themselves.

Research design is not only a specific time in a research translating into concrete terms the goals, questions, theoretical frameworks, methods, and techniques for identifying, acquiring, and analyzing evidences for its completion, but also a time to take into account what the research's presentation and generalization goals are. It is a specific time because as a wanderer, the researcher has often to come to terms with the limitations or even dead ends any of the dimensions of their research entails, and has to come back to certain crossroads where the question is changed, the theory adapted, the empirical cases and method techniques refined, the goal modified, or the presentation attuned in order to follow another road on the same pathway (Flick 2004). This temporality stands for different things depending on what expectations the wanderer had when they began their research walk. Most often, research designs are conceptualized as engaging with the logical problem of ensuring "that the evidence obtained enables [the social scientist] to answer the initial question as unambiguously as possible" (de Vaus 2001: 9). This emphasis on the logic of research links to a conception of science as a problem-solving exercise whereby specific research designs – experimental, longitudinal, cross-sectional, or case studies to name but the most known – are effective pathways to answering a research question (de Vaus 2001). In other words, research design helps the researcher to take a look back and forth to balance a specific research goal (explaining/understanding in a causal or constitutive fashion) and specific techniques for doing so (methods) with the empirical puzzles encountered along the way in order to improve the overall standing of the research as a scientific undertaking respecting internal and external validity criteria.

Stripped from its problem-solving shell, however, a research design is not only a form of checks and balances to attune a research with the methods to achieve an answer but, more basically, a reflexive mediation. This mediation is a guideline to a series of decisions "about how the research itself is conceptualized, the subsequent conduct of a specific research project, and ultimately the type of contribution the research is intended to make to the development of knowledge in a particular area" (Cheek 2008: 761). In this respect, research design is as much constitutive of the research itself as its problematique, its research question, or its empirical or theoretical methods and techniques. For instance, when faced with a specific research question such as "how has a Japanese political community formed, performed, and transformed in the nineteenth and early twentieth centuries?" (Guillaume 2011) the critical moment of the research design resides in the engagement with the concept *identity*, the inherent difficulties and ambiguities such a concept entail as it can be taken to be either as subjective, objective, or inter-subjective (Brubaker and Cooper 2000), its operationalization in a variety of empirical materials, and the necessity to avoid falling into the categories that the state, or any form of political authority, has set as prevailing historically.

Practically, a critical moment in designing identity-based research is the awareness that a form of objectification is necessary. In order to situate and grasp something as inherently fluid as identity, the researcher must, however, temporarily objectify it. Identity is both a category of social and political practice and a category of social and political analysis (Brubaker and Cooper 2000: 6). In other words, identity is a category that is used by social actors and by researchers alike. It is a category that evolves through time and space, is subjected to a variety of forms of constitutive power, is the object of contending definitions, etc. The challenge is thus to achieve this objectification of identity as a category of social and political analysis while at the same time avoiding reifying it, for which Berger and Luckmann (1990: 88–92) provide a classical definition, as a category of social and political practice; in that sense there is not such a thing as the Japanese identity, only different articulations by social actors who may, or may not, dominate the social and political space of the articulations of different Japanese identities. This type of reification is, however, common, and therefore researchers should seek to account for this process of reification. We should seek to explain the processes and mechanisms through which what has been called the "political fiction" of the nation (or "identity") can crystallize, at certain moments, as a powerful, compelling reality. But we should avoid unintentionally reproducing or reinforcing such reification by uncritically adopting categories of practice as categories of analysis (Brubaker and Cooper 2000: 5).

This is key as identity as a category of practice is precisely the type of category that is subjected to the state's ability to impose to other actors (and to researchers) lasting definitions of identity which conform to its vision of itself and its environment. We are precisely at this juncture where the researcher should act as a wanderer between the political questions of the potential effects of reifying identity as a practice into an objectified concept to study social reality, and the needs for the research to be operationalized. A critical research design engaging with the notion of identity should take into account this reification issue by precisely entering the fray of the multiple articulations of identity. There are a multiplicity of actors uttering what a Japanese identity might be, each with a different potential for this utterance to carry weight socially and politically; their relations with one another; how there might be contending articulations of what Japanese identity is and the shape of the Japanese political community; their context of enunciation, which channels (laws, literature, medias, institutional practices, everyday practices, etc.) are used to convey these articulations; who possesses privileged access to such channels, sociological, political, and economic contexts, etc.; and their multiple relations with what constitute difference: who are the *others* in these articulations.

Conclusion

Overall, critical research design distinguishes itself from a more *problem-solving* oriented research design by its emphasis on a continuous reflexive wandering between the different moments and dimensions of the research rather than on a form of checks and balances procedure to produce an answer via the use of specific methods. These steps, as illustrated in regards to the concept of identity, are to ensure that a critical research design is in tune with a critical engagement with our social world, an "engagement with the theorist's contemporary social world, recognizing that the existing state of affairs does not exhaust all possibilities, and offering positive implications for social actions" (Calhoun 1995: 35, Cox 1986: 208–210). This being said, however, it is important to note that criticality runs the risk of being limited in providing "constructive methodological suggestions" (Alvesson and Sköldberg 2000: 130), as such, suggestions are indeed difficult to devise prior to and outside the actual questioning at the heart of the research and the delimitation of the different previously highlighted dimensions. This has implications on the ways we tend to consider what research is. Critically minded scholars at the level of their research design should not consider research to be what Meyer (1986: 20) coins an apocritical undertaking, that is an undertaking which isolates different issues or problems, and by ways of answering to them seeks to "close the inquiry, stemming back and breaking away from the problems at stake" (Elias 1978: 112–116). On the contrary, a critical research design should open up inquiry, privileging the questioning rather than the answering, the doubt rather than the certainty that comes with an entrenchment in disciplinary practices.

Note

1   This contribution was inspired by on-going conversations in the International Collaboratory on Critical Methods in Security Studies (ICCM) (www8.open.ac.uk/researchprojects/iccm/) set up by Claudia Aradau, Jef Huysmans, Andrew Neal and Nadine Voelkner. I would particularly like to thank the members of the "situated knowledge" cluster – Christian Büger, Lara Coleman, Hannah

Hughes, Jef Huysmans and Manuel Mireanu – for the conversations we have had for the past two years. They have proven to be very engaging and stimulating and part of this contribution is based on my own reading of our conversations. All misinterpretations, mistakes, and misreadings are naturally mine.

Suggested reading

Alvesson, M. and Sköldberg, K. (2000) *Reflexive Methodology: New Vistas for Qualitative Research*, London: SAGE Publications.

Cheek, J. (2008) "Research Design", in L.M. Given (ed.) *The SAGE Encyclopedia of Qualitative Research Methods*, London: SAGE Publications.

Meyer, M. (1986) *De la problématologie. Philosophie, science et langage*, Paris: Pierre Mardaga.

de Vaus, D. (2001) *Research Design in Social Research*, London: SAGE Publications.

4 Do you have what it takes?

Accounting for emotional and material capacities[1]

Anne-Marie D'Aoust

Introduction

Emotions fly high during one's academic life. I, for one, can close my eyes and remember the anguish over getting admitted into my Ph.D. program. The pride and excitement I felt when my first English-language publication came out. The feeling of being totally lost and helpless during the dissertation-writing process. The gratitude I felt towards faculty mentors who gave me their time and support throughout my doctorate. Needless to say, these emotional highpoints were going hand in hand with intellectual and material processes as well: writing a Ph.D. application or an article, defending a dissertation, or interviewing for an academic position, to name but a few.

Keeping this in mind, this intervention seeks to address seldom openly-discussed aspects that nonetheless affect our capacities to conduct research and may influence its direction: emotional and material considerations. Of course, emotional and material concerns are not distinct spheres: such a division is done here for heuristic purposes. Material considerations should also be understood broadly and not limited to a narrow concern over travel expenses or tuition for instance, despite the fact that they are often major preoccupations. It can refer to one's geographic location (where you are pursuing your degree, with access to which intellectual resources, for instance), but also to concerns over the likelihood that one's research might help secure a stable, income-earning position, be it inside or outside academia, etc. As these examples make clear, these material concerns cannot be uncoupled from emotional ones.

These dimensions may certainly appear to some as either too pragmatic/cynical to be worth considering in designing a research project. If anything, they certainly challenge the romantic ideal of the dispassionate researcher pursuing knowledge for its own sake – and at any cost. They do represent, however, some inconvenient truths about research that lay behind the ideal of a detached pursuit of scientific knowledge. But the fact that they are informally discussed and talked about inside dissertation committees, in department corridors, and at conference bars justifies that we pay attention to them and examine how they might influence our research. As such, in this chapter, I discuss how they can possibly bear in the decision to use one specific method over another in the conduct of research. To do so, I first draw on Hochschild's concept of "feeling rules", which refers to "guidelines for the assessment of fits and misfits between feeling and situation" (1979: 566). I then briefly address materiality from a different angle, by examining the implications of what Yanow has labelled "the third hermeneutic", namely the way our potential readers will receive our work and give it the appropriate form of scientific legitimacy. Yanow identifies the first hermeneutic when the researcher interprets an experience during fieldwork, such as an interview or the analysis of written texts. The second hermeneutic occurs during the writing process or deskwork, when the researcher makes sense of her notes and analyzes her result. The third hermeneutic occurs at the dissemination stage, when the analysis is given to a given audience or readership (2009: 279).

Several scholars in anthropology and human geography have addressed how emotions might influence researchers' interpretation and data collection during fieldwork (Kleinman and Copp 1993, Rose 1997, Widdowfield 2005). Though critical security studies certainly welcome and embrace reflexivity on the researcher's part, little discussion has focused on the ways in which emotional components can be or should be considered alongside material considerations when designing and being engaged in a research project (for a notable exception in IR, see Soreanu and Hudson 2008). Addressing emotions still generally remains perceived as being opposed to rigour – the definition of which cannot be uncoupled from power relations inside the discipline. For instance, Vrasti (2008, 2010) astutely notes that the inclusion of ethnography in IR has, for the most part, remained limited to the idea of ethnography as yet another tool for data-collection in the IR toolbox. Feelings of doubt, uncertainty, improvisation, and happiness that characterize such work are usually silenced to conform to the discipline's norm that the selection of sites of study is simply the logical outcome of a well-planned and well thought-out research design, leaving unchallenged assumptions about the discipline, especially ways of knowing and writing about it (Vrasti 2010: 85–87). Taking ethnography seriously, she insists, should entail partaking in an "exercise in being truthful about the distance we travel from research questions to finished manuscript" (2010: 84), not shying away from material and emotional considerations when engaging in research and writing processes.

Keeping this in mind, we might want to consider how Hochschild's concept of "feeling rules" (1979, 2003) might apply to the planning and conducting of research. Feeling rules, Hochschild explains in her study of the workplace, are social guidelines that delineate zones of appropriate feelings in a given social environment (1979: 563). A feeling rule directs and "delineates a zone within which one has permission to be free of worry, guilt, or shame with regard to the situated feeling" (1979: 565) one is experiencing. Whatever the convention might be, she concludes, "the individual compares and measures experience against an expectation often idealized. It is left for motivation ('what I want to feel') to mediate between feeling rule ('what I should feel') and emotion work ('what I try to feel'). . . . But the attempts to reduce emotive dissonance are our periodic clues to rules of feeling" (1979: 565). Prevailing feeling rules thus entail emotional and material dimensions that warrant closer examination.[2]

Among the various feeling rules and emotion work experienced by academics and expected from them, the most obvious remains that emotions should not cloud the research process. Yet, we know that many research projects are triggered by an emotional reaction (a sense of injustice or shock, for instance, when confronted with an issue, or a sense of attachment if the topic was inspired by someone close to us). Such emotions are usually mediated through a rationalized explanation (authoritative scholar X neglected this element, variable, case study, etc.) to be deemed appropriate for research, rather than engaged in itself. Though such emotional dimensions seldom get mentioned in bona fide research design projects, they are often closely tied to what makes a puzzle a puzzle to you, and even influence how such research is presented to others. For instance, Muller (Chapter 18) illustrates well how his discomfort about the parameters set out by the Parliamentary Committee led to his concern about providing critical insights during his testimony, and affected several dimensions of his presentation. Muller also notes how a clear sense of the differential authority between him and other panelists led him to adopt certain presentation strategies to carry his points and dismiss others.

More pragmatically, emotional and material dimensions can become closely intertwined when it comes to designing a project that might entail fieldwork or long-term stays abroad. A prevailing feeling rule in IR consists in requiring researchers to detach themselves from their object of inquiry, and ensure that emotional and material considerations (deemed private) do not bear on their research (the rational *public outcome*). Yet, in her insightful study of women scholars conducting research abroad, Tripp underscores how women's personal arrangements often play a critical role in the direction and design of their research, and that the mediation between prevalent feeling rules and one's work might be greater than we think, for instance when motherhood comes into play (2002: 794). True, ensuring that one has the material capacities to conduct research entails varied components, such as how one can complete ethics clearance procedures, whether one can get the necessary visa or whether money can be secured to buy necessary software.

Prevailing feeling rules about childcare can also entail that considerations for children in research planning will be well-received when it comes from a woman, as women are often assumed to be the primary caregivers, but less so when it comes from a man. At the research design stage, these emotional and material considerations might make the difference between choosing, for instance, political ethnography or a two-week-intensive round of interviews, and are not unrelated to issues such as: can one bring a child along while undertaking research abroad? Will the child's presence hinder the research process or actually help it? In other words, sites and duration of research are not unrelated to negotiation practices taking place outside academia and involving, among others, partners, children, or relatives. As the example of childcare shows, dominant feeling rules go well beyond the immediate academic setting. However, we should keep in mind, following Orsini and Wiebe, that feeling rules are only part of an emotional landscape, not its totality, and that they are neither fixed nor static (Orsini and Wiebe forthcoming: 2).

The mediation between feeling rules, emotions, and research is certainly not limited to questions of parenthood or relationships management. Emotions such as fear, loneliness, or sympathy might also come into play in various ways. For instance, Nyers' activist socialization process highlights how a feeling of solidarity with the subjects of his research led him to purposively "design research questions that were responsive to and supportive of the needs of anti-deportation campaigns" (Nyers, Chapter 15). Feelings of exclusion, or fear of repression or violence based on one's racial and/or sexual identity also lead one to consider how fieldwork can be conducted, and where. As such, the materiality of the body is never disentangled from emotional dimensions. It can lead one to consider the settings in which bodily signs and markers of gender, race and class might be helpful in gaining confidence and access to certain settings and informants – though these aspects cannot be entirely known beforehand.

We should not assume that emotional and material considerations have to be negative by definition: the experience of joy, excitement, fulfillment, and pride, to name but a few, also come along with research! When it comes to research, we can certainly debate whether one should strive to adapt to prevailing feeling rules or whether certain emotions should be overcome in the name of research, if not explicitly expressed and taken into account when devising a research project. Nevertheless, discussions of emotional and material concerns should lead us to pause and wonder how, and to what extent, they might affect, at different levels: 1) one's research claims and findings, and 2) the reception to one's research.

Regarding this first concern, we might want to consider how securing a grant to carry on with a one-month trip abroad rather than a one-year immersion, or choosing to undertake a shorter research trip to stay close to one's family, might affect which respondents one has access to and what kind of information one might gather. It might ultimately prevent someone, as Allina-Pisano notes, from getting enough contextual knowledge to correctly understand certain situations or, when conducting interviews, from being able to differentiate between an implausible ritual speech told for outsiders and an original personal narrative (2009).

The second preoccupation brings us back to our point about the discipline's timid engagement with issues of emotions and uncertainty when it comes to research. Discrepancy in perceptions of "rigour" or lack thereof (Jackson 2011) on the reader's part – what Yanow calls the "third hermeneutic" (2009: 279) – carries with it several implications at the theoretical and practical levels. Much has been said about the former, especially how framing and writing one's research process sustains and encourages specific worldviews while obfuscating or dismissing others. The (in)famous Keohane/Tickner debate on the (ir)relevance of feminist scholarship in IR is a classic example of this (Keohane 1989, 1998, Tickner 1997, 1998, Weber 1994). Yet, little discussion has engaged the possible consequences of this third hermeneutic at the research design level: do concerns and anguish about what is perceived to be valid research affect how one decides which research project to pursue, and how one should go about studying it? As Schwartz-Shea notes, along with the passion that drives our research, we should also be careful not to lose sight of the fact that that "[t]he scholarly enterprise is built on the exercise of judgment. . . . [T]here are consequences of these judgments: some proportion of graduate students fails to receive degrees, some manuscripts are never published, and many research proposals go unfunded" (2006: 91).

Conclusion

We thus need to ask: what is gained, what is lost, and to what ends? Disciplining our writing to conform to certain standards because we keep the "third hermeneutic" in mind might help us secure the funding we need to conduct the research we really want to do, but it might also directly contribute to the further marginalization of some of the methods and methodology we would like to see become more prominent in the study of global politics. There are no easy answers to such dilemmas. But starting with awareness (rather than blindness) to the fact that emotional considerations and relations of dependency come into play when it comes to research might be helpful in weighing different research projects and strategies to ensure their completion.

Notes

1   I would like to thank Michael Orsini, Patrick Thaddeus Jackson, and David Grondin for their useful comments and suggestions. The usual disclaimer applies.
2   My use and discussion of feeling rules is indebted to Michael Orsini's insightful suggestion.

Suggested reading

Bleiker, R. and Hutchison, E. (2008) "Fear No More: Emotions and World Politics", *Review of International Studies*, 34(S1): 115–135.

England, K.V.L. (1994) "Getting Personal: Reflexivity, Positionality, and Feminist Research", *The Professional Geographer*, 46(1): 80–89.

Gould, D.B. (2009) *Moving Politics: Emotion and ACT UP's Fight against AIDS*, Chicago: University of Chicago Press.

Lutz, C. and White, G.M. (1986) "The Anthropology of Emotion", *Annual Review of Anthropology*, 15: 405–436.

Rose, G. (1997) "Situating Knowledges: Positionality, Reflectivities, and Other Tactics", *Progress in Human Geography*, 21(3): 305–320.

5 Attuning to *mess*[1]

Vicki Squire

"Mess is other to clarity, systematic study and knowledge. It defies knowing."
(Michel Foucault, quoted in Law and Singleton 2005: 333)

Introduction

A methodological emphasis on *mess* can be understood as a critique of what Law and Singleton call "methodological managerialism" (2005: 333). The latter is a form of knowledge production that is attuned to order, but that ironically makes a mess in seeking clarity. Rather than engaging a "nice and regular" world that clearly fits existing academic categories, projects that take the inconveniences and irregularities of mess seriously are able to explore how the object of analysis is enacted in ways that are both complex and multiple (Ibid: 333–334). This challenges managerial accounts that produce neat categories into which people, places, and things must fit. It also challenges the notion of "research design" in the conventional sense (Lobo-Guerrero, Chapter 2), which implies rationalist modes of knowing and a linear or neatly cyclical conception of the research process. Attuning our methodological approach to mess, in other words, can be a way to engage in research around a concrete object, *without presuming that we know what we are talking about*. In the case of the research that I draw on here, this object was sanctuary.

Not presuming to know means to acknowledge that research objects neither come neatly defined nor in terms that are easily disciplined to fit into existing academic categories. Sanctuary is a good case in point here. On the one hand, sanctuary can be understood as fitting relatively comfortably within the broad discipline of International Relations (IR). For example, we might trace the concept and practice of sanctuary as coming into being at the current juncture in relation to the practices of an international organization, the United Nations, as well as through practices of protection that are provided by (and within) a host state to those who have fled persecution in another (UNHCR 1951). From this perspective, sanctuary *qua* forced migration can be defined as a key object of research for scholars of IR (Betts 2009). On the other hand, sanctuary can be understood as entailing a much more complex array of discourses and practices, and as engaging a multiplicity of people, places and things; thus as belying any clear definition or disciplinary location. If sanctuary is enacted across a range of dispersed sites including churches (Lippert 2005) and cities (Darling 2010), for example, then it becomes more difficult both to create knowledge about *it* or even to define in any clear way what *it* is in the first place. As a research object, sanctuary is thus much messier than a disciplined mindset might presume.

Indeed, to assume that sanctuary forms a neat research object may be to risk inappropriately incorporating a multiplicity of people, places, and things as part of a unified series of phenomena, or to risk inappropriately reducing complex and heterogeneous discourses and practices to a single register. In order to undertake the process of researching sanctuary in terms that challenged my (and my discipline's) aversion to mess, I undertook a concrete analysis of how sanctuary is enacted and invested as such through an array of discourses and practices. This entailed a tentative identification of concrete relations of sanctuary as a research object, alongside the fostering of an approach that worked to de-invest the impulse to hold the object of analysis together as a coherent one. Focusing on the "City of Sanctuary" movement in the UK city of Sheffield allowed for an engagement with the people, places, and things through which sanctuary is (messily) constituted as such within a context marked by the re-emergence of such practices in a novel city-based form (Darling 2010). I was concerned with understanding how, why, and with what implications or effects people, places, and things enact and invest sanctuary in this context. The case thus provided a concrete entry point by which I could attune to the mess of sanctuary, while resisting the pull toward a disciplinary and methodological managerialism that would already presume to know "City of Sanctuary" Sheffield. This might be understood as a critical effort to open up questions about existing ways of thinking and enacting sanctuary (Guillaume, Chapter 3).

To attune to mess is less about getting to know a research object than it is about *cutting* into the ways in which an object of knowledge is constituted as such through existing discourses and practices. As Foucault's infamous quote at the beginning of the chapter implies, the production of knowledge is a political process that potentially cuts into existing ways of knowing and enacting sanctuary. Drawing on this insight, my aim was to engage in a mode of analysis that allowed both for a diagnosis as well as an intervention into existing discourses and practices of sanctuary. This double movement of diagnosis and intervention is critical, not in the sense that it is designed to advocate change in a specific or fixed direction, but rather in the sense that it is designed to open up cracks in existing ways of knowing and enacting sanctuary in order to explore alternative possibilities to which these give rise. Diagnosis and intervention can in this regard be understood in both oppositional and prepositional terms (Andrijasevic 2010: 25): as challenging uneven relations of power, as well as opening up possibilities for thinking and acting differently. This demands sensitivity as well as commitment on the part of the researcher, in my case to engage openly yet precisely with the discourses and practices of "City of Sanctuary" Sheffield.

How, then, can we undertake research in terms that maintains openness and precision, sensitivity and commitment, and diagnosis and intervention? How can we practically proceed with a diagnosis that exposes and opens up cracks in, or ambiguities of, existing ways of knowing and enacting sanctuary, to develop an intervention that brings the multiplicity and incoherence of mess to the fore? Indeed, why might we do this? I want to suggest that research that attunes to mess does not simply cut into knowledge about existing discourses and practices of sanctuary. Neither does it *cut* across multiple ways of knowing and enacting sanctuary, in their diverse manifestations. This is important for questions of criticality. Attuning to mess provides opportunities to excavate multiple realities; it can expose the disorder in order (Bonditti, Chapter 16), and can provide a perspective on alternatives that open to question the uneven relations embedded in existing discourses and practices. Translating this to questions of methodology, attuning to mess has implications for questions both regarding the relation between theory and empirics, as well as regarding the relation between methods and research design.

Just because the world is a mess does not mean that we cannot make theories about it. This is a somewhat frivolous statement, but the important point to take here is that research does involve theory, so how we do theory is important. Crucial in terms of the standard of clarity, is that theory is weaved into the design of research in a way that is explicit and relevant to the case at hand. For example, my diagnosis and intervention developed in part from an engagement with theories of statism, which allowed analytical purchase on the uneven relations embedded in sanctuary discourse and practices as well as a means to develop a critique of these relations.[2] The relation between theory and empirics in this regard was intimate, reflected in the on-going development of research questions as the research progressed. Questions were developed to allow for a cut into statist discourses and practices of sanctuary, without assuming these to be coherent, unambiguous or uniform in their practical manifestation. Rather than fixing questions at the start and testing hypotheses through a linear or circular research design, I worked with broad guiding questions as a means to focus the research without closing off new avenues to emerge through the research process. This reduces the risk of a researcher inappropriately imbuing coherence to the research object under investigation, and can act as a precaution against theoreticism.

Attuning to mess not only means to highlight the ambiguities of what has come to be called "sanctuary" in practice, but so also is it to examine the multiple realities that trouble a statist rendering of sanctuary taking a firm hold. Important here is the way in which theory and empirics are woven together to form a cut across, as well as into, sanctuary discourses and practices. Statism was a theoretical launch pad rather than a theoretical anchor for my project, remaining crucial to the diagnosis of uneven sanctuary relations rather than featuring as a set point to which the intervention must return. In my research, I was concerned to uncover discourses and practices that did not fit a statist frame, but that were nevertheless connected to sanctuary in this concrete case. By cutting across or between multiple discourses and practices, and by emphasizing their differences rather than simply their similarities, I built into the research design a means to challenge the tendency to fix statism in place as a coherent, albeit contested, frame of reference to one that brings multiple enactments of sanctuary into relation with one another. The aim of this was to develop an analysis that might expose the ambiguities, incoherence or cracks in sanctuary discourse and practices in an open and sensitive way, without losing the focus and precision involved in cutting into statist ways of knowing and enacting sanctuary.

My concern here, then, is not so much to take off my theory hat (Neal, Chapter 20), but rather to stress the importance of paying attention to detail in order that theory and empirics relate to one another in terms that are appropriate to the object in question. Mol's dual writing of her research in *The Body Multiple* is insightful here, since it allows the reader to consider the multiplicity of the research process itself in the interweaving of various theoretical and empirical engagements. To draw inspiration from Haraway's *Simians, Cyborgs and Women*, this weaving of theory and empirics through engaging research from a specific situation potentially facilitates the development of "a larger vision" by engaging "somewhere in particular" (1991: 196). This can be understood not simply as highlighting the importance of social positionality, but also as a means of valuing the wider significance of localized knowledge (Tsing 2005). But how does the development of situated knowledge, and of empirically and theoretically detailed analysis relate to methods and research design?

If Law and Urry are correct to suggest that methods "enact the social," the choice of method is central to the effective cut of a research design (2004). In my project, I triangulated different methods in order to foster research that was open while precise, sensitive while committed. Participant observation at "City of Sanctuary" activities and events, coupled with an analysis of textual material pertaining to the activities of (books/pamphlets, website entries, and audio/visual media outputs), fostered sensitization to different investments in sanctuary in this specific case. It also fostered engagement with potential interviewees, allowing for an identification of those likely to facilitate an understanding of the ambiguities of statist renderings of sanctuary, and of the multiple discourses and practices of sanctuary that was crucial to the cut of the research design.[3] Drawing inspiration from anthropologists such as Coll (2004), qualitative ethnographic methods allowed a consideration of discourses and enactments of sanctuary that exposed not simply the incoherence and ambiguities of a statist rendering of sanctuary, but also its limits. However, the cut of my research design remained pragmatic in its formulation, conditioned amongst other things by resources, fortune, and goodwill on the part of research participants. Research design in this regard cannot be understood in terms of a repeatable formula, but rather itself remains a messy process that demands openness and focus, as well as sensitivity and commitment.

Conclusion

To attune to mess is to challenge the methodological managerialism that comes with research design as conventionally conceived. This allows both for a diagnosis of the ambiguities of a research object such as sanctuary, and for an intervention into its discourses and practices that is at once critical in focus as well as open in design. This not only means that theory and empirics are intimate in their connections, but so also does it mean that methods are adapted pragmatically to the concrete case in question. Research design is thus an on-going and flexible process. This is not to advocate research that wanders aimless in the midst of mess and incoherence. Rather it is to point to the importance of research that is open and precise, sensitive and committed, diagnostic and interventionist. Attuning to mess in this regard is to both cut into and across a concrete object of analysis in terms that are critical yet unpredictable.

Notes

1   I would like to thank all participants of the New Methodologies in Critical Security Studies International Workshop, held at the University of Ottawa, 14–15 March 2011, whose insightful discussions provoked many of the interventions developed throughout the essay. Thanks also to participants of the International Collaboratory on Critical Methods Training School, held at the Open University on 3–4 March 2011. The essay is indebted to discussions of the Connectedness research group at the Open University, and to the inspiration and encouragement of Mark B. Salter and Can E. Mutlu.
2   By statist I here refer to a political logic characterized by the struggle to divide people into the categories of "citizen" and "noncitizen" and to render the state as a unified space through the containment and expulsion of its "excessive" elements. This notion of statism is inspired by James Scott's analysis of processes of standardization and categorization (1998), and is also influenced by debates regarding the "territorial trappings" of research (Agnew 1994).
3   In-depth semi-structured interviews were carried out between March and June 2009, and were then supplemented by a further series of interviews with six interviewees in June 2010. Staggering interviews allowed for the insights of interviews and observations carried out early in the research process to be fed into the design of interview questions and identification of interviewees as the research developed. I would like to thank Louise Richards, Gabi Kent (former Director/Producer for Angel Eye Media) and Yvonne Slater (Angel Eye Media), whose support with carrying out a selection of these interviews has been invaluable. The research for this project was funded by the Open University Pavis Fund as well as by the Open Politics podcast project. Full details of interviews can be found in relevant publications.

Suggested reading

Coll, K. (2004) *"Necesidades y Problemas*: Immigrant Latina Vernaculars of Belonging, Coalition, and Citizenship in San Francisco, California", *Latino Studies*, 2(2): 186–209.

Foucault, M. (1997b) "Nietzsche, genealogy, history", in D.F. Bouchard (ed.) *Language, Counter-Memory, Practice*, Ithaca: Cornell University Press.

Haraway, D. (1991) *Simians, Cyborgs and Women: The Reinvention of Nature*, New York: Routledge.

Law, J. and Singleton, V. (2005) "Object lessons", *Organization*, 12(3): 331–355.

Law, J. and Urry, J. (2004) "Enacting the social", *Economy and Society,* 33(3): 390–410.

6 Empiricism without positivism[1]

King Lear and critical security studies

Andrew W. Neal

Introduction

What are the costs of wearing a hat or not wearing a hat? By hat, I mean a role, identity, or mode of working. I might wear my poststructuralist hat, my International Relations hat or my sociology hat. More often than not in critical security studies, we wear theory hats. Theories and disciplines have costs.

Take securitization theory for example. This debate now has many experts. It has become a common starting point for research on a diverse range of security problems and practices. The classical definition of the theory involves three things: speech acts, an audience, and the legitimation of extraordinary means to deal with a (constructed) security threat (Buzan, et al. 1998, Wæver 1995). Every aspect of this definition has since been challenged, redefined, expanded, adapted, or deemphasized (Balzacq 2010a, 2010b, McDonald 2008, Salter 2008c, Stritzel 2007, Vuori 2008). We might wonder whether there is anything left of the theory, having perhaps died a death of a thousand qualifications. It remains popular, but at what cost?

The danger for critical security analysts is that using securitization theory to make sense of security problems and practices shapes our work in certain ways. It creates expectations about how the kinds of agency, discourse, or political organization we are studying work. This may have a constraining effect, limiting what can be said or thought about specific problematizations of security without yet another modification of the theory. The problem is that specific instances of security practice are always idiosyncratic in one way or another. Something may be lost when we try to make them fit a theory or a theory fit them. Perhaps it is better to let the peculiarities of these instances speak for themselves.

I would like to suggest that sometimes, when invoking the securitization of "x" as a starting point for research, all we really want to do is express the problematization of security: that somehow security has increased as a problem and is at the heart of important changes in social and political life. Yet we find ourselves encumbered with theoretical baggage.

So why the temptation to wear a securitization theory hat? Agreed, the theory can be useful and interesting. It has shed light on the way security problems are constructed and contested. But we should also consider the sociology of our own academic practices. Securitization theory provides a common working language and brings with it a body of prior scholarship, authority, and recognition. Putting on a securitization theory hat is perhaps a plea for identity and inclusion in all of this.

Leaving securitization theory aside, there is a broader question of why we feel the need to wear theory hats at all. What are the costs for our research? Here I want to argue that the spectre of Waltz still looms large, creating disciplinary expectations for theory to have a central explanatory role in research. For Waltz, the empirical is inferior. It expands endlessly, and we cannot say anything meaningful about it without theory. For this reason, Waltz argues that the empirical must be subordinated to theory.

Traditional IR justifies its methodologies through philosophy of science principles. The teaching of IR theory is still dominated by questions of epistemology and ontology. For the sake of argument we can attribute this to Waltz, who has been championed as the paragon of the *scientific* approach. My aim is not to critique Waltz, as that has been done extensively elsewhere. Rather I want to reclaim empiricism from the scientific IR tradition, to reclaim empiricism as a methodology that prioritizes the collection and analysis of data rather than its subordination to theory.

Empiricism and positivism are loose terms in IR. It is difficult to fix their definitions through reference to the literature. Often they are not distinguished from each other, functioning more as tags for a methodological persuasion towards objectivism or scientism. In fact Waltz disavowed both terms (Pond and Waltz 1994: 198, cited in Wæver 2009: 204). For the sake of argument I will clarify their meaning as follows.

Empiricism simply concerns the collection of data, information, or empirical material of some kind. Contrary to some disciplinary assumptions, there is nothing inherently numerical, statistical or correlative about this. Discourses are data, documents are data, practices are data. The term empiricism derives from a branch of philosophy concerned with the reliability of the information we receive through our senses and the difficult possibility of deriving truth from that. Well versed in this literature, Waltz critically argues that we could collect data *ad infinitum*, endlessly describing things that we see in the world without ever being able to explain what we have described (1979: 3–4).

In contrast to empiricism, positivism is the positive creation of laws, models, concepts, and most importantly theories for the explanation and sometimes the testing of data. For Waltz, theories cannot be derived from data or empirical descriptions themselves; they have to be created positively by the analyst in the attempt to provide meaning (1979: 6). Positivism is reductionist because it deliberately reduces the potential infinity of data to something manageable and, ideally, explicable. While there are few self-identified positivists or Waltzians in critical security studies (Wæver 2009), I would argue that many of us still in effect follow Waltz's prioritization of theory over the empirical.

Although Waltz has canonical status in IR, he is not the originator of this prioritization of theory. Waltz is above all a Kantian. This implies a certain relationship between the human and the world; between the possibility of knowledge (epistemology) and the stuff of which the world is made (ontology). For Kant, imposing theoretical categories on the world is what makes us truly human. Humans are able to use their reason to order the empirical chaos of the world. Human beings are like kings. They engage in sovereign acts of reason.

I would like to make a methodological plea for an inversion of the Waltzian-Kantian position to elevate the empirical above the theoretical. Sometimes describing something without explaining it *is enough* to say something politically and intellectually important. Sometimes documenting that something exists or is said or done is enough to contribute to our understanding of what happens in security politics and practice. There is an endless diversity in political life, social relations, and security practices. This diversity seems to be increasing, with new agencies, technologies, and power relationships built around the problematization of security. Often our knowledge and awareness of these developments is meagre. In critical security studies, we need methodologies that can do justice to this diversity.

When we look closely, we find that the fine grain of empirical detail contradicts theoretical assumptions, even critical ones. Theory risks clouding out detail. The world is always strange and interesting. The most exciting work in critical security studies describes rich empirical landscapes, unseen practices, and diverse knowledge systems. It describes things that are strange because they do not fit neatly into existing theoretical explanations or disciplinary expectations. We should revel in this and not constrain it. We should allow this diversity to speak without subjecting it sovereign ordering. Perhaps critical scholars are still too wedded to theory. Perhaps we have not yet escaped the spectre of Waltz. Perhaps we need to take off our theory hats.

Instead of continuing to ape Waltz's sovereign reason, instead of trying to be King, we should consider an alternative: to be heathen scholars. In *The Origin of German Tragic Drama,* Benjamin considers Baroque counterpoints to the rise of modern state sovereignty in the seventeenth and eighteenth centuries (1998). Instead of a masterful sovereign who is a mortal God, Benjamin explores alternatives from art and literature in which catastrophe and tragedy render the monarch impotent, unable to decide, cast down from divinity to the level of a creature, often in pastoral rather than courtly settings (Agamben 2005: 55–57, Neal 2010: 88–89).

King Lear is our lesson here. The King takes off his hat and relinquishes the crown. But he tries to hold on to the trappings of kingship, and ends up cast out on the heath. The literal meaning of being a heathen is to be on the heath. It implies being natural and undisciplined. "Unbonneted he runs" observes an onlooker: without his hat, Lear is no longer master of his realm but a frantic figure exposed to the elements. He "strives in his little world of man to out-scorn. The to-and-fro-conflicting wind and rain," but he is now only a man and cannot conquer these greater forces (Shakespeare 1937: 107).

Perhaps this is what we fear. Without a theory hat, without a crown, we will be unable to control the daunting volume of empirical phenomena. Perhaps we fear being cast out like Lear, rejected by those from whom we seek recognition.

Conclusion

In my methodological plea to elevate the empirical above the theoretical, I cannot excuse myself from all the problems of epistemology, objectivity and subjectivity that have troubled generations of thinkers. I am aware that there is no view from nowhere, and that we can never free ourselves from the assumptions, lenses or dispositions that shape our view of the world. I am also aware that the empirical world does not speak directly to us or reveal a legible face (Foucault 1981: 67). Neither do any of us have privileged, objective access to it. But Nietzsche feared that reason, indeed positivism, in its abstractions and reductions, had abolished the real world (Nietzsche 1990: 50–51). Let us develop heathen methodologies that allow us to inhabit it, rather than try to rule it.

All I ask is for us to be a little less disciplined by our disciplines. To be more troubled by the sociology of knowledge and less troubled by the philosophy of science. Perhaps sometimes to engage in a kind of naïve empiricism that worries less about commanding theory and more about doing justice to the richness and strangeness of social and political practices. We should design research that is less disciplined but has its eyes wide open. To quote a closing line from *King Lear*, we should try more to "Speak what we feel, not what we ought to say" (Shakespeare 1937: 228).

Note

1   I developed this essay from talks I gave at the New Methodologies in Critical Security Studies workshop at the University of Ottawa, 14–15 March 2011, and the 4th Annual Critical Voices in Swiss IR Conference, ETH Zürich, 19–20 May 2011. I must acknowledge the development of my thoughts through dialogue with the participants at both venues, in particular Chris Zebrowski, Philippe Bonditti, Vicki Squire, Claudia Aradau, Anna Leander, Joscha Wullweber and Mark Daniel Jager. These thoughts also emerge from a general background of thinking about critical methodology in the International Collaboratory on Critical Methods in Security Studies, an ESRC funded project (RES-810-21-0072): www8.open.ac.uk/researchprojects/iccm/

Suggested reading

Bourdieu, P. (1988) *Homo Academicus*, trans. P. Colier. Stanford: Stanford University Press.

Foucault, M. (2004b) *Archaeology of Knowledge*, trans. A.M. Sheridan Smith. New York: Routledge.

Latour, B. (2005) *Reassembling the Social: an Introduction to Actor-Network-Theory*, New York: Oxford University Press

Law, J. (2004) *After Method: Mess in Social Science Method*, New York: Routledge.

Veyne, P. (2010) *Foucault: His Thought, His Character*, Cambridge: Polity.

7 Engaging collaborative writing critically

Miguel de Larrinaga and Marc G. Doucet

Introduction

Collaborative writing has been an important part of academic research yet has been relatively unexplored (at least in our discipline) as a form of academic activity in and of itself. Since the final product is virtually indistinguishable from single authored work, the actual process of collaboration might appear as merely the practical matter of divvying up the work among authors and thus a technical issue that does not merit any particular analysis or examination. Indeed, when one thinks of collaboration in an academic setting the standard models most often entail arrangements in which some form of a division of labour is either explicitly or implicitly agreed upon. Among the standard models, one could think of a division by areas of specialization, turn-taking, or a form of refereed writing where authors react to something that has already been written (Hewett et al. 2010: 10–11). However, if the circumstances are propitious, a third more involved option of collaborative writing is available: one that entails the actual process of writing together, in real time, sentence by sentence, from the beginning of a text to its end. Despite what are some of its challenges and what could be perceived as an added burden to the writing phase of the research design, it has been our experience that this third approach is the most fruitful and rewarding in terms of developing rigorous and engaging scholarship and fostering an intellectual camaraderie over a long-term collaborative relationship. Beyond the written work that has been produced, the actual process of writing with this form of collaboration has become inextricable from the longstanding and sustained intellectual engagement that we share.[1]

In this chapter we engage critically with the ways in which we collaborate. In other words, we want to reflect upon the conditions of possibility that inform the methods that we use to do collaborative research and writing, and the consequences of these methods for the written work that is produced. We start by using the concept of the epistolary form of writing – letter writing and correspondences – as a starting point for how, in practical terms, we have approached our work. In this sense, we feel that the epistolary form provides a useful frame of reference and point of departure from which to examine the type of collaboration we have used in our writing.

The epistolary form, i.e., the writing and exchange of letters through regular or sustained correspondences, is well known in history as a central social and intellectual practice that many scholars, public intellectuals, and literary figures have used throughout the seminal years of their careers. The correspondence between, for example, Leibniz and Clarke, Newton and Boyle, Pascal and Fermat, Sand and Flaubert, Strauss and Voegelin, and Arendt and Jaspers can be seen as a central part of their oeuvres (and often published as such) where ideas are shared and explored and the exchanges produce more than the sum of their parts. As Stanley suggests, such exchanges are of interest in good part because the epistolary form they take is grounded in certain specific characteristics that are not found in other forms of writing:

> First, letters are *dialogical*. They are not one person writing or speaking about their life, but a communication or exchange between one person and another or others [. . .] an important feature of correspondences, rather than one-off letters, is their turn taking and reciprocity. Secondly, letters are *perspectival*. Their point is not that they contain fixed material from one viewpoint, nor that their content is directly referential, but that their structure and content changes according to the particular recipient and the passing of time. Letters fascinatingly take on the perspective of the "moment" as this develops within a letter or a sequence of letters [. . .] And thirdly, letters have strongly *emergent* properties. They are not occasioned, structured or their content filled by researcher-determined concerns. Instead, they have their own preoccupations and conventions and indeed their own epistolary ethics.
>
> (2004: 202–203)

It is precisely these characteristics of the dialogical, the perspectival, and the emergent that we would like to explore in relation to our collaborative work. Although the real time and visually interactive aspects of our exchanges provide a fundamentally different understanding of these characteristics, they nonetheless can give us some purchase upon the particularity of this type of intellectual activity.

Letters are *dialogical* insofar as they literally present a dialogue between two or more interlocutors that can be physically examined through the successive letters of the correspondence. The dialogue that can emerge from letters often resembles conversations to the extent that they involve turn-taking between interlocutors, but they are limited by time and space constraints and therefore are fixed and functionally structured in that each interchange comes as a package that most often includes a beginning, a body, and an end, and is sent in anticipation of a response. In real time online collaborative writing, the dialogical dimension is far more dynamic and fluid, and does indeed often take the form and flow of a face-to-face conversation. The conversation is an exchange punctuated by mutual interruptions motivated by the desire to complete a thought, describe a concept, or develop a segment of an argument (Ritchie and Rigano 2007). These conversations are scheduled and task-oriented. The task-oriented dialogue has as its immediate object the crafting of text for an article, conference paper, or book chapter. The dialogical aspect of this, therefore, is not revealed in a succession of letters but takes place before and through the crafting of the work constructed synchronously, often word-by-word, sentence-by-sentence. In this sense, the use of computer and web 2.0 technologies has made the dialogical in our work more immediate and consequential in that the writing is bound up with a real time discussion with the audiovisual of Voice over Internet Protocol (VoIP) playing a central role. Hand gestures, facial expressions, eye contact all play a part in the exchange. This telepresence can be seen as disturbing the binary of speaking and writing at the heart of the epistolary form as some of the conversation materializes as written word in a shared document that we as interlocutors both have access to, and write into, in real time. At first glance, the audiovisual may seem secondary and inconsequential to the actual written work that is produced. Yet, we have found that it has proven central in making the work engaging and sustainable insofar as the addition of video and audio to the writing process have often helped to strengthen the motivation needed to complete a given piece of work or surmount the writing and research blocks all authors generally face.

As with the exchange of letters, our collaborative work can also be seen as *perspectival* in that it is bound up with a labour of negotiation between viewpoints at a given moment in time and space. With that said, the moment as it operates in our work is in certain respects quite different from the classic epistolary form. Instead of a letter expressing a particular instant that is then responded to at another given point in time, the moment as it manifests itself in our collaborations is constantly deferred in the real time exchanges and is only arrested once the viewpoints are negotiated and inscribed in the document. Even then, the text itself remains malleable and changes are a constant element of the actual writing. As Internet file-sharing technology has advanced, structure and content are increasingly negotiated instantaneously (Kittle and Hicks 2009), and what results, although emanating from a tension between viewpoints and areas of knowledge, provides a text which is neither of ours in that typically we cannot isolate authorship of a given section or element of an argument. The collaboration is thus genuinely collaborative in that it is not only more than the sum of its parts but is also one in which we can only recognize it, and ourselves in it, as *our* work. Different from the epistolary form, the performative process of writing in this type of collaboration thus alters the perspectival dimension in that it disenables any claim to single authorship and as such brings to the fore the very question of the author and authorial ownership.

The final dimension of the epistolary form is its *emergent* characteristic. As Stanley suggests, letters are typically not conditioned or structured by research considerations but have their own preoccupations and conventions that are heavily shaped by their *milieu*. Indeed, one of the reasons an author's letters are apprehended as a distinct part of his or her oeuvre yet clearly associated to it, and revealing of certain aspects of it, is that they present themselves as something other than say a treatise, an essay, or a monograph. Within the context of our collaborative research and writing, there are certainly set research agendas, goals and timelines that motivate the relationship and structure the work. Yet, there is also an emergent quality to this work that is distinct and unconventional. Of course, any research can be seen as emergent in some form or another. Indeed, one of the primary reasons that, as academics, many engage in research is precisely a sense of curiosity or wonder (Lobo-Guerrero, Chapter 2) that often fuels a desire to pursue the learning process through an exploration of new ideas, concepts, and arguments. However, within the collaborative engagement there is also an additional element of mediation that emerges from the exchange itself and that takes this process of learning, of making known, in unanticipated directions for each of the interlocutors. It is an unfolding of ideas, concepts, and arguments that is contrapuntal in that the activity of researching and writing is one where the making known is affected through a series of points and counterpoints that unavoidably must move along a pattern in order to arrive at a conclusion. Yet, simultaneously, the different interlocutors experience a certain sense of contingency, or openness, in the moments of exchange. This element of openness brings to light an added dimension of self-conscious mediation in the critical posture that defines criticality in the research design as explored by Guillaume (Chapter 3). In the form of involved collaborative writing we have described here, mediation is not only between the different dimensions of the research (ontology, epistemology, and methods) but is also to be found in the continuous exchange between the researchers themselves. This added dimension of mediation leads to an element of openness in the trajectory of thought and argument that we feel has not only been an essential and productive aspect of our collaboration but that entails as well an element of shared responsibility. This shared responsibility is one that takes place through the collaborative process itself. It can be seen as a responsibility in that there is a shared element of burden towards maintaining our individual commitment to relinquishing some element autonomy of thought, control, and authorship in terms of the contingency of the process highlighted above. Yet ultimately, decisions have to take place in moving the work forward. It is in these decisions commonly arrived at, which apportion the written from the non-written, that we also find the responsibility towards *our* work.

Conclusion

One could argue that in the current academic climate in which research and publication is more closely monitored, counted, and assessed than ever before, a premium is clearly placed on single authored work. The classic image of the academic-researcher is that of a single figure even with the turn in recent decades towards more "team-centred" approaches to research (Ritchie and Rigano 2007: 126). Genuinely collaborative work is often at a disadvantage in the sense that the need for output and control in an environment increasingly marked by demands to compete for research funding and the requirements of regular career progression can work against the more open and deliberative labour examined above. Despite these considerations, it has been our experience that this form of engagement is not only fruitful but also brings a particular critical sensibility to the process of research and writing. Through an engagement with the categories of the dialogical, the perspectival, and the emergent, we have tried to reveal some of the ways in which this criticality manifests itself. As Salter points out in the introduction to Part I, one of the aspects of criticality is the emphasis on methodological openness and serendipity. The type of contingent creativity that emerges from the collaborative form of writing we have employed is very much akin to this understanding of criticality. As scholars engaged in critical work, it is incumbent upon us to not only reflect upon the way in which we research and write, but to take the time needed to find alternative ways to do so through genuinely collaborative experiences.

Note

1　Writing here is thus bound up with and is an extension of an ongoing discussion that for the past five years has been punctuated by the crafting of numerous calls for papers for interlinked panels at successive regional and international conferences, workshops and roundtables, conference papers, a journal article, book chapters, and an edited volume. In light of the other projects that we are both pursuing individually or with other colleagues, this output has been in our judgement considerable.

Suggested reading

Hewett, B.L., Robideaux, C., and Remley, D. (2010) "Principles for Exploring Virtual Collaborative Writing" in B.L. Hewett and C. Robideaux (eds) *Virtual Collaborative Writing in the Workplace: Computer-Mediated Communication Technologies and Processes*, Hershey: IGI Global.

Kittle, P. and Hicks, T. (2009) "Transforming the Group Paper with Collaborative Online Writing", *Pedagogy*, 9(3): 525–538.

Noël, S. and Robert, J-M. (2003) "How the Web is used to Support Collaborative Writing", *Behaviour and Information Technology*, 22(4): 245–262.

Ritchie, S.M. and Rigano, D.L. (2007) "Writing Together Metaphorically and Bodily Side-by-Side: an Inquiry into Collaborative Academic Writing", *Reflective Practice*, 8(1): 123–135.

Stanley, L. (2004) "The Epistolarium: On Theorizing Letters and Correspondences", *Auto/Biography*, 12(3): 201–235.

Part II

The ethnographic turn

Introduction

Mark B. Salter

Ethnography is an empathetic analysis of culture most often through participant observation, interviews, and archival or discourse analysis; it is the dominant methodology of anthropology. Geertz's *Interpretation of Cultures* describes both the aims and the activity of ethnography:

> establishing rapport, selecting informants, transcribing texts, taking genealogies, mapping fields, keeping a diary, and so on. But it is not these things, techniques and received procedures that define the enterprise. What defines it is the kind of intellectual effort it is: an elaborate venture in, to borrow a notion from Ryle, "thick description".
>
> (1973: 6)

It seeks to be holistic, and contextualize specific sets of language, practices, and habits into a recognizable pattern. One of the hallmarks of contemporary ethnography is the reflexive inclusion of the researcher in the analysis, understanding ethnography as a cultural exchange or embeddedness rather than a unidirectional extraction: a meeting, rather than the recording, of cultures; an examination of both self/other through the lens of difference; and also the study of particular cultures and organizations within the self, rather than exoticization of the other.

Anthropology is a formal stranger to International Relations (IR) despite being concerned with the dynamics of culture and identity; indeed one could argue that the entire discipline of IR is a political theory of the management of otherness (Walker 1993: 117). Neumann identifies an "ethnographic path" for understanding the self/other dynamic, and gestures towards area studies and nationalism studies before taking an "eastern excursion" into discourse analysis (1999). Autoethnography appears periodically, in Cohn's "Sex and Death in the Rational World of Defense Intellectuals" (1987), Beier's *International Relations in Uncommon Places: Indigeneity, Cosmology, and the Limits of International Theory* (2005), Neumann's "To be a Diplomat" (2005), Inayatullah's *Autobiographical International*

Table PII.1 Research design in ethnography

Object	Culture of self-defined group (institution, space, ethnic group, family)
Key concepts	Norms, identity (self and group; in-group/out-group)
Collection	Participant observation, interviews, discourse analysis
Data	Field notes, interviews, material culture
Relations	Hierarchy, relationships, structure, resistance, transversality
Fit	Self-identified group to which researcher can gain access

Relations: I, IR (2010), and Kratochwil's "intellectual biography" (2011), but there is not a wider disciplinary "ethnographic turn" (Vrasti 2008). Ethnography has come into the critical studies community – like so many of these methods – through reading of critical social theory outside of the discipline of political science. Like the feminism that inspires much ethnography in IR, the critical security studies community pays careful attention to writing as a practice: once we accept that there are power dynamics in writing and re-presentation, then we must come to use those writing tools purposively. Cohn breaks the fourth wall, and speaks to the reader directly (1987). Enloe reflects on her writing craft (2004), as do others inspired by her work.

Since the critical turn in IR in the late 1980s, there have been a number of studies analyzing the culture of IR and in particular the national cultures of IR theory (Wæver 1998, Crawford and Jarvis 2000, Tickner and Wæver 2009). One collection in particular attempted a kind of family tree or kin-structure of individuals within IR theory (Neumann and Wæver 1997), but the actual culture of the academic field is often not analyzed. An academic conference would not be decipherable from the discursive traces alone. For example, by being immersed in our academic community, we can see things that would not otherwise be immediately visible from an outsider's perspective.

Failure, for example, is not a surplus or exceptional aspect of academic life: rejection is aleatory, it circulates, it is productive; failure is the dominant culture of academe. Like insecurity, failure and rejection do not only haunt the dark forest at the edge of the green meadow of academic success, they are the condition for its possibility. Failure is inherent in entry to the field. According to the Association of American Medical Colleges, while it takes an average of 11 to 16 years to become a medical doctor, over 96% of all students registered in medical school succeed in their accreditation.[1] Segall reports figures for the legal profession that 93% of those who finish law school were employed within nine months of graduation.[2] Political Science doctoral students in Canada enjoy a 43% completion rate (Elgar 2003: 7). Lopez reported in 2003 that 65% of political science doctorates received some kind of academic position (Lopez 2003: 839). In the most recent survey by the American Political Science Association, only 48% of doctoral graduates won a permanent academic position, and 21% found a temporary position (Biggs and Jones 2010: 5). Failure is also crucial to the publication regime: journals measure their impact through citation reports and rates of rejection (ranging from 85% and above, *International Studies Quarterly* for example sets a 10% acceptance rate target); publishers reject a high proportion of proposals; rejection rates for the major annual conferences also range from 50% or higher. Publications and presentations are two of the primary ways that ideas are communicated and hiring, tenure, promotion, and status are accorded; these systems are built on the circulation of failure (Weeks 2006). Because of the internalization of these peer-critiques, these failures are rarely publicized or discussed, but they remain a powerful aspect of academic culture that structures access/entry to the field, and the distribution of status and position.

Part of the focus of the method of ethnography is its writing practice. Rabinow alludes to this in his introduction to *Reflections on Fieldwork in Morocco*, when he says "the book is a reconstruction of a set of encounters that occurred while doing fieldwork. At that time, of course, things were anything but neat and coherent. At this time, I have made them seem that way so as to salvage some meaning from that period for myself and for others" (1977: 6). Thus, one of the methodological precepts for contemporary reflexive ethnography must be to interpolate the writer into the social world that she/he is relaying. Johnson (Chapter 10) and Daigle (Chapter 13) are explicit about this concern in their contributions to this book. Johnson points out how she attempts to both interpellate herself into the everyday life in the camp, and also how she is mindful of the representation of her interlocutors in the writing practice. Because of the challenges of her field and object, Daigle is also conscious of her evolving understanding of the relation of her subjects to the Cuban state's control of sexuality and emotion, and so she chooses a narrative style that allows for that change in her thinking. We see three narrative strategies in contributions to this book: Johnson's authorial voice is present and empathetic to the vulnerability of her object of research; Ratelle (Chapter 12) specifically inserts himself into the research as an object of security practices; whereas Daigle reflects primarily on her role as a researcher. The writing practice of these projects becomes a central component to the research process. Vrasti has been an important commentator on ethnography in IR (2008), and she continues her engagement in this book. However, as we suggest above, the number of self-consciously-styled ethnographic projects in IR remain limited, and often confined to a solipsistic concern with the production of knowledge within the IR community.

Contemporary ethnography is less concerned with mapping familial, cultural, and economic relations in remote areas and more engaged with anthropologies of the present. Anthropology, in part because of its historical complicity in the colonial enterprise, is particularly sensitive to the legacy of both those imperial projects and the intellectual regimes of truth that supported them. The use of anthropologists to draft the Counter-Insurgency manual has led to a vigorous debate about the uses of ethnography and anthropology by the U.S. military, particularly in its "human terrain system" (González 2007). Contemporary American military counter-insurgency strategy relies on ethnographic research and embedded anthropologists in Iraq and Afghanistan, to understand the "human terrain" of conflict. As González sets out, the colonial resonance of this type of policy is worrying, particularly since anthropology had a similar public debate over the role of ethnographers during the Vietnam War:

> if history is any guide, it seems particularly likely that ethnographic intelligence will be used for social control methods reminiscent of those employed by the colonial powers of yesteryear . . . ethnography can quickly become a "martial art" under these conditions.
>
> (2009: 111)

Der Derian, Udris and Udris (2010) explore this issue in a documentary film *Human Terrain: War becomes Academic* to recount the story of their colleague Bhatia, a doctoral candidate in international relations and a fellow at Brown's Watson Institute, who was embedded as a social scientist with the US military in Afghanistan, and killed. The question of the complicity of anthropology in American military doctrine and operations has come to the fore since 2001, and the professional ethics of militarization has been an active site of debate in the discipline. As Gusterson states:

> the question for anthropology in our time is this: Will anthropology remain largely outside the orbit of the national security state, or has our turn at last arrived – following in the footsteps of physics, chemistry, engineering, political science, communications and psychology – to transform our discipline in response to initiatives from the Pentagon and intelligence agencies?
>
> (2009: 53)

Setting aside the disciplinary slight to political science, this questioning of the appropriateness of engagement with the military state embodies the critical, reflexive practice that is signal of ethnography.

Engagement and reflexivity are two of the core guiding ethico-methodological tenets of good ethnography. Kunz recognizes that her interviews with local community activists in Mexico on the impact of remittances on local development practices had the perverse effect of informing and motivating local activists to use remittances as an economic resource: she is engaged in the community, and comes to shape their practice in unexpected ways (Chapter 9). Crane-Seeber is illustrative of both the engagement with the military state, but also the self-reflection that is characteristic of the best kinds of autoethnography (Chapter 11). In understanding the lifeworld of pre-deployment American soldiers in Germany, Crane-Seeber reflects on how his fieldwork with these hypermasculine soldiers who would often use sexualized language was coming to affect his self-image. While seeking to understand the everyday of the soldier on their own terms, he was profoundly influenced by the codes of his adopted milieu.

Examples

Within this book, Ratelle provides a very clear justification for his research design. Within the critical community, we can point to two other important exemplars in the critical community: Der Derian's *Virtuous War*, which he describes in terms of a travelogue, and Gillem's *America Town*, which is self-consciously styled as an ethnography. Ratelle writes chiefly from the perspective of comparative politics, and in particular the subfield of political violence (to which he argues critical security studies does not pay enough analytical

Table PII.2 Examples of ethnographic research design

	Ratelle, Ethnography in Conflict Zones	*Der Derian*, Virtuous War *(2nd edition)*	*Gillem*, America Town
Object	Violence in Caucasus	Military-industrial-media-entertainment complex	Urban and architectural plans for persistent foreign American forces bases
Collection	Autoethnography, interviews, discourse analysis (newspaper)	Participant observation, interviews, discourse/policy analysis	Participant observation, interviews, discourse/policy analysis
Data	Fieldnotes, interviews, database of reported violent events	Interviews, policy and strategy documents, media reports, fieldnotes	Interviews, fieldnotes, policies, practices, photographs, graphic representation of urban plans
Relations	Heterogeneous field of security professionals and resistance in everyday	Professional links between military, industry, and media entertainment sectors; relations of ideas within military field	Institutional culture of US forces planning and relation to local space
Fit	Violent region with several ongoing conflicts; multiple language communities; high barrier to entry; public culture not easily legible	Restricted access to various fields with competing institutional cultures	Accessible through professional relations, networks, and practices; dispersed sites with common institution

attention); Der Derain writes as a research professor at the interdisciplinary Watson Institute; Gillem writes from a position within architecture and urban planning but is focused on foreign U.S. military bases. Interestingly, Gillem covers some of the ground of Enloe's *Bananas, Beaches, and Bases*, but from an ethnographic perspective, focused on spatial organization rather than gender.

Ratelle uses an autoethnography in the Caucasus to argue the analytical case for a wider use of ethnography and a consideration of actual political violence in critical security studies. He starts out with the intention of conducting a field analysis of violent actors in the Caucasus, particularly the conflict between Russian police, security, intelligence, and military forces and local ethnic and religious rebel groups, particularly in Chechnya, Dagestan, and Ingushetia. However, access is difficult and dangerous. The slippage between field analysis and ethnographic research practice becomes clear: Ratelle uses wide-ranging interviews and immersion in the everyday life, and while he is unable to gain access to either the government agencies or the rebel groups, he is able to embed in the everyday. Because of his physical similarity to the ethnic/religious groups targeted by Russian and government forces, Ratelle becomes subject not just to the everyday violence that living in the Caucasus entails, but of the specific profiling done by these agents of the state. Ratelle then puts himself at the centre of the analysis, and starts to examine systematically his detention and arrests: which agency is in charge, what are the questions being asked, what are the authorities to which they appeal, etc.? This is semi-covert ethnography, he does not immediately disclose his status as a researcher or his nationality, but when his identity documents are requested, then it becomes clear to the authorities that he is not a local. In some sense, Ratelle feels that this Canadian passport is recognized as a get out of Russian jail free card, but his narrative clearly indicates the uncertainty and fear that he experiences. This autoethnography allows him both to gather empirical material that was previously inaccessible and to experience the security system from the point of view of its objects.

Der Derian describes his own work as a "decade-long travelogue through the military-industrial-media-entertainment network" (2009c: xviii), and so is focused more directly on simulation and less on practices that transcend the military, the military-industrial complex, the media, and entertainment. As such, though the key argument could be made in terms of field and habitus, Der Derian self-consciously chooses an ethnographic form of writing, which he claims

> is not a scholarly treatise on international relations. Nor is it an op-ed article padded into a foreign policy book. . . From the start I sought to apply a critical attitude, developed outside the mainstream of American politics and scholarship, to current foreign and defense policies. My skepticism towards official stories was bolstered by empirical work in the field, where I was able to witness firsthand the concerted efforts and mixed results of powerful public and private institutions . . .
>
> (2009c: xix)

Der Derian's text is multiple: it includes philosophy, travelogues, interview transcripts, photographs, and features a clear first-person narrative. Der Derian is clear about his physical and emotional experiences during his fieldwork, his learning the vernacular of military-speak, his perceptions of the way that his subjects interact with him, and his conclusions and aspirations – he jokes, he wonders, he plans, he is frustrated, he is hopeful. Through his journey in the professional military-industrial-media-entertainment complex, in particular, focusing on the theme of simulation, Der Derian demonstrates a critical openness to the empirical field: he is able to approach the question of simulation from a variety of angles, and represents his research process as a journey rather than a test.

Gillem is a professor, a former Air Force Officer, licensed architect, and certified planner. Working from within the field of architecture, and a position he describes as his "outpost at the border of academia and empire" (2007: 283), Gillem writes about the planning and spatial organization of foreign American military bases. He self-consciously adopts an institutional ethnographic and autoethnographic method: combining his own personal experience as a planner for American forces, journalistic sources, visual, and photographic analysis, interviews, and an online survey. He demonstrates through three case studies of American bases that

> the United States has transported its socialspatial practices to diverse geographical settings, regardless of local concerns. . . America has exported its suburban land-use patterns, its version of home, across the globe, thereby helping engrave the military's incessant focus on command and control on distant landscapes.
>
> (2007: xx)

Gillem's object stems from his personal experience as an Air Force planner, but he chooses his case studies (Aviano, Italy; Osun, South Korea; and Okinawa, Japan) to reflect common practices across geographical scope. Mindful of his own position – both inside the institution and critical of it, an active officer and a researcher – Gillem uses his role as a university researcher to try and mitigate some of the bias that might emerge. He says,

> I wear the military uniform at times, but I am also an academic. Given these positions, I cannot eliminate my presence from the research. . . As an academic, I was able to develop a research agenda based on my own experiences. As an architect, I knew where to go for the answers. As an officer, I could go there.
>
> (2007: 281)

Conclusion

Ethnography, and in particular the foregrounding of the researcher, has become a more popular practice in contemporary critical security studies; it is particularly useful at representing unique but important bureaucratic, academic, or institutional cultures that acknowledge the role of the writer and the writing practice. The key assumptions about ethnography are that linguistic and material practices cannot be understood out of context, and that a culture must be experienced in order to be understood. Ethnography, then, is a meeting of cultures – the culture of the ethnographer and the culture of the object of research. As a science of singular instances, IR has avoided anthropology, but as Vrasti points out: "The radical promise of ethnography lies in its ability to expose IR as a culturally and historically specific ethnographic account of modern man and his political place" (2008: 301). The ethic of engagement and reflexivity can obviate the tendency of ethnographic IR becoming entirely onanistic and consumed with analyses of the tribal politics of the discipline. Because ethnography is an immersive and embedded practice, research design must include a methodological openness to the field, and thinking space for the process of writing.

The question of reflexivity and the engagement with the security apparatus of the state has not been tackled extensively in critical security studies. There is a robust debate concerning the role of experts in *Cooperation and Conflict* (Eriksson 1999a, 1999b, Goldmann 1999,

Wæver 1999, Williams 1999) and in the discipline more generally (Smith 2004), but this reflection is rarely evident in the writings of critical security studies scholars. Der Derian speaks clearly and powerfully about the impact of the field on his thinking and research, but little about his role in the development of the military's strategy. Gillem writes about this relationship in his methodological appendix because while researching and writing his doctoral thesis, he is problem-solving for the very Armed Forces that he criticizes. The question of engagement has been framed strictly in terms of emancipation in the debates surrounding securitization theory and the Welsh School of Critical Theory (Aradau 2004, c.a.s.e. collective 2006). There is still room within the critical security studies community, however, to engage more fully in the question of engagement with the security state.

Notes

1   AAMC (2011) "Exploring a Medical Career" www.aamc.org/students/considering/exploring_medical/ (accessed 16 June 2011).
2   David Segall (2011) "Is Law a Losing Game?" *New York Times* 8 January 2011. (accessed 16 June 2011). Segall points out the tension between those figures and reports of a more difficult job market.

Suggested reading

Appadurai, A. (1996) *Modernity at Large: Cultural Dimensions of Globalization*, Minneapolis: University of Minnesota Press.

Clifford, J. (1988) *The Predicament of Culture: Twentieth-Century Ethnography, Literature and Art*, Cambridge: Harvard University Press.

Geertz, C. (1973) *The Interpretation of Cultures*, New York: Basic Books.

Jackson, P.T. (2008a) "Can Ethnographic Techniques Tell Us Distinctive Things About World Politics?" *International Political Sociology*, 2(1): 91–94.

Madison, D.S. (2005) *Critical Ethnography: Method, Ethics and Performance*, London: SAGE Publications.

Network of Concerned Anthropologists (2009) *The Counter-Counterinsurgency Manual, or Notes on Demilitarizing American Society*, Chicago: Prickly Paradigm Press.

8　Travelling with ethnography

Wanda Vrasti

Introduction

Years ago, when I first became interested in ethnography, a colleague of mine who was flirting with similar ideas confessed he had realized that "[he] was not good enough of a writer to be doing ethnography". I rejected this notion out of hand as both elitist and defeatist, and went on to write a piece on "The Strange Case of Ethnography and International Relations" (2008). I was only in the second year of my Ph.D. and incredibly flattered to have made such a precocious intervention in the discipline. In the years that followed I wrote a couple of additional pieces clarifying my original position (2010, 2011). Before I knew it, I became an "ethnography person", somewhat of a trusted authority on the subject, although up to this point none of my *own* ethnographic research has appeared in print (2012). I want to use this opportunity to talk about some of the surprises and challenges I encountered during fieldwork, and explain how my view of ethnography has changed since the publication of the 2008 *Millennium* piece.

I wrote my dissertation on volunteer tourism, a booming business geared mostly to 18–25 year olds looking to spend their holidays doing charitable work in the Global South. A slew of studies discussing the ethical virtues and technical difficulties of this formula had already been published in tourism and hospitality studies, and I did not intend on stepping in their footsteps. Rather, what interested me were the types of subjects and social relations being produced in this encounter and how these furthered (or undermined) neoliberal modes of government and valorization. Mine were the classic Foucauldian questions: "How are we constituted as subjects of our own knowledge? How are we constituted as subjects who exercise or submit to power relations? How are we constituted as moral subjects of our own actions?" (Foucault cited in Nelson 2009: 130). It was clear to me from the very beginning that this had to be an ethnographic project. Ethnography, I hoped, would help me obtain first-hand experience of a practice I was not very familiar (or patient) with. At the same time, it would push me to write "stories about real people in real places" (Behar 2003: 16) to make global politics more palpable. This commitment to empirical grounding and democratic writing was already a radical departure from my initial ideas about what ethnography is and what it can do.

In the *Millennium* article, I criticized the so-called ethnographic turn in International Relations (IR) for being a narrow and selective adaptation of a much richer and ambitious ethnographic tradition in anthropology. International studies turned to ethnography just when critical anthropology was questioning the historic and textual authority of ethnographic texts, in the hope of capturing a more authentic, politically, but also policy-relevant version of social reality. This was a false hope, I argued. The task of ethnography was not to access the "really real" (Behar 2003:16), let the subaltern speak, or produce innocent knowledge outside the constraints of theory and representation (Scott 1992: 44). Instead, I argued, ethnography should be used to interrogate the stories IR likes to tell about the proper (read: modern, sovereign) configuration of political communities and identities by revealing their contingent history and spatiotemporal impermanence. Although I still consider this to be an important task, I no longer think it is sufficient for ethnography to limit its responsibility to polishing what is essentially an epiphenomenon of global politics, not its actual manifestation.

If in the beginning of my graduate studies I was seduced by all sorts of imports from continental philosophy, once I began doing fieldwork and was forced to build rapport with people who knew nothing about my profession, I became highly uncomfortable with the undemocratic grip higher education maintains over theory and knowledge production. My dissertation work was going to challenge this, I thought. Ethnography would help me repopulate IR scholarship with the voices and actions of *regular people*, neither the heads of states, diplomats, and military personnel usually credited with making global politics, nor the marginalized and dispossessed critical theory has discovered a fascination for, but white middle-class people not so different in their economic background, values, and tastes from those populating the academic profession. Using interviews and participant observation I would capture the everyday progression of volunteer experiences from compassion to boredom and, finally, to the development of multicultural sensibilities and other affective competencies congruent with liberal capitalism. This would show that the subjective condition and its everyday ontology is "the locus where the social link is forged" (Madra and Özselcuk 2010: 482), the place where political attachments are formed, and where political action acquires meaning. In the process, I would also defy the highly technical and esoteric language that academics like to dress up their theories in to make the end product relevant (and readable) beyond the narrow walls of academia, particularly for the participants, operators, and stakeholders of volunteer tourism. The end goal would be to make high theory, the usefulness of which I am still convinced of, amenable to personal reflection and political action.

Armed with these somewhat romantic aspirations, I signed up for two volunteering trips, one with a nature conservation organization in Guatemala, the other with a teaching program in Ghana. On each trip I spent about two months working as a volunteer by day and ethnographer by night – so to speak. Since it was going to be impossible to survey a "representative" number of volunteer tourism programs, I chose my sites by convenience, depending on location, timing, and pricing. The technicalities of participant observation and interviewing interested me less than the challenge of *writing* ethnography. Having read critical anthropology I knew that ethnography "is from beginning to end enmeshed in writing" (Clifford 1983: 120). Only writing can establish the authority of the ethnographic voice (or destabilize it), bring stories and characters to life, reconstruct the local colour, open up the text to the non-academic public, and translate theory into practice. During the period of fieldwork I would stumble upon many chance encounters and false expectations, but none would be greater than the realization that the ethnography I had intended to write when I left home would become impossible upon my return.

My first surprise realization was that ethnography does not have a political orientation or program of its own beyond a vague commitment to ethical representation. If I wanted to examine the conditions of possibility that allow volunteer tourism to function as a neoliberal strategy of subject-formation, I had to combine ethnography with Foucault's archaeological method. In contrast to ethnography, archaeology suggests that the minute description of everyday practices and experience is purely descriptive unless we take into account how these work in conjunction and disjunction with normative discourses, political institutions, economic regimes, and programs of government. It also implies that the ethnographer's responsibility does not stop at accurately transcribing fieldwork events, statements, and artifacts. No matter how urgent the demand for equitable representation, we cannot allow the spoken repertoires of our research subjects to sideline the material and discursive strategies involved in reproducing or subverting relations of power (Ferguson 2006: 19). To quote Bayart, "subjectivization is too important to be left up to the subjects" (2008: 199). Without a larger political ambition, even the most polyphonic of texts cannot help but become exercises in flatfooted sociology. This is why I ultimately opted for a dialogical method that moves between the narrative constructions of volunteer tourists and the governmental strategies involved in their subject-formation.

My second awakening was that my colleague, the one who had abandoned ethnography for not having the necessary writing skills, had been right after all. Ethnography may not require inborn talent, but it is a far more demanding genre than I had originally envisioned. Constructing a dynamic and dramatized representation of the temporal flows of international political life that is both theoretically astute and accessible is not as easy as doing away with jargon or "letting yourself go"; it is not about spilling one's guts out on paper or writing from the heart, as aficionados of ethnography's personalized tone would like to think (Behar 2003, Enloe 2004). Rather, it is a craft that requires training (editing work, professional audacity, political engagement, narrative skills, and even time), a type of training our graduate studies rarely provide because they are far more focused on getting the methodology right than helping us become better writers. But even when all these conditions are satisfied, ethnography can still fall short of lived reality either because textual representation forever defers our access to the "really real" (ethnography, like any other academic production, is also policed by certain textual and disciplinary conventions) or because theory (the dense, continental kind) turns out to be indispensable for the overall effectiveness of the project.

Conclusion

Instead of being discouraged by these realizations, I discovered a more humble and honest use of ethnography. I would use ethnography as a logistical strategy to piece together the disparate pieces of my research (field notes, library research, committee meetings, conference presentations, successive writing, and endless editing stages) while remaining honest about the windy and bumpy road I travelled from research questions to finished manuscript. This represents a radical departure from the idea of research as a "linear and deliberate accumulation" of insight usually presented in methodology courses (Cerwonka 2007: 37). The answers to our research questions rarely await us in the field. Often we return home more confused than we were in the first place. This is where ethnography comes in handy: recognizing that this is a man-made translation of social reality with no claims to scientific reliability, ethnography can afford to travel back and forth between the part and the whole, experience and text, fieldwork and theory, certainty and epiphany in ways that other methods cannot and which, in the end, can only add to the credibility and authenticity of this genre (Ibid: 15, 19).

Although the book that emerged from my dissertation research is a lot more theory-driven than I had originally envisioned and, therefore, will probably not end up in the hands of volunteers, parents, and tourism operators, my hope to correct the dehumanized (people-less, story-less, and emotionless) face of IR research and write user-friendly texts that transcend the boundaries of our profession is more alive than ever. Faced with the material hardships and political violence associated with the latest crisis of capital, we see a growing demand for knowledge that is empirically grounded in and politically vocal about the realities of our everyday lives. So far this demand has found most resonance outside university walls, through the continuous rise of new journalism, blogs, podcasts, free web and radio media, and the Global Autonomous University movement (spearheaded by the journal *edu-factory*). While the appeal to public responsibility in academia can also easily serve as a populist ploy to justify the corporatization of higher education, there remain many ways in which we can productively renegotiate the theory/practice divide without slipping into the anti-intellectual "all-these-theories-and-the-bodies-keep-piling-up" rhetoric (Zalewski 1996). Ethnography, with its ambition to repopulate international politics with human life and recreate the dramatic milieu of everyday experience, and, above all, its confidence in the power of writing to transcend disciplinary, professional and other spatiotemporal boundaries, I continue to believe, is one of them.

Suggested reading

Ehrenreich, B. (2001) *Nickel and Dimed: On (Not) Getting By in America*, New York: Henry Holt.
Ferguson, J. (2006) *Global Shadows: Africa in the Neoliberal World Order*, Durham: Duke University Press.
Graeber, D. (2009) *Direct Action: An Ethnography*, Oakland: AK Press.
Huynh, K. (2008) *Where the Sea Takes Us: A Vietnamese-Australian Story*, Sydney: Harper Collins.
Tsing, A. (2005) *Friction: An Ethnography of Global Connection*, Princeton: Princeton University Press.

9 Reflexive inquiry

Rahel Kunz

Introduction

International Relations (IR) was notoriously awarded the "dubious honour of being among the least self-reflexive of the Western social sciences" (Frost in Lapid 1989: 249–250). Since, a rich literature on the notion of reflexivity in IR has emerged, most notably in connection with the Third Debate and the ethnographic turn in IR (Ackerly and True 2008, Guillaume 2002, Neufeld 1993). Broadly defined, reflexivity means that "serious attention is paid to the way different kinds of linguistic, social, political, and theoretical elements are woven together in the process of knowledge development, during which empirical material is constructed, interpreted and written" (Alvesson and Sköldberg 2000: 9). This means that the research process influences the research object or situation, challenging established distinctions between object and subject, theory and reality, and author and text. Reflexivity makes us think about the (power) relations between the researcher and the researched, and the political nature of research (Aull Davies 1999, Marcus 1994).

The aim of this chapter is to highlight a number of elements of reflexive inquiry, particularly when conducting ethnography. First, I provide a brief outline of my research design. Next, drawing on my ethnographic fieldwork experience, I present a number of dilemmas encountered during the research process, and how reflexive inquiry was helpful in addressing them.

Over the last decade, a new trend has emerged within the international community: the Global Remittance Trend (GRT). Government institutions, international (financial) organizations, non-governmental organizations (NGOs), and private sector actors have all become interested in migration, remittances, and their potential for poverty reduction and development, and have all created institutions and devised policies to harness this potential (Kunz 2011: 4). While the current literature adopts a narrow problem-solving approach, my analysis sought to move beyond this narrow focus, first, by problematizing the GRT through an analysis of the process whereby the migration-development-remittances nexus has become an object of knowledge and intervention; second, by situating it within on-going transformations, such as global restructuring and neoliberalism; and third, by exploring the gender dimensions and implications of the seemingly gender-neutral GRT. Using Foucault's governmentality approach combined with insights from post-colonial and post-structural feminist theories, I analyzed the (gender-specific) implications of the GRT in the international realm and specifically in Mexico. To comprehensively trace the GRT – from its macro- to its micro-dimensions, from its conceptual to its institutional elements – I used a multi-method approach, combining textual and policy analysis with expert-interviews, and ethnographic fieldwork in rural Mexican communities. The main argument of this study was that the GRT has emerged as a regime of practices with concrete implications that stretch from the international realm to individual subjects, most notably, the reinforcement of gendered forms of neoliberal governmentality.

During the research process, I faced a number of challenges and dilemmas. First, being a non-Mexican and non-native speaker had both advantages and disadvantages. On the one hand, it was more difficult to gain access to the communities and earn the trust of informants, and it demanded additional efforts to understand the context of my informants. Often my respondents initially thought I was a *gringa* (a disparaging term referring to U.S. citizens), which sometimes facilitated the beginning of conversations. In other cases, it made it more difficult to establish trust. On the other hand, as a foreigner, I could often ask seemingly naïve questions regarding background or context that a Mexican could not have asked, and thereby gather valuable information. In the indigenous community where I carried out fieldwork, many inhabitants did not feel comfortable speaking Spanish, which meant that someone translated into Spanish. Yet, given that I am not a native Spanish speaker, this often created a sense of complicity between my informants and I, and some started talking Spanish to me after a while.

Given the gender focus of my research, being a woman was an advantage for conducting fieldwork research, as most women I have interviewed would not so readily have talked to male researchers, and even less given information about gender-specific issues. However, some interviews with men were more difficult to conduct. In addition, during my fieldwork, it was sometimes difficult to manage my feminist values, and to deal with the fact that as a foreign woman, I was able to move more freely than certain local women and do certain things that were taboo for local women.

This highlights the importance of self-reflexivity, i.e., awareness of the ways in which our gender, ethnicity, class, nationality, language, socio-cultural background, and beliefs and values have crucial implications for conducting research. This is an on-going process that intervenes at various stages of the research process, such as in the formulation of research questions, the selection of interview partners, and the conducting of interviews, as well as in the interpretation of replies. Thus, a first guiding question for reflexive inquiry asks: How do my identity, biography, socio-cultural background, assumptions, and values influence my research?

During my research I encountered another dilemma. For about a decade, countless research projects have been carried out in Mexico, collecting information about migration, remittances, and the lives of migrants and non-migrants. My interest was in the implications of this information collection in terms of its contributions to creating new objects of knowledge and creating normalization effects. These effects have the impact that the GRT acts as a disciplinary and regulatory power. Yet, the question is whether we researchers are also involved in spreading the norms within the GRT and reproducing the disciplinary power of the GRT, through rendering visible the activities of the people interviewed or by initiating dialogue and raising expectations to attract migrant remittances. Are we instrumental in reproducing the effects we study – in my case disciplinary neoliberal governing – even though the motivation behind our study is to expose and to a certain extent denounce these effects? Also, would taking this challenge seriously mean that we should not do research on this topic? Or is it the type of research that makes a difference?

During my own research, as well as during a collective research project in which I participated, we asked informants whether they knew about the possibility of establishing remittance-linked development projects and what they thought about them. Thereby, we implicitly informed those people who had not heard about such projects before. One could argue that we therefore indirectly promoted the Mexican government's neoliberal strategy of development through remittances. A statement by the local priest, who provided us with access to one of our communities, seemed to confirm this concern. During an interview, he said that he was happy that we had come to do interviews, because he felt it had "woken up" the inhabitants and incited them to become more active in establishing migration-linked development projects: "This study has contributed to raising awareness among the people . . . You can see how they have changed. And this is thanks to your investigation, it helped to motivate them and wake them up" (Interview with local priest, rural Mexican community, April 2006, my translation). This has to be understood in the context of a situation where the priest was actively engaged in attempts to organize the community, in order to initiate development projects with the help of migrants. Thus, to some extent, our research might have served his agenda.

In order to address this dilemma, I discussed with the priest the problematic impacts of the GRT that my research had revealed. I also made it clear during my interviews that I was not personally advocating such an approach, and discussed its potentials and pitfalls with my respondents. Oftentimes, I realized that my interviews created discussions and disagreement among informants regarding the GRT. I also highlighted various forms of resistance in my research, in order to not only expose the power implications of the GRT, but also emphasize counter-tendencies. This example highlights a second form of reflexivity: ethico-political reflexivity, which includes awareness regarding the implications of findings for informants and the research situation, and regarding the ways in which findings might be used for purposes other than intended. Thus, a second guiding question for reflexive inquiry asks: Which ethical, social, political, or economic implications might my research and my findings have?

This question is particularly relevant when researching resistance and empowerment. It is important to research resistance and empowerment in order to reveal that they exist, to emphasize agency, and potentially to express political support for certain forms of resistance and empowerment. This is particularly so in the context of research on neoliberalism that has tended to emphasize the homogeneous and all-powerful character of neoliberalism, which can be challenged through research on failures and contradictions of, and resistance to, neoliberalism. However, there is a risk of backfiring, whereby the space of resistance might be closed, or forms of empowerment rendered impossible, as a result of the publication of our research findings.

In my own research, I encountered a similar dilemma regarding the forms of resistance against the disciplinary power of the GRT in Mexico. Thus, for example, I reported how migrants use services provided by the Mexican government without cooperating with government officials in establishing remittance-linked development projects, or how non-migrants subvert and appropriate specific projects for their own purpose (Kunz 2011: 153ff). I attempted to reduce the risk of cooptation through a number of strategies, such as anonymity for respondents and vagueness regarding the exact form and place of resistance. In addition, I selected forms of resistance that are relatively well-known and have to some extent been acknowledged by the Mexican government, such as particular migrant groups that resist organizing and sending remittances or well-known organizations that officially counter the GRT discourse in Mexico. This was a way for academic work to provide space and support for such initiatives. In cases where forms of resistance or empowerment might be endangered through our publications, it might be better to renounce publishing such information.

Conclusion

Research might also have potentially liberating implications. Many women I contacted for an interview asked me why I was interested in what they had to say and suggested I should interview the head of the community instead. When I insisted, some respondents were flattered that I was interested in their views, feeling that their opinion mattered. Through our research we might also be able to give some voice to parts of the population that have hitherto been ignored and to trigger moments of discussion and awareness-raising. Thus, reflexive inquiry can guide us through the stormy weathers of research dilemmas.

Suggested reading

Ackerly, B.A. and True, J. (2008) "Reflexivity in Practice: Power and Ethics in Feminist Research on International Relations", *International Studies Review*, 10(4): 693–707.

Alvesson, M. and Sköldberg, K. (2000) *Reflexive Methodology: New Vistas for Qualitative Research*, London: SAGE Publications.

Guillaume, X. (2002) "Reflexivity and Subjectivity: A Dialogical Perspective for and on International Relations Theory", *Forum: Qualitative Social Research*, 3(3): Art.13.

Madden, R. (2010) *Being Ethnographic: A Guide to the Theory and Practice of Ethnography*, London: SAGE Publications.

Marcus, G. (1994) "On Ideologies of Reflexivity in Contemporary Efforts to Remake the Human Sciences", *Poetics Today*, 15(3): 383–404.

10 Listening to migrant stories

Heather L. Johnson

Introduction

At the end of a long day, my first day, in Nduta refugee camp in Tanzania I sat on a stool in front of the food distribution area, next to the information resource centre. I had spent the day in individual and group interviews, and had been in one place for more than three hours talking to large and small groups, some individuals, sometimes with the aid of translator, sometimes in English, occasionally in simple French. I ended my day more aware of my relative position of power and privilege than I had ever been, a position marked not only by my status as researcher/graduate student/visitor/Westerner, but also by the colour of my skin, my class status, and my gender. I was more aware of the power relations implicated within my study. It is this awareness, nascent in my project design and more deeply meaningful as time went on and these dynamics became more apparent, that profoundly shaped my methodological approach to my research. This approach began with a conscious privileging of narrative, and was pursued with a continued awareness of voice and of silence, under-standing narratives not as authentic statements of the *way things are*, but as subjectivities within an ongoing dialogue of meaning-making and knowledge creation in the global migration and asylum regime.

In 2007 and 2008 I pursued field research in three global sites: refugee camps in Tanzania, the border zone between Spain and Morocco, and detention centres in Australia. I wanted to pursue research that disturbed traditional security narratives of global borders, and to situate the non-citizen at the centre of analysis not as a problem, but as a powerful and transgressive actor who challenges the ways in which we understand political subjectivity. I also, however, wanted to understand global patterns of migration and border control from the *on the ground* perspective of the migrant. The challenges present were daunting. How was I to sensibly bring together several vastly different sites into one coherent study? More importantly, how could this be achieved while maintaining narratives at the centre of analysis without flattening migrant stories and experiences into abstract generalities? How, also, could I recognize my own role and power position within research that engages highly vulnerable populations?

Ethnography and the lessons it teaches suggests strategies and highlights concerns and priorities in research that I hope allowed me to tackle these challenges. I designed the project around particular spaces that illustrate border and asylum politics – refugee camps, border zones, and detention centres. In these spaces I take a snapshot of the dynamics of a border space, including the policies and practices that govern cross-border migration and the day-to-day lives of migrants. These snapshots allow me to glimpse how the global politics of migration and asylum are manifest on the ground and in the lived lives of individuals. I build upon an approach suggested by Marcus (1995) in his work on multi-sited ethnographies; I follow connections, relationships and experiences across multiple spaces to access the configurations of global regimes. It is the mobility, relationships, and changing position of the individuals who move through space that form the centre of the study.

I conducted research in Nduta Camp in Kibondo, Tanzania, complemented by policy interviews and research in Dar es Salaam; at the Spanish enclave of Melilla and Moroccan border city of Oujda with policy research in Madrid and Rabat; and in the Villawood Detention Centre in Sydney, Australia, with policy research in Melbourne, Sydney, and Canberra. Tanzania provides insight into refugee camps as the home of some of the largest and most long-term refugee camps in Africa. The border zone between Spain and Morocco provides insight into areas where the global North and South collide. Finally, Australia's detention regime provides a mirror of these dynamics in the context of the global North and a regime that serves as a policy leader for other regions. Together, they provide a picture of a global regime, of an example of how we can talk about the global together with the local, and of how particular, everyday migrant narratives can inform our understandings of border, migration, and asylum practice and policy.

I attempted to meet the challenge of ensuring continuity across all three sites, despite their differences, while carrying out interviews. Building upon Aberbach and Rockman (2002), I designed a program of open-ended interviews that remained guided by core questions. This allowed participants to more freely interpret my questions, and to guide the interview in directions that they felt were relevant. Such an approach is far better suited to accessing subjugated knowledges and the voices of the marginalized, as it does not presume that I, as the researcher, know what is important in their daily experience. In giving at least partial control of the interview to participants, a semi-structured, open interview enabled my participants to contextualize and represent her/himself as much as possible.

My policy interviews were scheduled, primarily, using cold call and snowballing (reference) strategies. In all three sites, however, interviews with migrants were more flexible. In Nduta I made some appointments, but most interviews were the result of being highly visible (for example, my afternoon described above) and spending time in the camp. In Morocco, I simply walked into the unauthorized migrant camp and approached people, who then introduced me to others. In Spain and Australia, particularly because the security context of detention not only limited my access to communities but also impacted the emotional and trust responses of migrants, I relied heavily on introductions from friends and allies in the community. In total I conducted 143 individual and group interviews, all open-ended, and engaged in participant observation at each site. I interviewed asylum seekers and unauthorized migrants, refugees and detainees, policy makers, practitioners, advocates, and support workers.

Taking a flexible approach to interview design required me to be open both to changing my focus and the questions I asked according to what information I received. I constantly assessed and reassessed my approach. I did not delete or remove questions, but only added them as needed. This maintained a baseline of consistency across interviews, while also enabling a learning process. I found that there was an unexpected dimension to this flexibility, however. Particularly during elite interviews with policy makers and implementers, I was frequently given advice about how to engage with migrant communities and warned against the information I would receive. The advice I was receiving was clearly located within the discourses that have marginalized and excluded the migrants I was working with, and so I was reluctant to adjust my approach in response. However, it was not advice that I could simply dismiss because it represents the understandings found in official circles, which directly impacts the experiences of migrants. In the end, the advice I received, and the attitudes it reveals, became a valuable part of my research in itself.

The greatest challenge I faced was that of trust; in a method based on interviews, this proved crucial. I work with a highly vulnerable population. Particularly for those individuals living illegally without official status, speaking with an outsider is a risk. The risks are serious; the consequences of speaking to the wrong person can include deportation and removal, police raids (usually with accompanying violence), and arrest and detention. I tried to address this barrier in several ways. I took active steps to minimize my own impact on migrant communities. I did not report illegal migrants or their migration strategies to the officials. Wherever possible, and at the advice of other researchers and advocates, I travelled as a tourist to minimize official attention. During the interviews themselves, I emphasized that my notes were my own and that participants could end interviews or choose not to answer any particular question. When I used translators, I required them to sign confidentiality agreements and ensured that they were fully aware of the dynamics and risks of the situation.

I did not tape record my interviews, relying instead upon very extensive handwritten notes. Within many methodological approaches, this decision could mean a loss of verifiability as the accurate recall of what was said becomes less reliable. It was, however, a conscious decision on my part. The daily experience of the migrants I was speaking with meant that I was not comfortable recording our conversations at risk of increasing their vulnerability. This was true particularly because we were speaking directly about their strategies and plans for further attempts to illegally cross borders. In addition to my concerns about vulnerability, a recording device would have negatively impacted an already cautious and fragile trust relationship, which was of greater concern to me than word for word recall. I did not ask their names or write them down if they gave them, and only requested their country of origin.

These concerns about vulnerability did not apply to the other groups of participants I spoke with. However, I felt that as I had not recorded migrant interviews, I could not record other interviews. This arose from the awareness of already present power relations that an ethnographic approach emphasizes. I felt that in a study that purports to privilege the migrant narrative, having complete transcripts of the already dominant voices of the policy makers and practitioners and not of migrant voices recreated a disparity in authority of voice and authenticity that undermined the intentions of my project. This concern was only exacerbated by the necessity for translators only for migrants, as all of my other participants were fluent in either English or French.

One consequence of the decision to not record interviews is that there are very few lengthy direct quotes in my final account. I only use false names. The other consequence, however, is that I have been privileged to hear, and then to share, very frank accounts of difficult experiences, but also of hopes and plans for the future.

Conclusion

I began my field research with the intention of focusing on refugees and asylum seekers. Several encounters that occurred during my fieldwork, however, gave me pause. In Australia, I met a detainee who had overstayed his visa and only then claimed asylum and so had been put in detention. He was on hunger strike in support of his final appeal against his deportation. In Spain, I met a group of children who had chosen to migrate across the border of Melilla, smuggling themselves beneath trucks and buses or swimming around the fence. They were living in the government migrant centre for unaccompanied minors, and challenging this space by demanding that local authorities take account of their complaints about living conditions, chanting, "we have rights!" In Tanzania, I met a young man who was refusing to participate in the repatriation program back to Burundi, choosing instead to live outside of the camp, effectively making himself illegal, and to work at local farms.

Not all of these individuals were refugees; not all of them were even asylum seekers, and those who had claimed asylum were having the legitimacy of that claim and that identity challenged by the state. They were all, however, irregular migrants, made irregular by their own migration choices and engaged in a politics of irregularity that I came to believe has more to tell us about contemporary border and migration politics than a more classic focus on refugees could. My focus shifted. This shift was made possible by a methodology founded in a deep awareness of how working with marginalized populations requires a different kind of attention to power and voice, not only in analysis of the research, but also in its actual carrying out.

This project is not about *giving* migrants voice; they have voices. The question is whether or not they are heard. By emphasizing dialogue and making particular choices in my method, I have attempted to engage in a politics of listening. I am thus part of the project myself. Who I am, what decisions I made, and how I reacted to my research encounters are part of my *data*. In this, I attempt to call attention to the dynamics of interpretation, not to discount the validity of my observations, but to emphasize their contingency. Moreover, in engaging with the migrant narrative in this way I hope to affirm the migrants' role as powerful actors within the politics of migration and asylum.

In this research I ask questions about participation, agency, and power. I look to the migrant experience to inform my understandings of the impact of policies and practices of management and control over migration on the everyday lives of those who cross international borders. I began the study intending to study refugee and asylum migration; I finished it with a deeper understanding of the ways in which irregularity has emerged as the central concept in migration politics. The central goal of my research, therefore, has become to work towards an understanding of irregularity not simply as a status, but as a way of being, of living through transversal border spaces that capture and attempt to regulate mobility. Achieving this objective relies upon a flexible and dynamic methodology in the field, and an attention to voice. But for every voice there is always a silence. An awareness of this is crucial, particularly in a study that centres the disruptive power of subaltern migrant narratives. It is not a limitation that must be overcome, but an inevitable by-product of any research. Research is mutable, by time and by space and also by absences, assumptions, perspectives, and subject positions. It is for this reason that any project is part of a larger field of study, and a larger conversation and dialogue that strives to engage and understand. One project cannot provide the complete picture, and should not attempt to do so at risk of making the silences it inevitably imposes permanent.

Suggested reading

Aberbach, J.D. and Rockman, B.A. (2002) "Conducting and Coding Elite Interviews", *PS: Political Science*, 35(4): 673–676.

Ashley, R.K. and Walker, R.B.J. (1990) "Speaking the Language of Exile: Dissident Thought in International Studies", *International Studies Quarterly*, 34(3): 259–268.

Bakewell, O. (2008) "Research Beyond the Categories: The Importance of Policy Irrelevant Research into Forced Migration", *Journal of Refugee Studies*, 21(4): 432–453.

Ghorashi, H. (2007) "Refugee Voice, Giving Silence a Chance: The Importance of Life Stories for Research on Refugees", *Journal of Refugee Studies*, 21(1): 117–132.

Marcus, G. (1995) "Ethnography In/of the World System: the Emergency of Multi Sited Ethnography", *Annual Review of Anthropology*, 24: 95–117.

Squire, V. (2010) "The Contested Politics of Mobility: Politicizing Mobility, Mobilizing Politics" in V. Squire (ed.) *The Contested Politics of Mobility: Borderzones and Irregularity*, New York: Routledge.

Tuhiwai Smith, L. (1999) *Decolonizing Methodologies: Research and Indigenous Peoples*, London: Zed Books.

11 Learning by feeling

Jesse Paul Crane-Seeber

Introduction

In 2003, I was living in a small German city that happened to host a US army base, and friends I had made there were preparing for the invasion of Iraq. At the time, Secretary of State Powell and others were saying that no final decision to attack Iraq had been made, but the Abrams tanks and Bradley fighting vehicles being loaded onto German freight trains suggested otherwise. As Secretary of Defense Rumsfeld aptly put it on September 12, 2001, "I'm inclined to think if you're going to cock it you throw it" (AP Staff 2001). I attended a few demonstrations against the war, and helped my best friend pack his bags for Kuwait. While the soldiers were gone, I stayed in touch with families who lived at an army family housing community, and after the invasion of Iraq got going, I followed the men I knew through the tangle of terror and bureaucracy that constitutes a soldier's life.

I spent my graduate school years talking to, studying, and struggling to comprehend those of my generation who fought in Iraq. I hoped to use graduate school to search for the methodological and theoretical tools necessary to interpret what I learned from people fighting this war, one that I, like many IR scholars, regarded as a mistake (Jackson and Kaufman 2007).

Since I started my research, the questions I work to answer have changed, because I learned a lot that surprised me along the way. As Vrasti (Chapter 8) and Johnson (Chapter 10) both describe, a certain methodological flexibility is a key requirement to doing ethnographic research. I began by asking how soldiers (including my friends) imagine and explain their participation in state-sanctioned violence, which drew me to the literature on why and how soldiers normalize killing (Browning 1998, Grossman 1995, Rose 1989: 15–52, Wong et al. 2003). These works describe loyalty to comrades, fear, repetitive training techniques, and ideological commitment as factors, but they build from historical case studies or large surveys. I wanted to offer a more intimate sense of how modern soldiers explained violence, by foregrounding their voices.

During my first fieldwork experience, I talked to recent veterans about combat, but the stories I elicited, as an outsider, were few and generic. I had hoped to analyze how they make sense of fighting, to understand their constructions of self and other, but it was not working. There are no doubt strategies I could have employed to salvage the original project, as others have managed to produce such studies (Bar and Ben-Ari 2005). However, I realized that my research plan was not yielding the information I was seeking, so I shifted the focus to mundane everyday life (Crane-Seeber 2011, Enloe 2011). Instead of trying to steer conversations, I sought opportunities to watch soldiers and their families as they approximated normal lives despite the strange rhythms and unique terrors of combat deployment. This was possible because I had a key informant who introduced me to people, took me to bars and private homes, brought me on base, and provided a certain amount of vouching.

At first I thought I was failing utterly, since most of my time was spent near (but not on) army bases, talking to soldiers and their families, and observing the social spaces they frequented. In bars, a pool hall, on the streets of German and US cities, in military family housing facilities, on-base grocery stores, and in private residences, I watched people interact, asked questions, looked at war photos, and got made fun of a lot... *a lot* (Ben-Ari, Taubman and Liora 2005).

I found that stereotypes about soldiers and gendered homophobia exist for a reason. Civilians were described as being "soft," and I was often called a "pussy" or "faggot" when talking with young soldiers. This may have been a way of taming an outsider, of asserting situational authority, or reducing the potential disruption my presence might have introduced. While these (usually) younger men lived with curfews, mandatory urine tests, 5:00am physical training, and very little individual freedom, they paradoxically mocked civilians for being too soft to surrender to the authoritarian discipline that military service entails (Sasson-Levy 2007).

As Salter notes in the introduction to Part II, participant-observation research is a recursive process, one that involves re-interpreting experience and seeking to impose some amount of retrospective order. After repeated visits to several US military installations in Europe and the US, I had learned a great deal about military family life, the various programs designed to smooth the transition back from war, and the unique political economy of base communities. I also, bit by bit, learned a few things about identity.

Without initially realizing it, my fieldwork began to affect my self-image. One morning on my first field visit, I found myself looking in the mirror and thought "what a chubby little pussy" – language that I normally do not use was transforming my self-conception. Despite engagement with feminist and queer theory, I found myself thinking that because they are physically stronger, and many had killed people in Iraq, these soldiers were in fact *real men* and that there was something wrong with me, in particular with my body.

The warrior-male image has a powerful hold on US culture, affecting numerous aspects of men's lives (Stump 2011). One effect of my proximity to military culture was an almost obsessive drive to be physically stronger. While conducting my first field study, I started to compulsively run and do push-ups or sit-ups. It was not a rational decision. I did not wake up one morning and decide that I would imitate the exercise regimen of soldiers, or try to measure up.

Anthropologists talk about "going native" when scholars lose their autonomous identity while engaging in participant-observation (Kondo 1990: 17). Similarly, away from the community I call home, I experienced a slippage of my self-image. I lost my detachment and came to evaluate myself, particularly my body, using the language of those I was studying. In short, the discursive environment in which I placed myself was undermining my self-image: I saw myself as less of a man than a 19-year-old sunburned soldier in tan boots.

The voice in my head, as I looked in the mirror and saw someone pathetic and weak, was neither my own nor any individual's. It was the voice of an inner-bully, which makes manhood a precarious and temporary achievement. Through fear of weakness, the feminine, and other men, a powerful cultural narrative polices masculinity through homophobia and violence (Kimmel 2000). Despite feminist and queer theory as potential antidotes, I felt the power of that fear activate within me.

I do not believe that anyone I talked to was trying to provoke an identity crisis. While the subjective experience of individuals can never be known from the outside, the function of a remark can be traced when researchers focus on observing interactions and how particular conversational moves produce local effects (Shotter 2008). But as I learned, subjecting oneself to someone else's cultural and social circumstances makes the emotional and embodied effects of discourse hard to ignore. I stumbled into the importance of reflexivity for any participant-observation, without anticipating its centrality for my future scholarship.

While the US military was the focus of my field work, the homophobic and self-disciplining style of masculinity soldiers exhibit is not isolated, but circulates throughout US culture (Boose 1993). Hollywood films, ancient myths, and religious imagery share a similar conception of the powerful heroic male who makes himself the instrument of political leaders' violence. This image of manhood provides a basis for judging oneself, for measuring peers, and for evaluating social rank. It is an ethically powerful story, with profound personal and social effects (Pascoe 2007).

Reflecting critically on my own reactions helped me make sense of what others experience. I went into my research trying to learn about war, but the soldiers I interacted with taught me more about manhood than about combat. Observing the community, and my own intense reactions to it, I came to understand how the psychological mechanism of self-labelling, as well as interactions in which others mock or denigrate us, shape and produce self-images. Where constructivists and others interested in meaning often talk about *identity* in abstract terms, my research helped me draw direct connections between intersubjective culture and subjective personal experience.

Simply showing up is not enough, however. A focus on mindful and reflexive self-awareness is required. By carefully developing field notes (Emerson et al. 1995), fieldwork produces a documentary record of both interactions and reflections on private experiences. This dual process provides the material for describing the community or institution under observation, as well as deeper insights into how those circumstances produce personal effects (Kraska 1998: 1314). As Jackson noted, "in interpretive research, the researcher is the research instrument, so attempts to minimize unique or idiosyncratic aspects of the researcher's individual experiences would make little sense" (2008a: 92).

Conclusion

Conducting such research requires putting oneself into an environment where unfamiliar practices, ways of talking, and background expectations are all present. Far from seeking to remove "bias" as philosophically dualist approaches would (Jackson 2008b), the goal is to analyze both our own experience and what we witness as indicative of the same social whole (Neumann 2008a).

Observing my reactions and contemplating my own struggles gave me an empathetic view of how militarized masculinities affect the experience of disciplining and training one's own body. For soldiers and other militarized professionals, this is so mundane as to be invisible. Yet in one of my later research trips, I encountered soldiers wounded in Iraq. In talking with them, there was a strong sense of mourning the loss of that hard, warrior self-image. Losing a leg or suffering severe shrapnel wounds makes the vulnerability and softness of human flesh impossible to ignore, destroying the feelings of power and control that military recruitment ads and Hollywood movies promise. Being a warrior is a matter of training weakness and doubt out of the body, of achieving self-mastery while submitting to authority (Sasson-Levy 2007). Being a wounded soldier, on the other hand, requires a re-imagining of what manhood might mean.

Accessing a community where I could immerse myself, while paying careful attention not only to what I heard and saw, but also to what I felt and what this meant, I came to understand the linkage between ways of talking and ways of being in a new way. Identifying how the vocabulary of militarized masculinity overshadowed my own self-image provided a key insight, one I never sought or anticipated.

For those interested in studying everyday life, particular institutional cultures, or the political practices at a given site, ethnographic participant-observation is likely the best tool to do so. As Ratelle's (Chapter 12) and my own experience highlights, however, the *participant* part of the equation may be intense. While ethnographic writing may or may not emphasize the personal to the extent that my chapter has, the reason that it is called *participant observation* is that this kind of research means using your own personality and body as research instruments. By placing ourselves in different contexts, we note how we change the interactions around us, and how they change us. It might be possible to observe a great deal in the field, but in keeping detailed notes and practicing reflexive writing, it is also possible to learn from what we feel.

Suggested reading

Kondo, D.K. (1990) *Crafting Selves: Power, Gender, and Discourses of Identity in a Japanese Workplace*, Chicago: University of Chicago Press.

Kraska, P.B. (1998) "Enjoying militarism: political/personal dilemmas in studying U.S. police paramilitary units", in J. Ferrell and M.S. Hamm (eds) *Ethnography at the Edge: Crime, Deviance, and Field Research*, Boston: Northeastern University Press.

Pascoe, C.J. (2007) *Dude, You're a Fag: Masculinity and Sexuality in High School*, Berkeley: University of California Press.

Sasson-Levy, O. (2008) "Individual bodies, collective state interests: the case of Israeli combat soldiers", *Men and Masculinities*, 10(3): 296–321.

Stump, J. (2011) "Weakness leaving my body: an essay on the interpersonal relations of international politics", in N. Inayatullah (ed.) *Autobiographical International Relations: I, IR*, New York: Routledge.

12 How participant observation contributes to the study of (in)security practices in conflict zones[1]

Jean-François Ratelle

Introduction

By using the case study of ethno-religious profiling in the North Caucasus, this chapter seeks to discuss how political ethnography rooted in participant observation could contribute to the study of (in)security practices in conflict zones. In order to do so, I will first explain how the Paris School provides valuable thinking tools but also has important limitations in the study of conflict zones. I will describe my thirteen months of fieldwork in Russia, which included six months in Kabardino-Balkaria, Chechnya, and Dagestan, with the aim of translating how political ethnography could be used to study (in)security practices. Finally, I will explain how political ethnography permits us to rethink our research question and concepts by utilizing an inductive and bottom-up process.

In the debate about securitization, the so-called Paris School describes the competition of security agencies and how it leads to illiberal practices in Europe (Bigo 2005). By using the concept of the field in the management of unease, Bigo explains how security actors compete to promote their heterogeneous interests. One can observe similar competitive interactions in conflict zones where borders between sub-fields such as criminal groups, state agencies, and insurgents are often blurred and porous. The Paris School offers a way to understand (in)security and violence in conflict zones by mapping out the field as where insurgents, security agencies and criminal groups interact (Campana and Ratelle 2010). These close interactions between sub-fields often lead to the involvement of security agencies in illicit activities, from simple corruption at checkpoints and arm deals with insurgents, to kidnapping and assassination cartels. Civil wars and insurgencies often make illegal business opportunities possible for both insurgents and soldiers. Checkpoints become an opportunity for security actors to impose their definition of threat and establish a lucrative shadow economy. Although valid, it is very difficult if not impossible to have access to security apparatuses in Russia and in most war zones. Political ethnography and participant observation, however, offers other alternatives in studying (in)security practices in conflict zones.

Bayard de Volo and Schatz explain that political ethnography is particularly useful when "government statistics are suspect [or inexistent], media outlets are controlled by political interests, [free media are also inexistent or strongly repressed]" (2004: 269). Studying structural violence at checkpoints and security controls implies having access to informal practices like illegal activities, corruption, or repression. Through participant observation, the political ethnographer immerses him/herself into the local life, travels throughout the region to identify security practices, and seeks to be controlled and arrested at various checkpoints managed by different security agencies. Immersion also offers a closer view and a unique perspective on political actors' and civilians' perceptions of their existence (Schatz

2009a). One can observe the internalization of patterns of violence, or as Bourdieu might term it "a habitus of violence" (1981) through ethno-religious profiling and security controls. Practices of violence and coercion become embedded in social practices through socialization and performances of social actors. Bigo (2005) has coined the term "*ban-opticon*" to describe these practices. The *ban-opticon* in the North Caucasus, and also in Russia itself, finds its roots in an important ethnic resentment, even hatred, against individuals of Caucasian appearance (dark skin, hair, eyes, and beard). This latter fact has been antagonized by recent events in Russia such as the two Chechen wars, the upsurge of terrorism, and the Caucasian migrant situation in Moscow. This violence against Caucasian-looking people is often forgotten by North Caucasus experts' analyses that mostly focus on physical violence and not structural violence. By structural violence I mean violence that is based on social structures, institutions, or practices (Galtung 1990, Russell 2007). This type of violence is embedded in social practices and thus becomes a part of daily life and social actors' behaviours and dispositions (Foucault 1975, 1978). Violence, just like Foucault's concept of power (1980b), is not something static but instead a contested concept that takes different forms in different contexts and cannot be restricted to its purely physical aspect. To paraphrase Nordstrom (1995, 1997) and Taussig (1987), as scholars we tend to reify, objectivize, and restrict our conception of violence. Structural and symbolic violence are always around us in conflict zones, while the same cannot be said for physical violence. Ethnographers working in conflict zones have insisted for decades on the need to ground our research "in people and the way they experience conflict and the [various] enactment of violence" (Nordstrom and Martin 1992: 5). Thus, ethnography offers a way to experiment, report, and deconstruct violence in its daily effect on people. By deconstructing the concept of violence, ethnography also seeks to enlarge and deepen our understanding of conflict zones away from the military-centric analysis and over-focusing on the frontline and battlefield.[2] In the last section, I will try to explain, based on my own fieldwork experience, how ethnography helped me realize the importance of structural violence compared to physical violence in conflict zones.

My research project was at first developed around the use of ethnography to uncover processes linked to political violence. By immersing myself into a conflict zone, I planned to get an insider perspective on the impact of political violence in people's daily lives. I could then map out, based on my immersion into the field, how insurgent and state violence affected local societies, why individuals participated in violence, and the impact of religion on violent engagement. I planned to travel across the North Caucasus to experience violence in its daily encounters and its impact on people. My research methodology was quite simple as I was looking to immerse myself in unstable republics like Ingushetia, Chechnya, and Dagestan in order to identify security agencies and insurgent groups who were perpetrating acts of violence and their various practices. I would also be travelling to local villages to collect testimonies about violence.

To be able to access these unstable republics I faced numerous police interrogations at checkpoints, security controls, searches, and continual ethno-religious profiling. This profiling has been the most difficult aspect of my fieldwork. My physical appearance, often labelled as "Caucasian" or as "Wahabist", was quickly identified as a security threat by security forces in Moscow, but also on public transportation throughout Russia and in the North Caucasus. Identifying these (in)security practices was part of my research design but had a secondary importance. The primary focus of my research was explaining the upsurge of insurgent violence in the North Caucasus. Even if this threat was imminently and constantly present around me, I could never experience the physical aspect of violence as a researcher. I perceived this as a major failure in my methodological planning. My first research objectives were impossible to attain even by using an ethnographic methodology mainly based on participant observation. I then realized that it was a completely different situation for the case of ethno-religious profiling, *random* interrogations, and detentions. This form of structural violence was not part of my initial research design but based on my interviews and participant observation I understood the importance of this topic compared to physical violence. I then decided to maintain a similar ethnographic methodology but I sought to map the various security agencies' practices. I travelled on a daily basis throughout the North Caucasus. At each checkpoint or *random* security control I made sure to identify which agency was involved and the type of security practices utilized, such as profiling, searches, or interrogations and who was labelled as a threat. On numerous occasions I was myself taken aside and interrogated along with other people identified as potential risks that were to be controlled. It offered me the unique experience to share time with these individuals and listen to their testimonies. For a very short moment of time, I was immersed in their daily life, felt how this profiling affected them and observed how they dealt with these (in)security practices. Even if I could understand the impact of profiling on those individuals based on their testimonies, and though I too was controlled and profiled on a daily basis and identified as a security threat just like them, I have to admit that my encounter of their daily lives was not complete. Indeed, my Canadian passport could always get me out of trouble while they had to bribe the police officers to do the same. It exemplifies why self-reflexivity occupies a central role in ethnographic research.

In participant observation, the researcher has to take into account his impact on the field and his research results. In the case of my research, my "Caucasian" physical features played an important role in the results I obtained. Other researchers using a similar research design might obtain drastically different results or interpret their fieldwork experiences in a different way. Therefore, a self-reflexive stance is crucial to interpret our impact on the field, how our experiences relate to ordinary people and how we report and describe them. Reproduction of the research results should not be focused on the duplication of the fieldwork experiences themselves but how we interpret and compare them.

In the case of my research, interpretive ethnography offered a unique perspective in understanding the impact of structural violence in conflict zones. What represented a research failure in my initial research results helped me understand that I was over-focusing my research on the physical aspect of violence based on an inherent bias coming from the literature about the North Caucasus and conflict studies in general (Nordstrom 1997). Throughout my fieldwork, I was controlled by security agencies on a daily basis simply because my physical appearance represented a threat as I was profiled as a possible radical Islamist or as an insurgent. Through my participant observation in the ethno-religious profiling I understood how (in)security practices represent something which is left outside of most academic research but has a major impact on violent engagement.

Conclusion

The importance of ethnographic methods and sensibility, which becomes a part of the researcher's mindset, has many crucial impacts on research, as well as research design. Ethnography not only offers a way to observe how people understand their daily life, how they give sense and meaning to it but it also permits the researcher to uncover processes which are hidden and not tangible to other methods. These processes are in the interstices of power and can be only uncovered by a prolonged immersion in our research environment. My fieldwork permitted me to uncover the importance of various (in)security practices which were central in understanding the actual upsurge of violence in the region. These practices were partially covered in the journalistic and human rights reports but were crucially lacking in conflict studies because of our insistence on speaking for the field instead of listening to it. As Wedeen explains, "practices, like human actions, are ultimately 'dual', composed both of what the outside observer can see and of the actor's understandings of what they are doing" (2009: 87). Ethnography offers a way to encounter and interpret the practices of political actors in the field through a double hermeneutic approach but it also permits the ethnographer to personally experiment them directly. This chapter has tried to emphasize how ethnography could contribute to the study of security in conflict zones, although ethnography as a methodology is not limited to dangerous fieldwork (Vrasti, Chapter 8, Kunz, Chapter 9). I did not seek to present ethnography as the only valid method to study security. Feyerabend explains through the metaphor of language how methods should be seen as complementary when he says: "the best protective device against being taken in by one particular language [or methodology] is to be brought up bilingually" (1979: 91 as quoted in Schatz 2009b: 303). I think that multi-method research design involving the use of ethnography to uncover processes allows us to deepen and widen our understanding of security. Methods should thus be seen as complementary and not mutually exclusive.

Notes

1   I would like to thank the Centre Franco-Russe de Recherche en Sciences Humaines et Sociales de Moscou for its logistical support, and Angela Franovic, Mark B. Salter, André Simonyi, Hélène Thibault, and John Dunlop for their helpful suggestions.
2   See Enloe (1990) and Cohn (1987) for a similar feminist critique, Nordstrom and Robben (1995) and Nordstrom (1997) for a comprehensive discussion.

Suggested reading

Nordstrom, C. and Martin, J. (1992) "The Culture of Conflict: Field Reality and Theory", in C. Nordstrom and J. Martin (eds) *The Paths to Domination, Resistance, and Terror*, Berkeley: University California Press.

Nordstrom, C. and Robben, A.C.G.M. (1995) "The Anthropology and Ethnography of Violence and Sociopolitical Conflict" in C. Nordstrom and A.C.G.M. Robben (eds) *Fieldwork under Fire: Contemporary Studies of Violence and Survival*, Berkeley: University of California Press.

Schatz, E. (2009a) "Ethnographic Immersion and the Study of Politics" in E. Schatz (ed.) *Political Ethnography: What Immersion Contributes to the Study of Power*, Chicago: Chicago University Press.

Sriram, C.L., King, J.C., Mertus, J.A., Martin-Ortega, O., and Herman, J. (eds) (2009) *Surviving Field Research: Working in Violent and Difficult Situations*, New York: Routledge.

Wood, E.J. (2006) "The Ethical Challenges of Field Research in Conflict Zones", *Qualitative Sociology*, 29(3): 307–341.

13 Dissident sexualities and the state

Megan Daigle

Introduction

My research topic first came to me while reading the fiftieth anniversary of the Cuban Revolution issue of the *Journal of Latin American Studies*. I now study the tourist-oriented sexual economy in post-Soviet Cuba – part of the broader network of black – and grey – market activities known locally as *jineterismo* – and how this economy and the state's reaction to it have served to condition the lives and subjectivities of young Cuban women of colour, bringing thinly-disguised prejudices of race and gender to the fore. While there was a certain amount of literature on this topic, most notably by Cabezas (1998, 2004, 2009), virtually none of it dealt with the political ramifications of the phenomenon, and nothing I could find engaged with the practicalities and challenges of carrying out fieldwork in Cuba.

Over the last fifteen years, the Cuban state has taken an increasingly punitive approach to romantic and sexual liaisons between Cubans and foreigners, employing mass arrests and rehabilitation centres, in an attempt to repress what it sees as prostitution – a stance which has had profound political implications for young Cubans, and which also brings special challenges to ethnographic study of the phenomenon. As even those engaged in traditional, long-term relationships are left with the burden of proving the legitimacy of their affective bonds in the eyes of the state, and particularly of the police, in order to avoid arrest and possible imprisonment, an atmosphere of fear has descended, meaning that many are unwilling to speak openly about their experiences. The *jineteras* are almost universally understood to be young, attractive, black or mixed-race women, and any such person seen in a heavily-touristed zone of the island runs the risk of attracting police scrutiny, if not arrest, based on racist and sexist assumptions about their sexual promiscuity and moral depravity. Predictably, reading voraciously and speaking to as many fellow researchers as I could find was helpful groundwork, but it still could not begin to prepare me for six months' fieldwork in Cuba.

Immediately upon arrival in Havana, in early February 2010, I met with a dean at the University of Havana in order to be enrolled as a visiting researcher, which was necessary to get an extended visa to do research. I had been cautioned to be vague when discussing my project at the university, but I had not been warned about what happened next, when the dean took me aside for a lecture, shaking his finger an inch from my face and sternly instructing me to abandon all pretence of fieldwork. I could go to libraries and speak to academics, but no one else; I was to do no fieldwork of any kind while in Cuba. Thoroughly chastized, I left the faculty in a panic and called the one contact I had in Cuba to whom I knew I could speak about this, a writer who had published several books and been a visiting scholar at universities in the US and UK. At the time, he was a total stranger to me, but over coffee the following day on the terrace of a hotel near the university, he told me that this is how it always is in Cuba for researchers: you arrive, you swear up and down that you will do no such thing, and then you do it.

So, I did six months of fieldwork in Cuba. I spent many days simply observing how tourists and young Cubans interacted in and around popular nightspots and tourist attractions, and also watching how police carried out their interventions on these people. I did archival research as well, visiting the documentation centres of several of Cuba's mass organizations. More importantly, however, I did as many unstructured interviews as I could with Cubans who had, or sought to have, relationships with foreigners. This was in itself a tricky proposition – gaining the trust of potential interviewees and attempting to mitigate the risk implied in speaking to me became my top priorities. I kept absolutely no written record of their real names, became proficient in concealing my documents and files, and did everything I could to keep myself and my interactions with my interviewees off the radar of the police and other state institutions. I also learned strategies for avoiding the gaze of the police while moving through public spaces.

Some of these interviews came by chance, via conversations I was able to strike up on my own, but the vast majority were the result of a network of contacts that I was able to build over time, snowballing into ever more connections and introductions. This proved to be the most effective method since it brought me into contact with more potential interviewees and, in turn, provided them with the safeguard of a mutual contact that could vouch for my trustworthiness. I quickly learned, however, as Cabezas had before me in the course of her research, that the "unified object of my research, the 'sex worker', did not exist, was ambiguous, or at the very least was quite an unstable subject" (Cabezas 2009: 8). Sexual-affective relations between Cubans and foreigners are ambiguous, ranging from long-term committed partnerships to fleeting and transactional affairs, none of which can be said to be devoid of emotional content, so attempting to determine who is and who is not a *jinetera* is useless. It is the *idea* of a category of people called *jineteras*, and the presumption of who fits the bill, that matters in effect. For that very reason, many young women who engage in sexual-affective relationships with foreign men reject the term *jinetera*, creating their own alternative names, or eschewing labels altogether. This is a discourse that has proved disciplinary and even repressive to a broad sector of the Cuban population in recent years, as I learned in conversation with so many young Cubans.

In terms of research design, the central question that my thesis poses is, as it turns out, fairly simple: how are bodies governed in Cuba? Or rather, why are these bodies, mostly young black or mixed-race women, governed differently and made available for state intervention? This has taken me down a very particular – anti-essentialist, feminist, critical race, queer, poststructuralist – path in terms of the theories on which I draw. In practice, my methodological approach has had to be flexible according to circumstances, a choice which I think is reasonable – even essential – when it comes to doing a project like this one. Doing field research in Cuba presents a special set of difficulties, and these difficulties are magnified when one is researching a topic that the Cuban state finds highly objectionable.

Conclusion

I learned two major lessons about fieldwork from my experience in Cuba. First, as a result of the challenges I faced, I very rarely had the luxury of naming the place and time of an interview. Opportunities were fleeting, so I had interviews which happened at 2a.m., which took place inside noisy clubs and bars, or on the beach; interviews where I took notes on the backs of bus tickets and receipts, and even one where answers came in the form of nods and shakes of the head. I learned something new from each of them, but not in ways that could have been predicted in advance, and I often did not learn what I set out to learn. Circumstances constantly changed, and the meanings of ideas, categories, and words shifted before my eyes. Flexibility had to be built into the design of my research, both methodologically and conceptually. On a related note, I have heard many Cubanists say, and I think it is true, that Cuba drives you to interdisciplinarity. The straightest path to the answers you want is rarely available. As another researcher-friend told me, you can never go straight up the middle, so you go sideways. I never anticipated using everything from newspaper articles and scientific studies to music, films, novels, and poetry in my work, but keeping an open mind as to what constitutes politics and political forms of expression has paid dividends. It was important to learn to be innovative when a door was closed in my face, to find new ways of asking taboo questions, and new ways of answering them too.

The second lesson I learned doing this project is that there is one element above all others that I cannot write out of it – and that is me. My fieldwork was a process of learning how to do this research – which questions to ask (and which not to ask), how to get interviews, how to understand these people and this scenario – and my own position as a white, female, Canadian researcher from a UK university undeniably affected the unfolding of that process (Lerum 2001, Mullings 1999). As an ethnographer, I struggled to make my interviews as reciprocal and conversational an experience as possible, in an attempt to mitigate the inherent power relationship between interviewer and interviewee. This almost unavoidably extractive, *colonial relationship* behoves the ethnographer to be mindful in taking a reflexive and self-critical approach to interviewing (Wahab 2003, Nencel 2005). Many of my interviewees asked me questions, which I always answered, and I often found these experiences as interesting as the questions I asked them. In Clifford's words, each was (and is) a "speaking [subject], who sees as well as is seen, who evades, argues, probes back" (2010:14). This project became so much more than just research, though; I could not escape my own subjectivity and partiality in Cuba, and it was through repeated and very personal moments of camaraderie, frustration, and even violence that my thesis became what it now is – as much autoethnography as ethnography.

To accurately portray my field experience, I have chosen to write my thesis loosely chronologically, according to the phases through which my work and life in Cuba progressed. I have done this for a number of reasons, but foremost amongst these is the need to foreground the personal elements. My writing in my thesis is conversational, almost novelistic, depicting my interviews as extended vignettes and allowing me to bring out entire stories that foreground individual experiences of the Cuban system. In this way, I can be honest about how fuzzy the line between work and life really was, how personal some of my field experiences were, how my position impacted on my work, how what I learned at each stage affected what happened later. In short, I do not have to pretend that I knew things at certain stages that I simply did not know yet. Throughout the story, I am always there, a character in the narrative who struggles, jumps to conclusions, fumbles interviews. This approach to both writing and ethnography is, I believe, not just a stylistic choice, but an ethical and a political one. I hope that bringing out the histories and personalities in my work will result in a more genuine representation of my interviewees' lives and the politics of their stories. That said, my authorial voice is always there as well. I was and am embedded in the story, and writing it in a way that acknowledges that embeddedness is, to me, another nod to the fact that objectivity will always remain elusive. "Ethnographic truths", according to Clifford, "are thus inherently *partial* – committed and incomplete" (2010: 7).

Suggested reading

Clifford, J. (2010) "Introduction: Partial Truths", in J. Clifford and G.E. Marcus (eds) *Writing Culture: The Poetics and Politics of Ethnography, 25th anniversary edition*, Los Angeles: University of California Press.

Lather, P. (2001) "Postbook: Working the Ruins of Feminist Ethnography", *Signs: Journal of Women in Culture and Society*, 27(1): 199–227.

Lerum, K. (2001) "Subjects of Desire: Intimate Ethnography, and the Production of Critical Knowledge", *Qualitative Inquiry*, 7(4): 466–483.

Nencel, Lorraine (2005) "Feeling Gender Speak: Intersubjectivity and Fieldwork Practice with Women who Prostitute in Lima, Peru", *European Journal of Women's Studies*, 12(3): 345–361.

Zalewski, M. (2000) *Feminism after Postmodernism: Theorising through Practice*, New York: Routledge.

Part III

The practice turn

Introduction

Mark B. Salter

Field analysis is a method that takes as its object the formal and informal practices within a structured, rule-governed, objective social sphere that is not pre-determined by institutional or national boundaries, but share a logic, or a sense of the rules of the game. Fields are constituted by sets of relations and positions in a given social sphere (such as security, academe, religion); social, symbolic, culture, and economic capital are up for grabs within the field. Multiple relations may be competitive, cooperative, hegemonic, and transversal (in relation to other fields), but all agents recognize that the field has a determinative effect on their positions and those relations – they are all playing the same game. The objective structure of the field is made practical by the *habitus*, the internalized and informal subjective dispositions of its embodied agents: the strategies, tactics, norms, best-practices of the game. Practices are most often studied through participant observation, wide-ranging interviews that seek background or tacit knowledge, and discourse analysis, particularly understood as discourse as a kind of practice.

Bourdieu populates multiple and overlapping lifeworlds with actors and institutions that exist in particular fields under objective conditions such as class, gender, and nationality, but which also understand those institutions and constructs both through unquestioned beliefs (*doxa*) and subjective understandings of the practice of those fields (*habitus*). Fields have particular logics, specific rules of the game, that structure the competition over the form of economic, cultural, social or symbolic capital at stake in that particular field. Bourdieu argues that in addition to economic capital, that is the ability to command economic resources, we can observe cultural, social, and symbolic capital. Cultural capital includes knowledge, experiences, and attitudes that command cultural resources. Social capital includes networks, relationships, and memberships that command social resources. Symbolic capital includes

Table PIII.1 Research design in field analysis

Object	*Field: Formal and informal practices within a structured, rule-governed social sphere*
Key concepts	**Habitus** (subjective dispositions or understandings about the objective field)
	Doxa (unconscious values and beliefs)
	Capital (economic, symbolic, cultural)
Collection	Participant observation, interview, discourse analysis
Data	Practices, discourses, norms, institutions, relationships
Relations	Competition, cooperation, domination, transversal
Fit	Professional sector united by common meta-identity (security, journalism, academia)

prestige, honour, and other forms of recognition. Within any single field, different kinds of economic, cultural, social, and symbolic capital are available, if subject to competition.

Field analysis was first proposed by Bourdieu, and promoted particularly within this critical community by Bigo and Walker, first in Bigo's independent work (1996, 2002) and in their collaborative work, particularly in the journal *International Political Sociology* (Bigo and Walker 2007: 1–5).[1] The practice turn in international political sociology, as well as the rise of the journal and the section in ISA and in the wider discipline in International Relations (IR), owe a great deal to Bourdieu (Leander 2005, 2008, Jackson 2008, Mérand and Pouliot 2008, Adler and Pouliot 2011, Eagleton-Pierce 2011).

This method places a great deal of emphasis on commonsensical or tacit and informal knowledges, those attitudes and beliefs that are a necessary supplement to the formal or explicit rules about a particular social field. We could not understand the lifeworld of an academic, for example, without understanding what is meant by the multiple discourses about professionalism, in terms of behaviour at conferences, mentoring and graduate training, teaching, publication, or the processes and norms of peer review. Rules police the limits of behaviour, and sometimes the best practices, but it is the soft-knowledge of the field that accomplishes a great deal of the work for the institution of the profession. The written program or the virtual archives of the American Political Science Association conference or the International Studies Association conference could not possibly hope to explain the behaviour or the meaning of those meetings. Similarly, in professional circles, there are a set of exemplars – both positive and negative – that the community shares, a kind of short-hand, that structures what is sayable, what is actionable, what gains social, cultural, or symbolic capital. Each field has a number of anecdotes or slogans that encapsulate informal knowledge – "we do not want another. . . (Pearl Harbour, Bay of Pigs, 9/11, shoe bomber, Maher Arar, etc.)" to which all the members of the field attach a similar meaning. Field analysis attempts to map through interviews and participant observation the unspoken beliefs and tacit knowledge that makes these systems of relations function. Interviews often take the form of life-histories, that illustrate not only the formal positions, qualifications, and institutions, but also the personal networks, connections, and forms of symbolic, cultural, and social capital that are developed and then utilized within the habitus of the field.

Practices and practical beliefs are, by necessity, bodily. "Practical sense, social necessity turned into nature, converted into motor schemes and body automatisms, is what causes practices, in and through what makes them obscure to the eyes of their producers, to be *sensible*, that is informed by a common sense" (Bourdieu 1990a: 69). To return to the conference example, presentations, questions, discussion, attendance, mealtimes, bathroom breaks, lodging, and travel, all play a role in the fabric of the conference and the capital up for grabs. Separate from the formal requirements that one presents a paper, there are a number of informal practices: thanking the organizer, the audience, and the discussant; apologizing for the quality of the paper and announcing a change in the title; the formality of the paper presentation, from talking through to reading to graphs or PowerPoint presentations; the arrangement of the panel in a line facing the audience (however few); the common disparagement of the time, the space, or the organization of the panel by conference chairs; the politics of who goes to lunch and dinner with whom; the selling of book projects at the fair; the drinking at the bar before, during, and after the day's panels; the journal and organizational meetings; the micropolitics of sections and receptions; who wears tweed, who wears jeans, and who wears a skirt. As much as these are cultural codes, they are also bodily practices: sitting or standing for presentations, sitting in the audience, rushing to eat, shaking hands in the corridor. In some ways, the entire structure of the program is meant to deny the corporeal in a particular way: the intellectual activity of conferencing, presenting, questioning, and debating, requires an obedient subject, who attends – in the sense of being present, caring for, and waiting on. Our consideration of the bodily practices of conference also reflects a concern with the conditions of the production of our own knowledge, symbolic, social, and cultural capital. Throughout his oeuvre, Bourdieu also places a great emphasis on reflexivity in the research activity (Leander 2005, Eagleton-Pierce 2011), including sociological analyses of the academic field in France surrounding the events of 1968 (Bourdieu 1988). In part, for Bourdieu, reflexivity is not simply about the engagement of the individual academic in the lifeworld of his research, but also serious analysis of the conditions for possibility of making authoritative knowledge claims within the social field of academe.

Plan

Field analysis is best suited to a social sphere or wider social institution that transcends institutions and/or national boundaries. Shah similarly follows the idea of the governance of the Internet, and follows these practices through international institutions and private companies (Chapter 30). Because fields are defined functionally, through their effect, the limits of a field analysis cannot be described before the empirical research. However, researchers can identify the sphere or the logic that they wish to investigate. Uncovering the habitus, the informal beliefs about the objective structure, must be done through an analysis of the condition of possibility for certain relations and positions, the necessary predicates for particular networks and actions. These two must be then analyzed holistically: the objective structure of the field and the subjective understandings of the rules of the game. Nyers demonstrates both the conditions for the possibility of his research agenda, and the communities with which he conducted that research (Chapter 15). He is thus reflexive about his own knowledge production and the collaboration needed by the community that he investigated. This reflexivity about the material conditions for the production of knowledge is also a hallmark of this kind of critical project. Bonditti explains how his research object shifted and changed through the design phase, until he could finally identify an object that was analyzable (Chapter 16). Salter (Chapter 17) and Muller (Chapter 18) also speak directly about the intersection of their scholarly field with the field of power, and talk specifically about the genre and reception of their interventions.

Bourdieu sets out three necessary steps for field analysis: (1) "analyze the position of the field vis-à-vis the field of power"; (2) "map out the objective structure of the relations between the positions occupied by the agents or institutions who compete for the legitimate form of specific authority of which this field [is] the site"; (3) "analyze the habitus of the agents, the different systems of dispositions they have acquired by internalizing a determinate type of social and economic condition, and which find a definite trajectory within the field under consideration a more or less favorable opportunity to become actualized" (Bourdieu and Wacquant 1992a: 105).

Pragmatically, the research process for a field analysis follows the same basic shape:

1   Clear statement of the research puzzle is supplemented by background research on the institutions, discourses, and positions in a particular area, which is hypothesized to be part of the same field.
2   Mapping of the dominant objective structures of the field through discourse, policy, historical, and legal research, which must be led by the empirical effect of the field and not any preconceived notions of institutional, public, or national boundaries. Field is

situated in relation to dominant field of power. Field is defined as a particular logic, set of rules, understanding of a game.

3   Participant observation and/or interviews with practitioners to develop preliminary sense of habitus, or the daily practice of actors within this field and the relations between them. Detailed analysis of economic, symbolic, cultural, and social capital at stake in relations of competition, cooperation, domination, and transversality. Researcher consolidates understanding of the everyday practice, habitus, within this field that constitutes the rules of the game and an observation of limits of field effects.

4   Reconsideration of primary research puzzle in light of empirical material; reflection on the conditions for production of knowledge about this field.

5   Communication of the results.

Examples

The clearest example in this book of the use of Bourdieu's thinking tools is Hughes' analysis of the International Panel on Climate Change (IPCC) (Chapter 14). Two strands of field analysis are influential in the community of critical scholars. The International Political Sociology School has its strongest and most powerful advocate in Bigo: his *Police en réseaux* (1996) is perhaps the most complete field analysis currently available. Williams (2007) and Mérand (2008) represent other successful and clear models of how this method can be applied to particular fields. A second strand is more positivistic and speaks to mainstream constructivism, represented by Pouliot.

Hughes' project articulates how the IPCC relates to the object of its mandate, international climate change. She clearly sets out how the IPCC relates to the field of power, and

Table PIII.2 Examples of research design in field analysis

	Hughes, Writing as Practice	*Bigo,* Police en réseaux	*Pouliot,* International Security in Practice
Object	International Panel on Climate Change	Professional managers of unease/insecurity	NATO–Russian diplomatic relations
Collection	Discourse/policy analysis, interviews, observation	Participant observation, interviews, discourse/ policy analysis	Qualitative interviewing, discourse/policy analysis
Data	Differentiated work, professional, and writing practices within different units of IPCC	Practices, formal and informal working groups, professional trajectories, networks	Practices and norms testing existence of NATO–Russia security community at NATO–Russia Council
Relations	Disaggregation of five (5) units within field of IPCC, transversal relations with institutional, national and disciplinary fields	Competition, cooperation, domination, transversal relations with national fields	Symbolic and practical competition, cooperation, transversal relations with national and bilateral fields
Fit	Institution at intersection of scientific and diplomatic fields	Professional sector united by common identity (security) instantiated in regional institutions (Europe)	Institution situated within diplomatic and security fields and particular regional dynamic

examines empirically if the limits of the field of the IPCC are the same as the limits of the institution: they are not. Through observation, interviews, policy documents, and discourse analysis, she concludes that there are five different sub-fields within the IPCC, and that the rules of the game are unique to each unit. The practice of writing about climate change demonstrates that each of these units relates to the object of analysis, climate change, differently, and that the cultural, social, and symbolic capital at stake in each sub-field is markedly different. Hughes makes the case that in each unit, the authority for the production of knowledge is different, or more precisely that the practice of writing authoritatively is different. Thus, the networks, the authority, and the practice of writing about climate change vary from unit to unit.

Bigo specifically adapts a Bourdieusian framework for analysis of the European security field, or in his words the "professionals of the management of unease".[2] He writes that "regardless of national or institutional differences, they share a common sense of a game that is radically different from all the others and which exerts a determinative influence on their ability to manage these risks" (Bigo 1996: 52*)*.[3] By tracing the practices, the common habitus of these professionals, Bigo is able to identify a security field that extends beyond particular national or institutional limits to encompass this community. One of the most striking conclusions of this empirical research is that in the realm of security professionals "the distinction between interior and domestic and the international has lost its meaning. . . These [false] distinctions between inside and outside, domestic problems and international problems, the world of police and the world of international affairs, the security of the state and societal security, serve only to prevent astute analysis" (1996: 16). Bigo uses multiple methods to interrogate this community: interviews, policy and document analysis, institutional analysis, but more specifically, analysis of professional meetings, networks, career trajectories, and personal connections. He does this through engagement at multiple sites, including government and intergovernmental institutions, academic communities, policy centres, advocacy networks, and think-tanks.

Pouliot adapts some of Bourdieu's thinking tools to the constructivist paradigm in IR, focusing on a very specific set of diplomatic practices at the NATO-Russia Council (NRC). Rather than a more traditional analysis that starts from professional practices and follows those empirical traces to the limits of the field, Pouliot tests the hypotheses of traditional security community theory by evaluating the diplomatic practices in this key bilateral institution. Guided by the search for the commonsensical and the doxic, Pouliot looks for the *self-evidence* of diplomacy, as the best way to resolve problems, as an indicator of a security community (in which war is not thinkable). His core claim is that "the theory of practice of security communities argues that peace exists in and through practice when security officials' practical sense makes diplomacy the self-evident way of solving interstate disputes" (2010: 42). Pouliot uses semi-structured interviews from within the NRC and think-tanks outside because participant observation is impossible, due to the secrecy of the actual content of NRC meetings, and discourse analysis. He encounters a number of obstacles directly interviewing Russian officials, and so interviews "think-tank directors, academic institute members, and senior consultants [as] proxies" (2010: 84). This distinction marks a difference from Bourdieu and Bigo, who would argue that these other professionals are members of the field of NATO-Russia diplomacy if not policymakers directly, whereas Pouliot uses them as proxies because he is interested in the actual, embodied members of the NRC. Because Pouliot is focused on the operationalization of habitus, he is less clear about the kinds or stakes of capital at play in the NRC, although he places a heavy emphasis on the informal or unstated assumptions about the use of diplomacy.

In each of these examples, the objective field is constituted through practices and an internalized habitus of its inhabitants, underpinned by a doxic structure of unquestioned assumptions. Relations amongst the various positions are epitomized by competition, dominance, cooperation, and transversal relations with other fields, including the field of power. Various types of capital are at stake, particularly the position to make authoritative statements about what counts within the field (as a scientific fact or economic consensus, as a risk or threat, or as self-evident way of problem-solving).

Conclusion

Field analysis has become an indispensible methodological tool in the practice turn of contemporary critical studies; it has been particularly useful at matching new empirical work to the theoretical suspicions of the dominance of state actors. Security professionals can be demonstrated to operate over, around, and through national and institutional boundaries, as the coding of threats as internal/domestic and foreign/international becomes increasingly blurred in the practice of policing/security. Migration, organized crime, drugs, money laundering, and surveillance specifically confound these inside/outside dichotomies. Because field analysis starts with and is led by the empirical, it might be characterized as a fundamentally materialist methodology. Field analysis could be misunderstood as inherently politically or rather philosophically conservative: it starts from what is rather than what should be. However, field analysis specifically brings questions to those habits, practices, and relations that are usually unquestioned. While not utopic or prescriptive, field analysis provides a radical and critical method with which to question the status quo, and to reflect on the position that enables such questioning. Displacing the usual categories of analysis (such as state/non-state, domestic/international, police/security), and following the actual empirical practices of agents on the ground, the practice turn can provide politically and theoretically salient critiques of contemporary international relations.

Notes

1   "International political sociology" as a term of art is a translation of the French term "sociologie politique de l'internationale" – which more literally means the political sociology of the international – in which "the international" is then the object of analysis rather than a modifier of what kind of politics is in question.
2   Bigo uses the term "des professionnels de la gestion de la menace" in *Police en réseaux* (1996: 51), although he translates the phrase as "professionals of the managers of unease" in "Security and Immigration" (2002).
3   All Bigo quotes from *Police en réseaux* in this chapter are translated by the author. English versions of these arguments can be found in Bigo (2002, 2008).

Suggested reading

Adler, E. and Pouliot, V. (eds) (2011) *International Practices*, Cambridge: Cambridge University Press.
Bigo, D. (2011) "Pierre Bourdieu and International Relations: Power of Practices, Practices of Power", *International Political Sociology*, 5(3): 225–258.
Boltanski, L. and Thévenot, L. (2006) *On Justification: Economies of Worth*, Princeton: Princeton University Press.
Bourdieu, P. (1977) *Outline of a Theory of Practice*, Cambridge: Cambridge University Press.
Bourdieu, P. (1990a) *The Logic of Practice*, Cambridge: Polity.

Bourdieu, P. and Wacquant, L. (1992a) *An Invitation to Reflexive Sociology*, Cambridge: Polity.

Leander, A. (2008) "Thinking Tools", in A. Klotz and D. Prakash (eds) *Qualitative Methods in International Relations: A Pluralist Guide*, New York: Palgrave.

Leander, A. (2011) "The Promises, Problems, and Potentials of a Bourdieu-inspired Staging of International Relations", *International Political Sociology*, 5(3): 294–313.

14 The practice of writing

Hannah R. Hughes

Introduction

This piece offers a personal account of how I put Bourdieu's thinking tools into practice through an investigation of the Intergovernmental Panel on Climate Change (IPCC). Bourdieu's notions of habitus, field, and interest, and the practical relation to the world that these tools were designed to interrogate, have helped me disaggregate the IPCC into its constituent parts and then re-assemble it into an analyzable whole. Emerging from this process of constructing a researchable object is an interpretation of the IPCC and its assessment process as a practice of writing. The term *practice of writing* is employed to characterize the people, pathway, and operations through which the IPCC compiles its assessments of climate change. I also intend to use the term practice of writing as a mode of analysis for exploring how this practice renders climate change practicable for social and political reality.

Initially, the central research question of the project was: how is the IPCC conceptualizing climate change? This question arose from a previous research project into climate change, in which I examined the British government's attempt to securitize climate change. What became clear from this research is that by invoking security, particular ministers and departments within the UK government were able to promote a conceptualization of climate change that served their interests. However, the British government is not the only actor seeking to control the meaning of this issue and security is not the only object mobilized to achieve this. Climate change is a contested concept and one that has the potential to impact every living being on the planet, making the stakes in assigning its meaning high. I wanted to study this struggle and to discern the processes through which issues like climate change are problematized to and by social and political reality. I could not study these processes by limiting myself to the British government or to the security concept, because climate change is too great an object of interest to be confined by a single actor, or a single notion. For this reason, the IPCC became the site of my research.

The IPCC describes itself as the "leading international body for the assessment of climate change" (IPCC 2011). Since its establishment in 1988 by the World Meteorological Organisation (WMO) and the United Nations Environment Program (UNEP), the IPCC has been producing assessment reports on the physical, technical and socio-economic aspects of climate change (Agrawala 1998a, 1998b, Bolin 2007, Skodvin 2000, Zillman 2007). This task is divided among three working groups:

1   Working Group I assesses the physical scientific basis of climate change.
2   Working Group II examines vulnerability, impacts and adaptation to climate change.
3   Working Group III focuses on the mitigation of climate change.

To date there have been four rounds of these assessments: 1990, 1995, 2001 and 2007, with a fifth scheduled for completion in 2014. The reports are compiled by hundreds of the leading scientists and other experts on climate change from around the world, although dominated by participants from North America and Europe (Yamineva 2010). Accompanying the three substantial Working Group assessments are summaries for policymakers, which are approved line-by-line by IPCC member governments – the intergovernmental constituent of the organization – in which the majority of the world's governments participate. The production of these assessments and the purpose they serve make the IPCC an ideal site for studying the processes through which climate change is being rendered a meaningful object for social and political life.

Converting interest in the IPCC into a researchable problematic was made easier by the work of Bourdieu.[1] Bourdieu regarded the social world as "the site of continual struggles to define what the social world is" (Wacquant 1989: 34). To reveal the social strategies that constitute this struggle and the forms of domination they perpetuate, Bourdieu developed a number of theoretical notions, such as habitus, field, and capital. These theoretical tools rest upon a relational ontology and Bourdieu's emphasis on the practical nature of knowledge, and are designed to orientate the construction of the research object in order to explore the making of the world in practice – making them ideal for my particular purposes.

Bourdieu emphasized the practical mode of knowledge, which he suggests is the "basis of ordinary experience of the social world" (1990a: 25). He posited this practicality against the dominant representation of the social world as either a subjective experience or an objective social physics. In order to perceive it in this way, he invited the researcher:

> to situate oneself *within* "real activity as such", that is, in the practical relation to the world, the preoccupied, active presence in the world through which the world imposes its presence, with its urgencies, its things to be done and said, things made to be said, which directly govern words and deeds without ever unfolding as a spectacle.
>
> (Bourdieu 1990a, 25)

Bourdieu uses the concepts of *habitus* and field to discern this practical relation to the world. Objects of knowledge are not objectively recorded, they are constructed through practice, "and the principle of this construction is the system of structured, structuring dispositions, the *habitus*, which is constituted in practice and is always orientated towards practical functions" (1990a, 52).

Initially, I did not recognize the significance and implications of knowledge as practice to my overall research problematic, and it was the notions of field and interest that were most useful in guiding the investigation. The IPCC is a large and unruly research object that is not easily characterized, and field and interest enabled me to disaggregate its constituent parts and discern the role of each in the assessment process. Bourdieu used the concept of field, understood as a particular "space of social forces and struggles" (Bourdieu and Wacquant 1992a: 102), to organize his empirical and theoretical study of social relations. A field may delineate a particular social realm or academic discipline, such as the realm of government or the discipline of climate science. These social spaces can be identified and delimited by the objects that interest those that occupy that space and by the shared practices through which understandings of these objects are generated. For example, the field of climate science can be delineated by identifying those experts with a shared interest in climate change as an object of research and by the scientific practices through which they study and produce knowledge on the subject. Interest in this sense is more than scientific curiosity; it structures the field and exerts a force on those invested.

Thinking in terms of interest and field, then, meant getting to know who and what the IPCC was and not assuming common characterizations of this organization as an epistemic community of scientists (Boehmer-Christiansen 1994a, 1994b, Lunde 1991, Paterson 1996, Haas 2000, Newell 2000), or as a component of the climate regime complex (Keohane and Victor 2011). A number of empirical techniques were employed to achieve this. Firstly, I read the assessment reports and accompanying summaries for policymakers, recording the nationality and disciplinary affiliation of the authorship. Secondly, I conducted interviews, trying always to visit interviewees in their place of work in order to situate them in their daily routines and relations. Thirdly, I attended an IPCC plenary meeting – a meeting of the government members of the institution – at which I observed the proceedings and recorded the type and length of government interventions. At each stage of this research Bourdieu's thinking tools guided the approach that I took, particularly in the types of questions I asked during the interview stage. The idea was not to obtain information about the IPCC as such, but rather to learn the participant's relation to the IPCC and contribution to its assessment process.

As a result of this research I began to disaggregate the IPCC as a single entity and see it instead as five units, divided according to the participant's style of work and contribution to the assessment process. I identified these five units as:

1 The secretariat, the organizational centre of the IPCC.
2 The government delegates and/or focal points that make up the panel and accept and approve the report outline and finished product.
3 The bureau, which oversees and manages the report's compilation, and is the bridge between scientific authorship and government oversight.
4 The authors who conduct the assessment.
5 The Technical Support Units (TSUs), responsible for the day-to-day technical, administrative and organizational requirements of realizing the assessment.

Each of these five units has a specific role to play in the assessment process and a set of rules and procedures for conducting its business. These units also have particular interests in the IPCC and climate change that may at times compete with the interests of others, drawing actors into struggles over scientific authority in and over the assessment process. However, the one thing that unites all IPCC actors and constitutes the IPCC as a *field of practice* is a shared interest in and contribution to the production of climate change assessment reports. For this reason, I began to characterize the IPCC both by its composition and its function as a practice of writing.

Conclusion

Viewing the IPCC's assessment process as a practice of writing has implications for how the data is employed and represented; if IPCC participants and the assessment process constitute a practice then I need to describe who these people are, what they do and how they write an assessment of climate change. This means mapping the pathway taken by the assessment report from the formation of the outline to the approval of the finished product, recording the access this pathway provides to each unit of the IPCC and describing the operations they perform in realizing the assessment. The purpose of this is to make the IPCC – its people, the pathway and the process – an analyzable object, so as to explore how this practice of writing renders climate change operable for and by social and political life.

Making the jump from constructing the IPCC as an analyzable object to analyzing this object's role in the construction of climate change, means accepting the practical mode of knowledge and our practical relation to the world as stressed by Bourdieu. After reading the IPCC assessment reports, interviewing many participants, and observing a plenary meeting, I found myself very stuck. I knew a lot about an organization called the IPCC and its assessment activities. What I did not know was how the data I had collected related to the central research question; how did these people and these assessments conceptualize climate change?

I began to realize there was something wrong in how I was approaching this problematic. I used the term "conceptualize" because I had imagined the IPCC was forming a knowable object of mind that once framed in discourse and comprehended as such, would be preceded by political action. However, whilst the frame of the research problematic assumed meaning was to be discovered at the level of thought or language I could not address the question I had set myself, because what I had observed through this investigation of the IPCC was not so much the creation of a way to think or speak climate change as a way to *do* climate change, which includes thinking and speaking. The IPCC's practice of writing, through its myriad pathways and activities, writes something that is suitable to the human way of doing life. Life is not a thought process, despite the fact that our disciplinary practices tend to constitute it as such. Life is the process and activity of living, in which thinking and speaking are two activities amongst many. Currently, I understand the IPCC's practice of writing to be a process of rendering climate change practicable to life – making it into something we know what to do with. I say currently, because as the above aims to illustrate, my engagement with the sociological approach of Pierre Bourdieu and my investigation into the IPCC has constantly forced me to re-evaluate the conclusions I would like to claim.

Note

1 For a brief biography and bibliography of Bourdieu's life and work see Wacquant 2002, 2007. For an introduction to Bourdieu and his theoretical approach to sociology see Bourdieu and Wacquant 1992a, Webb, Schirato and Danaher 2002. For more critical accounts of Bourdieu, see Calhoun et al. 1993, Jenkins 1992, Swartz 1997.

Suggested reading

Bourdieu, P. (1988) *Homo Academicus*, trans. P. Colier. Stanford: Stanford University Press.

Bourdieu, P. (1990a) *The Logic of Practice*, Cambridge: Polity.

Bourdieu, P. and Wacquant, L. (1992a) *An Invitation to Reflexive Sociology*, Cambridge: Polity.

Pouliot, V. (2010) *International Security in Practice: The Politics of NATO-Russia Diplomacy*, Cambridge: Cambridge University Press.

Wacquant, L. (1989) "Towards a Reflexive Sociology: an Interview with Pierre Bourdieu", *Sociological Theory*, 7(1): 26–63.

15 Researching anti-deportation

Socialization as method

Peter Nyers

Introduction

Over the past decade I have conducted research on the political mobilizations of non-status refugees and migrants,[1] specifically campaigns against deportation and detention, and for regularization and freedom of movement. Of particular interest to me have been campaigns that are initiated and led by self-organized groups of non-status people. These campaigns, I have argued, allow us to think critically about political subjectivity in relation to non-citizenship.

My research on anti-deportation has aimed to make both an empirical and theoretical contribution. Empirically, I have examined the specific ways that anti-deportation campaigns challenge some of the most exclusionary and coercive powers of the state. More to the point, I wanted to illustrate how these campaigns can, in fact, succeed (albeit with limitations) in a climate of securitized anxiety about refugees and non-status migrants. In doing so, I have avoided the temptation to formalize, assimilate, or integrate the political agency of non-status refugees into preexisted categories or frameworks. Instead, I have aimed to liberate some of the key concepts of political theory – citizenship, cosmopolitanism, and community – from their liberal pretensions, elitist enclaves, statist spatio-temporal orientations, and assumed subjects. Most fundamentally in this respect, I have sought to investigate citizenship as a site of struggle, and not as a settled status, in order to better understand the political agency of precarious subjects who mobilize to make claims, demand rights, and thereby constitute themselves as political.

How can we actualize such empirical theorizing about politics? I have always considered this task to require some creative experimentation with ideas, concepts, and methods. But while creativity is an infinite resource, I find that the more we socialize ourselves the more creative we can become. In this short chapter, I wish to elaborate on socialization as a method. While researching anti-deportation I have benefitted from a number of socializations, two of which – one activist, the other academic – will receive some elaboration here. Each socialization, in its own way, facilitated the process of thinking politically about non-status people not as subjects of humanitarianism or securitization, but as claimants of new rights and creators of new worlds in which to become political.

My interest in the rights of refugees and migrants is not just academic, but connected to my family's history of forced displacement as well as my own political commitments. Thus, the first socialization came from my involvement in the refugee and migrant rights movement in Canada, especially with groups working with non-status refugees and migrants (Basok 2009, Lowry and Nyers 2003, Wright 2003). While non-status refugees and migrants are often defined in terms of an absence of political voice or agency, the action committees of deportees challenged these expectations by organizing highly public anti-deportation campaigns (Nyers 2003, 2006b). As a result, studying these campaigns has challenged me to think of ways to theorize the political agency of people who are in a contentious relationship with the dominant category for expressing political subjectivity: i.e. state citizenship. For example, the socialization of activist groups and networks brought a concrete immediacy to the theorizations of absence of the refugee voice, especially in relation to that of the citizen (Nyers 1999, Nyers 2006c).

In practical terms – that is, how one goes about conducting research on anti-deportation – this form of socialization has challenged me to think critically about how academic production can work in alliance with the subjects of the research and in solidarity with their political aims. Indeed, much of the research I have conducted on anti-deportation has involved collaboration with researchers and activists from community-based organizations in Toronto and Montreal. It was important for everyone involved in these projects to design research questions that were responsive to and supportive of the needs of anti-deportation campaigns. For example, one project, for the "STATUS Campaign", evaluated the history and politics of regularization programs in Canada (Khandor et al. 2004, Nyers 2005). Another, for the "Don't Ask, Don't Tell" campaign in Toronto, evaluated the accessibility of city services to non-status migrants (Berinstein et al. 2006). For both projects, we consulted extensively with non-status people to understand their experience in Canada and also to get a sense of what kind of regularization program they would like to see implemented. The findings of these research projects were reported at press conferences and major community forums on regularization, and documented in plain-language reports that were widely disseminated among the public, the media, social justice groups, government, service organizations, and the policy community.

A variety of methods were utilized in these projects: historical and archival research, policy document and discourse analysis, participant observation, interviews, roundtable discussions, and so on. I would say that the key innovation was not so much the specific methods employed, but the choice of whom we talked to and to whom we held ourselves accountable. Salter, in his introduction to Part III, describes field analysis as a method to reveals the "unspoken beliefs and tacit knowledge that makes . . . systems of relations function". There is an important and rapidly emerging body of literature that critically examines the unspoken belief and tacit knowledge that makes the security field operable. However, the majority of this research focuses on the common habitus of security professionals (removal officers, border agents, etc.). In the field of anti-deportation, the security professionals are often the action committees of non-status refugees themselves, in the sense that stopping a deportation and regularizing one's status provides greater personal security. As a result, my research in this area has focused less on the common habitus of state security professionals and more on the acts that disrupt and challenge this habitus and seek to redefine what can be spoken and known.

The socialization of non-status refugee and migrant rights movements has been crucial to understanding how anti-deportation is a site for investigating shifts in the field of security and enactments of non-citizen political subjectivity. It is not, however, the only socialization that has been important to this research, especially in terms of the task of generating ideas or refashioning concepts that speak to the political acts of non-status refugees and migrants. While negotiating one's political commitments is unavoidable in this kind of research, so too is it important to be a part of the production and contestation of ideas, theories, and methods. Therefore, another important socialization for thinking creatively and politically in relation to anti-deportation was academic in orientation and came through my involvement in Isin's Citizenship Studies Media Lab at York University in Toronto. I joined "the Lab" as a CSML Fellow in 2002 and served as its Director in 2007.

The Lab provided a physical and virtual space for interdisciplinary engagement and collaboration for graduate students, post-doctoral researchers, and faculty at York. It was envisioned to be a space for conceptual experimentation, invention, and creativity. A geographer by training, much of Isin's scholarly work emphasizes the spatial practices that are key conditions of being political. But what are the spatial conditions for investigating citizenship as an object of study? He created the Lab to provide a social environment that would not only cultivate creativity and inventiveness but also help actualize these attributes. Indeed, the name "Lab" was intentionally chosen to indicate a sense of experimentation and inventiveness (Isin 2007). The Lab sought to be the kind of place where professors and students would come together to collaborate as equals and experiment as rivals. At its most ambitious moments, the Lab wanted to actualize the Deleuzian idea that thought is about creating concepts, and creating concepts demands and requires inventive spaces. By emphasizing the inventive aspirations of the Lab, the hope was not only for radical, progressive and critical attitudes to emerge but also irreverent, playful, indifferent, and ironic ones (Isin and Nielson 2008). I do not believe that my thinking about "abject cosmopolitanism" (Nyers 2003) or "accidental citizenship" (Nyers 2006a) would have emerged as it did without this kind of encouragement, example, and sociability.

The socializations I experienced at the Lab enabled some creative experimentation with concepts that, I hoped, would help me make sense of the forms of political subjectivity that were emerging in the anti-deportation campaigns I was researching. Concretely, I presented four papers that were later published as journal articles (Nyers 2003, Nyers 2006a, Moulin and Nyers 2007) or chapters in edited books (Nyers 2006b). It was through my engagement with the researchers at the Lab that I developed the strategy of working with conceptual paradoxes. Take, for example, the idea of "abject cosmopolitanism" (Nyers 2003), which I developed in the context of doing research on the anti-deportation campaign of the Action Committee of Non-Status Algerians in Montreal. The title of the article conjoins two seemingly contradictory concepts – abjection and cosmopolitanism. The concepts are not an easy fit. The act of abjection represents an expulsion or casting off; by contrast, cosmopolitanism signifies radical inclusion and universalism. The subjects of abjection appear as figures of excess, as remainders of the exclusionary practices of citizenship, capitalism, and sovereign power; cosmopolitans belong everywhere and enjoy a sense of worldliness. By pairing abjection and cosmopolitanism I sought to place the concepts into an agonist relationship with each other – i.e., a relationship characterized by contestation, disagreement, and tension. The aim was not for one concept to prevail and cancel the other out, but for each to challenge and transform the other. Such challenges and transformations were – and, I would argue, still are – necessary. The rampant securitizations of the war on terror and the politically disabling logic of bare life have resulted in some disturbingly pessimistic readings of political dissent. Abject populations of non-status refugees are especially subjected to paranoid fears or paternalistic advocacy. If nothing else, abject cosmopolitanism was an attempt to escape from this double blackmail.

Conclusion

Researching anti-deportation brings to the forefront two themes that are often in tension: a commitment to community-university collaborations and cross-socializations on the one hand, and a desire to create new ideas and concepts that speak to these socializations on the other. Since it is a challenge to sustain these dual efforts, I would like to conclude by reflecting upon the kind of dispositions, attributes, and attitudes that might help us in this endeavour. In this respect, a short story by Kafka is a good way to draw together these themes and tensions.[2] In "The City Coat of Arms", Kafka retells the parable of the Tower of Babel (1973). The great migrations and expulsions of the original biblical story already make this tale relevant to my research. In Kafka's telling of Babel, the idea of building the tower has the same captivating effect on the imagination as in the biblical version. But Kafka is keen to set the city and the tower into tension with one another. The city, after all, is built to house the workers while they build the tower. Over time, life in the city proves to have its own rewards and the tower becomes a perpetually deferred project. The idea of the tower does not die, however. In fact, it endures over many, many generations. For most of the story, Kafka's main point seems to be that once an idea gets hold it does not die. But then the parable continues and it turns out that the idea does die. At the end of Kafka's telling of Babel, the idea of the tower is abandoned entirely and the task – the ethos – of living in and building a city prevails.

The value of Kafka's story comes from how it forces us to be critically self-reflexive about the ideas (or concepts, or methods) that we hold so dearly. For myself, in addition to abject cosmopolitanism, I have utilized the strategy of conjoining conceptual paradoxes in the form of analyses of "irregular citizenship" (Nyers 2011a), "community without status" (Nyers 2008), "alien equality" (Nyers 2011b), and others. Each one of these concepts was invented not for its own sake (do we really need another buzzword?) but as a response to the world in which we find ourselves. But like all such responses, we have to be ambivalent about their future. Such concepts, Kafka would remind us, come and go. What is important is not their durability over time, but how they cultivate a disposition or an ethos toward thought, an ethos that requires certain attributes (sociability, solidarity) that cultivate certain attitudes (creativity, experimentation) towards thinking about politics.

But perhaps we should refuse Kafka's conclusion entirely. Perhaps we should not favour either the idea or ethos; indeed, the solution may be in refusing the choice between the two. Can we not have both? Maybe so. But if what motivates my political thinking is the belief that we can indeed have both, what sustains my broader scholarly and political commitments is the belief that the virtues of the ethos toward thought I have outlined above is much longer lasting than specific ideas or concepts.

Notes

1   Non-status refugees and migrants are referred to by a variety of names: undocumented migrants, illegal migrants, irregular migrants, *sans-papiers*, precarious status, autonomous migration, and so on (Nyers 2008: 126–128).
2   My thanks to Bonnie Honig for suggesting the relevance of Kafka's story for this line of analysis.

Suggested reading

Bigo, D. (2002) "Security and Immigration: Toward a Critique of Governmentality of Unease", *Alternatives: Global, Local, Political*, 27(1): 62–92.

Frampton, C., Kinsman, G., Thompson, A. and Tilleczek, K. (2006) *Sociology for Changing the World: Social Movements/Social Research*, Black Point: Fernwood.

de Genova, N. (2002) "Migrant 'Illegality' and Deportability in Everyday Life", *Annual Review of Anthropology*, 31: 419–447.

Isin, E.F. (2008) "Theorizing Acts of Citizenship", in E.F. Isin and G.M. Nielsen (eds) *Acts of Citizenship*, London: Zed Books.

Rancière, J. (1999) *Disagreement: Politics and Philosophy*, trans. J. Rose. Minneapolis: University of Minnesota Press.

16 Act different, think *dispositif*[1]

Philippe Bonditti

Introduction

Much has already been said and written about Foucault's methods of archaeology and genealogy, and how both might help renew our conception of knowledge, Man, and the (modern) subject. Too little attention has nonetheless been paid to the *dispositif*,[2] which I view as a decisive element in Foucault's method. In this chapter, I suggest what a research design conducted by means of the dispositif might look like. More specifically I want to argue that the dispositif can be understood as the operator of an archaeological research, conducted from a genealogical perspective. Thus understood, I shall argue the dispositif is likely to enable an empirical research that, contrary to most social theories advocating for empirical knowledge, does not assume the (Kantian) thinking subject as the origin of meaning. To better illustrate that claim, I will take a look back at the research on terrorism and US antiterrorism I have been involved in for more than ten years.

In the late 1990s, this research project grew from a diffuse and non-formalized set of questions about transnational violence structured by my own belief that *terrorism* existed as a specific category of violence. Quickly, I was asked to clarify my research object as well as the empirical basis on which I was to deploy my analysis. What was I to observe when expecting to do research on terrorism? Would I have to get in touch with terrorist groups? How then to contact and meet them? Where? And after all, who are they, particularly when no one has ever accepted this label? The task looked too enormous to be rigorously undertaken in the short period of time I was given to fulfil my master's dissertation, let alone the extreme abundance of academic literature on terrorism, which immediately raised the issue of the originality of any new research on that theme. My research was just beginning and I found myself caught in a deadlock that required clarifying the object.

Yet, terrorism was in fact everywhere around me in the overwhelming mass of discourses and narratives on the part of governmental agencies and media, academic analyses, expert's reports, military doctrines and strategy documents, laws and administrative regulations. An abundance of perceptions, injunctions, and limitations of all kinds about what terrorism is (and how to behave in front of it), which differed in space and time, needed to be looked at as expressions of specific interests, requirements and limits. Retrospectively, I can affirm that, at this stage of research, I had identified the plan – still mainly textual and discursive – on which the analysis was to be deployed; this plan provided me with an essential certainty: terrorism had little to do with some sort of violence – as it was often claimed – and more to do with those who were making claims about what it was supposed to be.

I progressively came to look at this textual and discursive web as an infinite archive of a research project that, by the same token, was morphing into a project about what was said about "terrorism". This archive and the network that connects the narratives together with no clear coherence at first sight, possibly reminding us of the *mess* Squire refers to (Chapter 5), thus came to be what needed to be probed to understand how terrorism was constituted in the given, a question Lobo-Guerrero might view as likely to open the possibility of "wondering" (Chapter 2) and, from there, as an area of investigation and intervention. As questions were swerving from terrorism to antiterrorism, I nonetheless found myself with the same kind of questions about antiterrorism that I had about terrorism, except that there were plenty of governmental agencies to claim responsibility for the fight against terrorism. This broadened the research design outside of the strictly textual and discursive order: the bureaucratic institutions with their buildings and agents, the routines, techniques, strategies/tactics, tools, and instruments they had been deploying for years to fulfill their antiterrorist missions in accordance with specific laws and administrative regulations. In other words, from then on, I was not just going to have to observe what was being said about terrorism and how, but the wider space of antiterrorism understood as both one of the multiple sites of the discursive emanation of terrorism, and a range of non-discursive practices of intervention on the space of terrorism as posed by the narratives.

Methodologically, the focus on the very heterogeneity of that archive first required that I articulate a method that would allow dealing with the discursive as well as the non-discursive orders constitutive of antiterrorism. Second, and more importantly, it required that I understand where and how to stand in relation to that heterogeneous whole. Was I really outside of it as suggested above when I affirmed that this archive was everywhere around me – thereby extending the modern/post-enlightenment split between the subject and the object? I am not sure at all. In fact, this archive was running through me, turning myself into one of its multiple relays and active mechanisms making itself work as a Foucauldian "regime of truth" about the legitimacy as well as the means and forms of violence and sovereign power. My own belief that terrorism existed as a specific kind of violence was only one expression of my ambivalent relation with that complex machinery that needs to be explored and deciphered from its inside but that also constitutes the thinking subject as one of its multiple insides. From then on, not only was I going to have to question the conceptual apparatus and the analytical categories I inherited, a move often referred to as reflexivism (Guillaume, Chapter 3), but also think of myself as being shaped by that same machinery. This led me at some point to conduct research on terrorism and US antiterrorism by means of the Foucauldian dispositif, which was going to become the operator of what can now be possibly looked as an archaeological research.

Foucault forged the dispositif during the 1970s. In his terms:

> [The dispositif] is, firstly, a thoroughly heterogeneous ensemble (. . .) The [dispositif] itself is the system of relations that can be established between [its constitutive heterogeneous] elements. Secondly, what I am trying to identify in this [dispositif] is precisely the nature of the connection that can exist between these heterogeneous elements. (. . .) Thirdly, I understand by the term dispositif a sort of – shall we say – formation which has (. . .) a dominant strategic function.
>
> (1980a: 194)

In Foucault's work, the dispositif is thus something much broader than what he had called the *episteme* in *The Order of Things* (1971): it is both discursive and non-discursive. Drawing on Foucault's propositions but also on their interpretation by Deleuze (1986), I would like to suggest not to limit the dispositif to its sole descriptive function but also to make use of it.

For Foucault, the dispositif is not a given. It is a network that has to be brought to light to reconstitute the strategically oriented overall coherence that allows for the construction of a particular issue (transnational violence in this case) into a (problematic) given (terrorism as a threat) and legitimate the development of procedures that the very orientation of the dispositif turns into appropriate ones. Thinking in terms of dispositif helps us to escape causal and linear thought by refusing to look at the perceived problems as being prior to solutions, or the contrary (when problems are said to be shaped by existing solutions). It is the very orientation of the dispositif that makes the construction of the problems converge with existing solutions, therefore reinforcing each other and rigidifying the strategic orientation of the dispositif eventually turned into a site where motion is enabled so that change can occur.

The concrete method associated with dispositif-thinking, first consists of gathering, among the infinite archive above-mentioned, a particularly extensive roll of reports, doctrines, laws and official statements, the data Neal refers to in his plea for empiricism in this book (Chapter 6). All together, these documents become the research corpus in which regularities in the enunciation of the constructed problem(s) are to be highlighted to better identify possible ruptures and eventually bring to light what Foucault called the archive in the *Archaeology of Knowledge*, i.e. "the law of what can be said" (2004b: 145). This is how I first came to look at terrorism as a word on which different know-how came to converge, progressively forging terrorism as a specific category of violence (neither crime, nor war) eventually associated with *trans*national practices of non-state actors.

At first, the approach consists of examining these texts for their very positivity to observe the conditions of possibility they pose for non-discursive practices to develop beyond language (in this case: counterinsurgency tactics, terrorism databases, antiterrorism centres, biometric machines, and specific architectural dispositions implemented in airports after 9/11 for instance). One follows here another Foucauldian piece of advice: to look at these texts as the traces of a much broader ensemble; traces that become a path towards the non-discursive dimension of the decidedly heterogeneous set of practices the research process gradually brings to light (1998).

Such an approach to and in terms of dispositif thus implies revealing and following the network, neither immediately visible nor really hidden, that tacitly connects these textual traces together and to the non-discursive order also involved. It allowed me to simultaneously engage with a 1963 US Army report on "Insurgency and Counterinsurgency", a 2004 DHS Report on "Biometrics and Border Security", military tactics, and the physical sites of contemporary mobility where biometric machines are being installed after a complete renovation of the architectural disposition of the actual site, establishing a renewed economy of movement for people and goods that echoes the one currently in the making at the international level. The challenge then is to understand how these heterogeneous elements, distributed in space and time come to resonate with, and activate each other so as to see what these dispositifs eventually *produce*: how a specific provision in law, based on the particular spatio-temporal characteristics discursively attributed to terrorism, made it possible for biometrics to be implemented, which in return implied for airports to be redesigned.

The archaeological research on terrorism and US antiterrorism eventually revealed the latter as an abstract site animated by the immanent motion by which the practices of state sovereignty are being reconfigured through a renewed narrative on enmity, with the emergence of traceability as the major technique of the art of governing people. Now, this approach raised the legitimate question of where, when, and if dispositifs stop, and therefore when we know that the research is done. Dispositifs do not stop. They might mutate but they do not stop, just like research never ends. Indeed, as Salter reminds us in his introduction to Part II, only external and institutional factors can terminate research. Therefore, only a *strategy of writing* will match the necessarily limited research budgets and institutional frameworks with the necessarily provisional results of a never-ending research project.

Conclusion

Bring out the dispositifs, follow them and look at what they produce as well as how they make it possible for power to operate: this is what I look at as the actual challenge of a Foucauldian method, a method that constantly strives to refuse the division between the thinking subject and the (research) object. As Deleuze suggested, this method requires one to situate oneself on the constitutive lines of the identified dispositifs and to think of oneself as one of their cogwheels, and not as what gives meaning to the real from a fantasized external point of view. Such an approach that folds the thinking subject back on the immanent plan he excavates and that shapes him in the same time, potentially offers to reorient dispositifs by working on what goes into the making of the given instead of on the given itself. Although certainly difficult to think of – as it might imply a deep critique of the Kantian subject – and implement, I nonetheless view this method as appropriate for a piece of research concerned with being politically involved in the making of our world.

Notes

1   I developed this chapter from talks I gave at the *New Methodologies in Critical Security Studies* workshop, University of Ottawa, 14–15 March 2011, and the 2011 ISA Annual Convention, Montreal. It also emerges from discussions within the *International Collaboratory on Critical Methods in Security Studies* (ESRC funded project; RES-810-21-0072): www8.open.ac.uk/researchprojects/iccm/. I want to thank R.B.J. Walker, Nicholas Onuf, and Victor Coutinho Lage for their precious comments on preliminary versions of this chapter.

2   In this chapter, "dispositif" (and not apparatus) "is retained for its unique capacity to refer simultaneously either to physical instrumentation (device, mechanism) or to abstract mean (plan or strategy)" (Virilio 1998: 72).

Suggested reading

Agamben, G. (2007) *Qu'est-ce qu'un dispositif?* Paris: Payot-Rivages.

Bussolini, J. (2010) "What is a Dispositive?" *Foucault Studies*, 10: 85–107.

Dean, M. (1994) *Critical and Effective Histories: Foucault's Methods and Historical Sociology*, New York: Routledge.

Deleuze, G. (1986) *Foucault*, Paris: Editions de Minuits.

Dreyfus, H.L. and Rabinow, P. (1982) *Michel Foucault: Beyond Structuralism and Hermeneutics*, Chicago: The University of Chicago Press.

Foucault, M. (2004b) *Archaeology of Knowledge*, trans. A.M. Sheridan Smith. New York: Routledge.

Shapiro, M.J. (ed.) (1984) *Language and Politics*, New York: New York University Press.

17 Expertise in the aviation security field

Mark B. Salter

Introduction

Field research in security studies is often particularly difficult, and so before the question of clarity or sufficiency can be engaged, researchers must gain access to the actual professional field. Building on the literatures on the role of security experts (Eriksson 1999a, 1999b, Goldman 1999, Wæver 1999, Williams 1999) and autobiography in IR (Inayatullah 2010), this chapter describes how I engaged the Canadian aviation security field, my accreditation as an expert in aviation security, and some of the consequences of those engagements.

When I arrived in Ottawa in 2003, after three years at the American University in Cairo, I had just completed and published a book on the history of the passport, and I was interested in pursuing a research project on the spaces where those passports were interrogated: airports and borders, and airport security as a special case of both. Theoretically, I was moving from a Foucauldian-inspired genealogy towards a Bourdieusian field analysis. Following Bourdieu, each field has its own specific language, its own habitus, its own processes of determining what counts as true and its own tactical politics of who can speak. I had a clear question (how has aviation security changed in response to the September 11th attacks?), a small but growing set of policy literature on the problem of aviation security and surveillance (Wilkinson and Jenkins 1999, Hainmuller and Lemnitzer 2003, Lippert and O'Connor 2003, Lyon 2003), some interesting cultural theory (Fuller and Harley 2004, Gordon 2004), but, in part because of my years in Cairo, I did not have a natural entrée into the professional field of Canadian aviation security.

The Canadian Air Transportation Security Authority (CATSA), a newly-formed crown corporation that took responsibility for certain segments of Canada's aviation security system, was headed by Jacques Duchesneau, an academically-minded former police chief. CATSA contracted the actual frontline services for which it was responsible, and so the core responsibilities of the executive team were strategic: understanding the risks to aviation security, operating within the regulatory environment, administering contractors, and managing new technologies. The International Centre for Comparative Criminology and the Chaire Raoul-Dandurand were hired to stage expert workshops, guest speakers, management simulations, and training for the new executive team, and I was enlisted (Brodeur 2006). Between 2003 and 2006, I gave lectures to the CATSA executive team, immersing myself in the field of practice, learning the daily language, plotting the struggles between agencies and ideas, understanding the deep well of specific commonsense beliefs that constitute the habitus. As a crown corporation, CATSA has a complex governance structure. Transport Canada is the lead ministry for aviation security, and writes the regulations that CATSA must follow, but as a crown corporation, CATSA has some independence. It is granted an operating budget that is approved by the Treasury Board, but only once Transport Canada has approved its annual report and corporate plan. Budgetary and strategic planning battles, which often take place out of the public eye, are crucial for understanding how CATSA presents itself, its mission, its strategies, and the problem of security. The rapport between CATSA, Transport Canada, and the Treasury Board cannot be explained simply by the formal relationships: the quotidian struggles and cooperation depends upon personal and professional relationships. The governing regulations of security procedures at the check-point, the Security Screening Order, are classified; however, the tasks of the organization, in terms of training, equipment, standards, and organization could be examined through policy document analysis, interviews, and internal documents. There were also a number of opportunities to observe the checkpoints, discuss the evolution of technologies, and strategy discussions. So, the technical standards for metal detectors or hand luggage scanners could remain secret, but the core ideas about risk management could be openly discussed. CATSA became seized by the issue of risk and risk management, just as the issue was becoming current in the critical security and sociology literature (Ericson 2006, Amoore and de Goede 2008, Aradau et al. 2008), which allowed me to analyze how this particular agency engaged with risk management (Salter 2007b). For example, European, American, and Canadian aviation security agencies all adopted a risk management approach, and roughly approximate hold-baggage scanners – but their fundamental idea about risk was different: European agencies scanned luggage with progressively more sophisticated equipment when an alarm was detected, American agencies scanned every piece of luggage with the most sensitive equipment. Canadian agencies were caught between two norms (Salter 2010: 70–71). Learning the field, thus, was a question of understanding quotidian language, personal and professional networks, historical perceptions and contemporary jurisdictional turf wars, as well as the bodily and technical practices at the security checkpoint.

Professional conferences, such as AVSEC World, the Canadian Aviation Security Conference, Passenger Terminal World, etc., sponsored jointly by governments and private firms, provided amazing snapshots of the technologies, norms, and practices of the field. Governments and international actors reported on pilot projects and new strategies, private firms demonstrated technologies and systems, experts provided data and analysis (though this was rare, as I was often the only professor at these conferences, and certainly the only social scientist). A barrier to entry to these conferences is the closed program selection process and the registration fees, which easily topped CAD $1,000. As a speaker, I received free or discounted registration and this reified my role as expert and the interpersonal connections that made subsequent entries easier. The formal presentations were incredibly useful, as was the interstitial informal conference-work: most surprising and helpful, however, were the trade shows in which vendors hawked systems and technologies. Promotional material was distributed that used the everyday language of the professional field, and provided a view as to how risk management technologies and systems were marketed, and to whom. Though no representatives ever followed-up with my request for further phone interviews, in the commercial space of the convention the representatives were frank about the state of their technology, the political state of play, and their commercial interests. This deep background reading in the field fleshed out the habitus of the aviation security professional, and helped demonstrate the relations of competition and domination between different actors. The more I spoke at professional conferences about risk and risk management, even though I was severely critical of the appropriateness of the risk framework for security issues, the greater access I got to key decision makers, policy leaders, and the risk professionals in the field. At one conference on the future of security screening, I won a prize – a free week-long course in airport security management at the International Air Transportation Association. My certification in airport security management was an ideal opportunity for auto-ethnography, and a deeper immersion in the field.

In 2006, immediately after my certification, which demonstrated my field-specific expertise, the Canadian aviation security field was opened to the public through a mandated five-year review of the empowering legislation for CATSA and a special examination by the Auditor-General of Canada. These two bureaucratic events made a series of interventions and positions suddenly publicly-accessible: the *CATSA Act* Review publicized submissions from a number of stakeholders (pilots, airports, private firms, experts, and consultants), CATSA itself issued a number of position papers, corporate strategies, and vision statements, and an expert panel provided a final report (Salter 2008c). These public statements made everyday struggles and languages suddenly visible. The Special Examination also engaged with the question of risk and risk management, in terms of quantification (Salter 2008d). My knowledge of the field allowed a contextualization of those public statements and bureaucratic struggles – and more importantly enabled me to demonstrate those struggles within the field.

While ongoing quotidian engagement with the field of aviation security constantly nurtured my sense of command of the issues, languages, and struggles, I judged that my field research was sufficient when (1) the actors and institutions recognized me as part of the field, and (2) as a researcher, I could contextualize the everyday practices in the field. For example, in addition to understanding the formal lines of authority, understanding the career trajectories of key individuals, education, training, background, and professional relationships explained the everyday rapport between different ministries. Rapport between offices had as much to do with tone, perception, and organizational culture as anything formal. Similarly, program or budget choices were often explained differently within institutions than between institutions or in public documents. CATSA, in particular, had a series of robust and sincere debates about the adoption and implementation of a risk management framework before it was publicly announced, which included a number of conversations with other ministries and even foreign agencies. In hindsight, I can see that one could enter the field through an analysis of policy documents and professional meetings, without engaging directly with government agencies. However, this would provide only part of the picture, because of a large number of closed-door meetings that would not be possible without the invitation or participation of government agencies. Similarly, a certain degree of social/cultural capital was required to gain access to those non-public struggles.

A self-reflection on criticality: during my period of intense involvement with the field, when I was presenting material at professional conferences, writing reports, and appearing in the media, I was deeply critical of the adoption of risk management for security, which went against the grain of government policy and common sense. I pointed out passionately in professional forums the problem of the quantification in the measurement of security as an outcome or result of policy. Passenger screening at airports, for which CATSA was responsible, had three incomplete and erroneous markers: screening rate (positives: successful screening indicating no prohibited items), screened items that were not threats to the system (false positives: confiscation of water bottles or gran's knitting needles), and disasters (failures: 9/11, Richard Reid the shoe bomber). None of these could actually measure the security of the aviation security system (Salter 2007a). While I hope that my academic writing had some impact, my policy presentations had no real policy impact. Whether or not it was possible to measure security, the empowering legislation and prescriptive regulations required measurement, and so the policy puzzle within the field was how to produce auditable data that could count as measurement. Audiences would agree that security was not measurable, but that did not change the legislative or regulatory imperative to produce measurements. My failure to convince them, however, did not harm my social capital within the field (a good lesson in itself). My identification of a core paradox at the heart of neoliberal attempts to govern risk and the political realities of security perception did not change the structure of the field: I understood in a thunderclap my position in the field. This failure helped me identify the difference between being critical of a policy and being critical as a position. Desecuritization is an important goal for critical security scholars, the publicizing of security issues. After this immersion in the field, however, I conclude that it is imperative to understand the field in order to be able to desecuritize. Without learning the bureaucratic codes for particular struggles, it would be impossible to speak authoritatively against securitizing moves, or even understand the bureaucratic or personal/professional struggles that underlay them.

Conclusion

In sum, my research design was both planned and opportunistic; I was able to access a professional field in which I had a scholarly interest, and I used my status as an expert to better understand the habitus of the aviation security field, going so far as to engage in its training and accreditation. Once inside the field, with an understanding of the language, discourses, and practices, I was able to articulate a clear research question, and use field research and auto-ethnography to map out the relations of competition and dominance, and in particular provide a clear empirical policy case to the theoretical literature on risk and risk management. The price of admission was policy-driven research that the field perceived as useful.

Suggested reading

Adey, P. (2010) *Aerial Life: Spaces, Mobilities, Affect*, Malden: Wiley-Blackwell.
Amoore, L. and de Goede, M. (eds) (2008) *Risk and the War on Terror*, New York: Routledge.
Augé, M. (1995) *Non-places: Introduction to an Anthropology of Supermodernity*, trans. J. Howe. London: Verso.
Fuller, G. and Harley, R. (2004) *Aviopolis: A Book about Airports*, London: Black Dog Publishing.
Pascoe, D. (2001) *Airspaces*, London: Reaktion.

18 Testifying while critical

Notes on being an effective gadfly

Benjamin J. Muller

Introduction

For many scholars, being referred to as an *expert* on a particular issue or field causes some trepidation. In media and policy circles, commentary from scholars is intermittently requested and repackaged as expertise, which through manipulation, editing, or the material restrictions of the exercise not only lead to oversimplification, but also discredit the academic enterprise in the process. To what extent can we maintain deconstructive, destabilizing, and emancipatory possibilities (to name just a few) once we accept the mantle of the expert? Does this mantle of expertise hinder the commitment to the Coxian notion of critical theory: unpacking and challenging the structures that underlie the world; or, is one forced down the road of what Cox (1986) labels "problem solving theory" and its avoidance of the underlying structures and economic and socio-political relations that underpin the knowledge claims and the existing order of things? Comfortably inhabited by the policy wonks, media hacks and hawks, and celebrated demagogues of the day, does our participation in media and policy forums force us to join this cast of characters, dooming us to be little more than a pesky gadfly, at best providing comic relief, and at worst the much needed counterpoint to legitimize the precooked sound bites and remedies of the bureaucrats?

The issues here are complex, and at times, raise concerns about our commitment to scholarship and the extent to which it is amenable with being a public intellectual. Can we maintain the commitment, for example, to Cox's notion of critical theory, which "does not take institutions and social power relations for granted, but calls them into question by concerning itself with their origins and how and whether they might be in the process of changing" (1986: 89). On the one hand, participation in media interviews, Parliamentary Committee testimony, and a host of other engagements might reify the institutions, let alone take them for granted. However, one might also consider the decision to include scholars with obvious commitments to critical approaches to particular issues as a sign that indeed the social power relations underpinning these institutions might "be in the process of changing". In his analysis, Cox clearly outlines the alternative to critical theory: problem-solving theory. In his words, this "takes the world as it finds it, with the prevailing social and power relationships" (1986: 88) and "limits the range of choice to alternative orders which are feasible transformations of the existing world" (1986: 90). To what extent can we insert ourselves with some effect, as critical scholars invited into these institutions that appear for the most part to be engaged in anything but a critical reflection on the social power relations responsible for their constitution? Moreover, how might we measure our own success or failure in this regard?

In what follows, I unpack these issues in light of my experience providing expert testimony to a Canadian Parliamentary Committee in May 2009. Part of the Committee on National

Security and Public Safety, my session was part of an ongoing dialogue on contemporary challenges in Canadian border security. I begin with some reflections on the genre of expert testimony, noting the challenges this presents to one with intentions of fostering criticality in the Coxian sense (and beyond), in addition to the more obvious material challenges of time, preparing statements, simultaneous translation, and so on. I follow this with some reflections on the statement I delivered, commenting on what constitutes criticality in such a context. In a related point, I consider the issue of effectiveness, what constitutes it and to what extent it can be measured in such a context.

Sharp, insightful critiques and critical engagements with contemporary borders and the bodies that cross them have arisen recently within academe. Indeed, many of the authors in this collection are among the leaders in this field (Muller 2009, Nyers 2006c, 2009, Salter 2004, 2007a, Squire 2010). Engaging in similar critiques when asked to provide expertise to either policy-makers or journalists is something altogether different. The register, tone, and genre of the Parliamentary Committee create dramatically different conditions for engagement and criticality than those afforded by the university classroom, the scholarly workshop, academic conference, or professional journal.

Testimony to the Parliamentary Committee cedes a certain verisimilitude, however unwarranted, to the expert providing it. Definitions of *testimony* invoke appeals to fact, evidence, declarations of faith, and some measure of truth. As a critical scholar, such unproblematized assumptions trigger discomfort, not soothed by the material limitations of the testimony: in this case, a ten-minute prepared statement. Moreover, the ties that bind genre to authorship are well worth noting (Derrida 1980). In my case, as a rather junior scholar at the time, I was seated between Perrin Beatty, a former Member of Parliament and erstwhile CEO of the Canadian Chamber of Commerce, and Michael Kergin, a career diplomat and nineteenth Canadian Ambassador to the United States, from 2000 to 2005. The differential authority among the panellists was both obvious to me prior to delivering my statement, and only emphasized by the dialogue over the course of the session. The power of authorship and legitimacy given to particular forms of expertise raises serious questions about the potential for critical engagement in such a forum.

Although the genre of testimony connotes some notion of factual evidence, both its delivery by experts and its reception by the audience – namely the Parliamentary Committee – seemed to stray somewhat closer to Stephen Colbert's notion of "truthiness", which refers to truth claims premised on intuition and common sense, in the absence of and with full disregard of evidence, logic, and intellectual examination (Colbert 2005). Under the cloak of expert testimony, and all that genre connotes, those with the microphone asserted partisan commitments, the private and commercial interests they represented professionally, and anecdotes that underscored their own historical claims to authority and access to power, but provided little if any insight into contemporary challenges in Canadian border management. The sort of conventions that keep us honest as researchers fell away: off-the-cuff anecdotes appeared to be granted equal weight with complex statistics and graphs about cross-border trade.

The extent to which one can maintain any sort of commitment to a research design, key questions, and considerations that compel one's participation is moot in light of the fact that the exercise itself, its limits and the governing structure of participation, inhibit one's ability to forward much of a self-directed enterprise. The manner in which knowledge claims and authorship are framed in the context of Committee testimony – or media interviews for that matter – fails to recognize fully the stripes earned as an academic. Whether tenured or not, the author of one or more single-authored books, etc., or simply a part-time instructor, one's ability to frame claims within the accepted strictures of the prevalent discourse far outweigh the sorts of baggage that aids one's claim to power and authority in academe. To what extent the cost to one's legitimacy in academe that results from reframing a critical engagement in the manners required for expert sound bites is not easily answered, but deserves serious consideration.

Reflecting on engaged research such as Der Derian's documentary *Human Terrain*, one wonders to what extent the expertise and scholarly cache is simply co-opted as part of the broader project? Being critically aware takes one only so far, as the institutional and organizational conditions of possibility create particular conditions for legitimacy and authority that generally tend to be disadvantageous to the scholar and more comfortable for those ensconced in the fields of lobbying and policy making. The performance of expertise is itself framed in terms of Cox's notion of "problem solving theory", where one's expertise is being elicited to solve or contribute to the solution of a particular problem. As such, there is little room for unpacking the social and political order that underpins the specific framing of the problem itself.

As noted earlier, the issue of audience and its interpretations is also relevant when reflecting on genre. The proceedings of Parliamentary Committees are publicly accessible, and therefore the Canadian people are in some nominal manner the audience. However, it is hard to imagine many Canadians spending their warm summer evenings gathered round the laptop listening to the proceedings of Parliamentary Committees. While this may be a rather pessimistic appraisal, I approached my testimony with the assumption that the committee itself and to some extent, my co-panellists formed the audience, and I framed my comments accordingly.

My statement to the committee begins with some brief points that serve to question expertise altogether, particularly in the field of terrorism and disasters, which had and to some extent continue to have disproportionate sway over policy makers. I then proceed to raise three questions with brief commentary: First, how appropriate is risk management to border security, particularly in relation to the focus on public safety? Second, to what extent has the call for improved border security and efficiency been answered by a rather uncritical embrace of identification and surveillance technologies? Third, to what extent have post-9/11 border security strategies been governed through bureaucratic changes such as the creation of the Department of Homeland Security and the Canada Border Services Agency, which contributed to a centralization of authority and legitimacy? Trying to play to the sound bite, or at least engage in the accepted vernacular, I ended my introduction with a few brief points regarding the need for scepticism towards strategies premised on predicting potential risks and any approach that fails to account adequately for public values in its construction.

In the case of each of the three questions, word choice is crucial. Rather than raise the importance of local communities, the input and values of those who regularly cross borders and inhabit borderlands – those who constitute borderlands – I simply used the policy friendly term: stakeholders. One cannot ensure that the members of the Parliamentary Committee simply hear what they want to hear when a term like this is used; however, time constraints make unpacking discourse, the grammatology of it all, far too ambitious. Similarly, in questioning the role of risk management I carefully indicated my comprehension of its mandated use, governed by the Treasury Board, and further extolling the virtues of its utility in terms of distributing scarce resources across a wide array of government ministries (Salter, Chapter 17). Only after framing it in this manner did I feel comfortable raising a series of questions about its appropriateness in the field of public safety, and commenting on the general manner in which public values tend not to enter into the discussion.

For me, the most challenging and pressing issue was to raise critical questions for the committee's reflection on the uncritical embrace of the wide panoply of identification and surveillance technologies. Having participated in a variety of government and commercial forums prior to my appearance on the Parliamentary Committee, the powerful private interests at stake in these decisions, the overlap with public officials, and the powerful lobbying was not at all lost on me. Indeed, it was as close to a "speaking truth to power" moment as I feel I could have hoped for. Raising the spectre of what Lyon regards as "social sorting", and the potentially nefarious misuses of mined data was part of my initial insight (2003). However, the simple fact that many accepted technologies tend to be unproven in the specific contexts of border security, as well as terribly costly, and substantiated by the fact that there have been no more 9/11s, was as much feather ruffling as I believed possible. Perceiving my contributions as those of a critical gadfly, sowing seeds of doubt, relaying hesitation and critical mistrust of certain strategies was what I believed possible under the conditions of possibility of expert testimony to the Parliamentary Committee.

Conclusion

Although one might not replace the seemingly more powerful hacks and hawks, whose commentary is ubiquitous in its vitriol and its Manichaean imaginaries of the border and the barbarians just on the other side, the influence of a nagging gadfly should not be underestimated. Sowing the seeds of doubt, raising critical questions, and highlighting the power embedded in the genre of expert testimony, one can maintain a commitment to the critical enterprise, and bring the experience *back* to one's own research agenda, and thus engage more critically in academic forums in ways only made possible through one's own participation. Measuring the effectiveness in any objective scientific manner presents obvious challenges. However, in terms of one's ability to maintain commitments to a series of critical questions and hesitations, an awareness of deeper considerations of genre and the power embedded in these institutionally reinforced conditions of (im)possibility, the stark relationship between the author and audience, and the way in which knowledge claims are articulated under such conditions, are not sacrosanct or beyond the limits of our critical engagement. Our participation can be disruptive not only in ways addressed here, as well as simply that of our own subject position, but also in terms of what we carry back to our research projects, classrooms, and scholarly conferences, where such experiences can be invaluable.

Suggested reading

Campbell, D. (1998) *Writing Security: United States Foreign Policy and the Politics of Identity*, 2nd edn, Minneapolis: University of Minnesota Press.
Der Derian, J. (2009c) *Critical Practices in International Theory: Selected Essays*, New York: Routledge.
Der Derian, J., Urdis, D. and Urdis, M. (2011) *Human Terrain: War Becomes Academic*, Urdis Film and Oxyopia Productions with the Global Media Project and the Watson Institute for International Studies. Online: http://humanterrainmovie.com
Inayatullah, N. (ed.) (2010) *Autobiographical International Relations: I, IR*, New York: Routledge.

Part IV

The discursive turn

Introduction

Can E. Mutlu and Mark B. Salter

Language is political, social, and cultural: discourse analysis is the rigorous study of writing, speech, and other communicative events in order to understand these political, social, and cultural dynamics. While discourse analysis can be traced to philology and philosophy, law, linguistics, and literature, as a method it primarily made its way into critical inquiry in international relations (IR) through the works of Foucault and Derrida, particularly the methods of genealogy and deconstruction. Within these approaches, discourse is a social practice that constitutes the social world, and is also constituted by other social practices.

Discourse analysis is a method to analyze these spoken, sign-based, or any other significant semiotic markers that provide meaning to the social world surrounding us. Cut loose from an easy correspondence theory of language (*this word means that thing, value, or relation in the real world*), discourse was understood to be a series of signs that could only be understood in relation to other signs, but that does not mean that words do not have real effects in the world. Linguists Austen and Searle are arguing for the ability of words to have action in their speaking, which they define as "performativity" (Austin 1975, Searle 1969). In one of his earliest works on the question of discourse, Foucault writes that our task is "no longer treating discourses as groups of signs (signifying elements referring to contents or representations) but as practices that systematically form the objects of which they speak" (1972: 49).

Today discourse analysis is used by a wide range of disciplines within social science and humanities, ranging from linguistics to human geography. In IR proper, discourse analysis is often associated with (social) constructivism (Ruggie 1998, Wendt 1999) and poststructural IR (Der Derian 1987, Der Derian and Shapiro 1989). As one of the core methods in critical security studies, discourse analysis has been used by a number of scholars in projects focusing on performativity of security threats (Buzan et al. 1998), deconstruction of self/other in relation to American foreign policy (Campbell 1998), or competing Western discourses on the Bosnian War (Hansen 2006). This book is no exception to this multiplicity; throughout this book contributors use different varieties of discourse analysis and multiple texts: policy documents, speeches, informal writing, practices, and visuals. In general, we have identified three dominant strategies of discourse analysis focusing on *continuity*, *change*, or *rupture*.

Table PIV.1 Research design in discourse analysis

Object	Studying linguistic origins of the socio-political world
Key concepts	Genealogy, intertextuality, speech-act
Collection	Archival research, interviews, content analysis
Data	Correspondence, publications, transcripts, policy documents, visuals
Relations	Continuity, change, rupture
Fit	Issues that have accessible linguistic and visual markers

Plastic discourse analysis seeks *continuity*: the identity of linguistic signs and tropes or the persistence of particular metaphorical schema. It often identifies an organizing principle through which deviation from this master narrative can be understood in terms of classification or typology. One of its primary tools is "intertextuality" – the connection of texts and meanings through reference to other texts, which also relates to questions of genre and form. An intertextual posture "takes a self-conscious step away from the dominant modes of formalistic and ahistorical trends in international relations theory that 'naturally select' hermetic, rational models over hermeneutic, philosophical investigations" (Der Derian and Shapiro 1989: 7). Analyses of self/other in Campbell's *Writing Security* (1998) and Neumann's *Uses of the Other* (1999) are exemplary of this technique. In his book, Campbell establishes a direct link between security-danger-identity and foreign policy by tracing the use of "danger" in discourses of American identity construction. Continuous use of the discourse of danger not only transforms identities but also re-affirms the role and purpose of the state and its foreign policy practices. To do this, Campbell uses a variety of policy documents, popular statements, and dominant tropes.

Elastic discourse analysis attempts to plot the *changes* or transformations over time of discourses, to trace the new relations between signs, tropes or metaphorical schema. Tracing the emergence or disappearance of a particular linguistic schema is typical, such as the securitization theory set out in Buzan, Wæver, and de Wilde's (1998) *Security: A New Framework for Analysis*. Building on speech-act theory developed by Austin (1975) and Searle (1969), securitization theory focuses on utterances of speech that associate an issue with a security value (societal, economic, political, military, or environmental security). These illocutionary speech acts, or securitization moves, represent moments of change, when an issue is removed from everyday politics and placed in the exceptional realm of security politics. Securitization theory is also concerned with the question of how issues ceased to be associated with a security value, the process of desecuritization.

Genealogical discourse analysis seeks *ruptures*, silences, breaks, marginalized voices or subjugated knowledges. While there is also a genealogical emphasis on historical change between signs and metaphorical schemes, there is a careful attention to the disappeared or silenced. Amongst Foucault's several definitions of genealogy, perhaps the clearest is:

> a form of history that can account for the constitution of knowledges, discourses, domains of objects, and so on, without having to make reference to a subject that is either transcendental in relation to the field of events or runs in its empty sameness throughout the course of history.
>
> (2000: 118)

Chilton demonstrates this clearly in his careful genealogy of "security" (1996); Der Derian (1987), Bartelson (1995) and Jahn (2000) also illustrate this in their respective genealogies of diplomacy, sovereignty, and the state of nature. In the case of each social institution or archetype, certain meanings or interpretations of diplomacy, sovereignty, or the state of nature are occluded, and their origins hidden. The search for silence is particularly difficult to manage. The point of the genealogy is not to assume that researchers can discover an origin or ur-text, from which all variants can be understood as deviants, but rather what disappears and what stays and the way these transformations occur with what effect.

In each of these strategies, plastic, elastic, and genealogical, the researcher must be open to the discursive evidence, and the selection of source texts will pull towards one conclusion or another. As a consequence, the question of fit remains important.

Fit

Discourse analysis takes textual, visual, or other semiotic data as its primary data. While discourse analyses focusing on *continuity*, *change*, or *rupture* all have a different focus, they all rely on similar sources for data. Personal correspondence, publications, newsletters, newspapers, magazines, memos, transcripts, policy documents, visual symbols, still and moving images, and PowerPoint presentations are valid sources for discursive approaches. The choice of texts is structured by necessity, accessibility, and the core object of the study. In our contributions, we see various uses of this method in a range of topics with an array of sources.

For example, Howell studies how psy disciplines came to be conceived as part of military operations in Iraq and elsewhere by looking at the *continuities* between different discourses in different types of documents, looking at the common underlying themes across these genres (Chapter 21); she asks how pre-existing practices of medicine and psy disciplines come to be understood and incorporated in pre-existing strategies of military practices. Howell often found important information pertinent to her project buried deep in secondary or *low* sources such as newsletters, technical documents, PowerPoint presentations, etc. Using a number of sources involved in the introduction and internalization of medical and psy practices into conflict zones and other *exceptional* spaces, Howell traces the continuity of the technical and scientific discourse in the face of new practices and fields.

Alternatively, as a good example of discourse analysis focusing on *change*, Vuori looks at the kinds of political functions security speech (in the political sector) served in the People's Republic of China (Chapter 22). To study various functions of securitization during four "spectacular" events in recent Chinese history, Vuori uses an intertextual method to focus on speeches, canonized ideological texts, historical discourses, newspaper editorials and articles, central documents, film, and news reports that primarily used securitization discourse. Through his analysis, Vuori discovers institutionalized master signifiers of securitization, such as "counter-revolution", "turmoil", and "well planned plots" are used to relate an issue to security and remove it from everyday politics thus changing the discourse surrounding an issue.

Finally, Lobo-Guerrero focuses on the use of marine insurance by the British government in times of war by going to the Lloyd's of London's archives (Chapter 19). Upon entering the archive, he faces the same difficulty as those using ethnography and field analysis: we do not know what we are going to find in the archive or the field until we get there. In his case, the difficulty arises from the fact that the specific archive he is looking for was destroyed as a result of a fire. Consequently, Lobo-Guerrero's research takes a different turn, and he tries to map out what would have been in that archive by tracing related documents and letting the documents speak to each other; he relies on the intertextuality of the documents in the archive by tracing footnotes, and trying to understand "the wider narrative articulating the complex and disperse body of correspondence" (Chapter 19). This genealogical approach results in the discovery of not a rupture but rather a *silence*, which was not previously in the discourse. His discovery leads him to trace a new articulation of a practice that became dominant but was not in the discourse.

As we see with each of these examples, there are a number of issues involved in designing a research project that uses discourse analysis as its primary method. First is the question of *which* texts to study. On any given socio-political topic, there are a multitude of official texts, critiques, media coverage, historical accounts etc. Often times the case study determines which texts are the appropriate ones – like in the case of Vuori, in which the institutional setting of the discourse is clearly identified, even if other sources have to be used for triangulation and contextualization. Other times, like Lobo-Guerrero, the archive is spotty, random, absent, or confusing, and requires a wider engagement in other kinds of sources. Alternatively, if the research object is contested, competing narratives can be examined, such as the case with Howell's description of the treatment of the mentally ill. These decisions are, inevitably, going to be shaped by the ontological and epistemological departure points of the researcher, but regardless, the process needs to be justified and re-traceable.

Good discourse analysis will also identify what the meaning is of the data collected through formal content analysis that measures: the appearance or dominance of a particular phrase or set of terms; the persistence of a metaphorical trope such as inside/outside, self/other, national security/international anarchy; or the development of a linguistic or visual practice. Vuori plots discourse on *spectacular* events in recent Chinese history by establishing a set of historically-determined linguistic signifiers that relate to security. Alternatively, Lobo-Guerrero conducts his research by searching wartime documents, related to a specific concept, "marine insurance". While each one of these authors has a different approach to this question, each project has a defined set of terms and ways of going through documents to trace the discourses surrounding these terms.

The question of reflexivity is equally germane to discourse analysis. To do serious discourse analysis, as Neumann states, the researcher must hold a certain degree of linguistic and cultural fluency (2008b). The informal and tacit knowledge that is the obvious target of ethnographic and field analysis approaches is equally important in the practice of reading and understanding genre, form, and irony. The almost random selection of the archive reinforces the importance of choice as to what counts within an author's oeuvre or within an institution's textual product. Each discourse analysis, then, must account for the role of speaker, audience, and form.

Examples

Within this book, Neal provides a clear description of his case selection and research design (Chapter 20). Within the broader critical security studies community, we can point to two other important exemplars: Huysmans' (2006) *The Politics of Insecurity*, which he presents as a critique of discursive approaches, and Jackson's (2005) *Writing the War on Terrorism*, which is a good example of critical discursive analysis of a signal event.

One of the clearest articulations of discourse analysis in this book is Neal's "Legislative Practices". Neal focuses on the history of anti-terror legislation in the British House of Commons. The British Parliament, with an official record – Hansard – that has been published in print for centuries and online for the last decade or so, is as well a site of multiple actors and discourses, collective groupings, differential relationships, and institutionalized practices that provide an accessible venue to trace debates surrounding implementation of anti-terror legislations. To narrow down the vast amount of information available to him, Neal identifies three bills that were each introduced in different security circumstances: when a period of major terrorist activity was seen to be coming to an end (2000), in the aftermath of a major terrorist attack (2001), and some time after that first attack (2008). He narrows down his data even further by focusing on the transcripts of second-readings of these bills, a formal stage in the British House of Commons lawmaking process. He contextualizes these transcripts with complimentary texts such as published political memoirs, general political histories, and his tacit knowledge of British politics, to understand some of the context for the discourses present in these second readings. Furthermore, Neal relies on his under-

Table PIV.2 Examples of discursive research design

	Neal, Legislative Practices	*Huysmans*, The Politics of Insecurity	*Jackson*, Writing the War on Terrorism
Object	Anti-terror legislation in the United Kingdom before and after 9/11	Discourses and practices of securitized migration in the European Union	Official discourses of the War on Terror
Collection	Discourse analysis	Interviews, discourse/ policy analysis, practice	Discourse analysis
Data	Transcripts of parliamentary debates, law, political memoirs, political histories	Policy documents, publications, interviews related to governance of migration and asylum through technologies of security	Written or spoken official documents, laws, policy documents, national strategy statements, official reports, briefing papers, internal reports and documents, official websites, interdepartmental memos, emails, letters, operations manuals, rules and standard operating procedures of all agencies and institutions involved in the counter-terrorism effort; symbolic and emblematic representations of the counter-terrorist campaign
Relations	Collective groupings, differential relationships, institutionalized practices in legislative practices	Discursive, technocratic, and technological aspects of security shaping the governance of migration and asylum	Symbolic: linguistic connection between self/other images, idea of exception and emergency, and war policies
Fit	A persistent institution that deals (parliament) with the same issue (terrorism) before and after a big event	Policy field that crossed bureaucratic jurisdictions, but has institutional, legislative, and popular discourses within a geographical scope	Policy area and identity dynamics that change over a short time, identifiable in popular support and discussion of new policies

standing of the institutional context of the House of Commons to prioritize which debates and documents are studied. From this analysis, Neal is able to demonstrate that counter-terrorism legislation is not solely the prerogative of executive power, and that the informal norms of the institution of Parliament instead have a structuring effect on the debate – an idea which runs counter to much of the academic work on this subject.

Huysmans' seminal work on the *Politics of Insecurity*, which focuses on the discourses and practices that result from the association of migration and asylum in the EU with security, is another good example of discourse analysis. Huysmans successfully traces the discourses and practices that connect concerns surrounding identity, welfare, and security to the evolution of European asylum and migration policy. The project is driven by a broad question: "What does it mean to politicize and regulate migration and asylum within a security framework?" (Huysmans 2006: 1). Huysmans supplements discourse analysis with practice-driven approaches because he believes that "discursive approaches tend to focus on political speeches and writings. [. . .] [t]hey thus have an implicit bias towards focusing on professional politicians and opinion makers" (Huysmans 2006: 8). He argues that this kind of discourse analysis fails to "theorize the power of language in relation to specific political processes" (Huysmans 2006: 91). In return, he suggests that discourse should be embedded in technologies of government. In Huysmans' approach, technologies of security – such as passports, visas, etc. – are not conceptualized as instruments simply implementing an already framed policy or discourse. Rather "they are themselves rendering the specific ways in which free movement can be exercised within the EU and between the Union and its external government" (Huysmans 2006: 93). While Huysmans is critical of discursive approaches to security, he uses discourse analysis as a method to focus on both discourses and practices surrounding government of migration and asylum in the EU.

Jackson's book is "about the public language of the 'war on terrorism' and the way in which language has been deployed to justify and normalize a global campaign of counter-terrorism" (Jackson 2005: 1). Looking at how the Bush administration gave meaning to the events of September 11, by providing the official account of events, Jackson demonstrates the role of language in shaping security practices. According to him, the language of the War on Terror "is a deliberately and meticulously composed set of words, assumptions, metaphors, grammatical forms, myths and forms of knowledge – it is a carefully constructed discourse" (Jackson 2005: 2). Jackson establishes a four-tiered pyramid as the data set to study the language of the war on terrorism. The first set consists of "any act of written or spoken speech, [. . .] whole corpus of official speeches, media interviews, press releases, radio and television addresses and articles written by leading figures in the administration" (Jackson 2005: 17). The second set includes laws, policy documents, national strategy statements, and official reports. The third set looks at briefing papers, internal reports, and documents, official websites, interdepartmental memos, emails, letters, operations manuals, rules and standard operating procedures of all agencies and institutions involved in the counter-terrorism effort. A final level consists of all symbolic and emblematic representations of the counter-terrorist campaign (Jackson 2005: 17–18). Through this four-tiered data set, Jackson creates an impressive archive, which he then uses critical discourse analysis to study. He demonstrates that the war on terror follows other established models for the incitement to political violence: the assertion of an in-group and out-group identity, the establishment of an emergency or exceptional circumstance, and a narrowing of the debated policy options. To answer how the policies for the war on terror were made possible, and given popular support, Jackson looks at the movement of official and public discourse.

Conclusion

Discourse analysis has become an enormously popular method among critical security studies scholars. A key assumption of discourse analysis is that language is constitutive of the social world surrounding us. Discourse analysis is especially useful for demonstrating the impact of language on discourses and practices of security; not only highlighting the linguistic origins of insecurities but also demonstrating the impact of competing narratives in shaping them. Given the textual and intertextual origins of security practices, discourse analysis provides a vigorous method for their understanding. However, because language is both social and political, we must pay attention to decisions we make along the way and be reflexive about our role as the researcher in the process to avoid misinterpretations and overemphasis on certain text while ignoring alternatives.

Suggested reading

Austin, J.L. (1975) *How To Do Things with Words*, Oxford: Oxford University Press.

Campbell, D. (1998) *Writing Security: United States Foreign Policy and the Politics of Identity*, 2nd edn, Minneapolis: University of Minnesota Press.

Fairclough, N. (1992) *Discourse and Social Change*, Cambridge: Polity Press.

Fairclough, N. and Wodak, R. (1997) "Critical Discourse Analysis", in T.A. van Dijk (ed.) *Introduction to Discourse Analysis*, London: SAGE Publications.

Foucault, M. (1981) "The Order of Discourse", in R. Young (ed.) *Untying the Text: A Post-Structuralist Reader*, New York: Routledge.

Hansen, L. (2006) *Security as Practice: Discourse Analysis and the Bosnian War*, New York: Routledge.

Jackson, R. (2005) *Writing the War on Terrorism: Language, Politics and Counter-Terrorism*, Manchester: Manchester University Press.

Neumann, I.B. (2008b) "Discourse Analysis", in A. Klotz and D. Prakash (eds) *Qualitative Methods in International Relations: A Pluralist Guide*, New York: Palgrave.

Searle, J.R. (1969) *Speech Acts*, Cambridge: Cambridge University Press.

Wæver, O. (2002) "Identity, Communities and Foreign Policy: Discourse Analysis as Foreign Policy Theory", in L. Hansen and O. Wæver (eds) *European Identity and National Identity: The Challenge of the Nordic States*, New York: Routledge.

19 Archives

Luis Lobo-Guerrero

> Dig into the archives of humanity in order to discover the complicated but humble origins of our lofty convictions.
>
> (Foucault, as read by Veyne 2010: 54)

Introduction

What constitutes an archive is not a settled matter.[1] To start with, an archive can be widely understood as a collection of data organized as *records* and the physical space where they are stored. The idea of record, however, deserves a short comment. Records are not simply a register of statements but constitute evidence of ways of thinking and ways of relating to the world. In other words, records are evidence of imaginaries, and imaginaries denote ways of understanding what is real and how that reality matters. Technically speaking, one could refer to records as representing orders of the real. From that perspective, archives are in principle depositories of evidence of how different ways of understanding and dealing with reality have taken place within specific locations and time-frames. Such an assertion implies already several assumptions worth making explicit.

If archives are depositories of how things have been thought of and dealt with in a past, it means that they are spaces from which to interrogate those imaginaries. They are not sites from which to derive final answers to general questions about issues and events. They are instead sites from which to "wonder" (Lobo-Guerrero, Chapter 2) about realities and experiences of how others, under different times and circumstances have related to the world. It follows that archives will not provide answers to preconceived questions formulated from our very present and life experience. Instead, they provide the possibility of an experience of discovery, an experience that will allow us to formulate exploratory questions that will in turn allow access to alternative ways of knowing the world. Knowledge here is of course not associated to objective truths but instead to the ways of life that experienced them, truths that are such within a particular logic and a specific rationality.

In this respect, archival research is not a neutral practice. The researcher is not there to depict objectively what he/she reads and observes since an archive becomes a mediated space between the records and the researcher's imaginary. It demands a creative attitude to understand why and how events were recorded and why were they recorded in their specific manner. Archival research demands resourcefulness to find out how to know more about the specific contexts under which records were created, contexts that lack secondary literatures in many cases. Weaving together the contextual histories of events allows the researcher to understand the singularities of the event; issues that might otherwise go unnoticed become the key to developing novel interpretations of the phenomena under study.

In that spirit, the archive becomes a field of surprise. Surprises are here understood as unexpected disruptions in the order of knowledge about phenomena. A researcher can foster the surprise by interrogating the minutiae surrounding the event. In making the detail productive, the archival researcher can gain access to a new order of truth that can help untangle apparently contradictory sets of events and help formulate productive questions on how to tackle a specific research problem.

My experience with archival research briefly explored below relates to the writing of a chapter of my book *Insuring War: Sovereignty, Security and Risk* (Lobo-Guerrero 2012). It began through a set of apparently unrelated encounters with events in which the British government employed marine insurance as an instrument of strategy in time of war. Some related to the time of the Napoleonic Wars in which the Board of Admiralty developed a strategic relationship with the Committee of Lloyd's of London to preserve the security of the Kingdom and its trade. Some others related to the two world wars in which the government became the reinsurer of the marine insurance industry in an attempt to save the country's credit and trade, and more recently to an emerging relationship between NATO and Lloyd's of London to counter piracy and illegal trafficking in the high seas. After initial conversations with current and retired senior officers at Lloyd's of London and with historians who were, if tangentially, familiar with the cases, I discovered the scarcity of secondary sources for my investigation. I began then to explore the existence of archival records with which to work.

I began conducting a set of exploratory interviews at Lloyd's of London. I was there reminded of its three-hundred-year history as a maritime insurance marketplace and of its centrality in British modern history – evidenced, for example, in their holding of the Nelson Collection. Through those contacts I negotiated access to what I expected to be Lloyd's historical archives. It is worth mentioning that Lloyd's of London is not a company as such but a marketplace with restricted membership. Although it has historically had an organizing committee, its administration has been quite basic over time and most of the documents I would be interested in would come from its organizing committee. In my dreams I assumed I would be entering an old and dusty basement room with long rows of volumes containing minutes of meetings, carefully dated boxes of correspondence, samples of marine policies over the centuries, documents registering agreements with British governments over time, and the odd painting and picture capturing moments well worth exploring – all of these, of course, neatly catalogued. Instead, I received a polite letter thanking me for my interest in the material and mentioning that the Lloyd's historical archives had been lost in numerous fires over the centuries. The last historical records, which had been commissioned for storage to a company specializing in storing corporate archives, were lost in a fire in London in 2006.

After confirming this fact with some historians and recovering from my disappointment, I decided to explore what of the material had been saved in private collections or at the Guildhall Library in the City of London. What I found was not very promising. Instead, through experience from a previous project I knew that Western states in the modern period have been extremely careful in archiving their records. This is evidenced, for example, in the dedicated use of buildings to store state records in the best possible conditions. A case in point is the Castle of Simancas in Valladolid, Spain, adapted in the time of Philip II to hold the archives of the Crown and the Spanish state. The British equivalent was the Public Record Office (PRO) established in 1838 on the site of the Chapel of the Rolls in Chancery Lane in London to centralize state records until then kept in diverse places such as the Tower of London. It is also worth mentioning in passing that the establishment of purpose-built facilities and infrastructure to collect, store, and access documents of state can be understood by what Foucault referred to as the memorialization of *monuments* of the past (Foucault 2004b: 7–8). As monuments (Nietzsche 1980: 17), they enact a form of continuous history, which is necessary for a sovereign form of power to operate.

With that knowledge in mind I resorted to visiting the former PRO which is now part of The National Archives operating from a purpose-built complex at Kew Gardens, London. My objective there was to explore any form of records that I could use to reconstruct the use of marine insurance by the British government in time of war. Here I was faced with a challenge familiar to many researchers intending to find answers to their questions when using search catalogues: I realized very quickly that if I were to be successful in my search I would have to understand the "logic of classification" around which the archive and its catalogue had been constituted. In the case of The British National Archives it is a logic that seeks to mimic the bureaucratic organization of the British state throughout time. Documents from the Admiralty are kept under the entry "ADM" and are classified thereafter by topic and year. If I were to find any clues to my project I would have to begin there and read my way through the structure of the boxes until I found what I wanted.

I found multiple boxes (more than would fit in the locker they assigned to my material) containing correspondence between the Board of Admiralty and Lloyd's in original form, in yellowed paper, handwritten, and in some cases faded ink. At first hand they seemed to contain what I wanted, and the only way to confirm that was by reading through the documents. In the back of my mind was the memory of my first experience with state records when researching forms of insurance used for Columbus's first trips of discovery. I was then exploring the formulation of a project on the early relationship between insurance and statehood and decided to follow a hint from a footnote I had read somewhere about a life insurance policy used in 1492 on the lives of prisoners who would venture with Columbus on his first voyage. I got myself a copy of the document from the Archivo General de Simancas, which had been labelled, in pencil "First Life Assurance Policy of the New World". I could hardly believe my luck, only to realize that I could not understand a word of the Elizabethan script in which it was written. With the help of a Spanish paleographer I discovered that whoever had labelled and classified the document as a life insurance policy understood something very different by this term. My lesson then was not to put too much hope on catalogues and labels but to go and *sniff* for myself. This is what I did with my collection of boxes at The National Archives.

I began by photographing all the documents – unconsciously, as a way to reassure myself they would not be lost in the next fire! I then spent months reading them, weeding out irrelevant material or taking notes for future projects, and trying to understand the wider narrative articulating the complex and disperse body of correspondence. My specific goal was to identify issues that seemed to be outstanding, singularities that disrupted the obvious, with the idea of then focusing on them to explore the details of the relationship between Lloyd's and the Board of Admiralty during the Napoleonic Wars. Once those singularities were identified I had to learn as much as I could about the context around which they were constituted in order to understand, in practice, the principles upon which the relationship operated. For example, I found something labelled as a "Bond of Exchange" which was an agreement between a French privateer who, after having captured a British merchant ship, liberated its master and crew in exchange for a document that granted him the same treatment if and when his ship was captured by the Royal Navy. I then found that the bond was actually used by the French privateer when imploring for his liberty after his ship was captured by the British months later. I also found requests from Lloyd's to the Admiralty to reduce or excuse the *impress* of certain sailors who had fought against capture of their ship by the enemy. The impress was a way forcing men to serve on Royal Navy ships, and sailors were usually recruited when approaching British ports. There is also a lengthy discussion about swords presented to Navy officers by the Committee of Lloyd's and their acceptance as part of the officer's uniform. Anecdotic as these cases might appear, the very fact that Lloyd's intervened in ways I could trace and evidence allowed me an entry-point from which to understand the complex political economy under which a marketplace became a partner in risk to the state. Singling out from the archives cases such as these opened up the possibility of writing a history of a relationship that had until now remained dormant in the understanding of international relations and security. Based on that narrative I could then proceed to theorize a power relationship which has a lot to offer to the modern understanding of sovereignty. I have labelled that form of sovereignty *insurantial sovereignty.*

Conclusion

When archives are approached as sites of interrogation rather than depositories of knowledge it is possible to explore through them avenues of thought that help unlock preconceived conceptions and ideas. In my projects, archival research has been an aide to thinking, a source of material from which to derive some of the elements that help me pose creative questions on what I am seeking to learn about. Ultimately, an archive becomes a space in which imaginaries are negotiated. The imaginaries of the researcher meet, if willing, the imaginaries of those who classified and stored the material, of those who recorded the facts and designed the recording systems (templates and forms), and of the actors involved in the narratives there contained. More importantly for the study of politics, international relations, and security, those imaginaries and the archives that monumentalize them enshrine the rationalities of power through which the conduct of individuals and collectives has been and is acted upon. If approached creatively and resourcefully they will provide the *stuff* for critical enquiry.

Note

1   For an extensive and constantly updated bibliography on archival science, see Abraham (2011).

Suggested reading

Abraham, T. (2011) *Archival Theory: Notes Towards the Beginnings of a Bibliography.* Online: www.uiweb.uidaho.edu/special-collections/papers/theorybb.htm (accessed 23 February 2012).
Daston, L., Vidal, F., Chamayou, G. and Mayer, A. (2012) *The New Sciences of the Archives.* Max Planck Institute for the History of Science. Online: www.mpiwg-berlin.mpg.de/en/research/projects/DeptII_Daston-SciencesOfTheArchives/index_html (accessed 23 February 2012).
Foucault, M. (2004b) *Archaeology of Knowledge*, trans. A.M. Sheridan Smith. New York: Routledge.
Hill, M.R. (1993) *Archival Strategies and Technique,* London: SAGE Publications.
Kirsch, G.E. and Rohan, L. (2008) *Beyond the Archives: Research as a Lived Process*, Chicago: Southern Illinois University Press.

20 Legislative practices

Andrew W. Neal

Introduction

My current research is on counter-terrorist lawmaking in the British parliament. Why this? For several reasons. First, this is an analytically neglected site in security studies that challenges some of the preoccupations of existing debates. In the last decade critical scholars have expended much energy discussing sovereign exceptionalism, detention camps, and other extreme security practices. My own work is a case in point (Neal 2010). Parliamentary lawmaking challenges this debate in several ways. Parliament is a site of multiple actors and discourses, collective groupings, differential relationships, and institutionalized practices. This contrasts with the singular executive decisionism considered in the Schmitt-influenced literature on exceptionalism and the "War on Terror". The practice of lawmaking also contrasts with the practice of making exceptions to law.

Second, Britain has a long history of counter-terrorist lawmaking because of the Northern Ireland conflict. Many other countries have only introduced specific counter-terrorism laws since 9/11. This gives the research a historical context and comparative angle that avoids overly focusing on the post-9/11 security environment. This is important because it avoids the kind of analytical exceptionalism that assumes the present to exhibit an especially pressing and urgent set of problems. Here, my work follows an important lesson from Foucault: not only is historical enquiry important for understanding the present, but our own particular present is not necessarily special. All times and places have their own pressing problems that animate them and make them unique or indeed "exceptional" (Veyne 2010: 6).

The third reason is a practical one. Being British and living in the UK means that I am familiar with its parliament and constitutional system. It also means I have access to legislative practices through the everyday media which I consume before I have even sat down to do *research*. This is an advantage for understanding a complex institution like Parliament. Much of the meaning that its actors produce is governed by convention and shaped by competing material and immaterial structures. While it is one thing to trawl the parliamentary archive to see who spoke, what they said and how they voted, its significance can be understood much more subtly if one has an idea of who they are and the history of their relationships with their party, the public, and the government.

A fourth reason for choosing Parliament as a research object, perhaps the most important, is to tackle a timely political problem. Security politics is not the same as it was ten years ago. What has happened to discourses of exception and illiberal security practices over time? Do the same logics apply or have they changed somehow? Research on the parliamentary archive offers the possibility to analyze security politics through the angle of duration rather than immediacy. A recent report of the Joint Committee on Human Rights used the subtitle

"Normalizing the Exceptional" for one of its sections (2010: 7), suggesting that parliamentarians are themselves reflecting critically on changes in security politics over time. This justifies research on security politics that is rooted in the historical, archival study of legislative practices.

There are many ways to construct a research question. While we may agonize over how to compose them for public consumption, the private questions that motivate our work are perhaps more important intellectually. My own is probably something rather simplistic such as: what is security politics like? There are nevertheless important methodological assumptions here. This is an empirical question that assumes there is not a core meaning or structure to security politics. It assumes that politics encompasses a great diversity of empirical situations and subjective experiences. In every instance, actors will have their own thoughts about security problems and their own idea of what they mean. Nevertheless, it is clear that for much of the time they make similar assumptions. We might call these assumptions *discourses*. So the aim of a simplistic question such as mine is to try to understand the discourses of security that seem to shape political opinion and action. These discourses may change over time or work differently in different circumstances (after terrorist attacks) or different power relationships (being in government or in opposition).

This kind of open research question precludes definitive testing or formal theorization. It is an implicit rejection of *positivism*. It reflects an empiricist assumption that political life is too complex to be formalized. This means remaining open to the possibility of being surprised at the findings, especially if they contradict theoretical assumptions.

An empirical, archival approach implies collecting and analyzing data, without implying that it will be fed any kind of scientific model or theory. In many projects, data collection is the main challenge because the practices under investigation may not be public or readily accessible. With the study of legislative practices this is not necessarily a problem because they are a matter of public record. Hansard, the official record, has been published in print for centuries and online for the last decade or so. It remains an under-utilized resource for political research.

Behind the scenes interactions, however, constitute much of the influence of the legislature over the executive and these are not captured in the official record. For example, it is the job of party whips not simply to enforce discipline but also to know in advance how government proposals are likely to be received in parliament. Thus "anticipated reactions" (Friedrich 1937) are often a more important shaping factor than publicly visible legislative interactions. Outright conflict or rebellions on the floor of the house are often a sign that these behind the scenes interactions have broken down (Norton 2005: 78–79). Studying this would require access to informants or recourse to published political memoirs, which could only be partial. But if security discourses are our research object, and not the policy process itself, then the prospects for research on legislative practices are somewhat different. If changing security arguments, constructions, rationalizations and justifications are what interest us, then the parliamentary record is a gold mine. Its discursive artifacts are indicators of how security is understood and how that understanding changes over time and in different situations.

In practical terms, the immediate problem is quantity. Typing "terrorism" or "security" into the Hansard search box returns tens of thousands of results, and not only about security politics but also about social security, finance, and so on. So we need to begin with an understanding of the institutional context to know which debates and documents are important. On this basis I began my research with a comparative analysis of House of Commons second readings of counter-terrorism bills. Second readings are the main debates on the principles of proposed legislation. I chose three bills introduced in different security circumstances: in the aftermath of a major terrorist attack (2001), when the last terrorist attack was at some remove (2008), and when a period of major terrorist activity was seen to be coming to an end (2000).[1]

Second readings begin in a structured way with the lead minister from the government department sponsoring the bill presenting the aims and content of the legislation to parliament. They may be interrupted by questions, especially if the bill is contentious. Statements from the main opposition parties follow, outlining their positions. Beyond this set piece opening, the debate becomes less formalized, with backbench MPs having more chance to intervene. In counter-terrorism there is a long-held parliamentary convention of consensus. Politicization is scorned. We cannot simply assume, therefore, that interventions are necessarily driven by tactical calculation against the government. Strong criticism of counter-terrorism bills is unusual and therefore all the more meaningful because it signals a challenge to this convention.

In the British system, nearly all members of the government (the executive) are appointed from the ranks of the legislature. Once so employed, these MPs (the *payroll vote*) cannot realistically challenge the governing party line without resigning their position. Shadow ministers and official spokespeople in the opposition parties are similarly tied to their party line. Backbenchers have fewer constraints but less power and influence. There are some who will always speak their minds and as a result will never be appointed to the frontbenches. It is in the speeches and questions of the backbenchers that the really interesting counter-discourses on security are found, yet they have to be taken in the context of unequal parliamentary power relations. They reveal a surprisingly diverse range of arguments about security. In critical security studies and discourse analysis we are often concerned with dominant discourses or general logics, but as a result we often miss interesting and more marginal instances that occur away from the centre of political activity. For example, to what extent have lessons from Northern Ireland been learnt in British counter-terrorism policy? Given the post-9/11 resurrection of discredited security practices such as detention without trial and unrestricted police stop and search powers, we might say not at all. But in the backbench debates there are many who remember the negative consequences of these practices only too well and warn against repeating them. In the debates we can see which of these interventions find traction, which are taken up by other members, which the government dismiss, and which the government has to defend against.

My research has only scratched the surface of the parliamentary archive, but it has yielded some interesting results. It revealed the existence of political principles and practices that went against certain theoretical assumptions. For example, the excellent critical literature on risk assumes that hypothetical future security problems have a powerful affective influence (Amoore and de Goede 2008, Anderson 2010, Aradau and Van Munster 2007, Lobo-Guerrero 2012). In the parliamentary debates, however, arguments about hypothetical future risks were not successful: they were too intangible and too difficult to authoritatively assert. They were met with incredulity. In contrast, successful security arguments were those made in the aftermath of major terrorist attacks. These did not need to construct an image of future risk because traumatic images of carnage where still fresh on the minds of parliamentarians. The nature of the present threat seemed obvious and did not need to be articulated in hypothetical terms. Another finding was the existence of a parliamentary principle that "exceptional measures require exceptional scrutiny". This always accompanies the old argument that "exceptional times require exceptional measures". It influences legislative practice after terrorist attacks, leading to the creation of special post-legislative scrutiny mechanisms such as sunset clauses and independent reviewers.

Conclusion

At first glance this research is a form of discourse analysis. There are many good books on how to pursue this in security studies (see suggested reading). In the course of my research, however, my approach moved away from a pure discourse analysis approach emphasizing language towards something more *structuralist*. In the works of Foucault, *discourse* is not only a matter of language but also of its supporting material, social and knowledge networks or *dispositifs*. In fact I found a straight Foucauldian approach limited too, because while good at analyzing broad social and historical developments, it did not seem very well suited to the heavily structured and institutionalized context of parliament. I came to lean more heavily on the work of Bourdieu in which symbolic power relations are structured and relational. The methodological lesson here is that as critical scholars we have to work these things out ourselves; there are no straightforward how-to guides.

Note

1   This research is published as: Neal, A.W. (2012) "Normalisation and Legislative Exceptionalism: Counter-Terrorist Lawmaking and the Changing Times of Security Emergencies", *International Political Sociology*, 6(3).

Suggested reading

Bourdieu, P. (1992) *Language and Symbolic Power*, J.B. Thompson (ed.), Cambridge: Polity.

Foucault, M. (2004b) *Archaeology of Knowledge*, trans. A.M. Sheridan Smith, New York: Routledge.

Hansen, L. (2006) *Security as Practice: Discourse Analysis and the Bosnian War*, New York: Routledge.

Jackson, R. (2005) *Writing the War on Terrorism: Language, Politics and Counter-Terrorism*, Manchester: Manchester University Press.

Veyne, P. (2010) *Foucault: His Thought, His Character*, Cambridge: Polity.

21 Medicine and the psy disciplines

Alison Howell

Introduction

This chapter provides an introduction to critical research on medicine and the psy disciplines in International Relations (IR) and security studies. The study of health and medicine is an emergent field of inquiry in IR. My research has focused particularly on psychology and psychiatry, and on how they function as technologies of security in multiple sites including: Western militaries, post-conflict situations, war zones, and detention facilities.

Psy disciplines include any discipline that is based on the ubiquitous but dubious and geographically – and historically – bound belief that a person's interior life can be reduced to a *psyche* and that psychologists or psychiatrists can tell whether a psyche is functioning normally or abnormally, as other medical sciences are supposed to do for bodies. In the case of a perceived abnormality, human behaviours and experiences are reduced to disorders. The psy disciplines include psychiatry and psychology, and their cognates and sub-disciplines: psychoanalysis, forensic psychiatry, and positive psychology, amongst numerous others. Although marked by diversity, all share a belief in the psyche and their authority over it. This authority is also expansive: any number of experts can take up and use the psy disciplines, from social workers, to nurses, chaplains, employment counsellors, aid workers, militaries, and educational institutions, airport security personnel, border guards, international development and conflict experts, and, even, subjects themselves, especially through new techniques such as cognitive behavioral therapy (CBT), or self-help. The authority of the psy disciplines circulates, and is diffuse. I have argued that this kind of diffusion is also taking place in the sphere of international and national security. Pupavac's (2002) work on therapeutic governance in Bosnia forms another excellent resource in this field.

While not necessarily anti-psychiatry per se, a critical approach to the psy disciplines begins by assuming that they have nothing of use to tell us. They should be treated as empirical artifacts rather than sources of theoretical guidance. This may seem like an absolutist stance, and as such, should be abandoned if it forecloses critical research possibilities rather than opening them. But it is a helpful starting point: because the authority of the psy disciplines is so ubiquitous, beginning by questioning such authority wholesale liberates us to pose critical questions. This also puts us in a position to see the systemic violence that the psy disciplines have often been implicated in, particularly as they have exercised authority over marginalized people.

This does not mean that psy practitioners are either duped or necessarily unethical: they are often, in fact, drawn to such professions by a desire to help. In present-day Western societies, the psy disciplines have an almost complete monopoly over providing such help. Still, some of the most vocal advocates of the limits of psy expertise are psy practitioners themselves. The psy disciplines become questionable, especially, when they are positioned as remedies at the level of the population, and when they are figured as solutions to political *problems* such as public safety, conflict, or security.

So, how can we pose critical research questions about medicine and the psy disciplines in IR? The role of health and medicine in IR remains under-explored. I have been interested in inquiring into the ways in which psychology, in particular, has been used as a technology of security in IR. This has involved posing the following questions:

- What happened? Or, what is the history or genealogy of the uses of the psy disciplines in any given site?
- Who was involved? What assemblages form around psy *problems* and how have a variety of actors come to be assembled around such problems (for example: human rights and humanitarian organizations, militaries, policy-makers, psy and medical experts, security and intelligence analysts, national departments of health, amongst others)?
- How have such arrangements, strategies or technologies been resisted or contested, often from unlikely quarters or through unlikely alliances?

These questions are empirical, not theoretical. They have little to do with the study of discourse as a set of representations, nor with deconstruction. My work has developed on from Foucault's shift away from the study of representations of madness, to his later work on psychiatric power, with its focus on modes of acting, authority, and institutions. In IR, we may similarly study the power of the psy disciplines and of medicine generally, and the ways in which they have increasingly come to occupy a place of authority not only over public safety or security within national settings, but over also national or international security.

There is no single way to research medicine or the psy disciplines, and no one type of source will reveal their workings. While policy documents are a useful place to begin, they can only tell us about the aspirations of their authors. In order to get at the *messy actualities* of governing, it becomes important to go beyond policy.

Important information will often be found buried amidst reams of dull or technical writing. Here are some examples of sources that I have found useful at getting at these kinds of messy actualities: military personnel newsletters, human resources newsletters, health services newsletters, local newspapers, publications associated with military bases, such as the Guantánamo Gazette, memos, the reports of NGOs, INGOs, and international organizations and their sub-groups, including topic-based, annual, and financial reports, PowerPoint presentations, blogs, and other *low* or niche sources. So, when I was researching the post-invasion reform of Iraq's mental health system, I read mental health surveys, medical, and psychiatric journals, US Department of Health newsletters, reports produced by IOs, INGOs, NGOs, and activist groups, as well as journalistic sources.

I first became interested in the story of the reform of Iraq's mental health system (Howell 2010), when I read a *New York Times* cover story on Baghdad's Al Rashad psychiatric hospital. The article was absurd but fascinating, not only because it represented the patients of Al Rashad as "dark and dangerous" in clearly racialized terms, but also because it represented the psychiatrists at Al Rashad as having experienced a loss at the hands of American marines, who let loose those incarcerated at the institution during the military occupation of the facility. The article, titled "In Baghdad's Anarchy, Insane Went Free", could have provided the basis for an analysis of representations of madness, anarchy, psychiatry, and warfare. But instead of the question of representation, I was more interested in what had happened at Al Rashad. I began looking at ICRC reports, because they had done some work on reforming the psychiatric hospital both before and after the US-led invasion.

I then became interested in how the US Department of Health and Human Services' Substance Abuse and Mental Health Services Administration (SAMHSA) came to be involved, which I traced in large part through their newsletter. SAMHSA was working closely with a number of expatriate Iraqi psychiatrists who had returned to Iraq, post-invasion, mainly from the UK, and also the US, and who were taking up positions of power within the Iraqi Ministry of Health, something which I ascertained both through government documents and news articles, not only from mainstream publishers, but also independent news sources. These experts were also working against the backdrop of broader global mental health programming by the World Health Organization, which had set "community-based care" as the example to be followed in their 2001 World Health Report (*Mental Health: New Understanding, New Hope*), as well as the International Organization for Migration (IOM), which had done studies on the mental health of Iraqi refugees. While keeping in mind this broader context, I was interested in tracing the specific assemblage of experts on Iraqi mental health reform, especially through a series of documents produced out of several Action Planning Conferences for Iraq Mental Health, and their production of an "Iraq Mental Health Action Plan". Furthermore, many of these experts were publishing in medical and psychiatric trade publications, newsletters and scholarly journals, such as *World Psychiatry*, *Psychiatric Services*, *Journal of Muslim Mental Health*, and *Psychiatric News*.

By tracing out these connections, I was able to ascertain: first, that an emergent cadre of experts was assembling around the problem of Iraq's mental health system; second, that they were defining the problem in particular ways (as a need to move urgently to "community-based care", despite ongoing warfare); third, the ways in which they were putting this plan into action, primarily through two means: by disaggregating the population of former Al Rashad patients, determining which could be let free into community care, and which would have to stay inside the hospital, and by reforming the hospital itself, from a space of confinement, to a space of treatment. To this point, I had traced a governmental rationality – that of moving to community-based care – and the actions taken through this ideational foundation, particularly the reform of Iraq's main psychiatric hospital. But I was interested in more than this: community care seemed an absurd aspiration, not only because of the imposition of Western-style psychiatric governance, or because of the context of ongoing warfare, but also because community services were entirely lacking. I was interested, therefore, in how these plans were implemented, or had failed in their implementation: the messy actualities. Some of the experts involved began to publish on problems with the plan, especially on the lack of community mental health resources. But in tracing this failure, the accounts of psy experts were not enough, so I also researched news reports.

Access to these resources is available through a number of databases, and through digital archives. Gathering and combing through masses of such sources in either physical or digital archives is often a labour. It is also an art. It is up to the researcher to determine what, amongst reams of information, is useful for understanding the problems they are researching.

The value of such sources is what they reveal about how people are thinking and communicating with their peers, about particular institutional cultures and about the problems experts see themselves as facing and attempting to overcome – particularly when direct access through interviews is not possible. It is important to look not only at *high* sources like policy documents or public pronouncements, but also *low* or niche sources that may give the researcher a handle on the more detailed workings of medical assemblages. Most often, these sources will reveal that the aspirations expressed in policies are just that: aspirational. This is not to say that they are irrelevant: the belief in such aspirations has real and tangible consequences, whether they produce the desired effect or unintended ones.

Omissions are also significant. For example, amongst the myriad medical journal articles, NGO reports, newsletters and documents outlining the US Department of Health's involvement in the reform of Iraq's health system, absurdly, the war was almost never mentioned as an obstacle to the move to community care for the patients.

Conclusion

Doing critical research on medicine, and specifically on the psy disciplines, raises the question of how to account for resistance. Anti-institutionalization, psychiatric survivor, and mad pride movements have been active for many decades now, and are increasingly international as well. Wherever we find medical or psychological interventions, we are also sure to find resistance. Though those subject to psychiatric and psychological interventions mount all kinds of refusals, researching resistance at the individual level is difficult because it is fraught with ethical quandaries: revealing such resistances, for example, can make it more difficult to mount them. At the same time, when I was researching the accounts of psychiatrists and health experts involved in Iraq, I noted that much lip service was paid to involving patients in informing these reforms, but I found no actual evidence of their inclusion. Keeping in mind the ethical quandaries outlined above, but also not wanting the replicate the psy disciplines exclusion of the voices of those who are subject to their power, it is important to include psychiatric survivors' own accounts where possible: one such account, by a former Al Rashad patient was published in *Time* magazine. There are also more systematically organized sources for such material, for example, the Guantánamo Testimonials Project, which includes the testimonials of former prisoners (as well as those of medical staff, military psychologists, and others). Additionally, resistance should not just be conceived at the individual level. It is important to account for how the psy disciplines are contested. Such contestation often takes place between psy experts, and through the varied use of psy expertise by any number of actors who are often at odds with one another. Paying heed to such contestation is vital because it exposes the contingency of psy authority.

The study of health and medicine is a growing field in critical security studies. There are innumerable topics that have not been touched by IR or security studies scholars. More could be said, for instance, on the role of medicine, and of psychiatry and psychology in international organizations, international law, borders, airports, militaries, detention and refugee camps, non-governmental organizations, wars and post-conflict situations, as well as the interactions between national health departments, diplomacy, espionage, and intelligence gathering. As security practices have increasingly come to be aimed at securing not only territory, but also the populations of territorial states, much more needs to be said about the role of medicine, and health in security practices.

Suggested reading

Elbe, S. (2010) *Security and Global Health*, London: Polity.
Foucault, M. (2006) *Psychiatric Power: Lectures at the Collège de France, 1973–74*, Basingstoke: Palgrave Macmillan.
Howell, A. (2010) "Sovereignty, Security, Psychiatry: Liberation and the Failure of Mental Health Governance in Iraq", *Security Dialogue*, 41(4): 347–367.
Howell, A. (2011) *Madness in International Relations: Psychology, Security, and the Global Governance of Mental Health*, New York: Routledge.
MindFreedom International. Online: www.mindfreedom.org (accessed on 14 March 2012).

22 Speech act theory

Juha A. Vuori

Introduction

Speech act theory[1] is at the heart of critical inquiry in the field of International Relations (IR). This has been explicit in how Onuf (1989) has studied the social construction of norms, but also in other social constructivist research, for example in the case of Ruggie (1998) through application of Searle's (1995) social theory. Like most other forms of social constructionism (Hacking 1999), these approaches are critical in the sense that they want to reveal the social constructedness of most of the things studied in the field of IR, and thereby the potential to alter world affairs. Such critical standpoints have led me to investigate the social construction of security. In the field of critical security studies, although there are other constructionist approaches, the most widely used theoretical framework that explicitly uses speech act theory is the theory of securitization (Wæver 1995, Buzan et al. 1998, Balzacq 2010a). In this chapter, I articulate the design and results of a decade of study that has investigated political security in the People's Republic of China (PRC) with the concomitant intention to develop the theory of securitization.[2]

The main bulk of my research has striven to enhance our understanding of the political use of language by focusing on a very specific aspect of human interaction, namely, the social construction of security issues, and even more specifically, the "power politics of a concept" (Buzan et al. 1998: 32). What such investigations have studied have been sets of techniques "concerned with exploiting the power of words to underpin or undermine the construction of our social world" (Skinner 2002: 5). These philosophical and theoretical engagements have taken place in the empirical context of the PRC, but my intention was to explicate the approach so that it could be used to study a variety of political orders without conceptual stretching. This suggests that students of securitization could use the explicated framework to investigate empirical cases that have so far remained without much scrutiny through the lens of securitization.

I have found the theory of securitization to be the most fortuitous approach to investigate the power politics of security. One way to distil the research programme of securitization studies is to note the general questions that it is interested in: the aim is to gain an increasingly precise understanding of who (securitizing actors) can securitize (political moves via speech acts) which issues (threats), for whom (referent objects), why (perlocutionary intentions), with what kinds of effects (interunit relations), and under what conditions (facilitation/ impediment factors) (Buzan et al. 1998: 32). The main purpose of my research has been to develop the theoretical model of this research programme, and to enhance the ways empirical study can be conducted in its remit.[3] The goal of such enhancements has been to allow the study of the Chinese political order without distortion to the model. My main empirical research question has been: what kinds of political functions have security speech (in the political sector) served in the People's Republic of China?[4]

The function of speech acts in Chinese politics has been studied before, and it has been found to be one of the best ways to comprehend the constitution of power structures in China (Schoenhals 1992). The theory of securitization provided a framework to study the political language of security, suppression, and resistance, both from the vantage point of authorities and social movements. This directs our attention to how issues of security are *made* in social fields of practice, which sets limits for what the approach can be: speech act logic (Searle and Vanderveken 1985) allows the analysis of what securitization *does* in texts, but does not allow access to other minds or to the *real* motives of political speakers. Thereby, while we cannot know what someone meant by producing, or indeed why someone elected to produce, an utterance, we can infer what an utterance does conventionally and thereby what it means conventionally. In the case of securitization speech acts, this is made possible by the fact that a security rationale or a security modality is dependent on a fairly stable constellation of meanings.

Theories of speech acts emphasize both linguistic and social aspects of language and its use. Accordingly, the research methods I have applied have combined both linguistic and socio-political analyses that are necessary to understand the performative of securitization in real situations and contexts. The method of inquiry has been based on cross-cultural pragmatics – the study of the ways in which meaning is derived from the interaction of utterances, with the contexts in which they are used – and not purely on semantics – the study of meaning – or universal linguistic rules (Wierzbicka 1991).

The way to study securitization is to study discourse, which has actually occurred through a "lens of security" (Buzan et al. 1998). While illocutionary logic has provided the means to study the *grammar*, or necessary culture independent meta-language for the cross-cultural study of securitization processes, I have used identity frame theory (Snow and Benford 1992) to decipher the specific *vocabulary*, the situated pools of resonant values (Stritzel 2007), or the heuristic artifacts (Balzacq 2010b, 2010c) of the empirical case under investigation. I have used the grammatical models of securitization (Vuori 2008) to identify relevant texts and discourse samples for analysis: it is necessary to be able to discriminate and separate security issues from non-security issues (Wæver 2004: 9). Once the relevant discourse samples were identified, collected, and analyzed with speech act analysis, the discourse samples could be analyzed further by sociolinguistic means to broaden the analysis beyond the discourse samples into the historically situated socio-political contexts beyond the specific samples of discourse.

Case-selection had a significant impact on the types of data that I deemed relevant, the corpuses of discourse samples, as well as the types of supplementary data. I selected the cases for scrutiny through a reading of the official history of the Communist Party of China. This was the basis for the mental map or model that guided the initial entries into the available data. In addition, *visible* major political outcomes were used as indicators of *spectacular* securitization. The selected cases represented ideological threats articulated by the party-leadership and included (a) the beginning of the "Great Proletarian Cultural Revolution" (1966), (b) the "Counter-revolutionary Political Incident at Tiananmen Square" (1976), (c) the "Tiananmen Counter-revolutionary Rebellion" (1989), and (d) the "Evil Cult of Falungong" (1999). These cases provided instances from three major leadership eras of the PRC, as well as examples of both the *success* and *failure* of the politics of securitization. This allowed the analysis of continuity and change in the grammar of securitization through the framework utilized in the research: the study of speech acts and language in a more general sense are important tools to identify conceptual changes at certain moments, or over periods of time (Brauch 2008: 67, Skinner 2002, Wæver 2008: 100).

The kinds of materials I used included speeches, canonized ideological texts, newspaper editorials and articles, central documents, film, and news reports. The texts chosen were central in the sense that a securitization discourse materialized in them. A relevant aspect of the discourse samples was their intertextual chains (Fairclough 1992: 232–233).[5] I related such aspects of the discourse samples to the framework of securitization theory, and to the political context, where theories of politics and models of political orders become relevant, as well as the capabilities and capacities of both agents and structures.

The investigation of spectacular instances of securitization in the political sector of security, during three major leadership eras of the PRC, revealed that "counter-revolution" was, for a long time, an institutionalized basis for securitization, onto which particular instances and chains of events were grafted. This demonstrates how, in one way, social artifacts – here issues of security – are sedimented into the *background* of social reality. Although labels like "turmoil" and "well planned plots" would not seem to fit well into European political rhetoric, the language Chinese officials have used to construct official security realities is remarkably consistent with the grammar that the theory of securitization would predict, making it unnecessary to distort culturally alien concepts to fit into the theory. Besides chaos or social instability, collusion with foreign powers is another oft-used political label for debasing opponents. Therefore, the PRC has its own set of institutionalized master signifiers, or watchwords, of security. The logic of such institutionalized categories can remain constant, but the signifiers that refer to institutionalized signified can change.

Moreover, while the vocabulary of threats and vulnerabilities may evolve, the underlying logic appears to remain remarkably consistent throughout the political transitions from the Mao to the post-Mao eras of Chinese politics. Securitization in the political sectors is no longer as present in the everyday as it was during the Cultural Revolution, but when political crises do escalate, the same logic appears to rise to the fore, more or less reliably. This suggests that securitization theory can be used to examine both Mao and post-Mao era politics through the same framework. However, the cases studied also suggest that there is a significant difference in how security arguments have been utilized in the two most definitive eras. In Mao's China, securitization was used as a means to mobilize the masses to fight inner enemies within the party and society, for example, through *rectification*. It seems that in post-Mao China, securitization is used as a reaction to more autonomous inputs or processes, which emanate from within its society. In Mao's China, security arguments were used as a means to mobilize society; in post-Mao China, they have conversely been used to suppress autonomous mobilization in society.

The political processes that I have studied illustrated how securitization speech acts can shift, and also how they can display various functions as the process goes on. Furthermore, outside the functions of any particular speech acts, the entire process of securitization can have various political functions: in the PRC, it has been used to foment social unrest and to legitimize changes in party leadership. It has also been used as a means of control and deterrence, both to mobilize bureaucratic systems and to quell autonomous social unrest. Negative labels, such as "counter-revolutionary", have been consistent tools in factional party-politicking, which many times resulted in the Golem of securitization getting loose and resulting in negative results. Political security has also been used as "autocommunication", as a means to compel bureaucracies to toe the line of a certain political formulation. It has also been used to reproduce a bond between the people and the party: the party has had many opportunities to present itself in a positive light as the guardian of all good in Chinese society against those who would do it harm, whether those be revisionists, counter-revolutionaries, foreign powers, or religious fundamentalists.

Conclusion

The main challenge of the research project was to use an approach that has mainly been applied to study liberal-democratic political orders in Europe and the U.S. in investigation of a political order, which differs in several ways from the implicit premises of most previous applications. This meant that theoretical development was necessary. Here the challenge was to adapt the model without distortion to its main premises. The speech act theory basis of the approach was key: elaboration of types of securitization acts in accordance with their political aims allowed the comprehension of Chinese politics and sensitivity to the socio-political context without distortion to the core of the theoretical model.

The experiences from the explication of the securitization approach, as well as from its empirical application to a non-democratic political order suggest that the approach can be used to examine other novel political environments too. In order to achieve this, students of securitization need to have a developed sense of the political order and environment the investigation takes place in, i.e., they need to be aware of what is relevant in the political order and how it operates. A further challenge is to find appropriate cases for study that allow for getting a sense of continuity and change, for getting a sense of which elements are plastic and which have ruptured within the realm of security under investigation. Cases over a longer duration of time seem to be appropriate to achieve this. They also enable the examination of institutionalized securitization and the specific *watchwords* of security that are prevalent in the particular socio-political order. Cases of longer duration also allow the operationalization of the abstract elements in the framework, and thereby the identification of the form securitization takes.

Notes

1   There is a vast literature on speech act theory and its variants. What is shared among the various approaches is the premise that language is used to do things beyond mere communication, e.g. to promise or to threaten. Speech acts can be categorized in many ways, but the most significant distinction is between locutionary (an act of saying something), illocutionary (an act in saying something), and perlocutionary (an act by saying something) aspects of speech acts (Austin 1975).
2   This decade of study can be traced through a number of publications that have either presented theoretical propositions or case studies: see Vuori (2003, 2007, 2008, 2010, 2011a) and Paltemaa and Vuori (2006). Vuori (2011b) collates the research into one monograph.
3   The main theoretical and methodological questions of this aspect of my research have included: how can political functions be inferred from political speech in general and in *security speech* in particular? In the absence of *security words*, how can we identify securitization, a *security modality* (Hansen 2000: 296) or a "security rationale" (Huysmans 2006: 147) in a sample of discourse? Other theoretical issues investigated have included: how is security achieved with words? How does securitization work in non-democracies and outside the "West"? How can shifting from one socio-political context to another be achieved without stretching the concept of securitization? How can the "messiness" of the "wild" in the model of securitization be dealt with? Can the theory be used to study securitization beyond the state?
4   I have used a battery of more specific questions as a heuristic device to assist in answering the main question: how is the issue constructed as a matter of security (speech act analysis)? What is the threat? What is the referent object of security? Who frames something as an issue of security – who or what is the securitizing actor? Who or what is the audience of securitization? Who or what are the functional actors (actors influencing securitization without being referent objects or securitizing actors)? What are the facilitation and impediment factors in the processes of securitization? How

do securitization moves affect the inter-unit relations of securitizing actors and the claimed threats present in securitization moves? How do securitization moves become part of the context of the subsequent stages of the process of securitization and its possible contestation or resistance? More specifically, how are securitization and desecuritization moves used to suppress social mobilization or to resist its suppression? Finally, how successful were the politics of securitization/desecuritization?

5   How is the sample connected to other texts and how does this facilitate, or impede, the possible aspect of securitization evident in it? How does the sample draw on culturally resonant ideas, cognitive maps, or precontracts? What kinds of signs are there of the assumed audience or audiences in the sample? Is it possible to determine who consumed the sample and "who" is speaking in the sample? What kinds of systems of knowledge and beliefs are evident in the sample? What about social relations and social identities (selves and others)?

Suggested reading

Austin, J.L. (1975) *How To Do Things with Words,* Oxford: Oxford University Press.

Buzan, B., Wæver, O. and de Wilde, J. (1998) *Security: A New Framework for Analysis*, Boulder: Lynne Rienner.

Sbisà, M. (2002) "Speech Acts in Context", *Language and Communication*, 22(4): 421–436.

Searle, J.R. and Vanderveken, D. (1985) *Foundations of Illocutionary Logic*, Cambridge: Cambridge University Press.

Vuori, J.A. (2011c) *How to Do Security with Words. A Grammar of Securitisation in the People's Republic of China*, Turku: University of Turku Press.

Part V

The corporeal turn

Introduction

Can E. Mutlu

Introduction

This chapter focuses on questions of method, research design, and case selection in an emergent research agenda within critical security studies: corporeal turn that covers affect, emotions, and the somatic. Corporeal research is relatively new to critical security studies; its origins are elsewhere in cultural theory, gender studies, geography, and psychology.

In recent years, starting with geography (Thrift 2004), but also in social and political theory (Connolly 2002, Massumi 1995, 2002, 2005), there has been an affective turn (Clough 2007) that introduced an affect and emotion-attuned methodology (Gregg and Seigworth 2010) to studying a wide range of questions concerning identity (Connolly 2002), objects (Bennett 2010), politics (Protevi 2009), torture (Scarry 1985, Butler 2009), looking at the role of affect and emotions in shaping our interpretations and perceptions of reality alongside rational calculations. Similarly, works on the somatic have originated primarily from gender studies looking at the body as a political site, specifically looking at the subjugation of women, as well as other marginalized groups such as the lesbian, gay, bisexual, and transsexual (LGBT) communities, by dominant gender and race groups within a society. In International Relations (IR) and critical security studies, this perspective led to works on the subjugation of certain colonial, female, subaltern bodies by the military, bureaucracy, international organizations, and non-governmental organizations.

There is a consensus on somatic methods originating from feminism. Feminist approaches to critical security studies focus on the role of the body. A clear research design on the

Table PV.1 Research design in corporeal approaches

Object	Bodily reactions and their socio-political meanings and interpretations
Key concepts	Affect: an intensity that exists in the body and is prior to any sociolinguistic fixity such as consciousness, emotion, feeling or language.
	Emotion: the mediated form of affect embedded within the constraints of the socio-linguistic domain
	Somatic: things that are of or relating to the body; especially distinct from the mind
Collection	Autoethnography, discourse analysis (textual and visual), practices
Data	Experiences, references in/to institutions, objects, practices, texts and visuals
Relations	Interpretations, perceptions, and subjugations
Fit	Corporeal origins of discourses, policies and practices that aim to control bodies and their relations with security

somatic takes discourses as institutions, cultural norms that shape knowledge, perceptions, and representations of the body. There is, however, no similar consensus in affect- and emotions-attuned approaches on what methods to use. On the one hand, affective research in political and social theory (Connolly 2002, Massumi 2002, Protevi 2009) has linked neuro-science with the philosophical canon on human behaviour as a method to study the socio-political impact of visceral or split-second reactions – affect. On the other hand, sociological perspectives have combined discourse analysis with concepts originating from social psychology to study socio-linguistic manifestations of visceral reactions – emotions. Any research on affect and emotions has to take this distinction seriously.

A clear and systemic research design on affect- and emotion-attuned approaches must first identify whether it is looking at emotions or affect. What is the research object? Is it love, hate, disgust, rage or their visceral counterparts? To focus on bodily reactions, the research object is affect. To study verbal or written expressions of those affective reactions, the research object is emotion (see Table PV.2). This is important, as the method that is used depends on this decision.

When studying affect, it is suitable to use auto-ethnography, interviews, participant observation, and a focus on practices to capture the interaction between the somatic and the social. Instead, if studying emotions, discourse analysis of texts and visuals along with analyzing practices are suitable methods. Interpretivist scholars, however, are predisposed to look at the social-linguistic reality as the source of our data. Critical inquiry in security studies is no exception; as such, critical security scholars are more likely to focus on emotions than affect. This does not mean that they cannot focus on affect or affect is of no concern for this community; given the methods available, this means that they are more likely to focus on socio-linguistic expressions of affect. Alternatively, instead of studying affect directly, given difficulties with collection of data – i.e. measuring affect – studying practices, such as airport security techniques that target affective signifiers as a marker, is a suitable alternative (Frowd and Leite, Chapter 23).

Upon deciding on whether to focus on affect or emotions, we need to establish a subjugated body politic or practice – our case study, whether it is indigenous tribes, immigrants, maternal bodies or travellers – that is subjected to a technique of government – bureaucratic, governmental or securitized – that targets or is shaped by affective and emotive dynamics. Before we go more deeply into these types of research designs, we must go over some of the key terms of corporeal research and how they fit into critical security studies.

Key terms and fit

Corporeal

Corporeal is an umbrella concept that covers concepts related to the body. This collection classifies three different methods as corporeal: affect, emotion, and somatic. While these terms are interrelated, they originate from different concerns related to questions of inter-

Table PV.2 Emotions and affective reactions

Affect	Smiling, crying, sobbing, frowning, changes of face colour, increase and decrease of blood pressure and body temperature, frozen stare, sweat, head movement
Emotions	Happiness, joy, sadness, anger, rage, hate, pain, fear, terror, shame, humiliation

pretation, perception, or subjugation, as well as ontological and epistemological departure points outside of IR – feminism(s), post-structuralism, psychoanalysis, and social theory. In critical security studies, we use these approaches to focus on the role of pre-conscious (affective), conscious (emotional), and bodily (somatic) reactions to construction, execution, and (re)evaluation of discourses, practices, and processes of (in)security.

Affect

Affect is a nodal concept that connects the social world with the somatic. It is an intensity that exists within our body and is prior to any sociolinguistic fixing such as consciousness, emotion, feeling, or language (Massumi 2002). It is experienced through bodily reactions that can be measured through visceral experiences (see Table PV.2). Critical security studies focuses on the role of affect in understanding the construction and execution of discourses, policies, and practices of security. Affect is a useful approach for projects researching security initiatives that target various types of visceral signifiers. As we see with various chapters in this section, affect is targeted by a number of actors – security professionals, government projects, militaries, and even members of the entertainment industry – during various stages of security practices – planning, execution, and evaluation. Several of these chapters approach affect from different perspectives looking at how affect is mobilized or targeted by various actors, such as Frowd and Leite (Chapter 23), who focus on how affect is operationalized in recent developments introduced by the Transport Security Administration to improve security at the airport.

Emotions

Emotion is, according to Massumi (2002), "the socio-linguistic fixing [of affect]" (28). In other words, emotion is affect filtered through the bounds of the sociolinguistic domain. Emotions are the expressed feelings. As such they present an opening in critical inquiry that allows us to understand the role of interpretations and perceptions in shaping seemingly rational behaviour by focusing on a wide range of feelings across the spectrum that create the backdrop for, and provide context to, security practices (see Table PV.2). In one of the few examples from IR, Saurette (2006) uses a Kantian perspective to examine the role of humiliation in post-9/11 global political discourse. When designing a research project that focuses on the role of emotions, discourse analysis – both textual and visual, autoethnography, and participant observation prove to be helpful in both gathering and analyzing data. Research projects on emotions bring out the multi-layered nature of the body politic.

Two chapters in this section focus on the role of emotions. Looking at the Aamjiwnaang First Nation reserve, Wiebe investigates the political and personal emotions that shape multiple social realities of the "Chemical Valley of Canada" (Chapter 25). Alternatively, Mutlu compares visuals from the *September 11 Photo Project* to the image of the Falling Man in order to understand the impact of acceptable *emotional optics* on shaping the socio-political climate that enabled a series of successful securitization moves in the United States after 9/11 (Chapter 24).

Somatic

Scholars that research the body focus on its role distinct from the mind. Traditionally, this line of inquiry has been associated with feminist critical theory (Butler 1993, Danto 1999,

Moore and Kosut 2010). Building on the work of gender studies scholars, security studies focuses on the role of gendered practices of security and externalities of these practices on marginalized or silenced groups (Enloe 1990, Hansen 2000). By using this approach, a group of scholars has documented the link between the personal and international, arguing that bodies – and especially female bodies – while heavily affected by practices of (in)security, are often missing from the analysis of issues surrounding conflict and war. Research into the somatic is generally reliant on archival research, discourse analysis, interviews, and participant observation as primary methods.

Several chapters in this section approach the body as a site of critical inquiry. Shinko focuses on the body as an essential site of IR while engaging with the question of power and how bodies react to power (Chapter 26). Managhan studies maternal reactions to casualties of war by focusing on the maternal body as a link between the private and the international while reflecting on what constitutes an *event* in International Relations (Chapter 27). Väyrynen focuses on the question of migration by looking at how the migrant's body is not solely a target of governmental practices, but is also political and capable of politics (Chapter 28).

Reflexivity

Reflexivity plays an important role in shaping research design in corporeal methods. In all of these approaches, the researcher plays an important role in both the activity of investigation and the narration of results. While the aim of corporeal research should be to produce inter-subjective concepts, the biases and preferences that shape the subjectivity of the researcher should be acknowledged and should not be in an either/or relation with methodological vigour. Wiebe does an exemplary job in this. Her emotive register is accounted for in her work; Wiebe's emotive responses from her lived experiences in the field are part of her critical posture, and she uses the anxiety, fear, and frustration she experiences to motivate her writing and political practice.

Similarly, the corporeal turn must also be reflexive about the institutional hurdles that are in place, such as the limited number of publication venues that accept this kind of research, or the difficulties of receiving grants through funding agencies due to the perceived lack of *policy relevancy*. This has to be written into the final product, to demonstrate the hoops that one has to jump through to arrive there. Related to the first and second points, the intellectual disposition of the researcher should also factor into the difficulties of speaking truth to power as well as taking – ethical – responsibility for the consequences of our work. Väyrynen's chapter is a good example of such reflexive disposition. Corporeal evidence added to the linguistic, so there is a greater opportunity for resistance to dominant practices. The inclusion of physical reactions of the immigrant into the analysis allows for consideration of affective and somatic communication, subsequently providing a greater sense of agency, ambiguity, and resistance.

Research design, case selection, and analysis

Given the virtually endless possibilities for case studies on the corporeal, we should focus on a set of core-questions to determine whether the case is worth the time and effort. These core questions are:

1   What is the object of study: the body, the body's reactions, the meaning of the body's reactions?

2   What is the operationalization of the somatic, affective, or emotional regime? What counts as data or signs of the body, emotion, or affect?
3   What are the conditions of possibility for doing this research, collecting and analyzing this data? To what extent is this study reproducible or generalizable?

For a successful project to have an impact, these questions should be addressed as clearly as possible without relying on jargon or convoluted theory. While this set of core questions can be adjusted to reflect the specifics of the research project, depending on the project, further questions should also be incorporated into the research design to reflect on the special requirement of the project.

In order to demonstrate how this set of questions is used in a successful research project, let us look at Managhan's chapter in this book. Managhan focuses on the maternal body because of the transformation of its perception over the last thirty years; demonstrating the socio-political significance of the maternal body by tracing "the way motherhood, as a discursive and inherently contested practice, has influenced American women's relationship to processes of militarism" (Chapter 27). She uses discursive methods to trace the signs of control over the maternal body. Moreover, by focusing on the maternal body, Managhan contributes to the literature on the somatic in IR by establishing a relevant case and furthering the knowledgebase of the field. Finally, her engagement with the dominant discourses of power – militarism, nationalism – has an inherently reflexive posture but more importantly her tracing of the changing discourses of motherhood from a voice of reason to madness is a reflexive act that challenges the established discourses within the body politic.

Managhan's clear articulation demonstrates how addressing these questions early on helps us be systemic and rigorous while maintaining our critical disposition. However, determining the case is only the first step towards a solid research project. Establishing the source and methods to analyze data is the second step. We must decide on what aspect of the corporeal turn we want to focus on. Critical security studies scholars generally focused on discourses, object, practices, and technologies of insecurity. But within these broad categories we need to determine what is the *it* of the project? Is it maternal, immigrant bodies? Is it love or hate? Is it disgust or certain visceral reactions that look suspicious to the observer? Is it the role of certain objects or technologies in shaping the *body politic* in a certain way? We can go about establishing this in two ways. We can either determine what it is that we *want* to study, or we can see what it is that we *can* study. As we see with some of the chapters in this section, sometimes the data is simply not out there, or even if it is, it cannot be accessible to the researcher either due to spatial, security-related, or temporal barriers. As we see with the Frowd and Leite chapter, however, there are often ways around these barriers, but these bypasses do take away from the rigour of the project and force it to rely on secondary sources or interpretations of others.

Examples

In this section of the chapter we look at three research projects that successfully use corporeal turn. First we look at Frowd and Leite's contribution on "Affect at the Airport" in this section (Chapter 23). Next we look at Scarry's (1985) work *The Body in Pain: The Making and Unmaking of the World*. Finally we summarize Protevi's (2009) *Political Affect: Connecting the Social and the Somatic*. Each one of these works presents a clear object and subject of research as well as a clearly articulated method.

Table PV.3 Examples of corporeal research design

	Frowd and Leite, Affect at the Airport	*Scarry,* The Body in Pain: The Making and Unmaking of the World	*Protevi,* Political Affect: Connecting the Social and the Somatic
Object	Role of affect in airport security	Political consequences of bodily pain's inexpressibility	Political implications of the interaction between the social and the somatic through affect
Collection	Discourse analysis	Archival research, discourse analysis (focusing on literary and autobiographical texts)	Discourse analysis, practice, interviews, and participant observation
Data	Policy documents, corporate advertisement materials and news sources	Amnesty International documents on torture and war, legal transcripts of personal injury trials, medical (patient and physician) and literary accounts of pain	Media coverage and first person accounts of the *Teri Schiavo* case, *Columbine high school* massacre and aftermath of *Hurricane Katrina*
Relations	The relation between affect, the technologies that "detect" those affective signs, and how that is being used to control bodies in motion	Bridges the mind/body split that is an important part of modern thought by focusing on the political ramifications of deliberately inflicted pain	Somatic, transversal, governmental
Fit	Technologized detection of affect explicitly incorporated into policing to obviate indeterminacy of security	Political significance of pain as a somatic experience that cannot be expressed and its ethical consequences	Role of affective/emotional cognition on the socio-political perceptions of the general public

One of the clearest articulations of the corporeal turn in this section is Frowd and Leite's chapter. By looking at two recent trial programs to improve American airport security, the Screening Passengers by Observation Techniques (SPOT) and Future Attribute Screening Technology (FAST), Frowd and Leite present an interesting case study on the role of affect in risk and security management at the airport since 9/11. By focusing on various policy documents related to behavioural profiling by the Transport Security Agency, the authors trace back the origins of these two programs and demonstrate an existing tension between various branches of the American government: concerns over the viability of behavioural and affective profiling, yet consensus on the desired outcomes of such security programs in the form of a docile, mobile subject. These trials explicitly attempt to manage the unknowability of security, the failures in current screening processes, and the limits of profiling by integrating pre-emotional bodily responses into screening technology. Affect, and its detection, is described in these policy documents as the solution to the problems of airport security. While they acknowledge the difficulty of conducting research on a classified topic, Frowd and Leite demonstrate the usefulness of alternative sources of information such as documents from the Government Accountability Office, analysis of corporate advertisement materials, and leaked news sources. In their project, the authors successfully map the connection between the security concerns of the US government, the field of airport security management and the role of experts in the implementation of behavioural profiling measures at US airports. On the down side, however, they fall into the trap of taking theory as method in their lengthy discussion of different theories of affect and how they influenced their project.

Scarry's work is one of the foundational texts that bring together the corporeal turn, specifically the question of infliction of pain surrounding war and torture. Scarry bridges the somatic/psychological split that has been an important part of modern thought by focusing on the political ramifications of deliberately inflicted pain through torture and war. While Scarry looks specifically at the visceral reactions of pain, her main argument brings affect and emotions together as she looks at the political implications of the difficulty of translating visceral reactions of pain into language; pain is an affect that we cannot explain through language. Scarry presents an insightful critical analysis of physical suffering and political consequences of its inexpressibility. She argues that pain is not only a medical term, but is an aspect of war, torture, and other explicitly political acts. To make her point, Scarry combines archival research and discourse analysis as her core methods. She bases her analysis of pain on a wide range of sources ranging from literature and art, to medical accounts of physicians and patients, documents on torture compiled by Amnesty International, and legal transcripts of personal injury trials among other sources. The first two chapters of her book, "The Structure of Torture: The Conversion of Real Pain into the Fiction of Power" and "Structure of War: The Juxtaposition of Injured Bodies and Unanchored Issues" especially stand out as exceptionally well articulated texts with clear method and research design as they establish the ways that pain comes to gain a political significance, in part because of its inexpressibility, and its internalization in the victim.

"The Structure of Torture" focuses on how torture "consists of a primary physical act, the infliction of pain and a primary verbal act, the interrogation" (Scarry 1985: 28). Within this structured act, consisting of the torturer and the tortured, the reality of the torture victim is reduced to an awareness of pain, while the torturer's world remains fully intact. Scarry is interested in the troubling political and ethical implications of torture as the act of torture is described as information-gathering even when the torturer insists on questions that for the tortured are no longer of any concern. As Scarry argues that torture's "immorality is so absolute and the pain it brings about so real that there is a reluctance to place it in conversation by the side of other subjects. But this reluctance [. . .] increases our vulnerability to power by ensuring that our moral intuitions and impulses [. . .] do not come forward enough to be of any help" (Scarry 1985: 60). Similarly, in the chapter on the "Structure of War" she claims, "the most obvious analogue to torture is war" (Scarry 1985: 61) in the sense that, similar to war, "rather than destroying physical facts of streets, houses, factories and schools, it [torture] destroys them as they exist in the mind of the prisoner" (Scarry 1985: 61).

In these two chapters, Scarry establishes her case study – the inexpressibility of pain inflicted through torture and war – elaborates on kinds of data – Amnesty International documents on torture and war, legal transcripts of personal injury trials, medical (patient and physician), and literary accounts of pain – her sources – archival research – and her method of analysis – discourse analysis focusing on literary and autobiographical texts in a clear and concise way while making a theoretically-informed argument that is grounded in rich empirical data. It is because of this clarity and vigour that we recommend her work as a good example of corporeal research.

Protevi's book *Political Affect: Connecting the Social and the Somatic* is another good example of a corporeal research project. Focusing on the political implications of the interaction between the social and the somatic through affect, Protevi presents a compelling argument on the role of affective/emotional cognition in the socio-political perceptions of the general public. Protevi focuses on "how our bodies, minds, and social setting are intricately and intimately linked" (Protevi 2009: xi). His research leads him to the intersection of (neuro)science, philosophy, and politics. Especially in the last three chapters, Protevi grounds theoretical discussions from earlier in the book in three empirical case studies: the case of Teri Schiavo, the Columbine High School massacre, and the events that happened in the aftermath of Hurricane Katrina.

The case selection, in this case, is based on some of the decisions that Protevi makes early on in the research design phase. Early on in the book, he introduces a three-layered structure or "compositions for political affect" – personal, group, and civic – along with specific emotional and technical foci, as well as a template to determine the relationship to the subject and the body politic. Protevi presents the Schiavo case to be representative of the *personal* level, as it looks at "how political institutions directly invest the organic life of Terri Schiavo without regard to consciousness or subjectivity, rendering it a simultaneously undead and obscenely mediatized body" (Protevi 2009: xvi). Here the medical and legal discourses take over the personal misfortune and evoke the political affect of the body politic. Columbine relates to the *group* level. Protevi questions how the killers maintained a cold rage during the massacre: "initiating the act of killing yet staying in enough control to carry out their plan" (Protevi 2009: xvi). He compares their preparation to military training and looks at desensitization through repetitive training. Finally, at the *civic* level, Protevi looks at "how a racialized fear contributed to delay in government rescue efforts in Hurricane Katrina until sufficient military force could confront thousands of black people in New Orleans" (Protevi 2009: xvi). He compares this fearful institutionalized response to the "massive empathy of ordinary citizens" (Ibid) that resulted in neighbours helping each other to get through the ordeal. To make his case, Protevi uses a number of sources combining media coverage with first-person accounts of the events. He then uses a multi-pronged approach that combines discourse analysis and a mapping of practices to make sense of the data.

Conclusion

Corporeal analysis, which brings together affect, emotions, and the somatic, provides an understanding of the body as both the subject and object of discourses, practices, and policies of (in)security. Given their central role and potential in relation to understanding various interpretations, perceptions, and subjugations, the corporeal turn has become a popular approach in critical security studies. A key assumption in this kind of research is the ontological primacy of the corporeal. In other words, corporeal projects focus on affect, emotions, and body because they consider them to be important signifiers for political analysis. The corporeal turn presents fertile ground for combining different methods such as discourse analysis, practice, or auto-ethnography, as they all have valuable insights into understanding the political agency of the body. Similarly, this multiplicity also demonstrates the difficulty of conducting corporeal research in general. Turning this frustration into reflexive vigour, complementing the usual assumptions of analysis on the role of rationality with an emphasis on the corporeal discourses and practices, will provide politically- and theoretically-grounded critiques of contemporary security studies.

Suggested reading

Ahmed, S. (2004a) "Affective Economies", *Social Text*, 22(2): 117–139.

Butler, J. (1993) *Bodies that Matter: On the Discursive Limits of "Sex"*, New York: Routledge.

Connolly, W.E. (2002) *Neuropolitics: Thinking, Culture, Speed*, Minneapolis: University of Minnesota Press.

Edkins, J. (2003) *Trauma and the Memory of Politics*, Cambridge: Cambridge University Press.

Enloe, C. (1990) *Bananas, Beaches and Bases: Making Feminist Sense of International Relations*, Berkeley: University of California Press.

Hansen, L. (2000) "The Little Mermaid's Silent Security Dilemma and the Absence of Gender in the Copenhagen School", *Millennium: Journal of International Studies*, 29(2): 285–306.

Leys, R. (2011) "The Turn to Affect: A Critique", *Critical Inquiry*, 37(2): 434–472.

Massey, D. (1994) *Space, Place and Gender*, Cambridge: Polity.

Massumi, B. (1995) "The Autonomy of Affect", *Cultural Critique*, 31: 83–109.

Sylvester, C. (1994) "Empathetic Cooperation: A Feminist Method for IR", *Millennium: Journal of International Studies*, 23(2): 315–334.

23 Affect at the airport

Philippe M. Frowd and Christopher C. Leite

Introduction

This chapter is concerned with the role of affect in the analysis of governmental strategies and presents our research design for a critical inquiry into two airport behavioural profiling programs. Affect is the physiological source of emotion, behaviour, feeling, or mood but is "not ownable or recognizable" on its own (Massumi 2002: 88). It is a non-representational and emergent intensity that exists in and through the body that is prior to any sociolinguistic fixity such as consciousness, discourse, emotion, or feeling. Affect is therefore not a material *thing*, but the origin of the underlying bodily events from which everyday human behaviours emerge. Due to the nature of the airport as a space of indeterminacy (Salter 2008b) and a space for the management of affective relationships (Adey 2008), being attentive to the role of affect is central to understanding the airport's security politics. Researching affect, in turn, requires methodological innovation.

We proposed an affect-attuned research lens that could coexist with common critical models of social organization (habitus, governmentality, and so on). As our research progressed, we found that simply identifying and looking for affect was not sufficient. Instead, our focus on affect forced us to rethink the types of intersubjective and subject-object relationships we were examining at the airport. This pushed us to think about models of causality that could account for the affective security relations of the airport. The sections that follow use our methodological trajectory as a way of discussing two things: a research design model that takes seriously the role of affect in shaping security practices; and an overview of the broader methodological conclusions that we came to by being attentive to affect in the airport security assemblage.

When the shoe bomber Richard Reid attempted to blow up a Miami-bound American Airlines flight in December 2001, it reinforced the perception that the US aviation system was facing a sustained threat. The post-9/11 climate reignited controversy around racial profiling, and what came to be known in 2003 as the Screening Passengers by Observation Techniques (SPOT) program was premised on the assumption that terrorists – such as Richard Reid – unintentionally display specific forms of hostile intent or *malintent* that trained professionals can detect. Although behavioural profiling was nothing new – originating in lie detection – its formalization in the context of airport security meant that passengers' affects and emotions were a new variable for risk profiling.

As part of the SPOT program, the US Transportation Security Administration (TSA) trains its Behavior Detection Officers (BDOs) to detect a set of suspicious behaviours. The program's behavior checklist[1] indicates, among other things, that a passenger who is "very arrogant and expresses contempt against airport passenger procedures" may be considered as behaving suspiciously (Ahlers and Meserve 2011) – highlighting the focus on the visible expressions of affect through the observation of specific emotions and behaviours. Airport security practices depend on observing and shaping affect, human behavioural profiling, and even the material architecture of the airport to perform these tasks.

Pinning down one definition of affect is tricky, and Bertelsen and Murphie (2010) find at least nine that draw from psychological, medical, sociological, and philosophical perspectives. We draw upon Massumi's (2002) definition of affect, outlined above, in the interest of parsimony and breadth, as the thread that runs through most definitions is intersubjectivity. Our focus on this intersubjective quality of affect is intended to emphasize that all social interactions operate on a sensory, affective register, and that social interaction and its context are co-constitutive. Our intersubjective focus questions the relationships engendered by the TSA's behavioural profiling programs. In the case of SPOT, there necessarily exists an affective relation between the passenger and the border agent. The TSA, cognizant of the drawbacks of profiling undertaken by humans, is developing a technical *tunnel*, the Future Attribute Screening Technology (FAST), to assess passengers' behaviours.

Beyond these immediate interactions, the broader field of airport security is also imbued with affect. Discursive justifications for behavioural profiling invoke fear of future attack stemming from hostile intent in the present. Setting aside the question of whether behavioural profiling prevents terrorism, we instead inquired as to what the drives towards this paradigm were, what relations it engendered, and how we could go about mapping and understanding them. The project's overarching question was: how does affect underlie airport security practices?

Our inquiry into affect at the airport began with a discursive mapping exercise that involved an analysis of airport security documents. We used policy documents from various US state organizations – the Department of Homeland Security (DHS), the Government Accountability Office (GAO), and the TSA itself – as well as corporate advertising materials. These documents illustrated a lack of consensus about the effectiveness of SPOT's affective profiling, but also a shared agreement that airport security programs should produce a docile mobile subject, as well as a consensus that affect and behaviour map onto hostile intent.

We also examined the psychology behind these practices by looking at the role played by experts such as psychologist Paul Ekman in providing scientific authority for SPOT. Ekman's pioneering approach to identifying and categorizing facial expressions of emotion is controversial within his discipline. Nevertheless, his Facial Action Coding System (FACS) constitutes a training manual of sorts for SPOT agents and has indirectly shaped the TSA's thresholds of acceptable and unacceptable forms of passenger behaviour.

Affect is not a phenomenon easily captured by empirical social science methods. Even the immediately visible expressions of affect – emotions, feelings, moods, or behaviours – are difficult to identify, trace, and interpret. Studying affect requires an attention to circumstance and relationality; the standard is therefore one of plausibility. For example, the analysis of SPOT and FAST does not locate affect as an epistemological *thing*, as outlined in the introduction to this chapter, even though the analysis is attentive to the role of affect. Rather, the analysis investigates: (1) the practices that seek out affect (the profiling), (2) the relationships that stem from this practice (between passenger and border agent), and (3) the material objects through which this process takes place (the airport's architecture, the FAST machine).

To embed the subjects in the field of airport security – passengers and border agents – we drew on Bourdieu's concept of the habitus. Conscious of the nature of affect as a bodily intensity, we challenge Bourdieu's view that individuals within fields exist solely as "agents

– and not as biological individuals, actors, or subjects" (Bourdieu and Wacquant 1992a: 107) by also seeing them as embodied. We drew from the literature on neuropolitics (Connolly 2002) to show the intimate linkages between social existence/identity and the affective register. By coupling Bourdieu's conceptual tools with an affect-attuned focus on embodiment and identity, we see how habits of interaction were entrenched – how they came to be habits. For example, we were able to note that border agents' interactions resulted from long-term imbrication of cultural and bodily training, what Protevi (2009) calls the mix of social institutions with somatic affect. The combination of the cultural tropes about terrorism that structure the airport security field with the bodily training agents undergo in behaviour recognition is an illustration of this logic.

Our argument, that programs like SPOT make race inextricable from the bodies it marks, is not one that could have been made without the twin assumption of subjects' embodiment and embeddedness. Specifically, this meant examining the larger airport security field, where we noticed that the physical structure of the airport was also engaged in the detection and management of travellers' affect, through its architecture and through technical forms of behaviour profiling such as the FAST tunnel. This forced us to confront the materiality of the subject-object interactions in passengers' airport experience.

Throughout our research, we were primarily concerned with adopting an affect-attuned lens to the subjects of our research and their habitus as well as to the materiality of the airport. This led us to a larger question about how the adoption of an affect-attuned approach could be so consequential for the analysis of security writ large. Our conclusion was that although an affect-attuned approach had its own methodological value-additions, there was a second payoff to be found in thinking through intersubjectivity and the questions of causality and human behaviour it engendered.

Using an affect-attuned lens made visible the contexts of, and relations between, subjects and objects at the airport. We came to see affective *managers* at the airport, be they subjects or objects, as *actants* (Latour 2005). Actants in the airport security field can shape behaviour by simultaneously being representative of and defining the field itself. This pushed us to conclude that the larger question we faced involved asking how the intersubjective nature of affect challenges our understanding of subjects and objects as discrete factors held together by clear causal relations. Drawing from Hopf (2010), we found that affect points to the neglected, understudied dimension of intersubjectivity as a field of social inquiry in its own right: "we have been ignoring what most people do most of the time in their *social* lives" (Hopf 2010: 540, emphasis added). This pushed us to adopt an understanding of affect as intersubjectivity in practice, since affect captures, and is expressed in, a multitude of social relations between people and their surroundings. In short, our approach presents a new angle for making sense of perception based on the understanding that "what is perceived as reality is already pre-cooked in our heads" (Hopf 2010: 541), independently of rational cost-benefit calculations.

This meant approaching causality as beyond strict causation between only human subjects, towards a complex causality accounting for the role of a range of *actants*. We drew on Latour's (2005) non-linear causality and Deleuze and Guattari's (2009) notion of emergence for this. Emergence is interconnectedness, resonance, and interdependence, where multiple phenomena resonate together, occur in tandem, or exist relationally (Connolly 2005, Deleuze and Guattari 1994, Massumi 1996). This "mutual imbrication and interinvolvement" characteristic of emergence "forg[es] a qualitative assemblage resistant to classical models of explanation" (Connolly 2005: 870). This nonlinear model of causality allowed us to account for the complex interactions between social institutions, material objects, and somatic affect.

Methodologically, this means approaching security practices from both discursive and practical standpoints. Contrary to Mutlu's argument in his introduction to Part V, we argue that studying representations of affect – emotions and behaviours, for example – helps us trace how affect is managed. Affect allows us to reframe our analysis of airport security practices, contrary to studies that focus on the *amount* of security that can be attained. Moving beyond this rationalism is what Mutlu has rightly identified as one of the value-additions of corporeal approaches such as ours.

Maintaining a reflexive methodology allowed us to return to the theory we were drawing on and make a different kind of contribution to the study of airport security: we made the management of the traveller's corporeal embodiment the focus of our study, focusing on what intersubjectivity concretely means for security practices. Maintaining a corporeal ontological focus to supplement a discourse analysis method revealed the political motivations behind sets of practices.

Conclusion

This chapter presents a methodology attentive to the importance of affect to social relations, allowing for a deeper practical understanding of intersubjectivity and of security relations as non-linear and emergent. Our original question asked how affect underlay airport security practices, but we realized that the more salient question concerned how the affective relations engendered by these practices could change our methodological bearings. We moved from looking only at the affective nature of airport security, towards understanding what payoff the study of airport security practices had for the analysis of security. This yielded two conclusions. First, security practices are complex relationships that imbricate the objects of security, security-producing subjects, and the ways they implicate the populations at which security measures are targeted. Second, the study of airport security practices should account for how they claim to provide security and what the contingency of different combinations of practices can be.

In sum, our attention to affect at the airport allowed us to conceptualize the myriad combinations of subject and object relations that are brought into play by SPOT and FAST. Through our original inclinations about the role of affect, and our reflexivity about the broader things our original approach necessitated, we highlighted some overlooked aspects of security politics: the role of emotionally resonant discourses of fear, the embodied nature of profiling practices, the way material space and practices interact, and the roles intersubjectivity and causality play in structuring security fields. With the addition of a case study, we were able to speak to broad questions about methodology for doing security studies.

Note

1   While information on suspect behaviours was closely guarded, these were listed in a DHS privacy assessment of SPOT, and the TSA's list of 70 suspect behaviours used by SPOT was leaked to CNN in April 2011.

Suggested reading

Blackman, L. and Venn, C. (2010) "Affect", *Body and Society*, 16(1): 7–28.
Gregg, M. and Seigworth, G.J. (eds) (2010) *The Affect Theory Reader*, Durham: Duke University Press.
Massumi, B. (1995) "The Autonomy of Affect", *Cultural Critique*, 31: 83–109.

Protevi, J. (2009) *Political Affect: Connecting the Social and the Somatic*, Minneapolis: University of Minnesota Press.

Walkerdine, V. et al. (2010) *Reflections on the Researching Affect and Affective Communication Network and Seminar Series*. Online: www.cardiff.ac.uk/socsi/newsandevents/events/innovation/seminar6/combined.document.doc (accessed 15 February 2012).

24 Emotional optics

Can E. Mutlu[1]

Introduction

While co-authoring a piece on *Psychoanalytic Theory and Border Security* with Mark B. Salter (Salter and Mutlu 2012), I came to appreciate the significance of the interaction between objects and our emotions, how rational actions are equally grounded in psychological and emotional registers. At the time, I suggested that a successful securitization move requires an *a priori* affective and emotional connection between the audience and the referent object.

A simple curiosity or interest in a subject is one thing, but it is another thing altogether to turn that spirit of inquiry into a project with a rigourous method. The process of research design and coming up with a research question is a lengthy process and one that is likely to involve numerous failures and shortcomings. I have started this project with the idea that focusing on affect, emotions, and securitization would be an interesting side-project along with my doctoral dissertation. At the time, I did not realize that it would be numerous drafts and almost two years before I had an article that is coherent and ready to be submitted for peer review.

During the early stage in the project, I made a few important decisions that helped me later on. At that time, I knew two things. First, I wanted to focus on the role of affect and emotions in securitization theory. Second, I wanted to include visuality, or more specifically still images, as the medium of analysis. Knowing the general topic that I wanted to study allowed me to come up with the general research question that I primarily wanted to focus on: what role do our emotions play in the construction of security threats? This is the core question of my project. While coming up with this question was a challenge in its own right, coming up with an object of study was a much harder challenge. Instead of rushing it, I decided to take my time and look into a couple of options.

I considered studying images of airport/border security or the War on Terror; these were the subjects that I have had previous experience with so they were natural departure points. At the time, a friend that knew about this idea recommended that I take a look at the *September 11 Photo Project* – "the Project". The Project was a community response to the tragic events of 9/11, designed to create an impromptu public shrine for those who passed away during the attacks, through "an open forum for display of photographs and words in response to the terrorist attacks of September 11, 2001" (Feldschuh 2002: vii). Anyone who wished to contribute was asked to send a tableau consisting of three photographs along with a paragraph.

By the time I started this project in the winter of 2009, however, the art gallery that originally hosted the Project no longer existed. Instead, the curator of the Project turned a selection of pictures from the gallery into an edited volume (Feldschuh 2002). After receiving a copy of the edited volume, I realized that images of September 11, 2001 were the images that I have been searching for. As one of the most memorable and (re)presented events in the last decade, images of September 11, 2001 emerge as a valuable "explanatory case" (Balzacq 2010b: 33) for studying the affective and emotional linkages that operationalize a successful securitization move: the policies and practices of the War on Terror. But the Project alone was not enough; while interesting, it was not clear exactly what the Project told me about affect, emotions, or securitization.

As I looked through the pages of the Project, I noticed something. This representation of 9/11, an event defined by destruction and death, did not include any explicit images of death. While death was implicit in almost every picture, it was as though there was something unacceptable about explicitly representing death when remembering September 11. It is important to note that the Project did not censor any images, but images of death were self-censored by submitters. While the Project captures the trauma of the American social imaginary after 9/11 through a pluralistic and inclusive approach – both in terms of participation and observation – the silences within the Project speak to what is regarded as (un)acceptable by the emotional economy of post-9/11 American collective memory.

Discovering these embedded silences in the Project opened up another avenue for my own project. I remembered a photo from the aftermath of September 11 that caused a public outcry upon publication. The Falling Man, which refers to a single photograph taken by Associated Press photographer Richard Drew, as part of a series of photographs that captured a man – whose identity remains uncertain – falling from the North Tower of the WTC at 9:41:15 a.m. on September 11. The image appeared on page 7 of the *New York Times* on September 12 and was faced with anger and criticism.

This was the last missing piece of my research design. After seeing the complete picture, I decided to juxtapose the acceptable images covered in the Project with the "tasteless" use of the image of the Falling Man, arguing that this demonstrates the role of acceptable images versus unacceptable ones in shaping the outcome of the mediated interaction between the audience and securitizing agent during a securitization move.

Once I got over this final hurdle in the research design phase, I readjusted the focus of the article to look at the impact of *emotional optics*[2] – images that evoke an emotional response upon exposure – on the outcome of the construction of (in)security. Consequently, the final product of this research project is the emotional economy that was at play in the origins and operations of post-9/11 securitization moves. In other words, following 9/11, why were certain images considered acceptable while others were not? What was the emotional economy behind the social and political reasoning in play? More importantly, what does non-use of certain images tells us about securitization moves?

Another challenge I had along the way was the question of incorporating the body of work on affect and emotions into the securitization literature. The issue was not that these two literatures were incompatible. It was, however, the question of intersubjectivity of emotions that puzzled me the most. I realized early on that the use of affect- and emotion-attuned methodologies in securitization theory raises two interrelated questions: how to study the ascription of value or identification between agents and objects – i.e. the legitimization process – and how to account for the intersubjective, as opposed to purely individual, origins and operations of emotions? While reflecting on the former question, a senior scholar of securitization theory posed me the latter question on intersubjectivity. At the time it presented a fundamental criticism of the role of affect and emotions in securitization moves. It is true that while the cognitive understanding and appraisal of the object is essential to securitization moves in the relationship between the audience and the referent object, it is the inter-subjective conception of emotions that is essential to understanding securitization at the societal level.

In facing this issue, I found Ahmed's (2004a) concept of affective economies to be a useful starting point to understand the intersubjective nature of affect and emotions. Ahmed engages the intersubjective nature of emotions and suggests that the crucial question is how emotions operate at a collective level, as she puts it: "[h]ow do emotions move between bodies?" (Ahmed 2004a: 117). Building on Ahmed's work, I looked into the emotional economies that are in play when we are expressing our emotions. For the most part, we express our emotions through a three-part sentence: "we love/hate/fear objects or people". I realized that there are two types of emotional economies in place in these statements. First is the interaction between the emotion and the object. In analyzing this sentence we often place the emphasis on this interaction. There is, however, a second economic interaction in this sentence: the relationship between the subject and the emotion. When we say "we love" or "we hate", the "we" in those sentences interacts with an intersubjective definition of love and hate that has a meaning that exceeds the subject, or *moves between bodies*; the subject is not the departure point of the emotion. Prior to the expression of our emotions, there is a collective under-standing on meaning of those emotions.

Once I was able to understand and translate my reflections on intersubjectivity, the time I have spent reading, reflecting, and sketching out my argument in the research design phase proved to be very useful. I was able to finish a first draft that clearly outlines the actors and fields that were involved in the post-September 11 securitization moves. These were: the bureaucratic and political field that links different branches of the US Government – *the securitizing agent* – with the American public – *the audience* – through the medium of sustained speech and visuality-based references to the "American way of life" and "home-land security" – *the referent object(s)* – that were presented as being under attack. I then juxtaposed two sets of images – the acceptable images of the Project and the unacceptable image of the Falling Man – and inquired about how and why one set – the Project – was referred to by securitizing agents whereas the other one was removed from the possibility of being a referent object.

In the article I concluded that different images of September 11 provoke different traumas and different affective and emotional responses. Our collective memory is capable of deal-ing with some of these traumas, while we chose to forget or ignore others. Anger, fear, and humiliation are emotions that connect with certain affective impulses, which in return provoke certain actions, whereas this line between affect-emotion-action is not as clear in instances of helplessness, hopelessness, and disconnectedness. At the personal level, we can either suppress traumas by forgetting, ignoring, or omitting feelings and objects associated with these feelings, becoming delusional and creating an alternative set of memories, or these traumas may cause post-traumatic stress disorder. At the societal level traumas may also manifest themselves along the same lines. Societies can mourn their losses, learn from them, or they can re-write history and omit traumas from those versions of history. Alternatively they can seek retaliation in the form of war or exceptional policy measures.

Conclusion

As an emergent research agenda, affect and emotion attuned-approaches present an opening into understanding corporeal origins of discourses, policies, and practices of security. In terms of reproducibility of this method, while I chose to focus on the juxtaposition of still-images from the Project and the Falling Man, moving images such as films, animations or literary accounts or graphic novels are equally fertile in terms of embedded discourses. In other words, visuality in general is an under-explored source in security studies. Similarly, specific references to certain events in major addresses by securitizing agents such as the President or the Secretaries of State or Defense would also be a more classical – as it is closer to the original methods used by the securitization theory – way of understanding the role of emotions in shaping security discourses, practices and policies.

Notes

1   Can E. Mutlu is a member of the ESCR funded *International Collaboratory in Critical Methods in Security Studies* (RES-810-21-0072).
2   Emotional Optics is a term that was used by a "senior British cabinet minister" (Wintour and MacAskill 2011) referring to images of the rebellion in Libya and was later picked up by David Campbell on his blog post *Target Libya*. Campbell defines the term as "visuals that prompt affective responses to international events" (Campbell 2011).

Suggested reading

Ahmed, S. (2004) "Affective Economies", *Social Text*, 22(2): 117–139.
Amoore, L. (2007) "Vigilant Visualities: The Watchful Politics of the War on Terror", *Security Dialogue*, 38(2): 215–232.
Butler, J. (2009) *Frames of War: When is Life Grievable?* New York: Verso.
Campbell, D. (2004) "Horrific Blindness: Images of Death in Contemporary Media", *Journal for Cultural Research*, 8(1): 55–74.
Edkins, J. (2003) *Trauma and the Memory of Politics*, Cambridge: Cambridge University Press.

25 Affective terrain
Approaching the field in Aamjiwnaang

Sarah Marie Wiebe

Introduction

Venturing beyond the classroom and into the field to conduct research can be understood as entering the *affective terrain*: field research is political and personal. On Mondays at 12:30 p.m. sharp, from inside the Aamjiwnaang First Nation's burial grounds, the drone of a siren warns that spills, accidents or explosions can take place at any time. A chain-link fence divides the cemetery from the adjacent stacks, flares, and plume. The reserve is pinched on all sides by this industrial zone, "Chemical Valley", an area known for Canada's highest concentration of chemical and petrochemical production, which is felt, smelled, and feared. Trains pass alongside the cemetery, sounding their whistles before crossing through the reserve as the wind frequently blows smoke South, pouring over citizens of Aamjiwnaang.

Spending time with members of this community is part of my field research strategy. Political ethnography is an interpretive and qualitative methodology that engages with humans embedded within political processes that affect their everyday lives (Schatz 2009a). Similar to Frowd and Leite's contribution (Chapter 23), this *intersubjective* methodology is an affective research design that takes scholars beyond text work into the shared, lived-experience of communities. Research in this context stems from a belief that social reality is multifold and its interpretation is shaped through how one experiences that reality; experiences are "lived in the context of intersubjective meaning making" (Yanow 2006: 23). In contrast to research that seeks to test a series of hypotheses, this logic of inquiry requires constant revision in light of emergent field realities and interrogates a multiplicity of viewpoints rather than develop *one* narrative or truth. As such, learning is a continuous process that takes place in the field. To ground theory in practice, developing knowledge from this framework tends to be a bottom-up process; concepts take on meaning, which become perceptible over time. To gain an in-depth understanding of the power relations and processes that affect the Aamjiwnaang First Nation's pollution burden in everyday life, after several site visits, this inquiry drew me into the field, where I chose to reside for a period of immersion.

Long-term relationship-building facilitated my entry to the field. As a research assistant conducting ongoing work in the community, I began to build trust and relationships with members of the Aamjiwnaang First Nation. Following a year of assistance and collaborative work with a professor and the Aamjiwnaang First Nation Health and Environment Committee, I developed my research strategy with the consultation of community advisors and the support of this committee. This kind of collaboration forced me to think critically about my expectations and to continuously rethink my strategy. Thus, a reflexive approach is important in this context. It requires, on the one hand, openness to the development of research design in close consultation with community members, and on the other hand, a level of confidence about the value and direction of the project. Striking the balance between outside *expert* and internal collaborator is crucial, but never simple.

Political ethnography is a personal research strategy. Ethnography provides a lens through which scholars can examine the micropractices of power. My entry into the field as a researcher is marked by an interest in the experiential knowledge of everyday life in a particular place. In order to understand struggles for environmental and reproductive justice on the ground, spending considerable time in the field became necessary. My involvement in the field entailed daily local media scans, constant contact with community activists, attending public meetings and community information nights, supporting and participating in community events with the Aamjiwnaang Green Teens youth group and working one day a week at the reserve health centre, while also setting up interviews with community members, officials, and policy-makers, and trips to the library and local archives. In this setting, almost everything becomes *data*; however, data is not something given, rather, it is something to be made sense of and interpreted.

Formally delineating between *participant* and *observer* in the field falls within a constantly shifting continuum. I participated in community activities both on and off reserve. In addition to attending public meetings and community events, as well as taking a weekly *Ojibwe/ Anishinaabemowin* class, like many residents, I smelled peculiar odours, noticed when the stacks flared larger and brighter at night and wondered about the health impacts. Conducting fieldwork in this manner involves engaging in practices of daily life that resemble those of locals. Thus, the only escape, or break, tends to be physical removal from the site itself.

The researcher places his or her body in a foreign or unsettling context, lending itself to experience a range of impulses, feelings and emotions, which may (re)shape the research design. Thus, immersion is an affective research method. Visceral or emotional drives may motivate the project's orientation. Affect in this case refers to the registered, yet often unconscious experience of emotions. It is part of the body's reaction to external stimuli, dealing with gut feelings, visceral impulses as they relate to cognition. By living in a new environment, one's relationships and habitus, or operating mode in a particular setting, become shaped by the field. As such, this kind of research is as much personal and emotional as it is political. Furthermore, in such a new and emergent setting, power relations are never absent from the research context. In addition to physically immersing one's body into the field, the separation between external expert researcher and internal community member becomes somewhat blurred, though never completely erased.

My own location as a white middle-class female researcher in this environment is important to situate. I am cognizant of my position of privilege and identity as a young female interested in studying the experiences of others living in a more precarious socio-economic context. Upon entering the field, I was motivated to conceptualize my experience as a researcher in the spirit of what Yanow refers to as "passionate humility", with the intention of revisiting my own assumptions (Yanow 2003). Passionate humility aligns with Foucault's reminder that scholars must conduct a critical ontology of the self as part of "personal decolonization" (Rabinow and Rose 1994, Irlbacher-Fox 2009). Moreover, my approach, a combination of interpretive analysis and political ethnography, coupled with a commitment to decolonizing methodology, seeks to contribute to social change and emancipation (Burnham et al. 2008, Madison 2005, Smith 1999). I aim to share voice, knowledge, and place with those kind enough to share their experiences with me and not just create "traveller's tales" that I take back to my privileged academic community (Tuhiwai Smith 1999). By taking extensive field notes that record my own thoughts, interpretations, and reflections, I continue to evaluate the views and values I bring to the study in order to challenge my assumptions, and make space for new meanings, ontologies, and epistemologies.

Examining the exercise of power depends on what a scholar takes to be axiomatic. Political analysis is commonly associated with the distribution and exercise of power; however, politics and policy increasingly occur across different spatial horizons (Orsini and Smith 2007). Conducting ethnographic research is a compelling way to understand power relations on the ground and how citizens ascribe categories of meaning to their daily lives. Such an approach offers a means for the researcher to evaluate discrepancies between expert, elite, and situated knowledges.

Interpretive methodologies are primarily concerned with the process of meaning-making. This involves positioning dominant discourses or narratives in relation to marginal or often ignored narratives to move towards a post-positivist or deliberative epistemology of knowledge and policy development (Fischer 2003, Orsini 2007, Yanow 2003). It entails considering the power relations involved in the formation and expression of privileged speech in relation to silences. This includes an exploration of local, or situated knowledges derived from lived-experience (Haraway 1991, Yanow 2003). Such an approach enables multiple viewpoints about a particular policy issue to come to the fore.

An interpretive approach builds from the premise that policy implications are neither transparent nor necessarily evident. Such analyses ask: "what are the meanings?" of a policy, rather than "what are the costs?" or "how can we evaluate policy?" (Yanow 2000). This emphasizes language, communication, rhetoric, argumentation, and the formation of contested meanings (Fischer 2003, Fischer 2009, Fischer and Forrester 1993, Yanow 2000, Yanow 2003). To unwrap these perspectives, interpretive analysts identify groups, stakeholders, and artifacts, which contain symbolic language, objects, and actions that determine how policies and processes are framed and understood (Yanow 2000). To understand these processes, interpretive research often includes textual analysis, participant observation, immersion, and semi-structured interviews with community-members and public officials.

As my research site takes place on and adjacent to a First Nations reserve, I am committed to an interpretive and ethnographic approach motivated by a decolonizing methodology. This stems from a collaborative, participatory-based model. Participatory research seeks to connect research to practice by sharing knowledge and authority about the research project with the community by involving communities in all stages of the process. The inclusion of community advisors allowed me to consult with *cultural navigators*, including Elders and partners from the community to facilitate a culturally appropriate approach to the research design. By including citizens of Aamjiwnaang at critical stages of the project's development, planning, design, analysis, and results dissemination I engage in the *field* with a spirit of reciprocity and relationship-building (Kovach 2009, NWAC 2009, Tuhiwai Smith 1999). This requires that I work with and not speak for the community.

Conclusion

After a year of research assistance, followed by a year of immersion, it is clear that the field has an emotional impact. Through ongoing engagement and immersion in daily site activities, I became fired up by various emotions that accompany this kind of ethnographic research – fear, humiliation, shame, passion, awe, disgust, and rage, among others. While I noticed a range of emotions expressed by those living there, I also paid attention to my own feelings, experiences, and attachments. As such, it became important for me to record my thoughts about this process on an audio recorder, to speak to academic and community-based advisors, and to practice self-care. At times it was challenging to separate my personal and professional entanglements, though it was necessary for me to gain some distance from the research context to have time and space to process, synthesize, and document daily events. During the first months of immersion, I often felt detached, isolated, and disconnected from the academic world I knew prior to the fieldwork stage. The experience has been challenging and rewarding as I became situated in an unfamiliar context, while trying to bridge the academic and field worlds.

Giving back in both theory and practice is a crucial part of any field-based research methodology. In addition to making theoretical and methodological contributions to scholarship, pressures emerge to make policy-relevant and meaningful recommendations and interventions in the spirit of social action. Throughout this process, the question of how to find my own place within this community as an external yet immersed researcher and how to give back remained present. I sought to give back to the community by creating a briefing note on the ongoing Lambton Community Health study, providing advice on the strategic direction for the Lambton Environmental Action Plan, and volunteering with the Aamjiwnaang Green Teens to assist with grant writing and event organizing. This also led to the production of a documentary film with community members. Throughout my immersion, I sought to contribute to public knowledge and awareness by using social media to disclose ongoing news stories and events, as well as concurrent information regarding real-time spills and accidents. Furthermore, in response to various spills, leaks, or accidents in Chemical Valley, I co-authored letters-to-the-editor with community members. Thus, sharing knowledge about my findings throughout the time of field immersion occurred within a continuous, intersubjective and dynamic process.

The research aims to speak truth to power in pursuit of social action and change. In consultation with my community and academic advisors, a report of my findings will be provided to the community. My intent is that these findings speak to policy gaps for First Nations environmental health in Canada and ultimately speak with, not for this community, about a multifaceted public policy issue. In this way, an interpretive method then seeks to contribute to the democratization of knowledge production by moving beyond technical researcher *expertise* to include the voices and stories from actors situated in the field throughout an emergent research endeavour.

Suggested reading

Fischer, F. (2003) *Reframing Public Policy: Discursive Politics and Deliberative Practices*, Oxford: Oxford University Press.

Orsini, M. and Smith, M. (eds) (2007) *Critical Policy Studies*, Vancouver: UBC Press.

Schatz, E. (2009a) "Ethnographic Immersion and the Study of Politics" in E. Schatz (ed.) *Political Ethnography: What Immersion Contributes to the Study of Power*, Chicago: Chicago University Press.

Schwartz-Shea, P. and Yanow, D. (2012) *Interpretive Research Design: Concepts and Processes*, New York: Routledge.

Tuhiwai Smith, L. (1999) *Decolonizing Methodologies: Research and Indigenous Peoples*, London: Zed Books.

26 Theorizing the body in IR

Rosemary E. Shinko

Introduction

I have chosen to focus on the body in a new line of research, which explores various aspects of embodied resistance. My research responds to the question posed by Campbell and Dillon: "where is the body in international relations?" (1993: 12). This highlights the absence of a sustained theoretical focus on the body which is, after all, quite puzzling since international relations is fundamentally about bodies, i.e., bodies marked as citizens, terrorists, refugees, illegal immigrants, enemy combatants, and so forth.[1] Burke identifies security "as an interlocking system of knowledges, representations, practices and institutional forms that imagine, direct and *act upon bodies*, spaces and flows" (2007: 28, emphasis added). Thus it is not a question of *bringing the body back* into International Relations (IR*)* so much as it is a recognition that the body has been the unacknowledged site on which and through which international politics has been conducted.

Thus this is not a reclamation but an acknowledgement of the significance of the body and its ideational/material position at the centre of our theoretical efforts in IR. It is quite confounding how much scholarly attention has been paid to the body in disciplines outside the purview of IR and that we have been very slow to take up this essential line of inquiry.[2]

My first objective is to explore how the body functions as an object/site of international politics. The next step is to focus on understanding the ways in which the body functions as an inscriptive surface on which and through which power operates to turn bodies into certain types of subjects. The third considers the ways in which bodies respond to these forms of power, operating as a counter-inscriptive surface in an effort to resist, contest, and/or transgress. Thus the goal is to understand this fundamental duality where bodies function as both absorptive surfaces produced by power and reflexive surfaces of resistance and struggle.

The most pressing question is how to "address the lack of theorization of the body in international relations" (Shinko 2010). However, the overarching aim of this research is to inquire about how embodied resistance practices might provoke ethical engagements between self and other which reveal those conditions under which the self is afflicted by the embodied performance of the other (Shapiro 1990: 80). This entails an understanding of the body, which takes into account the emergence of ethical relationships between bodies, how they respond to one another's location within various political, social, cultural, and economic structures of power and how they enact practices of contestation and transformation. In short, the research questions are: how do bodies both reflect and struggle against the operations of power?; how can we study these two intertwined sets of embodied practices as they unfold in international politics?

This project relies first and foremost on textual analysis in order to develop an understanding of core concepts such as autonomy, the body, and resistance. Feminist scholars such as McNay (2000: 151), who argue that we can think about autonomy as a site of inter-subjective relationships involving both affiliation and struggle, and Mackenzie and Stoljar (2000: 3), who conclude that "the notion of autonomy is vital to feminist attempts to understand oppression, subjection, and agency", reconfirm autonomy's centrality.

Foucault's discussion of the body offers a way to consider the complicated processes through which one constitutes oneself as a subject.[3] His later work on the aesthetics of care for the self provides insights into the ways in which we can identify our present "formulation of subjectivity and make determined choices to become the subject that we would ethically prefer to be" (Shinko 2011: 3). Thus, Foucault's work is essential to my larger project because "his examination of the body/power nexus enables us to consider how resistance emerges within, on and through the body" (Shinko 2010: 3).

Butler's concept of performativity and her analysis of the ways in which bodies not only occupy gender norms but actually transform those norms by enacting them in ways which contest or subvert accepted patterns of gendered behaviour are also significant.[4] Gender performativity involves "a process of repetition which can either repeat in ways which confirm existing cultural norms, prohibitions, or expectations or it can repeat in ways which provoke or question them" (Shinko 2010: 28). Reading Foucault and Butler together in this way enables me to draw upon aesthetic practices of self-making and performativity in order to analyze their potential for challenging, resisting and transforming structures of power and knowledge, as well as relations of power.

In conjunction with this theoretical framework, I developed a conceptual matrix that enables me to systematically identify and analyze instances of embodied resistance. I began with the body as a site of complicity/resistance and I identified what I thought were the most salient components related to the various aspects of embodied resistance. Mutlu, in his introduction to Part V, notes the significance of affect, emotion, and the somatic, but I would argue that we need a slightly more expansive framework in order to comprehensively study embodiment. I isolated the following components: intentionality, embodied acts as response/provocation, physicality, affectivity, responses to the embodied acts of resistance, meaning, and interpretation of these acts, and finally, their impact. The aim is to analyze how bodies are deployed, what they do, and how they do it. The focus is on the body or bodies, and what acts, movements, and/or poses they enact in various public spaces. This information is accessible via audiovisual documentation, participant interviews, diaries, personal writings, and written descriptions. The primary emphasis is on how bodies were used, noting where and how they emerged in public and what acts and counter acts occurred. This information addresses issues involving intentionality, embodied acts as response/provocation, physicality, and affectivity. But the second half of this research incorporates factual data about various responses to these enactments, considers what these embodied acts might mean and how they could be interpreted, and finally looks for evidence (changes in political leadership, laws, social norms, economic conditions) to begin to assess if and to what extent these acts have had an impact. Reading Gbowee's threat to strip naked in the hall outside the bogged down Liberian peace talks, through the proposed matrix, enables us to systematically analyze what such an embodied act of resistance entails, signifies, and impacts.

Conclusion

The challenge is to figure out how to work through the ways in which bodies can be deployed to resist, challenge and/or transform various structures of power. The key, then, is to conceptualize the body as an open-ended, relational site while acknowledging the body's physical materiality and its performative capacity to spark creative and eruptive moments of political resistance and transformation. It is difficult enough to detail the complicated and unfolding choreographies that develop when bodies emerge in public spaces to enact various forms of resistance, but quite another to assess their import, meaning, and impact.

I defined and provided examples to illustrate each component of the matrix. Intentionality explores how the resister emerges in the act of resistance. Act as response/provocation draws upon Foucault's formulation of actions upon actions. Physicality refers to the willingness to put the body on the line, while affectivity draws together what bodies do, feel, and think. Responses to the act consider how power responds to embodied provocations and meaning/interpretation of the act examines how embodied acts challenge structures of meaning. Impact asks how we know when an embodied act of resistance or a series of such acts results in stasis or change. Examples include Women in Black, lunch counter sit-ins, Mothers of the *Plaza de Mayo*, *Acevedo* Movement, *Encapuchados*, and Meira Paibi Women's Movement. This framework enables us to identify the bodies in international relations, to study them as sites/objects of resistance and transformation, and to assess the significance of embodied resistance practices.

Notes

1   Other scholars whose work explores the body in IR include Marlin-Bennett, Wilson and Walton (2010), Epstein (2007), Cooper (2006), Salter (2006), Zito and Barlow (1994) and Feldman (1991).
2   The following represents a mere sampling of work on the body outside the discipline of international relations: Moore and Kosut (2010), Noland (2009), Ballantyne and Burton (2005), Keane and Homer (2000), Danto (1999), Shildrick and Price (1999), Selzer and Crowley (1999), Komesaroff (1995), Burroughs and Ehrenreich (1993), Butler (1993), Shilling (1993), Young (1990), and Scarry (1985).
3   See McLaren (2002), Heyes (2007), Hengehold (2007), Bakare-Yusuf (1999), Riley (1999), Punday (2000), McWhorter (1989), and Montag (1995).
4   Analysis of Butler's theory of performativity includes Lloyd (2007), Carver and Chambers (2008), Dudrick (2005), and Meijer and Prins (1998).

Suggested reading

Bordo, S. (1995) *Unbearable Weight: Feminism, Western Culture and the Body*, Berkeley: University of California Press.
Guillaume, L. (2012) *War on the Body,* Abingdon: Routledge.
Shilling, C. (2007) *Embodying Sociology: Retrospect, Progress and Prospects*, Oxford: Blackwell.
Stoller, P. (1995) *Embodying Colonial Memories: Spirit Possession, Power, and the Hauka in West Africa*, New York: Routledge.
Young, I.M. (2005) *On Female Body Experience*, New York: Oxford University Press.

27 Reading the maternal body as political event[1]

Tina Managhan

Introduction

When the knock on the door came on April 4th, 2004, Cindy Sheehan, an American woman and a mother of three, said she already knew the message that was to come: her son, deployed in Iraq only five days prior, was killed in the line of duty. According to Sheehan (2006), a part of her died that day as well; she would or could never be the same. Such were the beginnings of a profound personal/political transformation that was born from a collision of the local and the global which would reverberate with both local and global effects. The events that were to follow were of weighty consequence for Sheehan, her family, the American anti-war movement, and the Bush Administration. These events were an instantiation of international politics. But what does it mean to say this? In other words, what within the field of International Relations (IR) constitutes an event?

This is not a question that IR scholars spend a lot of time thinking about, despite the increased prominence of interpretive approaches, the expectation has remained that *we*, in particular, can recognize what the significant events are, even if we question the meanings attributed to them and the processes by which certain events acquire significance. Certainly, post-positivist and feminist approaches have deepened our understandings of events, demonstrating that foreign policy decision-making is inextricably interrelated with domestic power relations and identity politics more broadly (Campbell 1998, Doty 1993, Enloe 2000). They have drawn our attention beyond events marked by formalized politics and acts of political violence, to the margins and the bedrooms in order to highlight, in Enloe's words, "the amounts and varieties of power it takes to form and sustain any given set of relations between states" (1996: 186).

But, while these types of analyses may help to draw our attention to marginalized events and interpretations, the matter of IR still tends to be prefigured within the discipline in important ways. This is what disciplinarity is. Within IR it is the ability to decipher the local and the global and, more currently, to analyze the ways in which they intersect. With reference to war, for example, *we* may talk about the impact of war *on* bodies, the so-called human costs of war, of which Sheehan and her son would be illustrative casualties. Alternatively, we may talk about the *politicization* of Sheehan and her impact on the antiwar movement and the Bush Administration. But, much like Shinko in this book (Chapter 26), I began to wonder what would it mean to invert the site of IR such that rather than it being that which impacts bodies or that which bodies effect, we take the body as an object/site of international politics. Specifically, my research was concerned with the following question: what would it mean to read the maternal body as a site of IR, as an instantiation of global politics, as the political event?

The initial object of my investigation was the shift that occurred between the height of the antinuclear movement in the early to mid-1980s when many women were organizing on the basis of their distinctive perspective as mothers and caregivers and the Gulf War in the early 1990s, characterized by a cheering re-affirmation of US militarism which women were also actively engaged in. From there, my project extended to a more general concern with motherhood as a discursive practice wherein maternal responsibility could be understood to demand protest against the military state in one instance and the pinning of yellow ribbons to support boys at war in another. I was concerned with the way motherhood has influenced American women's relationship to processes of militarism in different ways across bodies and even differentially within the same bodies across time. In the end, my analysis extended to encompass three distinctive foreign policy moments: the antinuclear movement of the 1980s, the Gulf War of the early 1990s, and the most recent US-led attack on Iraq.

For each period, I examined a particular female mode of embodiment and traced the ways such bodily forms came to surface in and through popular discourses of motherhood and in relation to sovereign articulations of power that were characteristic of the era.[2] Because I have been especially interested in hegemonic, or otherwise emblematic, variations of the ways female bodies have negotiated cultural articulations of motherhood and reasons of state, the bodies of white, middle-class women have featured centrally in my analysis.[3] The challenge was to make these bodies strange to trace the processes through which they emerged as gendered, raced, classed, and even more specifically *maternalized* in order to determine their implications for militarization process.[4]

This approach entails, for example, an investigation into the hystericization of the female body during the antinuclear movement as both a protest tactic and a performative act; it entails an interest in the cultural production of fear and the cultural production of bodies and, indeed, of highly particular bodies who would identify themselves as mothers of the nation in and through a very particular fear response; it entails attention to the dialogical nexus that was established between the female antinuclear protesters, the American public, and *the military men* – the identity markers, the dramatizations, and the various cultural resources mobilized to establish meaning and to thwart it. At this point, theory and ontology necessarily intersect with method as what it entails is an approach to IR that, in an extension of Enloe's analysis (1996), suggests that even if we want to understand what Walt (1991: 212) refers to as the *real stuff* of security studies (the "the threat, use, and control of military force"), we have to understand something about the subjects who speak the nation – those who can define it and its (constitutive) threats. This may include the mothers of the nation, but, of course, it also includes the foreign policy makers who speak on their behalf within the twin logics of protection and representation: ways of life must be defended. My concern has been with the conditions of possibility of foreign policy articulation that enabled nuclear deterrence to be heralded as the lynchpin of cold war security strategy for years and then recast as madness or, worse yet, a sign of men's *missile envy* or lack (Caldicott 1986).

As Doty (1993) has aptly outlined, a concern with the conditions of the possible moves us away from *why* questions – which, in this case, might include "why were a particular group of women able to mobilize a 'rationality of care' to resist militarization in one instance and not another?" This type of question too often situates a woman/women as a dependent variable such that while women's perceptions and behaviour may change subject to external manipulation, the subject of analysis (white, middle-class woman) may herself be held reasonably constant. This takes far too much as given: power, interests, women – when it is precisely the ways in which these have been articulated, understood and reassembled that are the object of my investigation. Here, theory and ontology intersect with method, because my approach assumes a particular understanding of the body, one that is inherently plural, such that what may be understood as woman and/or the aims to which this subject is put (including the nebulous aims of care and peace) cannot be held constant. Seen thus, we might understand why Foucault conceptualizes the body as both the material point of power's investment and application, and also always inherently resistant – as it is always both more and less than any singular cultural imprint or understanding (Foucault 1980a, Foucault 1997b, Foucault 1997d, Butler 1989, Stone 2005).

This has important implications. On the one hand, if we take the human body to be inherently resistant – to the extent that it cannot be contained within our social categories and the various purposes to which it is put – we must ask questions of how this unruly matter is made intelligible and useful at all. Following Foucault, the issue is not one of exposing power and liberating the human subject; at issue are "the different modes by which, in our culture, human beings are made subjects" (Foucault 2003b: 126). On the other hand, to the extent that human bodies are also culturally inscribed bodies – subject to various classification schemes, diets, habits, types of work and caring labor, and social and sexual norms – we must ask what it might mean for bodies to talk back within the very discursive frameworks that enable them to be. At the heart of the matter, expressed by Gordon (1980: 255), is the fact that "the human material operated on by programmes and technologies is inherently a resistant material. If this were not the case, history itself would become unthinkable." The moment that Sheehan (2006: x–xi) was, according to her own narrative, reborn (*becoming* a "public peace mom" who would stay silent no longer") and the moment that, in a process of reciprocal recognition, the nation recognized her as "the grieving mother in all of us" (CodePink 2005), the grounds of foreign policy formation and legitimization irrevocably shifted.

The methodological task then is to read IR in terms of the surfacing of bodies and to read the body, in and of itself, as a discursive event. Rather than taking a clash of civilizations or a war between two nations as *the* event, one might begin by asking how a civilization or nation is made body not only at the level of the body-politic, but also at the level of the individual – such that collective bodily formations become lived and material realities in our everyday lives.[5] It is to trace the processes by which culture is imprinted on bodies in ways that *make subject* and to trace the emergence of the particular bodily forms that, at any given time period, come to embody, subvert, and otherwise negotiate predominant cultural meanings and norms. To show that the body is political *all the way down*, not only extends the realm of the political, but also extends the sites wherein IR occurs. If metaphorically, we can still understand foreign policy decision-making as issuances from the *head* of the body politic – as that which acts on its behalf and speaks its name (constituting its inside and outside within the structures of language) – we must nevertheless ask empirical questions about the conditions of possibility that underlie specific foreign policy speech acts. What are the processes by which individual and collective bodies surface in ways that augment, mitigate, and/or in some way fundamentally alter sovereign articulations of nation? To read international relations as a history of bodies is to move beyond relations *between* bodies (the treaties, the ceasefires, and the hostile acts) and to read the emergence of particular bodies with interests, desires, surfaces and intensities as international politics.

Conclusion

When choosing my cases I selected three distinctive and seemingly defining foreign policy moments in U.S. history, spread across three decades. These were moments when, in one form or another, the performative force of the United States was on the line – via its threats or acts of war. For each of these moments, I traced the emergence of the real/imagined maternalized bodies (ranging from the hysterical antinuclear protester in the early to mid-1980s, to the figure of Supermom in the early 1990s, to the rise of Sheehan as leader of an antiwar movement in 2005) who laid claim to or were otherwise positioned within the space of *mothers of the nation*.

There was, however, nothing straightforward about the occupation of this space – as both its status and the status of those occupying it was both contested and always better imagined than lived by the actual bodies who have to inhabit several sites, desires, and discourses at once. But, I argue that it is precisely for this reason that we can map something of the workings and limits of sovereign representation and indeed sovereignty's performative force as it is constituted and contested by those who literally and metaphorically give it life. What emerges from the research project is precisely the instability of the grounds of sovereign representation, but also and contrary to some feminist analyses, the limitations of dichotomized under-standings of the relationship between the female body and the military state. While such constructed dichotomies can be and have been powerfully employed to challenge various forms of militarization, they also work to limit understanding of the ways in which women are militarized and the significant ways in which practices of care are entangled in sovereign violence. My research suggests that reading the maternalized body as a political event unsettles sovereign logics of representation not by pointing to an inherent contradiction between the violent aims of the military state and the life-affirming practices of women, but by highlighting their points of mutual constitution and simultaneous disruption.

Notes

1   The critical inquiry summarized here is the product of the research design and theoretical framework that has informed the research conducted in my book (2012).
2   The concept of bodies that "surface" is a concept I take from Ahmed (2004b).
3   This is not to suggest that non-white, non-middle-class women do not have to negotiate hegemonic articulations of "American motherhood" and "reasons of state"; clearly, they do. It is, however, to point to "American motherhood" as a classed and raced construct, variously intertwined with *reasons of state* – and one that is accessed through enactments of race and class (constituting these and nation, in turn). For more, see Managhan (2012).
4   The point should perhaps be emphasized that unlike some texts within the literature on "women and militarization", the primary intention of this study is not to trace the effects of mothering discourses and/or militarization *on* white, middle-class women as though these bodies might somehow precede the discourses and practices through which they emerge. For more, see Managhan (2012).
5   I take the phrase "made body" from Susan Bordo, who is quoting Pierre Bourdieu, in Bordo (1989: 13).

Suggested reading

Ahmed, S. (2004b) *The Cultural Politics of Emotion*, New York: Routledge.
Butler, J. (1999) *Gender Trouble: Feminism and the Subversion of Identity*, New York: Routledge.
Foucault, M. (1997b) "Nietzsche, Genealogy, History", in D.F. Bouchard (ed.) *Language, Counter-Memory, Practice*, Ithaca: Cornell University Press.
Foucault, M. (2003a) "Questions of Method", in P. Rabinow and N. Rose (eds) *The Essential Foucault*, New York: The New Press.
Stone, A. (2005) "Towards a Genealogical Feminism: A Reading of Judith Butler's Political Thought", *Contemporary Political Theory*, 4(1): 4–24.

28 Corporeal migration

Tarja Väyrynen

Introduction

L: *There isn't a life for us in Bosnia anymore. It's a free country but we don't have any freedom. A gypsy isn't respected anywhere. And my children [. . .]* [cutting her throat with her hand] *are afraid.* [showing her crossed wrists as in handcuffs]. *They are scared that if they return they will be butchered. I don't have anything else to say.*

I: *During your basic interview you told that you never went abroad. Can you confirm that?*

L: *I can't remember. I don't remember. I swear to you. I swear on the life of all my children.*

I: *Nevertheless, you have a child who was born in Berlin. This isn't insignificant. And you have another child who was born in another state. Which country?*

L: *I don't remember. I can't remember.* [lifting her hand high up, hitting the air] *12 years ago or more, I was in Germany. Oh my God, phew.* [shrugging and drawing away from the table]

I: *It's a shame that you don't cooperate more in this procedure.*

In the scene described above, a Bosnian family has lodged an asylum claim at the refugee registration and processing centre in the Swiss town of Vallorbe[1] and now they are heard in order to establish the validity of their claim. The dialogue takes place between a middle-aged Bosnian woman and a migration official. The scene can be read as an attempt of the migration official to categorize the migrant's body in order to find its proper place in the national order of things where there are clear-cut distinctions between those who belong in the body politic of the state and those who can be cast outside (Malkki 1995). The categorizing process proves to be difficult as the Bosnian lady interrupts the smooth functioning of the official power by refusing to make a coherent claim and acting offended when the interviewer does not believe her. The woman's corporeal choreography, affective and somatic enactment, is rich and it indicates her outright disapproval of the hearing.

For me and my interdisciplinary research group,[2] mundane scenes like this have come to form a core for critical research design that examines how the migrant's body is not solely a target of governmental practices, but also political and capable of politics (Shinko, Chapter 26). After having done empirical fieldwork among asylum seekers, paperless immigrants, refugees, skilled migrants, and migration officials we started to wonder why International Relations has been so indifferent towards the micropractices of power and resistance that can be read from the type of scenes described above. For us, the encounters open up a rich field of research material on the "corporeal choreographies" (Puumala and Pehkonen 2010) that characterize the migrant's corporeal interface with the representatives of sovereign power.

Theoretical categories of corporeality, agency, choreography, and the political have come to inform us as we seek to bring International Relations (IR) to visit this interzone, i.e., the body-space that is not only constraining or conditioning, but also enabling and transformable (Nancy 2008).

By examining migration as a corporeal and embodied phenomenon it is possible to show that the migrant's body is a highly political site on which different forces, e.g. the international system of sovereign states, the practices of migration governance, population control, inscribe their marks. Critical IR often relies on Foucault's (1980a, 2009) and Agamben's (1993, 1998, 1999) theorizing when it looks at migration and its control. If the migrant's body is seen from the Foucauldian perspective, the body's yielding to the practices of power is emphasized. In this critical corpus of IR scholarship, it is argued that the techniques of control are constitutive of the materialization of the power of the nation-state. The focus is often on the biometric techniques of surveillance that transform nation-states to biometric states where extreme *identity management* takes place. The migrant's body in this branch of study is seen largely as a target of control, although the productive function of power is also recognized: the securing of populations requires surveillance and the accumulation and analysis of data concerning migrants' bodies and behaviour.[3]

When the migrant's body is examined from the Agambenian perspective, it is always already caught in the deployment of power, which is why it is a biopolitical body, bare life. Agamben evokes the notion of *homo sacer* that denotes a naked life that is depoliticized. *Homo sacer* is the excess of processes of political constitution that create a governable form of life. *Homo sacer* is thus exempt or excluded from the normal limits of the state. At the same time, however, *homo sacer* is not simply cast out but is held in particular relation to the norm: it is through the exclusion of the depoliticized form of life that the politicized norm exists. The migrant's body plays an important part in this process where the body of the citizen is heavily prioritized over other bodies.[4]

Following our fieldwork, we arrived at a critical stance where the Foucauldian emphasis on political technologies of control proved to be insufficient. As Diprose et al. (2008: 274–275) argue, the view fails to articulate the ways both human and non-human material life contest regimes of governance and control. In a similar vein, the means of opposition to the functioning and demands of sovereign power are scarce in Agamben's thought. His emphasis on sovereign power and the camp as a space where human life becomes depoliticized and politicized simultaneously offers few possibilities for thinking the value, or even the possibility, of migrants' bodies as political actors – particularly when their bodies are categorized as belonging to the subcategories of refugees or asylum seekers.[5]

The notion of *choreography* is vital for us to construct a research design that appreciates the corporeal practices of migrants' bodies as well as the forces that inscribe the bodies, while simultaneously focusing on the micropractices of power and resistance. Choreography implies non-linear embodied relationality, extending and reaching out towards others. When theorizing bodily movements in these terms it is possible to seek political agency in acts and places where it often is not found. Choreography assists us in the envisioning of spaces for political agency that do not simply pre-exist, but are articulated through bodies' movements. In this version of choreography, the body resists pre-definitions of political agency in terms of fixed categories. Choreography then suggests that even the motionless and silent body is always not only eventually in motion, but also already in "movement-with" its surroundings (Puumala and Pehkonen 2010, Puumala et al. 2011, Manning 2007, 2009).

The migrant body's fractional and mundane choreographies that refuse to move become firmly and unambiguously located at the centre of our research design. The state seeks to take over the body and create a hierarchical bond of reciprocity, whilst in the processes of exscription the body starts to create and relate to other bodies and worlds containing a possibility of speaking or acting back to the governmentality (Nancy 2008). Hence the theoretical research questions we ask concern: how do bodies relate to other bodies? How is the migrant's body a site of the political when it becomes a target of governmental practices? How does the body find its subtle ways of resisting the practices of control? We examine how the embodied agency of the migrant is not only in relation or opposed to governmental body politics, but also moves beyond this framework.

When migration is studied as an embodied phenomenon where the focus is on the body and its choreographies, purely textual analysis or a focus only on administrative rationality is bound to offer limited tools for the analysis of governmentality. This is bound to leave out possible variations and expressions of political agency. We start our research design with an understanding of discourse that accommodates both the statements produced through the programmes and rationalities of governmentality and the everyday operations of power that take part in the inscription and exscription of the migrant's body. In order to examine the micro-politics of everyday encounters we rely on ethnography, and particularly the critical and activist variants of it.

We try to avoid the naïve understanding of ethnography that reduces ethnography to data collection, a style of writing, or simplified sensibility to the details of everyday action (Vrasti 2008) by establishing three procedures that guarantee its validity. First, we always embed the research in discourse analysis that works on public texts in search of "the rules governing what can be said and what not" (Wæver 2002: 26–29). Although our research may look like it arises out of empirical fieldwork, the first – and often the most tedious – part of the research concerns mapping out the conditions under which something can be said about the migrating body. Second, the ethical-political issues related to the research procedures and writing are clearly spelled out in our research. We are aware of the asymmetrical relations of domination and subordination of our research setting as well as of the possibility to contest, challenge, and negotiate them. In other words, we locate the "work in the inherently political connections between selves and others" (Bleiker and Brigg 2010: 785). Third, our aim is to think radically about the foundational categories that bind, discipline, and normalize the mode of inquiry in IR. We are particularly interested in re-thinking the category of the international and the limits it sets for our political imagination concerning mobile bodies.

In this type of research design, a richer variety of research material such as narrative interviews, documentary films, policy documents, participant observation and field notes, photographs, poetry, graffiti is needed, as it provides a means to approach the multi-sitedness of the object researched. The design calls forth a form of ethnographic fieldwork where fields can be fuzzy and consist of different sets of research materials. According to Marcus (1995, 1998), this kind of multi-sited ethnography is mobile and it moves out from the single sites and local situations of conventional research designs, so as to examine the circulation of cultural meanings, objects, and identities, and in our case also bodies, in diffuse time-space. In this methodological tradition, the researcher spells out his or her subject position, hence not pretending to have an authorized and original knowledge of the object examined.[6] Given our interest in imagining and articulating possibilities for *what has never been*, our research design has elements of activist ethnography too: we collaborate with research subjects in order to rethink possibilities for agency and action.

The researchers in our research group have worked in a registration and processing centre (participant observation); interviewed migrants in their temporary shelters and camps, homes, work places and asylum centres; worked with and interviewed migration officials;

contributed to transnational NGO work; organized meetings between the migrants and officials; and written policy reports. Hence a substantial set of research material that includes field notes, interviews, policy reports, and photographs has been accumulated. This material has been complemented with documentary films, novels, poems, and visual art. We believe that all this material carries with it many sites of connotation and meanings that allow multiple, and even contradictory interpretations (Gadamer 1979). Our task as researchers is to establish a dialogue between the material and us and demonstrate the steps of our interpretative processes. Furthermore, many of the connotations are felt, particularly in the visual material, rather than recognized or perceived through cognition (Bennett 2005b, Bleiker and Brigg 2010, Möller 2007), and it is often this affect that throws us into the unknown that allows us to rethink the multiple relationships between the governmental practices, the migrant body, and its political agency.

Conclusion

Our research design seeks to study migrants' bodies and their affective and somatic political agency. In terms of reproducibility, our research design calls for double contextualization. First, the researcher maps out the discursive domain within which something can be said about the migrating body in the chosen case. Second, the researcher enters to the field and locates his or her body in relation to the bodies examined. A variety of research material is needed in order to grasp the corporeal choreographies and affective and somatic enactments from which the migrant body's political agency emerges. This kind of corporeal approach requires constant awareness of the researcher's own ethical-political choices, namely reflexive disposition, which often leads to close collaboration with the research subjects.

Notes

1   The dialogue is adopted from director and producer Fernand Melgar's documentary film *The Fortress* (*La Forteresse* 2008).
2   The research group consists of researchers Anitta Kynsilehto, Samu Pehkonen, Eeva Puumala, and Tiina Vaittinen.
3   See Bell 2006, Bigo 2002, Ceyhan and Tsoukala 2002, Dauphinee and Masters 2006, Dillon 2007, Dillon and Lobo-Guerrero 2008, Dillon and Reid 2001, Edkins et al. 2004, Elbe 2008, Huysmans 2006, Rajaram and Grundy-Warr 2007, Salter 2004, 2006, 2007, Security Dialogue 2008 and Soguk 1999.
4   See Rajaran and Grundy-Warr 2004, Epstein 2007, Norris 2000, Pugliese 2002.
5   See Agier 2008, Edkins 2000, Edkins and Pin-Fat 2005, Squire 2009, Sylvester 2006.
6   See Ackerly et al. 2006, Jutila et al. 2008, *Review of International Studies* 2010, Vrasti 2008, Wedeen 2010.

Suggested reading

Ackerly, B.A., Stern, M. and True, J. (eds) (2006) *Feminist Methodologies for International Relations*, Cambridge: Cambridge University Press.
Behar, R. (1996) *The Vulnerable Observer: Anthropology That Breaks Your Heart*, Boston: Beacon Press.
Bennett, J. (2005b) *Empathic Vision: Affect, Trauma, and Contemporary Art*, Stanford: Stanford University Press.
Marcus, G. (1998) *Ethnography through Thick and Thin*, Princeton: Princeton University Press.
"Forum on Autoethnography and International Relations" (2010), *Review of International Studies*, 36(4): 777–818.

Part VI

The material turn

Introduction

Can E. Mutlu

Objects have a social life that expands beyond their material existence. In Bennett's (2010) words, objects have *thing-power*. They are central to our identities; we practise and perform our identities through objects. Soldiers use weapons; air traffic controllers rely on their radar; cab drivers have cars; programmers use computers. Objects play a central role in these repetitive performativities; they define and mediate our relationships with our core identities and practices. The material turn, as an emerging research agenda, looks at the co-productive relationship between the origins and everyday functioning of objects while tracing the transformation of their purpose and justification. In particular, we look at the agency of actants in three instances of security practices: emergence, continuity, and transformation. Some of the driving questions of the approach challenge the constructive and destructive power of objects, their centrality to socio-political life of human societies, and the ecology of these objects as actants in security economies.

The material turn we are presenting in this chapter looks at the social and political lives of objects. In particular, we look at the mediating and constitutive role of security objects in shaping assemblages consisting of actors and networks. This emergent research agenda in critical security studies is pertinent for scholars with research projects studying the role of objects, at the intersection of identities, practices, and materialities, in shaping networks.

Object analysis, as a research method, is central to the material turn presented in this chapter. The central question for this kind of research is: what is the role of a given object in shaping social relations? In return, two concepts help us answer this question: actants and agency.

Actants are material mediators between actors *that act* and systems *that behave*. Based on Actor Network Theory (ANT), a branch of Science and Technology Studies (STS) primarily developed by Callon (1986), Latour (2005), and Law and Hassard (1999), the *actant* concept looks at the mediating role of objects in how material-somatic networks come to exist and act together. In particular, STS scholars place their emphasis on the agency of objects through

Table PVI.1 Research design in material cultures

Object	Material objects, assemblage of human and non-human actants
Key concepts	Actants (material mediators between actors and systems), agency (capacity of a thing/person to impact its surrounding)
Collection	Tracing, discourse analysis, mapping, participant observation
Data	Objects, infrastructure, networks, technologies
Relations	Emergence, continuity, transformation
Fit	Networks that include practices and objects

their mediational role. By an object's agency, they refer to its capacity to operationalize associated discourses, fields, and practices.

Similar to other approaches covered in this book, the material turn and its key concepts also have their origins elsewhere in sociology and political theory. There are two emerging patterns of studying the material turn in social science and humanities: (1) the ANT approach; and (2) the philosophical approach that looks at the "ecology of things" (Bennett 2010). These approaches differ in two aspects: the way they conceptualize the agency of objects, and the way they measure the impact of objects.

On the one hand, STS scholars primarily focus on the *mediating* role of objects in scientific spaces such as the laboratory (Latour and Woolgar 1979), or fish farms (Callon 1986), and the role of technology in managing epidemics such as the foot and mouth outbreak in the UK (Law and Mol 2011). In this approach, material objects are not placed in a dualism in relation to other actors and systems. Instead, objects function as nodes that mediate the interaction between actors and systems. On the other hand, the philosophical approach of Barad (1998, 2003, 2007) and Bennett (2004, 2010) focuses on the relations of objects with each other and their physical surroundings. In this perspective, the social agency of actants is measured through their potential impact on their surroundings. Unlike STS, the philosophical approach places its emphasis on the distinction between humans and non-humans by highlighting the agency of both and placing them in a dualist relationship. Bennett's account of the 2003 electrical blackout in Canada and the American northeast is a good example of this distinction; she highlights the agency of non-human actants, by arguing that "the elements of this assemblage [the electricity grid], while they include humans and their (social, legal, linguistic) constructions, also include some *very active* and *powerful* nonhumans: electrons, trees, wind, fire, electromagnetic fields" (2010: 24, emphasis added).

Both approaches make forceful yet different contributions to the methods of social inquiry that we have covered in this book. The ANT approach contributes to the debates on the identity/performativity/practice nexus. By suggesting the placing of emphasis on the agency of objects as a mediator between actors and systems, the ANT approach bridges the divide between corporeal and practice-driven approaches covered in this book. Latour and Woolgar argue that "it is not simply that phenomena depend on certain material instrumentation; rather the phenomena are *thoroughly constituted* by the material setting [. . .] the artificial reality, which participants describe in terms of an objective entity, has in fact been constructed by the use of inscription devices" (quoted in Law 2004: 21). While complimentary to both corporeal and practical approaches, the material turn also presents a strong critique of these approaches for omitting the agency of objects from their analysis. Similarly, the philosophical approach makes a point on the attribution of agency. Scholars of this canon look at the constitutive role of non-human agency in shaping their environment. This approach also presents a direct challenge to corporeal, ethnographic, and field/practice-driven approaches that exclusively focus on human agency.

These approaches present a strong challenge for the critical security studies scholars in the decades to come. From the ANT perspective, the challenge is to focus on the mediating role of objects. Whereas the security discipline has focused on the role of bodies, emotions, events, practices, and technologies in shaping (in)securities, it has, for the most part, ignored the objects through which these actions are made possible. From the philosophical perspective, the challenge is to broaden the object and subject of security practices even further beyond the state/human division. Whereas one of the original goals of critical security studies was to broaden the focus of agency to include different levels of analysis such as human and societal security, it has not broadened the discipline's vista to extend agency to objects.

Acknowledging the distinctions between these two approaches and then clearly selecting to use one should be the first step in doing a research project that focuses on the material turn, grounding the research in one of these two traditions.

In terms of methods, object analysis uses a combination of discourse analysis, mapping, and participant observation to trace the genealogy and quotidian uses of security objects. Once again, the specific method that we can use depends on the approach we want to take: ANT or philosophical? Each approach presents a different set of challenges and short-comings. Whereas the ANT approach is comprehensive and meticulous in its data collection through participant observation (Latour and Woolgar 1979), similar to the difficulties of ethnographical research, successful application of this approach involves a level of scholarly embeddedness that undoubtedly tests material limits – financial and temporal – of a research project. Similarly, as Salter's (Chapter 17) discussion of access into security fields in this book demonstrates, the level of inside access required in conducting an in-depth research on security objects is often very difficult, if not impossible, due to the imposed secrecy of these procedures.

The research from the philosophical perspective, while contributing to the conceptualization of an ecology or *dispositif* of actants, often fails to meet the challenge of methodological rigour imposed by the positivist canon. Measurement of social agency through potential impact of objects on their surroundings generally fails to meet the positivistic rigour for two directly related reasons: first, the philosophical approach is event driven – we cannot measure the agency of objects prior to their impact on their surroundings; and second, the fact that their agency has to be measured by us, humans, undermines the very dualism established by this approach – what counts as non-human agency is measured through their interference with human agency. In other words, based on this approach, there is no non-human agency, beyond its interaction with human agency. Bennett (2010) answers this question through her "willingness to theorize events (a blackout, a meal, an imprisonment in chains, an experience of litter) as encounters between ontologically diverse actants, some human, some not, though all thoroughly material" (xiv). In other words, rather than engaging with this line of criticism based on the binary upon which it is based, Bennett argues for an ontological shift in perception that regards human and non-human actants alike as *material* actants. As Bennett also acknowledges, however, objects have agency beyond human cognition, "since they do in fact affect other bodies, enhancing or weakening their power" (2010: 3). In other words, non-human actants have agency simply because they impact their surroundings.

In this chapter we propose three points that capture important stages of the actor-network relationship as they are mediated by actants or as actants impact their surroundings. These three stages of object analysis are: *emergence*, *continuity*, and *transformation*. *Emergence* is the initial moment an actant is introduced into an actor-network relationship. This moment co-produces the actor-network relationship, as the actant has a constitutive role in mediating this relationship. *Continuity* is the period in which the actant's role is stable and the actor-network interaction is sustained. As mentioned earlier, however, conflict and discrepancies are organic parts of the actor-network relationship. As such, *transformation*, or the re-invention of the system, is inevitable. In other words, unstable systems inevitably breakdown and re-generate, albeit through different alignments and assemblages.

Whereas the positivist critiques of the philosophical approach apply to the emergence stage due to lack of precedence, once we witness the agency of an object based on its effects on its surroundings, we can trace its continuous existence and transformations. These temporal categories are important for both the ANT and philosophical approaches. Object analysis through these three temporal stages allows the material turn to complement corporeal, ethnographic, and practice-driven research projects.

The debate surrounding the installation of backscatter x-rays and millimetre wave units – or full body scanners as they are commonly known – at American airports by the Transport Security Administration (TSA) is a good example to see the value of the material turn. In early 2010, full body scanners were installed in various airports across the United States as a security measure. A more advanced type of airport security technology, full body scanners were introduced as a way to improve aviation security. The TSA, however, faced an almost instant backlash against their use. The seemingly-indistinguishable pictures of human bodies produced by the machine were deemed too intrusive of personal privacy and generally unethical; the images were compared to pornography. Similarly, exposure to radiation was also listed as a concern.

The full-body scanner presents a case-study that can be studied from multiple perspectives covered in this book: field-analysis (looking at the competition within and among different fields resulting in their implementation and subsequent reactions), practice-driven (looking at the practices involved in aviation security), ethnographic research (looking at the quotidian practices of airport security), and corporeal approaches (focusing on the somatic and emotional subjectivities). The material turn, however, provides an insight that bridges most of these approaches by shifting the exclusive focus of agency away from human actants and looks at the agency and the mediational role of the non-human actant scanners.

In this particular case, by introducing these machines, the TSA introduced a new *non-human* actant into a previously existing eco-system – the mobility security assemblage at the airport. From the philosophical perspective, the reaction of human actants to the introduction of this new technology is the moment of *emergence*. Whereas, as scholars did not know the impact of this non-human actant on its surroundings prior to its introduction, once it was introduced, it became a legitimate object of analysis with an impact on its surroundings. Focusing on the backscatter x-rays and millimetre wave units bridges the divide between the corporeal – bodies and emotions – the discursive – policy and public – and the practical – airport security practices – aspects of an airport security operation. As such, as a node within the *ecology* of actants, the full-body scanner presents an opening, or a point of departure to observe the everyday activities of airport security.

Full-body scanners, however, are one of the many objects that operationalize and mediate everyday security practices. Aradau (2010), on critical infrastructure, and Walters (2011), on e-passports elsewhere, are both exemplary works on object analysis that combine theoretical openness and reflexivity with clarity and methodological vigour. In critical security studies, researchers using this approach can focus on the social life of security objects such as CCTV cameras, walls and barriers, material manifestations of crime prevention through spatial design (CPTED), critical infrastructures, biometric identity systems in identification documents such as passports, lethal and non-lethal weapons, networks, databases, and other various technologies used in everyday governance of security. More specifically, this approach is most suitable for research projects that focus on the *byproducts* of security, such as objects, infrastructure, networks, technologies of security: the actual material *things* that are being secured and used in the act of securing.

Within this book we see six chapters that fit well with the concept of material turn. Aradau looks at the construction of critical infrastructure as an object of insecurity (Chapter 29). Shah's chapter looks at the role of Internet *protocols*, as a combination of rules, norms, and practices that shape the everyday functioning of the Internet as a material network consisting of cables, routers, and computers (Chapter 30). Grondin's chapter on Unmanned Aerial

Vehicles (UAV) looks at the construction of drones as objects of warfare (Chapter 31). Anaïs' chapter, discussed below, deals with non-lethal weapons and how they shape common conceptions of the battlefield (Chapter 32). Vuori engages with the semiotic perception of objects in his analysis of the Doomsday Clock of Atomic Scientists in his study of macro-securitization moves (Chapter 33). Voelkner examines how the traces of human security are dispersed through international institutions, local governmental institutions, and non-governmental organizations (Chapter 34).

Examples

Along with Anaïs' chapter on non-lethal weapons in this book (Chapter 32), we present short summaries of Bennett's book *Vibrant Matter: A Political Ecology of Things* (2010) and Matthew Paterson's *Automobile Politics: Ecology and Cultural Political Economy* (2007) as good examples of research that use the material turn.

Anaïs's chapter on non-lethal weapons is one of the clearest articulations of object analysis in this book; as such it deserves particular attention. In Anaïs' work, non-lethal weapons refer to *devices* such as tear gas, electrical stun technologies, kinetic impact weapons, and rubber bullets. She uses non-lethal weapons as a departure point to study the complex linkages between "technology, security, the governance of insecurity, and broader regimes of governance" (Chapter 32). In particular, her excellent analysis makes sense of "spatio-temporal contact zones where objects, devices, ideas, and human beings become entangled, locating non-lethal weapons within a web of events, accidents, and contingencies" (Chapter 32). She pays particular attention to politically and historically contextualizing non-lethal weapons by following the *life story* of non-lethal weapons. The emphasis on non-lethal weapons as objects allows for a traceable *mapping* that combines genealogical research with

Table PVI.2 Examples of material cultures research design

	Anaïs, Non-Lethal Weapons	*Bennett,* Vibrant Matter	*Paterson,* Automobile Politics
Object	Non-lethal weapons	Non-human actants: the electricity grip, the garbage dump, etc.	The automobile
Collection	Archival research, critical discourse analysis	Discourse analysis, ethnographic research	Archival research, discourse analysis, field analysis, and mapping
Data	Policy documents, patents, secondary literature	Field research, newspapers, interviews, policy documents, and participant observation	Policy documents, secondary literature, and field research
Relations	Relations between discourses and practices of non-lethal weapons	Untangling a complex web of actors, systems, and networks by focusing on a single "actant"	Deconstruction of different discourses of ecology, mobility, and political economy
Fit	Political and historical contextualization of non-lethal weapons by following their "life story"	Establishing the material agency of non-human actants: natural bodies and technological artifacts	Focus on a single object of (auto)mobility to make broader claims about cultural political economy

practice-driven analysis. In other words, Anaïs' use of non-lethal weapons as her central point of analysis allows her to deconstruct the complex web of discourses, practices, feelings, and identities that are central to the social structures surrounding these objects. As a point of departure, then, these objects present a fixed point upon which she builds her research project.

Bennett's *Vibrant Matter* focuses on the agency of matter. As a project, *Vibrant Matter* is an ambitious philosophical project aiming to re-interpret the meaning of materiality beyond the tradition of *historical materialism* of the Hegel-Marx-Adorno axis. Instead, Bennett pushes for a "public value in following the scent of a nonhuman, thingly power, the material agency of natural bodies and technological artifacts" (Bennett 2010: xiii). In short, using Latour's terminology of *actants* Bennett sets out to describe the agency of non-human *things* beyond their relationship to humans. This approach has sparked a debate on the ontological significance of "vitality of matter and the lively powers of material formations" (Bennett 2010: vii) in political philosophy. In the book, Bennett's analysis is grounded in a number of case studies – the electricity grid, metals, and stem cells, among other *vital matters*. In each case, Bennett's object-analysis allows her to untangle a complex web of actors, systems, and networks by focusing on a single *actant*. In terms of her practical methodology, she gathers her data from field research, primary documents, interviews, and participant observation; she relies on a combination of discourse and ethnographic analysis to get through the data. In critical security studies, her work found resonance in scholars working on critical infra-structure (Aradau 2010, Coward 2009, Lundborg and Vaughan-Williams 2011) especially in relation to her articulations on the vitality of networks as complex assemblages consisting of numerous non-human actants. Bennett's philosophical approach to the agency of matter provides an elaborate theoretical framework that is compatible with the existing literature on the ANT and the broader material turn.

The object-driven analysis presented in this section is an emergent research agenda in IR in general and critical security studies in particular. There are, however, some exceptions to this. Paterson's *Automobile Politics* (2007) is one of the exemplary accounts of the material turn perspective. In Paterson's analysis, "cars act as a 'vehicle'" (Paterson 2007: 24) for linking debates in different fields of analysis. In other words, Paterson's focus on the automobile as an object of mobility allows him to map out a complex analysis that touches on environmental politics, international political economy, and poststructuralist approaches to IR; the car, as the object of his analysis, is central to the analysis of more general themes of (auto)mobility – the emergence of car dominated societies – environmental politics – the green movement – and cultural political economy – the culture of car ownership. One of Paterson's core contributions to his field of study is his attempt to bring back material practices as a legitimate object of study. Given the centrality of material elements in environmental change, he argues that omitting them from the analysis is shortsighted. He argues that the scholarly work on environmental politics should "start with an account of the individual and collective subjects, and the political institutions, structures and discourses [. . .] which is abstracted from the material practices of their everyday lives which are principal immediate sources of environmental change" (Paterson 2007: 15–6). In his analysis, Paterson uses policy documents, secondary literature, and field research as his data. In return, he successfully uses discourse analysis, field analysis, and mapping to make a compelling argument about the cultural political economy (auto)mobility.

Conclusion

The recent practice turn in IR has presented an opportunity towards more methodologically reproducible research for post-structuralist scholars. Along with the practice turn, the material turn presents an alternative to the agency/structure binary that is central to the IR discipline. Increased dialogue between sociology, a discipline that had its fair share of methodological debates a decade earlier, and IR has led to the fertile and vibrant International Political Sociology (IPS) approach. One of the emerging approaches within the IPS community is the material turn in IR. The material turn is based on the understanding that objects are central to our identities; as such, they are central to our practices.

Object analysis presents a method for studying the agency of objects. As such, it is a starting point for a radical reorganization of our social hierarchies, one that recognizes both human and non-human actants as agents of impacting our social world. Within the broader field of IR, the material turn presents an opening for studying circulations and mobilities beyond the specific focus on *regimes*. As such, we are starting to see theoretically informed and methodologically vigorous projects on material aspects of currency circulation (de Goede 2012) and migration and mobility (Walters 2011). Given the *a priori* emphasis on (in)security practices within critical security studies, analysis of insecurity objects presents an opportunity for a methodological study of insecurity practices. As observable nodes in a complex system of variables, objects are invaluable for the critical security studies.

Building on this potential, this chapter provided a brief introduction to two related approaches to the study of material turn: the ANT and philosophical approaches. While these approaches differ in some of their practices, they both position themselves in such a manner that studies the agency of matter beyond its economical value. In particular, we paid attention to two different types of agency measures through mediation and direct impact. These approaches allow us to look at the co-productive relationship between the origins and everyday functioning of objects while tracing the transformation of their purpose and justification. As such, the material turn will play a central role in the increasing of methodological rigour in critical security studies in the decades to come.

Suggested reading

Barad, K. (2003) "Posthumanist Performativity: Toward an Understanding of How Matter Comes To Matter", *Signs: Journal of Women in Culture and Society*, 28(3): 801–831.

Barad, K. (2007) *Meeting the Universe Halfway: Quantum Physics and the Entanglement of Matter and Meaning*, Durham: Duke University Press.

Bennett, J. (2004) "The Force of Things: Steps Toward an Ecology of Matter", *Political Theory*, 32(3): 347–372.

Bennett, J. (2010) *Vibrant Matter: A Political Ecology of Things*, Durham: Duke University Press.

Callon, M. (1986) "Some Elements of a Sociology of Translation: Domestication of the Scallops and the Fishermen of St. Brieuc Bay", in J. Law (ed.) *Power, Action and Belief: A New Sociology of Knowledge*, New York: Routledge.

Latour, B. (1987) *Science in Action*, Cambridge: Harvard University Press.

Latour, B. (2005) *Reassembling the Social: an Introduction to Actor-Network-Theory*, New York: Oxford University Press.

Law, J. and Hassard J. (eds) (1999) *Actor Network Theory and After*, Oxford: Blackwell.

Law, J. and Singleton, V. (2005) "Object lessons", *Organization*, 12(3): 331–355.

Paterson, M. (2007) *Automobile Politics: Ecology and Cultural Political Economy*, Cambridge: Cambridge University Press.

29 Infrastructure[1]

Claudia Aradau

Introduction

Action to combat terrorism has increasingly mobilized attention to things: liquids in airports, critical infrastructure protection, products in shopping bags, circulation of money, building design, architectural plans, databases, flight tickets, and so on. All these objects do not simply inform counter-terrorism responses but also produce the *globality* of terrorism. Among the objects that have recently emerged as privileged targets of terrorism and sites of vulnerability are locales of critical infrastructure. "Terrorists seek to destroy, incapacitate, or exploit critical infrastructure and key resources across the United States to threaten national security, cause mass casualties, weaken our economy, and damage public morale and confidence", noted a Homeland Security Presidential Directive in 2003 (DHS 2003). Since then, terrorist attacks in London, Madrid, and Mumbai have prioritized *critical infrastructure* on the international security agenda. Agencies and experts strive to select, locate, and define critical infrastructure among the socio-economic infrastructures of a country, region, or sub-region. "Which infrastructures are critical and to be protected from terrorist attacks and which are not?", ask counter-terrorism experts. At the same time that critical infrastructures have emerged as an object of insecurity given their vulnerability to terrorist attacks, we have witnessed numerous infrastructures collapsing across the world: Hurricane Katrina in the US brought to international attention the decaying state of urban infrastructure, the lack of funds and the role of material resources in the differential chances of survival of populations facing disasters (Elliott and Pais 2006, Graham 2006). Moreover, many areas of the world lack the infrastructures taken for granted in counter-terrorism policy as support for urban and social life.

How to study the materiality of critical infrastructure in the securitization of terrorism? International Relations (IR) students often start their analyses – the way I have started this brief discussion – with discourses of security professionals, or, to use the terminology of the Copenhagen School, with securitizing speech acts. Others start with practices and consider the governance of critical infrastructure and its effects. In this way, it is possible to analyze the rationalities that have propelled critical infrastructure to the height of security agendas. It is also possible to analyze the policy and media discourses that constitute infrastructures as endangered as well as the subjects – humans or networks – that endanger them. The method adopted is dependent on the theoretical approach adopted and the research question one formulates. Different chapters in this book take some of these different positions: analyzing discourse (Shah, Chapter 30, Anaïs, Chapter 32), images (Vuori, Chapter 33), and genealogy (Grondin, Chapter 31).

What I was interested in was how to analyze things in a critical way without falling back upon a positivist separation between reality and language, or assuming the predominance of representation over materiality. Although analyses of security and risk have incorporated discussions of technologies and institutions, non-human objects have been relegated outside the realm of securitization, either as simply *facilitating* conditions for securitization (Buzan et al. 1998), or as remnants of mainstream positivism. Even the literature drawing on Foucault's notion of the dispositif has been less interested in the role that objects played in the definition of the security dispositif (Aradau and van Munster 2007, 2011, Dillon 2008, Dillon and Lobo-Guerrero 2008). Discussions of rationalities, technologies, and subjec-tivities in the governance of security did not lead to an engagement with the role of "things" in security constructions.

My question was then how to analyze the status of objects in processes of securitization in ways that do not subsume them to discourse? How can we make sense of the securitization of critical infrastructure in the war on terror? I addressed these questions in an article published in 2010 (Aradau 2010).

As the first section has started to outline, research questions emerge out of the intersection of theoretical and practical discordances. On the one hand, my questions were sparked by the prominence critical infrastructure had gained in counter-terrorism policies. On the other, there was little debate in security studies about the materiality of critical infrastructures. When materiality played an active role within IR theory – from realist debates about capabilities to Marxist discussions about resources in the war on terror – it appeared as separated from the discursive, or it was subsumed to ideas, values, and policy and media discourses. Placing the question within the IR literature also made clear two methodological precautions. First, not to revert upon a positivist understanding of materiality which is at the heart of many discussions of materiality. Materiality can be used in a sense reminiscent of a positivist ontology, as in many expert reports on critical infrastructure protection. "Not all infrastructures can be protected from all threats. For example, electricity transmission networks are too large to fence or guard", notes a European Commission Communication (European Commission 2004). Second, not to analyze materiality as simply socially or discursively constructed. Materiality often risks being folded back upon either static physicality or social conditions. By consequence language is seen as establishing a relation of adequacy with these *foundations* or *conditions*. Therefore, in analyzing the materialization of critical infrastructures in counter-terrorism it is important to privilege neither discourse nor objects as separate entities but to analyze them relationally, as processes.

How to think about research design? I would like to argue that there is not a recipe for a method to study materiality critically. Methods develop in close relation to theoretical approaches, epistemological positions, and empirical problems. Method, Rancière (2009) has argued, can be seen as a path that one constructs rather than a path that is pre-given and one follows. You will find in the research design discussed here some overlap with the methods used in other chapters in this section. You will also see that I have widely relied on documents – policy documents, media discourses, social scientific and scientific texts, and parliamentary debates. Yet, these have been used in different ways to make sense of the theoretical conceptualizations I was working with and the empirical problem of critical infrastructure.

How to set out studying the materiality of infrastructure? I started with a different conceptualization of materiality, which had been inspired by Barad's work (2007). Barad is a feminist physicist who has been writing on questions of language and materiality, and political agency. Barad was particularly interesting as she proposed not to think of things, objects, or materiality but to analyze processes of materialization. Hers is one approach among other theoretical approaches that have turned an analytical eye to the existence and role of materiality. Bennett, Latour, Law, Mol, Bakker, Mitchell, and Barry are a few of the scholars who have focused on objects and materiality in their work across the political theory, sociology, or geography. While close to Foucault's notion of the dispositif or Bennett's reworking of the concept of assemblage, Barad's analysis of discursive material entanglement is not exactly the same as the emergence and stabilization of a dispositif that brings together heterogeneous elements. For Barad, objects are dynamically produced through intra-action and are open to rearticulation and reshaping. This recognition is derived from Bohr's acknowledgment that the nature of light (waves or particles) depends on the apparatus used for its observation (Barad 1998: 90). Barad's approach was particularly interesting as she analyzes discourse and matter as co-constitutive. Objects do not precede subjects or vice-versa – both emerge as particular types of objects or subjects through processes of materialization. In this approach, critical infrastructures emerge through particular discursive material arrangements, which include risk assessment techniques and computer modelling for instance. The particular materialization of critical infrastructure in counter-terrorism can be analyzed both synchronically and diachronically.

I selected four types of documents to analyze the securitization of critical infrastructure: EU reports on critical infrastructure protection; UK parliamentary debates about critical infrastructure protection; newspaper coverage of the terminology of "infrastructure" and "critical infrastructure"; and academic publications by social scientists, computer scientists, and engineers on critical infrastructures.

This selection of materials allowed to me to approach critical infrastructures both synchronically and diachronically. The newspaper coverage from *The Times* database was useful to trace different uses of infrastructure in particular historical contexts. Similarly, accessing social scientific and scientific literature from both before and after 9/11 allowed me to trace changes in how critical infrastructures evolved. While the article did not do a genealogy of critical infrastructure (Grondin, Chapter 31), I have made use of some historical material to indicate changing materializations of infrastructure.

At the same time, selecting a variety of documents that can be largely located post-9/11 allows for an analysis of different materializations of infrastructures. Critical infrastructures are not the same in the EU reports and the UK parliamentary debates. This has consequences for what materializes as protected infrastructures and what not. This also affects the particular infrastructures that are produced or reinforced. For instance, critical infrastructure is materialized as interconnected: gas flows, energy supplies flow, oil flows, transport flows, and so on. It is this interconnectivity of modern infrastructures that is seen to potentially lead to catastrophic failures if a node in this infrastructure is under attack and stops functioning. Integrated circulatory processes appear indeed to be at the heart of the securitization of critical infrastructure, as many security scholars have noted in the wake of Foucault's analysis of biopolitics (Dillon and Reid 2009, Lundborg and Vaughan-Williams 2011). I have argued that the materialization of infrastructure as interconnected, circulating, flows that need to move unimpeded but can be stopped by *bad circulation* (for example, hostile vehicles) effaces the materialities of production. Discussions of electricity in relation to critical infrastructure protection, for example, efface the materialities of energy production, particularly the relation between generation and use (Graham and Thrift 2007). The materialization of energy as simply flow obliterates the material connections that exist in the generation of energy, the nodes and lines contained in the grid, their physical properties and connections. The materialization of infrastructure in critical infrastructure protection also effaces another materialization, in which infrastructure is not adaptable or resilient, but it is slowly degrading, breaking down, in fact disconnected through processes of neoliberalization and privatization.

Tracing these different materializations of infrastructure was made possible by the varied selection of documents. For Barad, materialization implies boundary drawing and a reconfiguration of the world. This insight shaped my research and led me to consider how boundaries are drawn in the securitization of critical infrastructure. In critical infrastructure protection, infrastructures become materialized through their capacity for being disrupted and their effects upon the smooth functioning of society. This materialization misses the processes of degradation, decay, lack of infrastructure, as well as dis-connectivity that under-lies the regular, smooth functioning of most infrastructures.

Why did I use a whole selection of documents to talk about materiality? Is this not a contradiction? As I have argued, the discourse and matter, subject and object are always entangled. Neither pre-exists, rather, both emerge through discursive-material arrangements. Another way to analyze the materialization of critical infrastructure would have been to analyze the instrumentation that is used to designate what counts as critical infrastructure – risk assessments and computer modelling and simulation that treat infrastructures as complex adaptive systems. Or I could have taken a genealogical approach, which focuses on the discontinuities, the contestations, and struggles over the production and extension of infra-structure, their material shape and role in society. Either of these two other methodological approaches would have required more in-depth analysis of processes than was possible to include within the limited space of an article. The methodological precautions and research design outlined in this chapter could be used to analyze the securitization of a whole series of other objects: from the policing of dangerous objects at airports to the use of biometrics for border control, and from the securitization of crowded spaces to that of photography.

Conclusion

The argument about materialization of critical infrastructures in counter-terrorism securi-tization aimed to show other materializations are or have been possible. This was not the only way in which a critique of critical infrastructure protection could be formulated. Lundborg and Vaughan-Williams have recently argued, for instance, that attention needs to be paid to the mistakes, mishaps, and backfires in critical infrastructure protection. Whether it is false positives or absurd lists of critical infrastructures that include a flea market, the materiality of infrastructure, they argue, cannot be contained or controlled. Their approach is inspired by Bennett's theory of the "vitality of matter" (Bennett 2010) and their research focuses on locating these mishaps and backfires within the very process of securitizing infrastructures. While there is always variation in methods and research design, depending on the questions one asks and the theoretical approach one adopts, all these need to be considered in con-junction to construct the path of research.

Note

1 I would like to acknowledge the "Discourses and materialities" cluster (Martin Coward, Eva Herschinger, Nadine Voelkner and Owen Thomas) of the ESRC-funded International Collaboratory on Critical Methods in Security Studies for stimulating a discussion on methods and materiality. I am also grateful to the participants of the workshop on "New Methodologies in Critical Security Studies", Ottawa, 14–15 March 2011.

Suggested reading

Bakker, K. and Bridge, G. (2006) "Material Worlds? Resource Geographies and the 'Matter of Nature'", *Progress in Human Geography*, 30(1): 5–27.

Barad, K. (1998) "Getting Real: Technoscientific Practices and the Materialization of Reality", *Differences: A Journal of Feminist Cultural Studies*, 10(2): 87–128.

Bennett, J. (2004) "The Force of Things: Steps Toward an Ecology of Matter", *Political Theory*, 32(3): 347–372.

Lundborg, T. and Vaughan-Williams, N. (2011) "Resilience, Critical Infrastructure, and Molecular Security: The Excess of 'Life' in Biopolitics", *International Political Sociology*, 5(4): 367–383.

Mitchell, T. (2009) "Carbon Democracy", *Economy and Society*, 38(3): 399–432.

30 The Internet as evocative infrastructure

Nisha Shah

Introduction

The Internet is often viewed as a material infrastructure facilitating contemporary globalization. Its decentralized and distributed networks of routers, cables, and servers, enabling the unprecedented volume and speed to the circulation of goods, peoples, and ideas, are said to contribute to the transformation of political order from a system of sovereign territorial states to a novel planetary community (Castells 2001, Friedman 2005, Nye 2011, 2004).

Infrastructures, however, are never just made of *materials*. Although comprised of physical components (cables, routers, computers) that facilitate the transport of information, the Internet is characterized by protocol: agreed upon rules, norms, and practices that specify how Internet technology is implemented and used (Galloway 2004). Furthermore, as rules, norms, and practices, protocols reflect broader cultural and political values about appropriate Internet use, produced and enforced by institutions, such as technical standards organizations, corporations, or even governments (Lessig 1999, Thacker 2004). Along these lines, infrastructures are better understood as "institutional-technical complexes" that propagate particular political ends (Edwards 2003, 2006).

This understanding of infrastructure relates to work that views technologies as *artefacts*: composites of relationships between people, devices, and practices (Bijker et al. 1987, Latour 1987, 1999, Mol 1998). Situated in broader social and political forces, this approach explores the normative aims – the legitimate goals, practices, and actors – that are built into the design and use of infrastructures, shaping what they are for, how they should be managed, etc. (Lakoff and Collier 2010). This approach in turn implies that as infrastructures are adopted and become embedded, their related physical and institutional elements structure societies (Edwards 2003). Consider, for instance, how highway systems relate to cars, a consumer economy, and a political culture of "mobile subjects" (Paterson 2007).

Approaching infrastructure in this way suggests that the "spatial transformations" associated with globalization – from territorial to global orders – must involve more than the physical reach – or *stretching* – of the Internet's networks around the world. Following the view that spatial frameworks – territorial or global – install political categories (Driver 1985, Elden 2001, Foucault 2000a), I assessed how the Internet has evolved with the normative goals expressed in novel "global" ideas of political community and authority. I therefore studied Internet infrastructure as more than emblematic but evocative of the hopes and fears of global political life (Edwards 2003, Turkle 2005, 2010).

This investigation of the relationship of Internet infrastructures and globalization required two tasks: (1) uncovering why global emerges as a normative category that legitimates different – non-territorial – objectives for political authority; and (2) determining if this normative shift has implicated the evolution of the Internet. Taken together, the central focus of this project was to determine how and why the Internet and globally oriented political objectives interact and reinforce each other so that the Internet becomes part of the *matter* of and something that matters for global politics.

My central research objective was to identify the political categories embedded in protocols, their influence on the Internet's institutional-technical complexes, and their relationship to broader understandings of global political order. Infrastructures tend to be taken-for-granted platforms that enable a wide range of activities. When they work well, they are invisible, black boxes that are opaque to inquiry (Latour 1987). Excavating political categories induces visibility by revealing how and why infrastructures are assembled, implemented and used in certain standardized ways. As Star and Bowker put it, "It is not just the bits and bytes that get hustled into standard form in order for technical infrastructure to work. People's discursive . . . practices get hustled into standard form as well" (Star and Bowker 2006: 234, Star 2002).

I therefore illuminated the political categories embedded in infrastructures with a research design based on the methods and tools of discourse analysis (Hansen 2006). Discourses are systems of ideas, images, and vocabularies that are connected to practices and material things. They establish specific identities and behaviours, and not others, as normal, even incontrovertible (Foucault 1972, 1975, 1994). Although primarily a study of texts – written and oral, official and popular – discourse analysis does not reduce *matter* to ideas. Discourses illuminate the normative conditions under which material elements are taken up within and combined with the goals of a political society (Lakoff and Collier 2010, Lash and Lury 2007, Grondin, Chapter 31, Anaïs, Chapter 32). Applied to infrastructure, discourse analysis provides an approach to studying how a political order's material requirements are prioritized and forged, and how they align with political practices and institutions (Walters 2002). In my study, it allowed for exploring the goals and practices through which material elements such as routers, cables, servers, and regulatory practices combine to become built pathways of contemporary globalization and how they in turn inscribe global political objectives.

Discourses accordingly do not lay over the top of technical-material components – their political categories assemble actors, regulatory norms, and material factors into specific configurations and hold them together. Uncovering this practically, I examined the global as a spatial discourse in four overlapping dimensions. Each dimension involved specific analytical tasks that parsed out political categories, technical priorities, institutional frameworks, and regulatory practices to reflect on how the Internet has become operative as a global political infrastructure.

Spatial logics are the broader contexts that embed global political space as "commonsense" (Foucault 2000a). I identified the circulation of metaphors and their *literalization* in a set of linked terms that provide shared vocabularies that define political order (Rorty 1989). To determine how these vocabularies challenge the states-system, I examined how and why they were juxtaposed to "territory", and the related concepts of "state", "sovereignty" and "borders". As globalization is publicly debated, texts analyzed included official documents (policy reports, legislation and intergovernmental agreements), statements by civil society actors, and scholarly texts. A related task involved considering how discussions about globalization refer to the Internet, delineating how vocabularies in the documents listed above were used to describe the Internet. I also consulted popular sources such as *Wired* and cyberpunk literature, evaluating the way popular understandings of the Internet invoked global community. Analysis of the Charles Babbage Institute archive (www.cbi.umn.edu) assessed the degree to which Internet pioneers saw their efforts as radical and global.

Spatial products emerge as ideas of space become "reified" (Lefebvre 1996). As infra-structures are artefacts that bring together multiple components, this step examined how institutional-technical complexes become consolidated. I studied consolidation by examining the incorporation of broader global vocabularies in technical discussions. I identified how certain issues become technical priorities and assessed how links between vocabularies and technical priorities provided contexts in which protocols were formulated, and which institutional sites were deemed necessary for their enforcement. I focused on three sets of documents: technical standards, interviews, and vital texts. Standards documents illustrated how global vocabularies identified above specified technical priorities and protocols. Interviews explored how respondents described the Internet, and how technical issues connected to policy issues in respondents' involvement in technical activities, civil society, the private sector, and/or government. Vital texts occupy a pivotal place in the development of technical and institutional protocols. Uncovering their discursive structures provided another way to consider how an emerging global common sense brought together technical specifications, physical devices, and different actors.

Spatial practices involve the propagation of discourses through routines, whose regular repetition legitimate political order (Gregson and Rose 2000). Emphasis was placed on why operational procedures of regulatory institutions prescribed certain protocols, regulatory principles, and practices as logical and necessary for the Internet to function. This step provided additional evidence for reification, as routines stabilize technical-institutional complexes and their global "shape" (Law 2002). Evidence of routines stabilizing effects rested in whether the Internet was described as a singular object (*the* Internet), taken as a *cause* for regulatory practices (Latour 1999). Analysis focused on vocabularies and rules outlined in constitutions, policy directives, memoranda, and procedure oriented standards documents. Assessing operational procedures as themselves protocols illuminated the routines through which understandings of global order have been ratified within Internet regulation, which in turn revealed how the Internet has been taken to be an infrastructure of global order more generally.

Spatial variation explains how artefacts are transformed: artefacts mutate as ideas evolve, actors leave or join, and technical and political priorities change. A goal of this research was to contest the view that the Internet is inherently *global*. Through the documents gathered, I scrutinized vocabularies and practices historically, beginning with the initial development of the Internet in the US military to the present. This uncovered how the presumed "global" reach of the Internet has been contingent upon the dissemination of diverse categories that displaced *territorial* policy objectives, reassembling and reconstituting relationships between people, material factors and practices.

Conclusion

The above analysis demonstrated that the Internet has evolved alongside political categories contained in three visions of global political order – *global village*, *global marketplace*, and *global war*.

In the global village humanity, not competitive, conflict-prone territorially delimited com-munities, defines the basis of political authority. Influenced by cybernetic theories (McLuhan 1962), the spread of new communications technologies is tied to the rise of a peaceful, planetary society (Turner 2006). The Internet's pioneering engineers reflected this worldview in their commitment to openness. Initially about publicly available technical specifications, openness became a debate about who would standardize specifications. Divesting authority over the Internet from defence agencies to the National Science Foundation allowed newly devised TCP/IP protocols to extend network access beyond US space. Bringing Internet standards to the attention of the International Standards Organization, as an intergovernmental body it was criticized as being beholden to national interests and bureaucratic inefficiency – and, consequently, failing to include the input of a burgeoning worldwide user community. As decentralized control and end-user empowerment became both technical design principles and political criteria (Clark 1992, Crocker 1993, IETF Secretariat 1994), the user-based Internet Engineering Task Force (IETF) emerged as the authoritative site for standards development. A mission that continues to state that the "Internet will help build a better *human* society" through a "commitment to *openness*" (Alverstrand 2004, emphasis added), the IETF has been touted as evidence of the Internet's capacity for generating inclusive and participatory global governance (Barsook 1995).

By prioritizing market-share over territory, the mid-1990s enthusiasm for a competitive global marketplace popularized the Internet as a cyber shopping mall. Publicity in this new commercial realm required the right domain name (URL). Initially freely available on a first-come-first-served basis, entrepreneurial individuals acquired famous names (e.g., www.mcdonalds.com) in the hope of selling them back to corporations for a profit.[1] Corporations responded by claiming that competition required a system of property rights, and one that did not disrupt the domain name system's cross-border space with varying national regulations. The creation of the Internet Corporation for Assigned Names and Numbers (ICANN) resolved the debate by creating a privately governed competitive market for domain names, structured through transjurisdictional trademark protection rules. ICANN's authority therefore exemplifies how the Internet's technical (domain name) dimensions have been institutionally shaped and regulated to ensure the operation of global commerce more generally.

The fight against terrorism is a global war. Networks, and not territory, define the topography of danger. The Internet is said to play a strategic role in the new field of danger, enabling "[connections] . . . throughout the world [that] offer opportunities to build relationships and gain expertise" and radicalize citizens to plan attacks both abroad and in their home countries (US Senate Committee 2008, UK Home Office 2009). Addressing terrorist use of the Internet, security efforts aim to prevent terrorist activity by targeting communications *data* (user names, message pathways, location of equipment). Once considered to be neutral information conduits, new policing roles for Internet Service Providers (ISPs), including data retention and potentially censorship, have been proposed and legislated (European Union 2006, UK Home Office 2009).[2] Developed with new capacities to address present-day security concerns, the Internet is becoming a frontline in a battle not simply between states, but civic and "dark networks" (Deibert and Rohonzinski 2008).

The technical-institutional complexes uncovered – standards-IETF, domain names-ICANN, data-ISPs – reveal that political categories – humanity/openness; commerce/competition; prevention/security – affect relationships between the administrators, protocols, and regulatory mechanisms. More generally, this shows how evolving understandings of the scope and character of political community influence why Internet infrastructure has been formed in certain ways, and how, once institutionalized, the Internet's global character can structure a set of broader global political practices.

This research faced challenges that also provide avenues for future research. First, technical and regulatory discussions overwhelmingly occur in English. As non-roman web addresses are accommodated in the domain name space, it is worth reflecting on whether global discourses translate across different languages. Do other metaphors come to the fore? Do they produce different *Internets*?

Second, my limited technical expertise prevented an analysis of the Internet's software programming (computer programs, algorithms, etc.). Examining how software evolves alongside concerns for openness, competition, and security would provide greater understanding of how global political objectives shape and are reproduced by institutional-technical complexes.

Finally, the focus on discourse only partially explores how infrastructure constitutes practice. Complementing the analysis above with ethnographical methods that study patterns of Internet use could discern with greater depth how, even in everyday routines, the Internet evokes a global political order.

Notes

1   Interview with Bob Maher, former outside counsel for McDonald's Corporation.
2   This extends similar efforts to address digital piracy and child pornography.

Suggested reading

Hansen, L. (2006) *Security as Practice: Discourse Analysis and the Bosnian War*, New York: Routledge.

Lakoff, A. and Collier, S. (2010) "Infrastructure and Event: The Political Technology of Preparedness", in B. Braun and S. Whatmore (eds) *Political Matter: Technoscience, Democracy and Public*, Minnesota: University of Minnesota Press.

Lash, S. and Lury. C. (2007) "Method: Ontology, Movement, Mapping", in *Global Culture Industry: The Mediation of Things*, Cambridge: Polity.

Star, S.L. (2002) "Infrastructure and Ethnographic Practice: Working on the Fringes", *Scandinavian Journal of Information Systems*, 14(2): 107–122.

Walters, W. (2002) "The Power of Inscription: Beyond Social Construction and Deconstruction in European Integration Studies", *Millennium: Journal of International Studies*, 3(1): 83–108.

31 The study of drones as objects of security

Targeted killing as military strategy

David Grondin

Introduction

Over the past few years, drone[1] attacks in Afghanistan and Pakistan have been regularly featured in news headlines. While it is true that the vast majority of drones in service are used for reconnaissance and surveillance missions,[2] new prototypes such as the MQ-9 Reaper are designed for combat missions and have become remote-controlled weapon systems specifically made to kill people and take out targets with advanced guided weaponry.

This chapter reflects on my work on drones as *objects of security*. The research presented here stems from previous work on air power and space (Grondin 2009) and from my ongoing research project on the transformation of the American way of war (Grondin and Racine-Sibulka 2011). The first section presents how I chose to study drones as objects of security. The next section exposes how I framed the research process, how it was theoretically and empirically informed, and how I actually conducted my research. The final section discusses the conclusions and challenges encountered during the process of research.

As material and cultural artifacts (Miller 2005), drones can be studied in multiple ways. They can simultaneously be media objects, artifacts, weapon systems, aircrafts, discursive objects, and policy discourses. As a result of their use in the American fight against Al Qaeda operatives, the use of drones has become a highly mediatized topic. Furthermore, because of their status as politically reprehensible high-tech weaponry, and their use in illegal practices of warfare, drones can be studied as *objects* in themselves, but also as *discourses*, when we reinsert them in the transformation of the "virtuousness" and cleanliness (Der Derian 2009c: xx) of the American way of war. Finally, as "defense policy options" (Shore and Wright 2011), drones are also part of military and security strategies of irregular warfare and have in fact become inseparable from the targeted killing policy pursued consequently by the Bush and Obama administrations in the war on terror.

Conceiving of drones as objects of security has allowed me to take them head on as objects in themselves and as objects of discourses and of military strategies. More importantly, this project provided me with an excellent platform for further research on the increased blurring of the boundaries between spaces of war and non-war, or between liberal and illiberal practices of liberal states (Bigo and Tsoukala 2008, Guild et al. 2009) that the Revolution in Military Affairs (RMA) has enacted with the global circulation of technologies of war and surveillance.

The majority of the scholarship on drones has so far focused on the legality of their use (Melzer 2008), while the remainder consists of journalistic accounts of drone attacks in Pakistan and Afghanistan. I was, however, more interested in understanding how drones are made to operate as part of aerial unmanned warfare in a military strategy of targeted killing.

I wanted to find out how drones emerged as offensive weapons and came to be the eyes or snipers in the sky of the US military. My research on drones thus aimed to undertake a careful genealogical study of this object of security that is the drone.

The question of the objects of security has either been assumed or dismissed altogether in the fields of International Relations (IR), critical security studies, and critical geopolitics. My genealogical work on drones taps into the recent *material-semiotic turn* in critical security studies (Collier and Lakoff 2008, Grondin 2010). In this project, similar to Shah's study of the Internet in this book (Chapter 30), genealogy is methodologically understood as the process that interpellates both the discursive and material actors, objects, and institutions by which drones came to be conceived as part of a military strategy of targeted killing. Thus, instead of restricting itself to semiotic analysis (Vuori, Chapter 33), this project follows the *material-semiotic turn* in security studies alluded to by Walters in his study of migration (2010, 2011). In this approach, the study of security discourses does not stop at language and symbols, but aims to look at both "the ideal *and* the material, discourses *and* institutions" to analyze assemblages and configurations of power, mappings of territory and space, social arrangements, regimes, bureaucracies, and networks of actors, etc. (Walters 2010: 220–221, emphasis added).

By using the material-semiotic approach I was able to figure out how drones came to be part of aerial unmanned warfare by thinking about how drones made possible killing at a distance – through *abstraction* as a "materially lived relation" (Cooper 2002: 5). Although this project follows Gregory's (2011) work on the history of bombing upon which his work on drones is based, my work is focused specifically on the further integration of information and military technologies (Boot 2006). As such, the project takes into account how drones are a part of the ongoing robotic RMA (Singer 2009a) as weapons and weapon systems that may be construed as weaponized, robotized technologies even if pilots still remotely fly them.

To undertake this research, I relied on Latour's (2004) material-semiotic approach to sociological research and the actor-network theory, and on historical and sociological works on military revolutions and technologies (Singer 2009a, 2009b, Boot 2006, Blackmore 2005). As Latour explained,

> [t]he observer of technologies has to be very careful not to differentiate too hastily between signs and things, between projects and objects, between fiction and reality, between a novel about feelings and what is inscribed in the nature of things. [. . .] The R-312 [a bus built by Renault] was a text; now it's a thing.
>
> (Latour 1996: 24)

But to understand how drones came to operate as part of a targeted killing military strategy, I reverted to a discourse analysis of drones as weapons of choice for irregular warfare, which required delving into the military-industrial complex involved in the conception and production of drones – as drones were developed by research companies supervised by DARPA, the Pentagon's research and development arm – and into the US defence policy process of the Global War on Terror (GWoT).

The use of drones, however, is a matter of national security and defence. As such, aspects of weapons development such as research, development, and production are usually kept under a veil of secrecy. This also means that there is obviously a great part of the data gathering that can only be derivative. Hence, for the collection of primary source data for my research, I had to rely on several and spread out sources: on the work of investigative journalists covering national security and defence affairs, for example the work of Turse; on data accumulated from the steady watch of specialized blogs or websites like Shachtman's national security blog *Danger Room: What's next for national security?* on Wired.com, now run by Ackerman; on technical accounts found in popular science magazines (*Popular Mechanics*); on first-hand accounts of weapons used; on promotional material found in defence journals and professional defence magazines (*Air and Space Power Journal*); on defence industry magazines (airforce-technology.com); on the work of people who were once insiders and who have had privileged accesses afterwards (like Singer, a Brooking Institute fellow who used to be in the US Office of the Secretary of Defense during the Bush administration and is now a leading expert on robotic warfare); on information found on websites of think tanks and independent research facilities (Center for Defense Information, globalsecurity.org); on data assessed from written testimonies (in Congress); and, interestingly enough, a significant amount of data came from the weapon designers' webpages (General Atomics for Predators and Reapers and Lockheed Martin for the Global Hawk). Through an analysis of these documents I was able to familiarize myself with the different technical specificities of a MQ-1 Reaper in comparison to the forthcoming Boeing's X-45A or Northrop Grumman's X-47. Furthermore, through a first-hand account of drone pilots (Martin and Sasser 2010), I got to learn about the actual routine and systemic operation involved in combat operations of a Predator drone. Doing sensitive research on ongoing weapons development and weapon systems used to orchestrate targeted killings like drones leads to the conclusion that just tracing and mapping the information is, in and of itself, part of the challenge. There is, however, no other way to access the data, other than publicly available and de-classified documents, especially if you are an outsider to the defence community and industry.

My research on drones as objects of security demonstrated how they have become indispensable instruments of warfare to which we had to accustom ourselves when thinking about the new American ways of war (Coker 2007, 2008). In conceiving drones as weapons systems, I had to look at the technological path development of drones. I traced the evolution of drones by looking at the first armed drone. With the introduction of the armed Predator drone in Afghanistan in 2002, however, it seemed that we had reached a new stage: killing at a remote distance without risk. We ought to be reminded that the first test of any weapon system or military strategy is the battle, where the battlefield serves as a laboratory. Obviously, the Afghanistan and Iraq wars, as well as the fight against Al Qaeda in Pakistan, have proven their worth as laboratories for unmanned systems in combat operations, for reconnaissance mission mainly, but also for intelligence collection and targeted killings.

The hype surrounding the promise of drones, however, is equally linked to the fact that they are economical objects (Engelhardt 2010). Drones are the next-best aerial weapons after expensive weapon systems like the F-35 Joint Strike Fighter that will cost more than 100 million dollars per unit. As drones are able to fly for longer durations, require differing amounts of instruction from the ground, and can carry different types of payloads, ranging from surveillance gear to guided missiles (Blackmore 2005: 130), they have become instrumental to the adaptation of the US armed forces to new military terrains, and drone and robotic warfare owe much to the new practices of urban warfare; for example, one need only look at Graham's work on this new military urbanism (2010).

Conclusion

Over the course of my inquiry, I was able to highlight how drones revealed themselves as a flexible, capable, and adaptable solution to an extended and mobile battlespace that is anything but secured. Drones deployed in US military operations in Iraq and Afghanistan represent the smooth, nomadic, fluid, virtual, and global character of the new American way of war (Coward 2009). This so-called network-centric framework of drone warfare enables a global information grid rendering the networking of people and machines possible and making possible the waging of war with precision, from a remote distance, if not from anywhere in the world.

This is what led national security journalist Scahill to state that the doctrine of targeted killing stemmed from a logic where "the world is a battlefield" (Jerving 2011, Gosztola 2011, Rogers 2006). In effect, a sense of shared humanity is lost to the technologies of seeing and targeting offered by the drone gaze that visually frames the screening of a world that is both at a remote distance and virtual. In doing so, drones enable the United States to do pre-emptive and extra-judicial remote killings outside of the United States. Future research should further inquire into the legal and extra-legal basis of drone warfare, as drones are here to stay, especially as they are affordable and may prevent the loss of soldiers' lives on the ground, making them popular objects of security for state leaders and governmental powers of the world. One major challenge this research faces thus lies in the legal groundings and debates that will delimit the use of drones in the increasingly blurred spaces of war and non-war. More scholarship done in other disciplines like geography and international law will help us expand our grasp of drones as objects of security.

Notes

1   Armed drones are Unmanned Combat Aerial Vehicles (UCAVs) and the surveillance drones are referred to as UAVs (unmanned aerial vehicles).
2   Unmanned aerial drones are also increasingly being deployed for civil surveillance and policing in urban spaces (in the UK, France, and Germany notably) and borderland contexts (in the US especially), for visual mapping and reconnaissance in disaster and trauma relief (such as the tsunami in Japan in 2011), as well as for image collection for the scientific study of birds and other natural processes, among other things.

Suggested reading

Collier, S. and Lakoff, A. (2008) "Distributed Preparedness: Space, Security and Citizenship in the United States", in D. Cowen and E. Gilbert (eds) *War, Citizenship, Territory*, New York: Routledge.
Cooper, S. (2002) *Technoculture and Critical Theory: In the Service of the Machine?* New York: Routledge.
Latour, B. (1996) *Aramis or the Love of Technology*, Cambridge: Harvard University Press.
Miller, D. (2005) "Materiality: An Introduction", in D. Miller (ed.) *Materiality*, Durham: Duke University Press.
Shore, C. and Wright, S. (2011) "Conceptualising Policy: Technologies of Governance and the Politics of Visibility", in C. Shore and S. Wright (eds) *Anthropology of Policy: Critical Perspectives on Governance and Power*, New York: Routledge.

32 Objects of security/objects of research

Analyzing non-lethal weapons

Seantel Anaïs

Introduction

Recently, social historians, sociologists of science and technology, and social scientists working in critical security studies have turned their attention towards an unconventional class of weapons designed not to maximize killing potential in war and domestic conflict, but rather those which fall under the term "non-lethal" (Rappert 2001, 2003, 2004, Davison 2009). My research focuses on the role of non-lethal weapons in the government of American cities and in international interventions carried out by the US military. It does so by locating them within the context of a set of political and historically-specific relations between technology, security, the governance of insecurity, and broader regimes of governance. It follows the life story of objects of security by asking how they come together and how they sometimes fall apart, and what this means for them and for the sets of practices of which they form a part. Included in the broader class of non-lethal weapons are familiar devices such as tear gas, electrical stun technologies, kinetic impact weapons such as bean-bag rounds, and rubber bullets. Newer and less well-known non-lethal weapons include vehicle-mounted active denial devices which deter crowds by directing sound or microwave beams at them, slippery and sticky foams meant to dissuade crowds or mobs from entering particular areas, and weaponized calmative agents such as the anesthetic Fentanyl.

Scholars working in International Relations (IR), critical security and governmentality studies, and the sociology of science and technology have generated growing interest in the technological artifacts of security and governance, recently turning their attention to the technological artifacts that make "governing through insecurity" practicable (Barry 2001, Lentzos and Rose 2009). Often these accounts concentrate on technological depictions and predictions of threats to security: biometrics, surveillance-at-a-distance, the creation of "zones of governance", and remote and real-time algorithmic and enactment-based renderings of risk (Amoore 2009, Barry 2001, Collier 2008). This thread in critical security studies has turned much needed attention towards the often taken-for-granted objects of security. It is perhaps not surprising that non-lethal weapons have a political dimension. The more radical claim would be to suggest that they do not. I suggest that an interesting aspect of the political life of non-lethal weapons is that they do not operate solely in the realm of the material, but instead embody a shifting set of ideas that exist in a complex relationship to the physicality of the objects themselves. Moreover, like Shah in this book (Chapter 30), I am concerned with the connection between the materialities of security and the legitimation of political authority. My research attempts to make sense of the spatio-temporal contact zones where objects, devices, ideas, and human beings become entangled, locating non-lethal weapons within a web of events, accidents, and contingencies.

My research is guided by a cluster of questions that can be organized into two groups. First, concerning the development and use of non-lethal weapons themselves: What kind of regulatory and governmental functions do non-lethal weapons serve? What contestations do non-lethal weapons serve as a surface for? How do they take shape, change, come into being, and fall apart? What kind of political life do these weapons lead? What kind of legitimating function do they provide, and what programs of political action do they make possible? Second, related to discourses concerning non-lethal weapons in institutional texts: On what basis are they legitimized, and in response to what kinds of ethical or political crises? What kinds of social and political subjectivity do these weapons putatively guard against, and what kinds do they protect?

I analyze institutional texts using a qualitative research design that combines two methodological approaches: genealogy and critical discourse analysis (CDA). Although genealogy is generally more popular as a methodological choice for philosophers, a number of social scientists have taken it up as means of approaching the study of institutional texts in sociology (Dean 1992), critical pedagogy (Scheurich and Bell McKenzie 2005), anthropology (Palmié 2006), critical security studies (Walters 2006), and psychology (Hook 2005). By genealogy, I refer to a methodological process concerned with telling the story of how a set of discursive and non-discursive practices come into being and interact to form a set of political, economic, moral, cultural, and social institutions which define the limits of acceptable speaking, knowing, and acting. By CDA, I refer to the analysis of texts, whether written or spoken, and their power to shape "situations, objects of knowledge, and the social identities of and relationships between people and groups of people" (Fairclough and Wodak 1997: 258). At least two existing challenges are alleviated through this pairing. First, the combination of genealogy and CDA serves to redress the ahistoricism apparent in much critical discourse analytic work. Second, as a post-positivist critical approach to qualitative social scientific research, CDA can systematize and clarify genealogy, making it less likely to be misunderstood by a culture of "methodological conservatism" (Lincoln and Cannella 2004), or dismissed by a variety of audiences who read it as too theoretical, difficult to assess, "philosophically ambiguous" (LeGreco and Tracy 2009: 1520), or beyond understanding (Denzin and Lincoln 2005). Below, I briefly discuss the data-collection stage of my research before outlining the three main components of data-analysis.

For my research on the history of non-lethal weapons, I collected and digitized over 3000 pages of documents as a broad data set, most of which came from the National Archives and Records Administration (NARA) in College Park, Maryland. Some documents pertaining to non-lethal weapons in the NARA holdings remained classified when I started my research there. I applied through Freedom of Information Access (FOIA) requests to have roughly 500 pages of documents declassified and made publicly available. Some of the documents that I analyzed came from more open sources, including publicly available patent filings that detailed the development of as-yet-unrealized plans for new non-lethal weapons technologies and documents proactively released by private civilian defence and policing research and development agencies.

The data set that I assembled for my research was *living* in the sense that new source materials were constantly being added and no prior decisions regarding what should be included were made. There are two reasons for this liberal approach to data collection. First, rich materials may never be uncovered if a closed data set is chosen before the collection stage begins. Second, a veil of secrecy shrouds military and police research and development programs, even when they have long been decommissioned. Most researchers who deal with matters of *national security* face tremendous barriers in terms of their ability to access documents. Researchers using data sources that are limited by the exigencies of secrecy do not always have the luxury of being discerning. Further, documents that are deliberately kept from the public eye are telling in that they contain information that has not yet formed a part of existing analyses. More importantly, they reveal a great deal about how governmental institutions attempt to manage public impressions of the procedures and policies that guide their actions. For this study, I isolated three practical elements from CDA and used them to analyze my raw archival data: attending to systematicity, analyzing genre, and reading for silence.

Attending to systematicity involves approaching texts not as passive objects but as actors with a role to play in the enactment of various social configurations. This textual agency, I argue, is made possible by the various systematic elements enmeshed in their physical form. Taking a critical approach to the systematicity of texts involves uncovering and discussing the power relations inherent in their production and circulation. This focuses attention on the organization and form of texts, what Halliday and Hasan (1976) call their *texture*. I focused on the reciprocal constitution of content and texture. As Fairclough suggests, content cannot be studied as distinct from form because "contents are always necessarily realized in forms" (1992: 188) and as Geertz (1973: 4) put it, forms of knowledge are "indivisible from their instruments and their encasements".

Analyzing *genre* involves paying attention to the relationship between the content and materiality of the text to the extent that it conforms to or helps shape particular modes of communication appropriate to a given activity. Scholars working in the field generally referred to as *genre analysis* concern themselves with knowledge production and its codification in forms of writing (Swales 1990, Berkenkotter and Huckin 1995). Many discourse analysts, including Fairclough, define genres as socially sanctioned ways of using language "in connection with a particular type of activity" (1992: 14). Genres, according to Berkenkotter and Huckin, are inextricably linked to "a discipline's methodology, and they package information in ways that conform to a discipline's norms, values, and ideology" (1995: 4). Berkenkotter and Huckin draw on Bakhtin (1986) to argue that most analyses have treated genre as a reified entity, immutable, and mainly of interest to linguists. I use the notion of genre to position institutional texts as dynamic actors that work to produce coherence within an organization. This view of genre is significant to my work because it provides a framework for thinking through the role of content and form in stabilizing meaning within an institutional setting. Like Berkenkotter and Huckin (1995), I see knowledge of and facility with genre as a form of situated practice – or craft-work – enmeshed in institutional text and embedded in the actual activities of actors within institutions such as the Department of Defense and its related branches.

Finally, *reading for silence* involves first reading the content of a text and deciphering the meanings it attempts to convey (Tonkiss 2004). This involves creating a conceptual schematic of the terms it uses, the assumptions it asks its readers to take for granted, the basic message that it delivers – and to whom. It also requires the active analysis of – and active resistance to – the forces in a text that serve to captivate the audiences that they were produced for (Curtis 2004). In reading for silence, I borrow two distinct approaches from other critical discourse analysts (Tonkiss 2004). Reading along is a partially passive step, in that it involves an examination of the text from a position that is simultaneously critical and uncritical. The critical manoeuvre consists in performing an uncritical reading of the text. This strategy involves a complex of practices discussed in the section above – attending to the systematicity of a text – part of what Curtis (2004) identifies as a kind of craft knowledge that involves acquainting oneself with the construction and mobilization of official documentary systems. The second strategy might be called reading against the text. It involves looking for silences, taking a critical stance towards the claims made therein, interrogating the assumptions that make it function, questioning the serialization of events, considering accounts which might run counter to the official position portrayed in the text and deliberating on what accounts might be usurped by a proactive rhetoric or baldly excluded by omission (Tonkiss 2004). Of course, while CDA encourages a practical approach to reading for silence, the notion that texts should be analyzed in such a way as to disrupt the collective memory, to disturb history, and to resurrect the voices of the marginalized is one that Foucault embraced and that genealogy exemplifies.

Conclusion

My research shows that non-lethal weapons are often envisioned as a solution to widespread outrage over the use of conventional weapons and strategic use of force in domestic civil disturbances throughout the twentieth century. Through a genealogically informed critical discourse analysis of text, I was able to discern a series of discourses that ran through, in various ways, the documents that I collected. I concentrated on ethics, distinction, and humanitarianism. My exposition of the research took the form of a series of case studies that reveal how these discourses operate in some combination to constitute non-lethal weapons as legitimate means of intervening on to bodies and sites at various moments throughout the twentieth century. These case studies reveal the power of the ethico-political discourses of non-lethality (ethics); the means through which distinctions between combatant and civilian are inscribed in discourses concerning which forms of political subjectivity should be guarded against and which should be protected using non-lethal means of intervention (distinction); and, finally, the mobilization of humanitarian discourses in policy documents concerning non-lethal weapons (humanitarianism).

The methodological and theoretical approaches favoured in political sociology and security studies have often proved insufficient to the study of objects, which are more or less unknowable, or what Law and Singleton (2005) call *messy*. I see this as a valuable point of departure for the study of non-lethal weapons: they change, they are reconfigured, they are put to uses other than those for which they are designed, they break; they produce outcomes other than those for which they are approved; they are changed by the behaviours of the user; they in turn change the behaviours of the user; they fall out of use for periods of time and in particular places only to find reinvigorated purpose in other places and at different times. In sum, objects – like most things – are not a straightforward business.

Suggested reading

LeGreco, M. and Tracy, S.J. (2009) "Discourse Tracing as Qualitative Practice", *Qualitative Inquiry*, 15(9): 1516–1543.

Lincoln, Y.S. and Cannella, G.S. (2004) "Dangerous Discourses: Methodological Conservatism and Governmental Regimes of Truth", *Qualitative Inquiry*, 10(5): 5–13.

Scheurich, J. and Bell McKenzie, K. (2005) "Foucault's Methodologies: Archaeology and Genealogy", in N.K. Dezin and Y.S. Lincoln (eds) *The SAGE Handbook of Qualitative Research*, London: SAGE Publications.

Swales, J. (1990) *Genre Analysis: English in Academic and Research Settings*, Cambridge: Cambridge University Press.

Tonkiss, F. (2004) "Analysing Text and Speech: Content and Critical Discourse Analysis", in S. Seale (ed.) *Researching Society and Culture*, London: SAGE Publications.

33 Pictoral texts

Juha A. Vuori

Introduction

The research presented in this chapter draws on my previous engagement with securitization theory, and retains the goal of critically developing ways it can be applied to new types of investigations. After explicating the speech act fundamentals of the approach in order to apply it to broader types of political orders and functions, I have been interested to see how insights from other theories beyond speech act theory could be added to the securitization framework without distortion to its main premises. In order to do this, I have explored how pictoral text has been interwoven with security arguments, and how semiotics can be used to expand the range of methods available for students of securitization (Vuori 2010a, 2011b).

Discourse is not limited to verbal or written texts, but can include any type of symbols that contribute to meaning making. This means that securitization studies needs be more inclusive in terms of the types of data that is analyzed by its means. Indeed, students of security who want to utilize discourse analysis in their work should include the production and reception of images in their examinations. Relevant issues here include how visual means can present security arguments, embody threat images, and increase or decrease the plausibility of such claims. Similarly important is how images portray, amplify, and form cultural resonance and symbolic capital within processes of securitization (Balzacq 2010b, Stritzel 2007).

Semiotics, or the study of signs, suggests itself as an appropriate field of thought to render the visual for students of security. While linguistics has been of major importance for discourse analysis approaches to security, semiotics can be used to study materials beyond written and spoken objects. Indeed, anything that can convey meaning can be investigated via the various methods developed within the empirical, linguistic, philosophical, and cultural approaches to semiotics.

In order to get a grasp of how to study such a broadened field of inquiry, I set out to find an example of a visual representation of a security argument. I was looking for an *object*, a symbolic sign lodged in the flow of meaning, or semeiosis in Peircean terms. As I was also interested in the notion of "macrosecuritization" (Buzan and Wæver 2009), I came to think of the Doomsday Clock of the Atomic Scientists (Vuori 2010a). As a widely recognized visual symbol, and with a long history of use, the Clock seemed to be an ideal entry point for the investigation of a visual master signifier of securitization. Of interest was how its image has been connected to securitization in the presentation of nuclear weapons as a threat to human civilization since 1947: how does the visual symbol of the Clock weave into the verbal-textual securitization moves of the Atomic Scientists?

Once I had settled on the Clock as my *visual sign*, I selected the recent issues of the *Bulletin of the Atomic Scientists* as the corpus, or archive of empirical data from which to gain a comprehensive view of the evolution of the security argument, and the aesthetic evolution of the Clock itself. Although the securitization move of the "Emergency Committee of Atomic Scientists" was made in the issue of the Bulletin that displayed the Clock for the first time, the argument has been maintained for over six decades in the form of the Clock and the brief textual description of it.

My main point of interest was how the sign of the Clock was anchored to the security argument of the Scientists: if an image should have an influence on an act of securitization, in a Barthesian sense, it must be *anchored* to a meaning – that is, the "floating chain of signifieds" has to be affixed to a preferred reading of the image (Barthes 1977: 38). Since images can convey emotion, affective images especially can have a facilitation effect in securitization processes, where threats and fear, on the one hand, and certainty and relief, on the other, play major roles. Just as with standard advertisement practice, when bound to securitization processes images can evoke emotions that thereby facilitate the *purchase* of a securitization argument, in addition to the provision of either evidence or a degree of plausibility for the claims of the securitizing actor.

Explicit views of the Clock presented by the Atomic Scientists exhibit how securitization arguments can be interwoven with visual symbols, and how an image can become an institutionalized marker for a security discourse: the task set for the symbol by the Scientists was "to frighten men into rationality". The elements of the symbol have contained the same elements as the security argument of the Scientists: the lateness of the hour (the nuclear genie is out of the bottle) and impending doom (nuclear war would end our civilization), as well as the possibility to reverse course by moving the hands of time far away from midnight (nuclear war can be prevented by strict international control of nuclear technology and the alteration of the international system).

The pilot type study of the Doomsday Clock revealed that there indeed are visual signifiers of security arguments, and that a single image or symbol can contain such an argument. Although the Clock is a special symbol with its own particular history, there are plenty of other symbols and systems of symbols that can be rendered with the type of analysis discussed here. Military insignias and various warning systems come readily to mind, but there are whole symbolic secondary architectures of security that can be investigated.

It seems that images are an efficient way to communicate meanings and to bring affective aspects into security arguments. For example, through the symbol of the Doomsday Clock, the Atomic Scientists have been able to combine their social capital as voices of reason and objectivity with that of the soothsayer to influence society and behaviour. While science deals with concepts, the symbol of the Clock relates to emotions; while the Scientists' textual arguments try to awaken the reason of their audience, the symbol of the Clock tries to reach its bare sensibilities. Thus, with their Clock, the Atomic Scientists could combine the aesthetics of science and prophecy. Display of the Clock evokes and thereby facilitates all of the crucial ingredients involved in a securitization plot: the lateness of the hour (urgency) and impending doom (existential threat), as well as the possibility to reverse course by moving the hands of time far away from midnight (way out). This has made the Clock a potent symbol and a "standing speech act" (Searle 2011: 86) for the anti-nuclear macrosecuritization discourse. Yet the meaning of the symbol has not remained constant: it is no longer only about nuclear conflagration, but also about the threat of climate change, and even bio-technologies.

While the interest here has been on how symbols can be interwoven into security arguments, other symbolic aspects of security practices can be studied in this manner as well. Thereby, there is a need to provide the framework of securitization with the means to take a stand on signs beyond speech acts and for the approach to tackle the role of images just as systematically as it has tackled language in general and speech acts in particular. I have deployed the semiotics of Peirce (1985) for this purpose (Vuori 2011b). The secondary architecture of security could be engaged through typologies of images, and the systematic investigation of how they relate to security practices and processes. Mitchell's (1986) semiotic typology of images[1] could be enhanced with other dimensions through Peirce's (1985) various typologies of signs for this purpose. For example, the classificatory scheme of icon-index-symbol suggests an empirical research project to examine how felicitous each type of sign is for securitization processes: do iconic, indexical, or symbolic signs that can be deemed to perform or be part of securitization moves vary in their usefulness to bring about success for the move? Do indexical signs (photographs as *evidence*) function differently from symbolic signs (political cartoons as commentary) in processes of securitization?

In order to grasp how such images operate in securitization processes we have to investigate how the image under examination relates to the textual *anchor* of securitization (for example, "does the image function as an institutionalized securitization?"): we need to be able to deem that the image is somehow a part of a securitization move or process. After such identification of the form has taken place, we have to examine what type of an image we are dealing with. We should then determine which functions the image serves in the process: does the image present a whole securitization argument, does the image work towards reassurement (presentation of protective means) or unease (presentation of threat images), does the image work towards facilitation of the securitization move (advertisements and the *purchase* of a security argument) or towards its impediment (does the image represent *evidence* or *plausibility* for or against the securitization move)? Such questions allow us to examine how images become part of securitization processes via four components: the image itself and the immediate intertext of the image, of the wider policy discourse, and of the texts that ascribe meaning to the image (Hansen 2011: 19).

It is, however, not enough to read representations of security. Already Barthes (1977) proposed that the social study of images should entail three aspects: sociological means should be used to study the production and reception of images, while semiology should be used to read and decode them. This basic approach still seems sound. A problem with studies of images has previously been that most studies merely produce semiological readings, while the sociological study of both production and reception remain absent. There also seems to be a general lack of enthusiasm for empirical studies that would go beyond the interpretations of single scholars. These kinds of studies have justifiably been criticized for the mere production of readings by elite analysts, which may be quite detached from how the same images would be received by people less versed in philosophy and social theories (Bignell 2002: 31, Chandler 2007: 222). Indeed, a major difficulty with the investigation of pictoral texts is their polysemiousness and the openness of their interpretation (Barthes 1977). This has indeed been one of the key discoveries of the study of signs and images. Another discovery within this field may alleviate this problem though: interpretative communities seem to, to a degree, converge in interpretations of certain images (Fish 1980). A shared interpretation may even be a necessity to understand a certain sign or symbol.

Such a view is connected to the more general debate within Securitization Studies on the issues of context, situatedness, and intertextuality: just as in standard instances of securitization, visual acts also depend on conventions. In Peircean terms, securitizing signs are part of a process of semeiosis where meanings flow or stream and are based on each other, whereby they form the ground of their meaning, i.e. the relation between the "representamen" and the "object". This is where the sophisticated analytical frame of Peircean semiotics can be operated to uncover how images become a part of the meaning making of security issues. The combination of speech act theory and Peircean semiotics can be used to investigate what an image does together with its securitization anchor in an elaborate manner (Vuori 2011b). This allows us to investigate new types of materials within the Securitization Studies framework, and enhances the means available for students of securitization to denaturalize signs that pertain to security.

Conclusion

Just as in discourse analysis in general, students of semiotics can examine the coding and decoding of visual signs in terms of plasticity, elasticity, and rupture: synchronic and diachronic semiotic analysis of signs can reveal how the meaning of signs is constrained by codes and how their meaning depends on their relations with other signs and meanings. Here, both the pessimism of structuralist views on consumers of signs as victims and the optimism of the capacities of emancipated spectators (Rancière 2011) have to be avoided: these are empirical questions and cannot be resolved with philosophical fiat. Yet, the semiotic analysis of security remains a powerful tool for students of security to show how meanings are communicated by signs and read in relation to social codes as well as other structures in society.

Note

1   (1) graphic images (pictures, statues, designs); (2) optical images (mirrors, projections); (3) perceptual images (sense data); (4) mental images (memories, ideas); (5) verbal images (metaphors).

Suggested reading

Chandler, D. (2007) *Semiotics: The Basics*, New York: Routledge.
Hansen, L. (2011) "Theorizing the Image for Security Studies: Visual Securitization and the Muhammad Cartoon Crisis", *European Journal of International Relations*, 17(1): 51–74.
Innis, R.E. (ed.) (1985) *Semiotics: An Introductory Reader*, London: Hutchinson.
Kangas, A. (2007) *The Knight, the Beast and the Treasure: A Semiotic Inquiry into the Finnish Political Imaginary of Russia, 1918–1930s*, Tampere: Tampere University Press.
Mitchell, W.J.T. (1994) *Picture Theory: Essays on Verbal and Visual Representation*, Chicago: Chicago University Press.

34 Tracing human security assemblages

Nadine Voelkner

Introduction

How does one analyze the effects of security when it encapsulates the global such as the policy discourse of human security? Human security is a governmental logic that is concerned with the management of conflict and underdevelopment through mechanisms of global governance (UNDP 1994). Human security is an elusive concept that has attracted an array of definitions, interventions, and political purposes. From the multiplicity of meanings and activities associated with human security, I decided to concentrate on the work of the UN and affiliated agencies. These transnational agencies have adopted a broad understanding of human security, which principally entails the inclusion of people and their everyday concerns for security including unemployment, famine, diseases, earthquakes, flooding, rape, and gun crimes in processes of (global) governance. Implicit in human security is an aspiration to shift political authority away from the traditional centre of the nation-state to multilayered, networked configurations with, and through, a host of (inter)governmental, para-governmental, nongovernmental, and private organizations. Indeed, accounts of global governance including human security often rely on the idea of a shift in the locus of political power and authority. This has prompted many of those debating human security to argue that its agenda is eroding the state and state sovereignty. Yet, if we conceptualize human security as a form of *governmentality* (Foucault 2009, Rose 1999, O'Malley et al. 1997), it then gives rise to security practices that reconstitute existing forms of political subjectivity including the state and sovereignty, the human and international order, engendering new iterations of the latter. In order to trace and analyze this effect of human security in the world, I examined the intersections between its macro- (at UN headquarters) and micro-politics (onsite where human security is implemented) by drawing on the notion of (global) assemblage in which I emphasized materiality.

My aim was to bring to light the way human security practices depend on a specific governmental logic and associated technologies of power that are much broader in scope than what I would find if I were to focus only on formal governing authorities such as those associated with the state. Traditional categories like the state embody specific assumptions about political life such as the division inside/outside in international relations, which I wanted to avoid from the outset. Moreover, if I were to only consider programmatic logics and top-down flows of power such as are evident in the texts of large-scale programmes and international policies, I would de-emphasize the incoherence and contingency of power as well as the invention of governing practices from below. Considering this, it was necessary to design my research to emphasize the variability and instability of human security flows. Consequently, much like Hughes in this book (Chapter 14), I adopted a flexible research strategy that evolved in the research process (Robson 2002: 163–200). This way, there would be space to be surprised and led by what I encountered on the research path. Indeed, it was only in the field that I began to observe the way human security emerged as a messy, contingent, and at times absurd political strategy that was in the process of setting up and arranging a set of heterogeneous elements into a multiplicity of assemblages around specific governmental problems – each comprising their own set of, amongst others, global programmes and expertise, situated histories and (knowledge) cultures, as well as material objects.

Having read *Aramis or the Love of Technology* (Latour 1996) on my way into the field, I was sensitized to the possibility of material objects playing a role in the way governance is practised and shaped. In this context, although such things as small arms and viruses are emphasized in the human security discourse, they tend to appear only as inert objects that either benefit or risk (global) human security. Rather than seeing them as passive entities, I came to see them as giving human security concrete form. Indeed, human security comprises assemblages of "men and things" (Foucault 2009: 96) in which material objects, just like human beings, play a constitutive role. For example, I was struck by the importance of information technologies including the Internet (emails) and mundane paraphernalia (electricity, computers, office furniture) as well as viruses (HIV, SARS) and human bodies in setting up and shaping human security interventions. Though Foucault implied the composite role of all elements – human and nonhuman – in giving rise to power effects such as governmentalities, others have more decidedly commented on how the interrelation between differential elements produces forces that help to constitute specific political subjectivities (Mitchell 2002). Considering this, I began to look particularly to Bennett (2005a, 2010) in interpreting human security as open-ended assemblages that are always in the process of (un-)becoming, absorbing, discarding, and transforming disparate human and nonhuman elements. It is partly in this way that human security assemblages and their effects in the world can be seen to be circumstantial, unstable, and unpredictable.

How and to what effect does the governmentality of human security matter concretely? I visited the Human Security Unit (HSU) at the United Nations headquarters in New York to begin to understand the programming of human security. The HSU administers the UN Trust Fund for Human Security (UNTFHS) which, to date, has committed over US $350 million to projects managed by UN and UN-associated agencies in over seventy countries, disseminating and embedding the human security outlook with variable effect to South and Central America, Sub-Saharan Africa, the Balkans, Eastern Europe, Central Asia, South Asia, Southeast and East Asia. Judging by the work of the HSU, human security interventions have taken or are taking place in multiple, dispersed, and shifting vernacular sites. Thus, by conducting a multi-sited field study of selected sites of practice, it became possible for me not only to see how the application of human security varies from the (global) programme as well as between vernacular contexts. It also allowed me to see in what way the micropolitics of human security are linked to the broader rationalities, processes, and power assemblages associated with its global politics.

I decided to trace the workings of human security in two UNTFHS-funded projects tackling issues arising specifically from forced migration. Migration, forced migration at that, brings into sharper focus the question of political order: it raises "the fundamental ethical question of the membership of a political community, so also reflecting on the character of its justice, as well as the technical question of ordering and disciplining large mobile or potentially mobile populations" (Dillon 1995: 327). Indeed, it problematizes the very distinction between the inside and outside as a way of enframing political issues such as are embodied in state security programmes. Specifically, I looked to human security projects tackling insecurity relating to forced migration including human trafficking within and out of Southeast Asia. The current increased human mobility within the region is considered a key element in the rise of global migration. Southeast Asian governments, which operate under a diversity of political orders including liberal and communist regimes, have responded by attempting to manage the problem of migration and related issues with varying strategies and efforts including human security (Regional Thematic Working Group on International Migration including Human Trafficking 2008).

The first project in which I sought to trace the human security flows dealt with the double circulation problematic embodied by Burmese migrants in Thailand whose travelling bodies are both desired for the labour to be yielded and repulsed and criminalized for the diseases they are said to carry. The second project dealt with the circulation problematic relating to Vietnamese women and children at risk of human trafficking whose travelling bodies were both desired in a booming pleasure industry and repulsed for the "social evil" and lack of traditional Vietnamese femininity they are believed to represent. In order to capture the miniscule shifts in political order associated with human security as applied to issues of forced migration in Thailand and Vietnam, I followed Foucault's cue and focused on the "incessant transactions which modify, or [...] insidiously shift sources of finance, modes of investment, decision-making centres, forms and types of control, relationships between local powers, the central authority and so on" (Foucault 2008: 77).

Specifically, in order to grasp the ways political subjectivities such as the human, the state, and global order are formed, I looked to the ways of seeing, understanding, and managing forced migration. My position as researcher and my endeavour to understand was made known to the research subjects from the outset. The advantage of this approach lies in the possibility of gaining a deeper understanding of the complexity of particular social phenomena (Geertz 1973) otherwise unobtainable through conventional methods such as questionnaires. The challenge of adopting this approach, however, lies in understanding, as D'Aoust notes in this book (Chapter 4), how I, as a researcher, am influenced by and affect the situation under observation. This is especially so in the case of research in a sensitive political area such as forced migration where migrants are seen either as illegal or morally doubtful and knowledge is not easily or safely come by. Moreover, the primary material collected will be the interpretation of the researcher. There is the problem of bias and the potential for distortion of research findings (Haraway 1998). Indeed, security is an expression for what and how to protect in the world that is particular. In the case of migrants in both Vietnam and Thailand, the meaning and proposed activities of (human) security differed from the proposed UN programmes. It thus required an open mind to deviate from agenda-setting parameters.

In order to locate these incessant transactions and given also the global character of human security, I decided to trace them not only customarily by identifying and interviewing relevant groups of people involved in the networks that were established and by examining relevant primary and secondary literature but also by following the material objects that were produced or appropriated in the name of human security. For example, I was interested in the emails sent from New York to Bangkok to Ranong, the management tools employed, the software developed in Geneva and transferred to Bangkok where it was reconfigured and transferred to Samutsakhorn, and so on. Governmental notions that invoke the global such as human security operate along dramatic distances. When the object of analysis is the global, a focus on the materiality of events helps to explore how the global is localized. At the same time, a focus on materiality opens up the opportunity to explore how the local materializes.

Not only does it show the way governmental logics are performed, it also demonstrates their inherent situatedness and instability. Thus, the interplay between localizations and materializations disrupts the logics that underlie governmental processes. By looking at the emergence of the global assemblages that human security comprises, tracing the multiple transactions and relations that assemble the heterogeneous elements including the material objects into nearly stable organizational and institutional practices (Li 2007), it becomes possible to capture where and how power operates and where human security is performatively produced. It helps to understand the distinctive interplay between the micro- and macropolitics of global human security.

Conclusion

How does tracing assemblages in the way suggested above matter to critical security studies? Tracing the workings of security through the material objects it produces or appropriates allows for (better) appreciating the variability and contingency as well as the complex interplay between differently levelled security flows. It is possible to see the way the micropolitics of security and macropolitical rationalities and processes relating to international and global security are intimately related. By adopting a flexible research strategy, the contextual particularities of security can be considered. The researcher remains open to unexpected encounters with the research field. The differences in interpretive environments can be taken into account and creatively utilized towards finding new avenues of research otherwise obscured. For example, not only do global programmes only tangentially become adaptable to local settings, but governance is frequently also invented from below, producing hybrid forms of governance in which global and local security cultures become intertwined.

Suggested reading

Bennett, J. (2005a) "The Agency of Assemblage and the North American Blackout", *Public Culture*, 17: 445–465.

Foucault, M. (2009) *Security, Territory, Population: Lectures at the Collège de France 1977–1978*, London: Picador.

Li, T.M. (2007) *The Will to Improve: Governmentality, Development, and the Practice of Politics*, Durham: Duke University Press.

Mitchell, T. (2002) *Rule of Experts: Egypt, Techno-Politics, Modernity*, Berkeley: University of California Press.

Robson, C. (2002) *Real World Research: A Resource for Social Scientists and Practitioner-Researchers*, London: John Wiley and Sons.

Bibliography

www.aamc.org/students/considering/exploring_medical (accessed 16 June 2011).

Aberbach, J.D. and Rockman, B.A. (2002) "Conducting and Coding Elite Interviews", *PS: Political Science*, 35(4): 673–676.

Abraham, T. (2011) *Archival Theory: Notes Towards the Beginnings of a Bibliography*. Online: www.uiweb.uidaho.edu/special-collections/papers/theorybb.htm (accessed 23 February 2012).

Ackerly, B.A. and True, J. (2008) "Reflexivity in Practice: Power and Ethics in Feminist Research on International Relations", *International Studies Review*, 10(4): 693–707.

Ackerly, B.A., Stern, M., and True, J. (eds) (2006) *Feminist Methodologies for International Relations*, Cambridge: Cambridge University Press.

Adey, P. (2008) "Airports, Mobility and the Calculative Architecture of Affective Control", *Geoforum*, 39(1): 438–451.

—— (2010) *Aerial Life: Spaces, Mobilities, Affect*, Malden: Wiley-Blackwell.

Adler, E. and Pouliot, V. (eds) (2011) *International Practices*, Cambridge: Cambridge University Press.

Agamben, G. (1993) *The Coming of Community*, trans. M. Hardt. Minnesota: Minnesota University Press.

—— (1998) *Homo Sacer: Sovereign Power and Bare Life*, trans. D. Heller-Roazen. Stanford: Stanford University Press.

—— (1999) *Potentialities: Collected Essays in Philosophy*, trans. D. Heller-Roazen. Stanford: Stanford University press.

—— (2005) *State of Exception*, trans. K. Attell. Chicago: University of Chicago Press.

—— (2007) *Qu'est-ce qu'un dispositif?* Paris: Payot-Rivages.

Agier, M. (2008) *On the Margins of the World: Refugee Experience Today*, Cambridge: Polity Press.

Agnew, J. (1994) "The territorial trap: The geographical assumptions of International Relations theory", *Review of International Political Economy*, 1(1): 53–80.

—— (2003) *Geopolitics: Re-Visioning World Politics*, 2nd edn, New York: Routledge.

—— (2009) *Globalization and Sovereignty,* Lanham, MD: Rowman and Littlefield Publishers, Inc.

Agrawala, S. (1998a) "Context and Early Origins of the Intergovernmental Panel on Climate Change", *Climatic Change*, 39: 605–620.

—— (1998b) "Structural and Process History of the Intergovernmental Panel on Climate Change", *Climatic Change*, 39: 621–642.

Agrawala, R., and Teitelbaum, E. (2010) "Trends in Funding for Dissertation Field Research: Why Do Political Science and Sociology Students Win So Few Awards?" *PS: Political Science and Politics*, 43(2): 283–289.

Ahlers, M.M., and Meserve, J. (2011) *TSA Security Looks at People who Complain About. . .TSA Security*. Online: http://articles.cnn.com/2011-04-15/travel/tsa.screeners.complain_1_tsa-security-behavior-detection-officers-airport-security?_s=PM:TRAVEL (accessed 17 April 2011).

Ahmed, S. (2004a) "Affective Economies", *Social Text*, 22(2): 117–139.

—— (2004b) *The Cultural Politics of Emotion*, New York: Routledge.

Albrow, M. (1996) *The Global Age: State and Society Beyond Modernity*, Stanford: Stanford University Press.

Allina-Pisano, J. (2009) "How to Tell an Axe Murderer: An Essay on Ethnography, Truth, and Lies", in E. Schatz (ed.) *Political Ethnography: What Immersion Contributes to the Study of Power*, Chicago: University of Chicago Press.

Alvesson, M. and Sköldberg, K. (2000) *Reflexive Methodology: New Vistas for Qualitative Research*, London: SAGE Publications.

Alvestrand, H. (2004) *IETF Mission Statement*, RFC 3935. Online: www.ietf.org/rfc/rfc3935.txt (accessed 17 July 2005).

Amoore, L. (2007) "Vigilant Visualities: The Watchful Politics of the War on Terror", *Security Dialogue*, 38(2): 215–232.

—— (2009) "Algorithmic War: Everyday Geographies of the War on Terror", *Antipode*, 41(1): 49–69.

Amoore, L. and de Goede, M. (2005) "Governance, Risk and Dataveillance in the War on Terror", *Crime, Law and Social Change*, 43(2–3): 149–173.

—— (eds) (2008) *Risk and the War on Terror*, New York: Routledge.

Anderson, Ben (2010) "Security and the Future: Anticipating the Event of Terror", *Geoforum*, 41(2): 227–235.

Andrijasevic, R. (2010) *Migration, Agency and Citizenship in Sex Trafficking*, Basingstoke: Palgrave.

AP Staff (2001) *Rumsfeld Talks of Heroes to Come; Forces on Alert*, USA Today. Online: www.usatoday.com/news/nation/2001/09/11/attack-alert.htm (accessed 1 May 2007).

Appadurai, A. (1996) *Modernity at Large: Cultural Dimensions of Globalization*, Minneapolis: University of Minnesota Press.

Aradau, C. (2004) "Security and the Democratic Scene: Desecuritization and Emancipation", *Journal of International Relations and Development*, 7(4): 388–413.

—— (2010) "Security That Matters: Critical Infrastructure and Objects of Protection", *Security Dialogue*, 41(5): 491–514.

Aradau, C., Lobo-Guerrero, L., and van Munster, R. (2008) "Security, Technologies of Risk, and the Political: Guest Editors' Introduction", *Security Dialogue*, 39(2–3): 147–154.

Aradau, C. and van Munster, R. (2007) "Governing Terrorism through Risk: Taking Precautions, (Un)Knowing the Future", *European Journal of International Relations*, 13(1): 89–115.

—— (2011) *Politics of Catastrophe: Genealogies of the Unknown*, New York: Routledge.

Ashley, R.K. and Walker, R.B.J. (1990) "Speaking the Language of Exile: Dissident Thought in International Studies", *International Studies Quarterly*, 34(3): 259–268.

Augé, M. (1995) *Non-places: Introduction to an Anthropology of Supermodernity*, trans. J. Howe. London: Verso.

Aull Davies, C. (1999) *Reflexive Ethnography: A Guide to Researching Selves and Others*, New York: Routledge.

Austin, J.L. (1975) *How To Do Things with Words*, Oxford: Oxford University Press.

Bainbridge, W.S. (2010) "Introduction", in W.S. Bainbridge (ed.) *Online Worlds: Convergence of the Real and the Virtual*, London: Springer.

Bakare-Yusuf, B. (1999) "The Economy of Violence: Black Bodies and Unspeakable Terror", in J. Price and M. Shildrick (eds) *Feminist Theory and the Body: A Reader*, New York: Routledge.

Bakewell, O. (2008) "Research Beyond the Categories: The Importance of Policy Irrelevant Research into Forced Migration", *Journal of Refugee Studies*, 21(4): 432–453.

Bakhtin, M. (1986) *Speech Genres and Other Late Essays*, trans. V.W. McGee. Austin: University of Texas Press.

Bakker, K. and Bridge, G. (2006) "Material Worlds? Resource Geographies and the 'Matter of Nature'", *Progress in Human Geography*, 30(1): 5–27.

Ballantyne, T. and Burton, A. (eds) (2005) *Bodies in Contact: Rethinking Colonial Encounters in World History*, Durham: Duke University Press.

Balzacq, T. (ed.) (2010a) *Securitization Theory: How Security Problems Emerge and Dissolve*, New York: Routledge.

—— (2010b) "A Theory of Securitization: Origins, Core Assumptions, and Variants", in T. Balzacq (ed.) *Securitization Theory: How Security Problems Emerge and Dissolve*, New York: Routledge.

—— (2010c) "Constructivism and Securitization Studies", in V. Mauer and M. Dunn Cavelty (eds) *The Routledge Handbook of Security Studies*, New York: Routledge.

Bar, N. and Ben-Ari, E. (2005) "Israeli Snipers in the Al-Aqsa Intifada: Killing, Humanity and Lived Experience", *Third World Quarterly*, 26(1):133–152.

Barad, K. (1998) "Getting Real: Technoscientific Practices and the Materialization of Reality", *Differences: A Journal of Feminist Cultural Studies*, 10(2): 87–128.

—— (2003) "Posthumanist Performativity: Toward an Understanding of How Matter Comes To Matter", *Signs: Journal of Women in Culture and Society*, 28(3): 801–831.

—— (2007) *Meeting the Universe Halfway: Quantum Physics and the Entanglement of Matter and Meaning*, Durham: Duke University Press.

Barnett, C. and Inderjit, B. (2009) *Becoming a City of Sanctuary: A Practical Handbook with Inspiring Examples*, North Yorkshire: Plug and Tap.

Barry, A. (2001) *Political Machines: Governing a Technological Society*, London: Athlone Press.

Barsook, P. (1995) "How Anarchy Works: On Location with the Masters of Meta-verse, the Internet Engineering Task Force", *Wired*.

Bartelson, J. (1995) *Genealogy of Sovereignty*, Cambridge: Cambridge University Press.

Barthes, R. (1977) *Image–Music–Text*, London: Fontana.

Basok, T. (2009) "Counter-hegemonic Human Rights Discourses and Migrant Rights Activism in the US and Canada", *International Journal of Comparative Sociology*, 50(2): 183–205.

Bayard de Volo, L. and Schatz, E. (2004) "From the Inside Out: Ethnographic Methods in Political Research", *PS: Political Science and Politics*, 37(2): 267–271.

Bayart, J-F. (2008) *Global Subjects: A Political Critique of Globalization*, New York: Polity Press.

Behar, R. (1996) *The Vulnerable Observer: Anthropology That Breaks Your Heart*, Boston: Beacon Press.

—— (2003) "Ethnography and the Book that Was Lost", *Ethnography*, 4(1):15–39.

Beier, M.J. (2005) *International Relations in Uncommon Places: Indigeneity, Cosmology, and the Limits of International Theory*, New York: Palgrave Macmillan.

Bell, C. (2006) "Surveillance Strategies and Populations at Risk: Biopolitical Governance in Canada's National Security Politics", *Security Dialogue*, 37(2): 147–165.

Ben-Ari, E. and Sion, L. (2005) "'Hungry, Weary and Horny': Joking and Jesting among Israel's Combat Reserves", *Israel Affairs*, 11(4): 655–671.

Ben-Ari, Orit Taubman and Findler, Liora. (2005) "Proximan and Distal Effects of Mortality Salience on Willingness to Engage in Health Promoting Behavior Along the Life Span", *Psychology & Health*, 20(3): 303–318.

Benhabib, S., Butler, J., Cornell, D., and Fraser, N. (1995) *Feminist Contentions: A Philosophical Exchange*, New York: Routledge.

Benjamin, W. (1998) *The Origin of German Tragic Drama*, trans. J. Osborne. London: Verso.

Bennett, J. (2004) "The Force of Things: Steps Toward an Ecology of Matter", *Political Theory*, 32(3): 347–372.

—— (2005a) "The Agency of Assemblage and the North American Blackout", *Public Culture*, 17: 445–465.

—— (2005b) *Empathic Vision: Affect, Trauma, and Contemporary Art*, Stanford: Stanford University Press.

—— (2010) *Vibrant Matter: A Political Ecology of Things*, Durham: Duke University Press.

Berger, P.T. and Luckmann, T. (1990) *The Social Construction of Reality: A Treatise in the Sociology of Knowledge*, New York: Anchor Books.

Berinstein, C., Nyers, P., Wright, C., and Zeheri, S. (2006) *Access Not Fear: Non-Status Immigrants and City Services*, Toronto: "Don't Ask, Don't Tell" Campaign.

Berkenkotter, C. and Huckin, T. (1995) *Genre Knowledge in Disciplinary Communication: Cognition/ Culture/Power*, Hillsdale: Lawrence Erlbaum Associates.

Berry, J.M. (2002) "Validity and Reliability Issues in Elite Interviewing", *PS: Political Science and Politics*, 35(4): 679–682.

Bertelsen, L. and Murphie, A. (2010) "An Ethics of Everyday Infinities and Powers: Félix Guattari on Affect and the Refrain", in M. Gregg and G.J. Seigworth (eds) *The Affect Theory Reader*, Durham: Duke University Press.

Betts, A. (2009) *Forced Migration and Global Politics*, London: Wiley-Blackwell.

Biggs, J.R. and Jones, V. (2010) "Whether and Whither an Applied Career Track for Doctoral Political Scientists", *The Forum*, 8(3): 1–17.

Bignell, J. (2002) *Media Semiotics: An Introduction*, 2nd edn, New York: Manchester University Press.

Bigo, D. (1996) *Polices en résaux: l'expérience européenne*, Paris: Presses de Sciences Po.

—— (2001) "The Möbius Ribbon of Internal and External Security(ies)", in M. Albert, D. Jacobson, and J. Lapid (eds) *Identities, Borders, Orders: Rethinking International Relations Theory*, Minneapolis: University of Minnesota Press.

—— (2002) "Security and Immigration: Toward a Critique of Governmentality of Unease", *Alternatives: Global, Local, Political*, 27(1): 62–92.

—— (2005) "La mondialisation de l'(in)sécurité: Réflexions sur le champ des professionnels de la gestion des inquiétudes et analytique de la transnationalisation des processus d'(in)sécurisation", *Cultures et Conflits*, 58: 53–101.

—— (2008) "Globalized (in)security: the field and the ban–opticon", in D. Bigo and A. Tsoukala (eds) *Terror, Insecurity and Liberty: Illiberal Practices of Liberal Regimes after 9/11*, New York: Routledge.

—— (2011) "Pierre Bourdieu and International Relations: Power of Practices, Practices of Power", *International Political Sociology*, 5(3): 225–258.

Bigo, D. and Tsoukala, A. (eds) (2008) *Terror, Insecurity and Liberty: Illiberal Practices of Liberal Regimes After 9/11*, New York: Routledge.

Bigo, D. and Walker, R.B.J. (2007) "International, Political, Sociology", *International Political Sociology*, 1(1): 1–5.

Bijker, W.E., Hughes, T.P., and Pinch, T. (eds) (1987) *The Social Construction of Technological Systems: New Directions in the Sociology and History of Technology*, Cambridge: MIT Press.

Binford, L. (2004) *Para Salvar la Economía Mexicana: La Trampa de las Remesas*, Online: http://meme.phpwebhosting.com/~migracion/modules/seminar ioe/binfordleight.pdf#search=%22 binford%20leigh%20trampa%20de%20las% 20remesas%22

Blackman, L. and Venn, C. (2010) "Affect", *Body and Society*, 16(1): 7–28.

Blackmore, T. (2005) *War X: Human Extensions in Battlespace*, Toronto: University of Toronto Press.

Bleiker, R. (2001) "The Aesthetic Turn in International Political Theory", *Millennium: Journal of International Studies*, 30(3): 509–533.

Bleiker, R. and Brigg, M. (2010) "Autoethnographic International Relations: Exploring the Self as a Source of Knowledge", *Review of International Studies*, 36(3): 779–798.

Bleiker, R. and Hutchison (2008) "Fear No More: Emotions and World Politics", *Review of International Studies*, 34(S1): 115–135.

Boehmer-Christiansen, S. (1994a) "Global Climate Protection Policy: The Limits of Scientific Advice Part 1", *Global Environmental Change*, 4(2): 140–159.

—— (1994b) "Global Climate Protection Policy: The Limits of Scientific Advice Part 2", *Global Environmental Change*, 4(3): 185–200.

Bolin, B. (2007) *A History of the Science and Politics of Climate Change: The Role of the Intergovernmental Panel on Climate Change*, Cambridge: Cambridge University Press.

Boltanski, L. and Thévenot, L. (2006) *On Justification: Economies of Worth*, Princeton: Princeton University Press.

Boose, L. (1993) "Techno-Muscularity and the 'Boy Eternal': From Quagmire to the Gulf", in A. Kaplan and D.E. Pease (eds) *Cultures of United States Imperialism*, Durham: Duke University Press.

Boot, M. (2006) *War Made New: Weapons, Warriors, and the Making of the Modern World*, New York: Gotham Books.

Bordo, S. (1992) "Review: Postmodern Subjects, Postmodern Bodies", *Feminist Studies*, 18(1): 159–175.

—— (1995) *Unbearable Weight: Feminism, Western Culture and the Body*, Berkeley: University of California Press.

Bourdieu, P. (1972) *Esquisse de la théorie de la pratique*, Paris: Éditions Droz.

—— (1977) *Outline of a Theory of Practice*, Cambridge: Cambridge University Press.

—— (1981) *Questions de sociologie*, Paris: Minuit.

—— (1988) *Homo Academicus*, trans. P. Colier. Stanford: Stanford University Press.

—— (1990a) *The Logic of Practice*, Cambridge: Polity.

—— (1990b) "The Scholastic Point of View", *Cultural Anthropology*, 5(4): 380–391.

—— (1992) *Language and Symbolic Power*, J.B. Thompson (ed.), Cambridge: Polity.

—— (1994) *Raisons pratiques: Sur la théorie de l'action*, Paris: Seuil.

—— (1998) *Homo Academicus*, Cambridge: Polity Press.

—— (2005) "Habitus", in J. Hillier and E. Rooksby (eds) *Habitus: A Sense of Place*, Aldershot: Ashgate.

Bourdieu, P. and Wacquant, L. (1992a) *An Invitation to Reflexive Sociology*, Cambridge: Polity.

—— (1992b) *Réponses. Pour une anthropologie réflexive*, Paris: Seuil.

Bourke, J. (1999) *An Intimate History of Killing: Face-to-Face Killing in Twentieth-Century Warfare*, New York: Basic Books.

Brauch, H.G. (2008) "Conceptual Quartet: Security and its Linkages with Peace, Development, and Environment", in H.G. Brauch, Ú.O. Spring, C. Mesjasz, J. Grin, P. Dunay, N.C. Behera, B. Chorou, P. Kameri-Mbote and P.H. Liotta (eds) *Globalization and Environmental Challenges: Reconceptualizing Security in the 21st Century*, New York: Springer.

Brodeur, J-P. (2006) "Introduction", *Canadian Journal of Criminology and Criminal Justice*, 48(3): 323–331.

Browning, C.R. (1998) *Ordinary Men: Reserve Police Battalion 101 and the Final Solution in Poland*, New York: HarperPerennial.

Brubaker, R., and Cooper, F. (2000) "Beyond 'Identity'", *Theory and Society*, 29(1): 1–47.

Burgess, J.P. (ed.) (2010) *The Routledge Handbook of New Security Studies*, New York: Routledge.

Burke, A. (2007) *Beyond Security, Ethics, and Violence: War against the Other*, New York: Routledge.

Burnham, P., Grant, W., and Layton-Henry, Z. (2008) *Research Methods in Politics*, 2nd edn, New York: Palgrave Macmillan.

Burroughs, C. and Ehrenreich, J. (1993) *Reading the Social Body*, Iowa City: University of Iowa Press.

Bussolini, J. (2010) "What is a Dispositive?", *Foucault Studies*, 10: 85–107.

Butler, J. (1989) "Foucault and the Paradox of Bodily Inscriptions", *The Journal of Philosophy*, 86(11): 601–607.

—— (1993) *Bodies that Matter: On the Discursive Limits of "Sex"*, New York: Routledge.

—— (1999) *Gender Trouble: Feminism and the Subversion of Identity*, New York: Routledge.

—— (2004) *Precarious Life: The Power of Mourning and Violence*, London: Verso.

—— (2009) *Frames of War: When is Life Grievable?* New York: Verso.

Buus, S. (2009) "Hell on Earth: Threats, Citizens and the State from Buffy to Beck", *Cooperation and Conflict*, 44(4): 400–419.

Buzan, B. and Wæver O. (2009) "Macrosecuritization and Security Constellations: Reconsidering Scale in Securitization Theory", *Review of International Studies*, 35(2): 253–276.

Buzan, B., Wæver, O., and de Wilde, J. (1998) *Security: A New Framework for Analysis*, Boulder: Lynne Rienner.

Cabezas, A.L. (1998) "Discourses of Prostitution: The Case of Cuba", in K. Kempadoo and J. Doezema (eds) *Global Sex Workers: Rights, Resistance and Redefinition*, New York: Routledge.

—— (2004) "Between Love and Money: Sex, Tourism and Citizenship in Cuba and the Dominican Republic", *Signs: A Journal of Women in Culture and Society*, 29(4): 987–1015.

—— (2009) *Economies of Desire: Sex and Tourism in Cuba and the Dominican Republic*, Philadelphia: Temple University Press.

Cairncross, F. (1997) *The Death of Distance: How the Communications Revolution is Changing Our Lives*, London: Orion Publishing Group.

Caldicott, H. (1986) *Missile Envy: The Arms Race and Nuclear War*, New York: Bantam Books.

Calhoun, C.J. (1995) *Critical Social Theory: Culture, History and the Challenge of Difference*, Oxford: Blackwell Publishers.

Calhoun, C.J., LiPuma, E., and Postone, M. (1993) *Bourdieu: Critical Perspectives*, Cambridge: Polity.

Callon, M. (1986) "Some Elements of a Sociology of Translation: Domestication of the Scallops and the Fishermen of St. Brieuc Bay", in J. Law (ed) *Power, Action and Belief: A New Sociology of Knowledge*, New York: Routledge.

Campana, A. and Ratelle, J-F. (2010) "Political Violence in the North Caucasus: a Political Sociology Approach", Association for the Study of Nationalities Convention 2010 (Unpublished Paper).

Campbell, D. (1998) *Writing Security: United States Foreign Policy and the Politics of Identity*, 2nd edn, Minneapolis: University of Minnesota Press.

—— (2004) "Horrific Blindness: Images of Death in Contemporary Media", *Journal for Cultural Research*, 8(1): 55–74.

—— (2011) "Thinking Images v.13: Target Libya". 22 March 2011, www.david-campbell.org/2011/03/22/thinking-images-v-13-target-libya (accessed 4 July 2012).

Campbell, D. and Dillon, M. (1993) *The Political Subject of Violence*, New York: Manchester University Press.

Carver, T. and Chambers, S. (2008) *Judith Butler's Precarious Politics: Critical Encounters*, New York: Routledge.

c.a.s.e. collective (2006) "Critical Approaches to Security in Europe: A Networked Manifesto", *Security Dialogue*, 37(4): 443–487.

Castells, M. (2001) *The Internet Galaxy: Reflections on the Internet, Business, and Society*, New York: Oxford University Press.

Cerwonka, A. (2007) "Nervous Conditions: The Stakes in Interdisciplinary Research", in A. Cerwonka and L.H. Malkki (eds) *Improvising Theory: Press and Temporality in Ethnographic Fieldwork*, Chicago: University of Chicago Press.

Ceyhan, A. and Tsoukala, A. (2002) "The Securitization of Migration in Western Societies: Ambivalent Discourses and Policies", *Alternatives: Global, Local, Political*, 27(1): 21–39.

Chambers, S. and Carver, T. (2008) *Judith Butler and Political Theory: Troubling Politics*, New York: Routledge.

Chandler, D. (2007) *Semiotics: The Basics*, New York: Routledge.

Cheek, J. (2008) "Research Design", in L.M. Given (ed.) *The SAGE Encyclopedia of Qualitative Research Methods*, London: SAGE Publications.

Chilton, P. (1996) "The Meaning of Security", in F.A. Beer and R. Hariman (eds) *Post-Realism: The Rhetorical Turn in International Relations*, East Lansing: Michigan State University Press.

Clark, D.D. (1992) "A Cloudy Crystal Ball: Visions of the Future", presented at the 24th Meeting of the Internet Engineering Task Force, Cambridge, Mass., 13–17 July, Online: http://ietf20.isoc.org/videos/future_ietf_92.pdf.

Clark, G. (2004) "Insurance as an Instrument of War in the 18th Century", *The Geneva Papers on Risk and Insurance*, 29: 247–257.

Clearwater, D.A. (2010) "Living in a Militarized Culture: War, Games and Experience of the U.S. Empire", *TOPIA: Canadian Journal of Cultural Studies*, 23–24: 260–85.

Clifford, J. (1983) "On Ethnographic Authority", *Representations*, 2:118–146.

—— (1988) *The Predicament of Culture: Twentieth-Century Ethnography, Literature, and Art*, Cambridge: Harvard University Press.

—— (2010) "Introduction: Partial Truths", in J. Clifford and G.E. Marcus (eds) *Writing Culture: The Poetics and Politics of Ethnography, 25th anniversary edition*, Los Angeles: University of California Press.

Clough, P. (2007) "Introduction", in P. Clough and J. Halley (eds) *The Affective Turn: Theorizing the Social*, Durham: Duke University Press.

CodePink: Women For Peace. Online: www.codepink.org

Cohn, C. (1987) "Sex and Death in the Rational World of Defense Intellectuals", *Signs: A Journal of Women in Culture and Society*, 12(4): 687–718.

Coker, C. (2007) *The Warrior Ethos: Military Culture and the War on Terror*, New York: Routledge.

—— (2008) *Ethics and War in the 21st Century*, New York: Routledge.

Colbert, S. (2005) *The Colbert Report*. Online: www.colbertnation.com/the-colbert-report-videos/ 24039/october-17-2005/the-word—-truthiness (accessed 16 June 2011).

Coll, K. (2004) "*Necesidades y Problemas*: Immigrant Latina Vernaculars of Belonging, Coalition, and Citizenship in San Francisco, California", *Latino Studies*, 2(2): 186–209.

Collier, P. and Hoeffler, A. (2004) "Greed and Grievance in Civil War", *Oxford Economic Papers*, 56(4): 563–595.

Collier, S. (2008) "Enacting Catastrophe: Preparedness, Insurance, Budgetary Rationalization", *Economy and Society*, 37(2): 224–250.

Collier, S. and Lakoff, A. (2008) "Distributed Preparedness: Space, Security and Citizenship in the United States", in D. Cowen and E. Gilbert (eds) *War, Citizenship, Territory*, New York: Routledge.

Commission on Human Security (2003) *Human Security Now*, New York: United Nations.

Connolly, W.E. (2002) *Neuropolitics: Thinking, Culture, Speed*, Minneapolis: University of Minnesota Press.

—— (2004) "Method, Problem, Faith", in I. Shapiro, T.E. Masound, and R.M. Smith (eds) *Problems and Methods in the Study of Politics*, Cambridge: Cambridge University Press.

—— (2005) "The Evangelical-Capitalist Resonance Machine", *Political Theory*, 33(6): 869–886.

Cooper, M. (2006) "Pre-empting Emergence: The Biological Turn in the War on Terror", *Theory, Culture and Society*, 23(1): 113–135.

Cooper, S. (2002) *Technoculture and Critical Theory: In the Service of the Machine?* New York: Routledge.

Covino, W.A. (1994) *The Art of Wondering: A Revisionist Return to the History of Rhetoric*, Portsmouth: Heinemann.

Coward, M. (2009) "Network-Centric Violence, Critical Infrastructure and the Urbanization of Security", *Security Dialogue*, 40(4–5): 399–418.

Cox, R.W. (1986) "Social Forces, States and World Orders: Beyond International Relations Theory", in R.O. Keohane (ed.) *Neorealism and its Critics*, New York: Columbia University Press.

Crane-Seeber, J. (2011) "Everyday Counterinsurgency", *International Political Sociology*, 5(4): 450–453.

Crawford, R.M.A. and Jarvis, D.S.L. (eds) (2000) *International Relations – Still an American Social Science?*, Albany: SUNY Press.

Crocker, D. (1993) "Making Standards the IETF Way", *StandardView*, 1(1), 48–53.

Curtis, B. (2004) "Reading Reflexively", *Journal of Historical Sociology*, 17(2/3): 240–263.

CVECO (2011) *Chemical Valley Emergency Control Organization*. Online: www.caer.ca/cveco.html (accessed 19 April 2011).

Dalby, S. (2007) "Ecology, Security, and Change in the Anthropocene", *Brown Journal of World Affairs*, 13(2): 155–164.

Danto, A. (1999) *The Body/Body Problem: Selected Essays*, Berkeley: University of California Press.

Darling, J. (2010) "A City of Sanctuary: the Relational Re-imagining of Sheffield's Asylum Politics", *Transactions of the Institute of British Geographers*, 35(1): 125–140.

Daston, L. and Park, K. (2001) *Wonders and the Order of Nature, 1150–1750*, New York: Zone Books.

Daston, L., Vidal, F., Chamayou, G., and Mayer, A. (2012) *The New Sciences of the Archives*. Max Planck Institute for the History of Science. Online: www.mpiwg-berlin.mpg.de/en/research/ projects/DeptII_Daston-SciencesOfTheArchives/index_html (accessed 23 February 2012).

Dauphinee, E. and Masters, C. (eds) (2006) *The Logics of Biopower and War on Terror*, London: Palgrave Macmillan.

Davison, N. (2009) *Non-Lethal Weapons*, London: Palgrave Macmillan.

Dean, M. (1992) "A Genealogy of the Government of Poverty", *Economy and Society*, 21(3): 215–251.

—— (1994) *Critical and Effective Histories: Foucault's Methods and Historical Sociology*, New York: Routledge.

Deibert, R. and Rohonzinski, R. (2008) "Good for Liberty, Bad for Security? Global Civil Society and the Securitization of the Internet", in R.J. Deibert, J. Palfrey, R. Rohonzinski, and J. Zittrain (eds) *Access Denied: The Practice and Policy of Global Internet Filtering*, Cambridge: MIT Press.

Deleuze, G. (1953) *Empirisme et Subjectivité*, Paris: PUF.

—— (1986) *Foucault*, Paris: Editions de Minuits.

Deleuze, G. and Guattari, F. (1994) *What is Philosophy*, trans. H. Tomlinson and G. Burchell. New York: Columbia University Press.

—— (2009) *A Thousand Plateaus: Capitalism and Schizophrenia*, trans. B. Massumi. Minneapolis: Minnesota University Press.

Denzin, N.K. and Lincoln, Y.S. (2005) "Introduction: The Discipline and Practice of Qualitative Research", in. N.K. Denzin and Y.S. Lincoln (eds) *Handbook of Qualitaitve Research*, 3rd edn, Thousand Oaks: SAGE Publications.

Department of Homeland Security (2003) *Homeland Security Presidential Directive 7*. Online: www.dhs.gov/xabout/laws/gc_1214597989952.shtm (accessed 1 September 2011).

Der Derian, J. (1987) *On Diplomacy: A Genealogy of Western Estrangement,* Oxford: Blackwell Publishers.

—— (1989) "Textualizing Global Politics" in J. Der Derian, and M.J. Shapiro (eds) *International/ Intertextual Relations: Postmodern Readings of World Politics*, New York: Lexington Books.

—— (1992) *Antidiplomacy: Spies, Terror, Speed, War*, Oxford: Blackwell Publishers.

—— (2009a) "Cyberwar, Videogames, and the Gulf War Syndrome", in *Critical Practices in International Theory: Selected Essays*, New York: Routledge.

—— (2009b) *Virtuous War: Mapping the Military-Industrial-Media-Entertainment Network*, 2nd edn, New York: Routledge.

—— (2009c) *Critical Practices in International Theory: Selected Essays*, New York: Routledge.

Der Derian, J. and Shapiro M.J. (eds) (1989) *International/Intertextual Relations: Postmodern Readings of World Politics*, New York: Lexington Books.

Der Derian, J., Urdis, D. and Urdis, M. (2010) *Human Terrain: War Becomes Academic*, Urdis Film and Oxyopia Productions with the Global Media Project and the Watson Institute for International Studies. Online: http://humanterrainmovie.com

Derrida, J. (1980) "The Law of Genre", *Critical Inquiry*, 7(1): 55–81.

Dillon, M. (1995) "Sovereignty and Governmentality: From the Problematics of the 'New World Order' to the Ethical Problematic of the World Order", *Alternatives: Global, Local, Political*, 20(3): 323–368.

—— (2003) "Virtual Security: A Life Science of (Dis)order", *Millennium: Journal of International Studies*, 32(3): 531–558.

—— (2007) "Governing Through Contingency: The Security of Biopolitical Governance", *Political Geography*, 26(1): 41–47.

—— (2008) "Underwriting Security", *Security Dialogue*, 39(2/3): 309–332.

Dillon, M. and Lobo-Guerrero, L. (2008) "Biopolitics of Security in the 21st Century", *Review of International Studies*, 34(2): 265–292.

Dillon, M. and Reid, J. (2006) "Global Liberal Governance: Biopolitics, Security and War", *Millennium: Journal of International Studies*, 30(1): 41–66.

—— (2009) *The Liberal Way of War: Killing to Make Life Live*, New York: Taylor and Francis.

Diprose, R., Stephenson, N., Mills, C., Race, K., and Hawkins, G. (2008) "Governing the Future: The Paradigm of Prudence in Political Technologies of Risk Management", *Security Dialogue*, 39(2–3): 267–288.

Dittmer, J. (2010) *Popular Culture, Geopolitics, and Identity*, Lanham, MD: Rowman and Littlefield.

Dodge, M. and Kitchin, R. (1998) *Mapping Cyberspace*, New York: Routledge.

Doty, R. (1993) "Foreign Policy as a Social Construction: A Post-Positivist Analysis of U.S. Counterinsurgency Policy in the Philippines", *International Studies Quarterly*, 37: 297–320.

Dreyfus, H.L., and Rabinow, P. (1982) *Michel Foucault: Beyond Structuralism and Hermeneutics*, Chicago: The University of Chicago Press.

Driver, F. (1985) "Power, Space, and the Body: A Critical Assessment of Foucault's Discipline and Punish", *Environment and Planning D: Society and Space*, 3(4): 425–446.

Ducheneault, N. (2010) "Massively Multiplayer Online Games as Living Laboratories: Opportunities and Pitfalls", in W.S. Bainbridge (ed.) *Online Worlds: Convergence of the Real and the Virtual*, London: Springer.

Dudrick, D. (2005) "Foucault, Butler and the Body", *European Journal of Philosophy*, 13(2): 226–246.

Dyer-Witheford, N. and de Peuter, G. (2009) *Games of Empire: Global Capitalism and Video Games*, Minneapolis: University of Minnesota Press.

Eagleton-Pierce, M. (2011) "Advancing a Reflexive International Relations", *Millennium: Journal of International Studies*, 39(1): 1–19.

Eckl, J. (2008) "Responsible Scholarship after Leaving the Veranda: Normative Issues Faced by Field Researchers – and Armchair Scientists", *International Political Sociology*, 2(3): 185–203.

Edkins, J. (2000) "Sovereign Power, Zones of Indistinction, and the Camp", *Alternatives: Global, Local, Political*, 25(1): 3–25.

—— (2003) *Trauma and the Memory of Politics*, Cambridge: Cambridge University Press.

Edkins, J. and Pin-Fat, V. (2005) "Through the Wire: Relations of Power and Relations of Violence", *Millennium: Journal of International Studies*, 34(1): 1–24.

Edkins, J., Pin-Fat, V., and Shapiro, M.J. (eds) (2004) *Sovereign Lives: Power in Global Politics*, New York: Routledge.

Edkins, J. and Vaughan-Williams, N. (eds) (2009) *Critical Theorists and International Relations*, New York: Routledge.

Edwards, P.N. (2003) "Infrastructure and Modernity: Force, Time and Social Organisation in the History of Sociotechnical Systems," in T. Misa, P. Brey, and A. Feenberg (eds) *Modernity and Technology*, Cambridge, Mass.: MIT Press.

—— (2006) "Meteorology as Infrastructural Globalism", *Osiris*, 21(1): 229–250.

Egner, D. (1977) *The Evaluation of Less Lethal Weapons*, Maryland: Human Engineering Laboratory Aberdeen Proving Ground.

Ehrenreich, B. (2001) *Nickel and Dimed: On (Not) Getting By in America*, New York: Henry Holt.

Elbe, Stefan (2008) "AIDS, Security and Three Concepts of Risk", *Security Dialogue*, 39(2–3): 177–198.

—— (2010) *Security and Global Health*, London: Polity.

Elden, S. (2001) *Mapping the Present: Heidegger, Foucault and the Project of a Spatial History*, London: Continuum.

—— (2010) "Land, Terrain, Territory", *Progress in Human Geography*, 34(6): 799–817.

Elgar, F.J. (2003). PhD degree completion in Canadian universities (Final Report). Dalhousie University: Graduate Student Association of Canada.

Elias, N. (1978) *What is Sociology?* New York: Columbia University Press.

Elliott, J. R. and Pais, J. (2006) "Race, Class, and Hurricane Katrina: Social Differences in Human Responses to Disaster", *Social Science Research*, 35(2): 295–321.

Emerson, R.M., Fretz, R.I., and Shaw, L.L. (1995) *Writing Ethnographic Fieldnotes: Chicago Guides to Writing, Editing, and Publishing*, Chicago: University of Chicago Press.

Engelhardt, T. (2010) *The American Way of War: How Bush's Wars Became Obama's*, Chicago: Haymarket Books.

England, K.V.L. (1994) "Getting Personal: Reflexivity, Positionality, and Feminist Research", *The Professional Geographer*, 46(1): 80–89.

Enloe, C. (1990) *Bananas, Beaches and Bases: Making Feminist Sense of International Relations*, Berkeley: University of California Press.

—— (1996) "Margins, Silences and Bottom Rungs: How to Overcome the Underestimation of Power in International Relations", in S. Smith, K. Booth, and M. Zalewski (eds) *International Theory: Positivism and Beyond*, Cambridge: Cambridge University Press.

—— (2000) *Maneuvers: The International Politics of Militarizing Women's Lives,* Los Angeles: University of California Press.

—— (2004) *The Curious Feminist: Searching for Women in a New Age of Empire*, Berkeley: University of California Press.

—— (2011) "The Mundane Matters", *International Political Sociology*, 5(4): 447–450.

Epstein, C. (2007) "Guilty Bodies, Productive Bodies, Destructive Bodies: Crossing the Biometric Borders", *International Political Sociology*, 1(1): 149–164.

Ericson, R. (2006) "Ten Uncertainties of Risk-management Approaches to Security", *Canadian Journal of Criminology and Criminal Justice*, 48(3): 345–357.

Eriksson J. (1999a) "Observers or Advocates? On the Political Role of Security Analysts", *Cooperation and Conflict*, 34(3): 311–330.

—— (1999b) "Debating the Politics of Security Studies: Response to Goldmann, Wæver, and Willams", *Cooperation and Conflict*, 34(3): 345–352.

European Commission (2004) *Communication from the Commission to the Council and the European Parliament: Critical Infrastructure Protection in the Fight against Terrorism*. Com702. Online: http://europa.eu/legislation_summaries/justice_freedom_security/fight_against_terrorism/l33259_en.htm (accessed 12 March 2010).

European Union (2006) "Directive 2006/24/EC of the European Parliament and of the Council of 15 March 2006 on the retention of data generated or processed in connection with the provision of publicly available electronic communications services or of public communications networks and amending Directive 2002/58/EC", *Official Journal of the European Communities*, L 105.

Ewald, F. (1991) "Insurance and Risk", in G. Burchell, C. Gordon, and P. Miller (eds) *The Foucault Effect: Studies in Governmentality, With Two Lectures and an Interview with Michel Foucault*, Chicago: The University of Chicago Press.

Fairclough, N. (1992) *Discourse and Social Change*, Cambridge: Polity Press.

Fairclough, N. and Wodak, R. (1997) "Critical Discourse Analysis", in T.A. van Dijk (ed.) *Introduction to Discourse Analysis*, London: SAGE Publications.

Feldman, A. (1991) *Formations of Violence: The Narrative of the Body and Political Terror in Northern Ireland*, Chicago: University of Chicago Press.

Feldschuh, M. (2002) *The September 11 Photo Project*, Toronto: HarperCollins Canada.

Ferguson, J. (2006) *Global Shadows: Africa in the Neoliberal World Order*, Durham: Duke University Press.

Feyerabend, P. (1979) "Dialogue on Method", in G. Radnitzky and G. Anderson (eds) *The Structure and Development of Science*, Dordrecht: Reidel.

Fierke, K.M. (2007) *Critical Approaches to International Security*, Malden, MA: Polity.

Fine, G.A. (1993) "Ten Lies of Ethnography: Moral Dilemmas of Field Research", *Journal of Contemporary Ethnography*, 22(3): 267–294.

Fischer, F. (2003) *Reframing Public Policy: Discursive Politics and Deliberative Practices*, Oxford: Oxford University Press.

—— (2009) *Democracy and Expertise: Reorienting Policy Inquiry,* Oxford: Oxford University Press.

Fischer, F. and Forrester, J. (eds) (1993) *The Argumentative Turn in Policy Analysis and Planning,* Durham: Duke University Press.

Fish, S. (1980) *Is There a Text in this Class? The Authority of Interpretive Communities*, Cambridge: Harvard University Press.

Flick, U. (2004) "Design and Process in Qualitative Research", in U. Flick, E. von Kardorff and I. Steinke (eds) *A Companion to Qualitative Research*, London: SAGE Publications.

"Forum on Autoethnography and International Relations" (2010) *Review of International Studies*, 36(4): 777–818.

Foucault, M. (1966a) *L'archéologie du savoir*, Paris: Gallimard.

—— (1966b) *Les Mots et les Choses. Une archéologie des sciences humaine*, Paris: Gallimard.

—— (1971) *L'ordre du discours*, Paris: Gallimard.

—— (1972) *Archaeology of Knowledge and the Discourse on Language*, trans. A.M. Sheridan Smith. New York: Vintage.

—— (1975) *Surveiller et punir: Naissance de la prison*, Paris: Gallimard.

—— (1976) *Histoire de la sexualité I. La volonté de savoir*, Paris: Gallimard.

—— (1978) *Sécurité, Territoire, Population*, Paris: Gallimard.

—— (1980a) *The History of Sexuality, Volume I: An Introduction*, trans. R. Hurley. New York: Vintage Books.

—— (1980b) *Power/Knowledge: Selected Interviews and Other Writings, 1972–1977*, Brighton: Harvester Press.

—— (1981) "The Order of Discourse", in R. Young (ed.) *Untying the Text: A Post-Structuralist Reader*, New York: Routledge.

—— (1988) "Practicing Criticism", in L. Kritzman (ed.) *Michel Foucault: Politics, Philosophy, Culture: Interviews and Other Writings 1977–1984*, New York: Routledge.

—— (1991) "Governmentality", in G. Burchell and C. Gordon (eds) *The Foucault Effect: Studies in Governmentality*, Chicago: University of Chicago Press.

—— (1994) *The Order of Things: An Archaeology of the Human Sciences*, New York: Vintage.

—— (1995) *Discipline and Punish: The Birth of the Prison*, trans. A. Sheridan. New York: Vintage.

—— (1997a) "Michael Foucault: An Interview by Stephen Riggins", in P. Rabinow (ed.) *Ethics: Subjectivity and Truth, Essential Works of Michel Foucault 1954–1984, Vol. I*, New York: The New Press.

—— (1997b) "Nietzsche, Genealogy, History", in D.F. Bouchard (ed.) *Language, Counter-Memory, Practice*, Ithaca: Cornell University Press.

—— (1997c) "What is an Author?", in D.F. Bouchard (ed.) *Language, Counter-Memory, Practice*, Ithaca: Cornell University Press.

—— (1997d) *"Society Must Be Defended": Lectures at the Collège de France 1975–1976*, New York: Picador.

—— (1998) "Aesthetics, Method, and Epistemology", in J. D. Faubion (ed.) *Essential Works of Michel Foucault, Vol. 2*, New York: The New Press.

—— (2000a) "Space, Knowledge, Power", in J.D. Faubion (ed.) *Power: Essential Works of Michel Foucault 1954–1984, Vol. III*, New York: The New Press.

—— (2000b) "Truth and Power", in J.D. Faubion (ed.) *Power: Essential Works of Michel Foucault 1954–1984, Vol. III*, New York: The New Press.

—— (2003a) "Questions of Method", in P. Rabinow and N. Rose (eds) *The Essential Foucault*, New York: The New Press.

—— (2003b) "The Subject and Power", in P. Rabinow and N. Rose (eds) *The Essential Foucault*, New York: The New Press.

—— (2004a) *Abnormal: Lectures at the Collège de France, 1974–1975*, New York: Picador.

—— (2004b) *Archaeology of Knowledge*, trans. A.M. Sheridan Smith. New York: Routledge.

—— (2006) *History of Madness*, trans. J. Murphy and J. Khalfa, J. Khalfa (ed.) New York: Routledge.

—— (2006) *Psychiatric Power: Lectures at the Collège de France, 1973–74*, Basingstoke: Palgrave Macmillan.

—— (2008) *The Birth of Biopolitics: Lectures at the Collège De France, 1978–79*, Basingstoke: Palgrave Macmillan.

—— (2009) *Security, Territory, Population: Lectures at the Collège de France 1977–1978*, London: Picador.

Foucault, M., Gutman, H., Hutton, P.H., and Martin, L.H. (1988) *Technologies of the Self: A Seminar with Michel Foucault*, Amherst: University of Massachusetts Press.

Frampton, C., Kinsman, G., Thompson, A., and Tilleczek, K. (2006) *Sociology for Changing the World: Social Movements/Social Research*, Black Point: Fernwood.

Friedman, T.L. (2000) *The Lexus and the Olive Tree*, New York: Anchor Publications.

—— (2005) *The World is Flat: A Brief History of the Twenty-First Century*, New York: Farrar, Straus and Giroux.

Friedrich, C.J. (1937) *Constitutional Government and Politics: Nature and Development*, New York: Harper and Brothers.

Fuller, G., and Harley, R. (2004) *Aviopolis: A Book about Airports*, London: Black Dog Publishing.

Gadamer, H-G. (1979) *Truth and Method*, London: Sheed and Ward.

Galloway, A.R. (2004) *Protocol: How Control Exists after Decentralization*, Cambridge: MIT Press.

Galtung, J. (1990) "Cultural Violence", *Journal of Peace Research*, 27(3): 291–305.

Geertz, C. (1973) *The Interpretation of Cultures*, New York: Basic Books.

de Genova, N. (2002) "Migrant 'Illegality' and Deportability in Everyday Life", *Annual Review of Anthropology*, 31: 419–447.

Ghorashi, H. (2007) "Refugee Voice, Giving Silence a Chance: The Importance of Life Stories for Research on Refugees", *Journal of Refugee Studies*, 21(1): 117–132.

Gibb, D.E.W. (1957) *Lloyd's of London: A Study in Individualism*, London: Macmillan and Co. Ltd.

Gilbert, E. (forthcoming) "Geographic Insights into Political Identity", in C. Flint (ed) *International Studies Compendium*, Oxford: Blackwell.

Gillem, M.L. (2007) *America Town: Building the Outposts of Empire*, Minneapolis: University of Minnesota Press.

de Goede, M. (2012) *Speculative Security: The Politics of Pursuing Terrorist Monies*, Minneapolis: University of Minnesota Press.

Goldmann, K. (1999) "Issues, Not Labels, Please!: Reply to Eriksson", *Cooperation and Conflict*, 34(3): 331–333.

Goldstein, K. (2002) "Getting in the Door: Sampling and Completing Elite Interviews", *PS: Political Science and Politics*, 35(4): 669–672.

González, R.J. (2007) "Towards Mercenary Anthropology", *Anthropology Today*, 23(3): 14–19.

—— (2009) "Embedded: Information Warfare and the 'Human Terrain'" in the Network of Concerned Anthropologists (eds) *The Counter-counterinsurgency Manual: Or Notes on Demilitarizing American Society*, Chicago: Prickly Paradigm Press.

Gordon, A. (2004) *Naked Airport: A Cultural History of the World's Most Revolutionary Structure*, New York: Metropolitan Books.

Gordon, C. (1980) "Afterword", in C. Gordon (ed.) *Power/Knowledge: Selected Interviews and Other Writings, 1972–1977*, New York: Pantheon.

Gosztola, K. (2011) *Jeremy Scahill: The Obama Doctrine Is No Different Than Bush's*, thenation.com, Online: www.thenation.com/video/159638/jeremy-scahill-obama-doctrine-no-different-bushs (accessed 2 April 2011).

Gottmann, J. (1973) *The Significance of Territory*, Charlottesville: University Press of Virginia.

Gould, D.B. (2009) *Moving Politics: Emotion and ACT UP's Fight against AIDS*, Chicago: University of Chicago Press.

Graeber, D. (2004) *Fragments of an Anarchist Anthropology*, Chicago: Prickly Paradigm Press.

—— (2009) *Direct Action: An Ethnography*, Oakland: AK Press.

Graham, S. (2006) "Homeland Insecurities? Katrina and the Politics of 'Security' in Metropolitan America", *Space and Culture*, 9(1): 63–67.

—— (2008) "Cities and the "War on Terror", in M. Sorkin (ed.) *Indefensible Space: The Architecture of the National Insecurity State*, New York: Routledge.

—— (2010) *Cities Under Siege: The New Military Urbanism*, London: Verso.

Graham, S. and Thrift, N. (2007) "Out of Order: Understanding Repair and Maintenance", *Theory, Culture, Society*, 24(3): 1–25.

Grayson, K. (2011) "Targeted Killing and the Scopic Regime of Counter–Terrorism", *Chasing Dragons: Security, Politics, Culture blog*, Online: www.chasingdragons.org/2011/07/targeted-killing-and-the-scopic-regime-of-counter-terrorism.html (accessed on 7 July 2011).

Grayson, K., Davies, M., and Philpott, S. (2009) "Pop goes IR? Researching the Popular Culture–World Politics Continuum", *Politics*, 29(3): 155–163.

Gregg, M., and Seigworth, G.J. (eds) (2010) *The Affect Theory Reader*, Durham: Duke University Press.

Gregory, D. (2004) *The Colonial Present: Afghanistan, Palestine, Iraq*, Oxford: Blackwell.

—— (2006) "The Black Flag: Guantánamo Bay and the Space of Exception", *Geografiska Annaler B*, 89: 405–427.

—— (2011) "From a View to a Kill: Drones and Late Modern War, Theory, Culture, and Society", presented at the Association of American Geographers annual meeting, Seattle, WA, April 12–16 (made available by the author).

Gregory, D. and Pred, A. (eds) (2007) *Violent Geographies: Fear, Terror and Political Violence*, New York: Routledge.

Gregson, N. and Rose, G. (2000) "Taking Butler Elsewhere: Performative Spatialities and Subjectivities", *Environment and Planning D: Society and Space*, 18(4): 433–452.

Grix, J. (2002) "Introducing Students to the Generic Terminology of Social Research", *Politics*, 22(3): 175–186.

Grondin, D. (2009) "The (Power) Politics of Space: The US Astropolitical Discourse of Global Dominance in the War on Terror", in N. Bormann and M. Sheehan (eds) *Securing Outer Space*, New York: Routledge.

—— (2010) "The New Frontiers of the National Security State: The US Global Governmentality of Contingency", in M. Doucet and M. de Larrinaga (eds) *Security and Global Governmentality: Globalization, Governance and the State*, New York: Routledge.

Grondin, D. and Racine-Sibulka, P. (2011) "A Virtual Geography of Aerial Unmanned Warfare with the World as Battlefield: The Rise of Killer Robots and Killing Drones, the End of the Warrior Ethos?" presented at the Association of American Geographers annual meeting, Seattle, WA, April 12–16.

Grossman, D. (1995) *On Killing: The Psychological Cost of Learning to Kill in War and Society*, Boston: Little, Brown.

Grosz, E. (1994) *Volatile Bodies: Toward a Corporeal Feminism*, Bloomington: Indiana University Press.

Gubrium, J.F. and Holstein, J.A. (2001) *Handbook of Interview Research: Context and Method*, London: SAGE Publications.

Guibert, N. and Zecchini, L. (2011) *La guerre à longue distance*, Le Monde.

Guild, E., Groenendijk, K., and Carrera, S. (2009) *Illiberal Liberal States: Immigration, Citizenship and Integration in the EU*, Aldershot: Ashgate.

Guillaume, L. (2012) *War on the Body*, New York: Routledge.

Guillaume, X. (2002) "Reflexivity and Subjectivity: A Dialogical Perspective for and on International Relations Theory", *Forum: Qualitative Social Research*, 3(3): Art.13.

—— (2011) *International Relations and Identity: A Dialogical Approach*, New York: Routledge.

Gusterson, H. (2009) "Militarizing Knowledge", in the Network of Concerned Anthropologists (eds) *The Counter-counterinsurgency Manual: Or Notes on Demilitarizing American Society*, Chicago: Prickly Paradigm Press.

Haas, P.M. (2000) "International Institutions and Social Learning in the Management of Global Environmental Risks", *Policy Studies Journal*, 28(3): 558–575.

Hacking, I. (1999) *The Social Construction of What?* Cambridge: Harvard University Press.

Hainmuller, J. and Lemnitzer, J.M. (2003) "Why Do Europeans Fly Safer? The Politics of Airport Security in Europe and the US", *Terrorism and Political Violence*, 15(4): 1–36.

Halliday, M.A.K. and Hasan, R. (1976) *Cohesion in English*, London: Longman.

Hansen, L. (2000) "The Little Mermaid's Silent Security Dilemma and the Absence of Gender in the Copenhagen School", *Millennium: Journal of International Studies*, 29(2): 285–306.

—— (2006) *Security as Practice: Discourse Analysis and the Bosnian War*, New York: Routledge.

—— (2011) "Theorizing the Image for Security Studies: Visual Securitization and the Muhammad Cartoon Crisis", *European Journal of International Relations*, 17(1): 51–74.

Haraway, D. (1991) *Simians, Cyborgs, and Women: The Reinvention of Nature*, New York: Routledge.

—— (1998) "Situated Knowledges: The Science Question in Feminism and the Privilege of Partial Perspective", *Feminist Studies*, 14(3): 575–599.

Hay, C. (2006) "Political Ontology", in R.E. Goodin and C. Tilly (eds) *The Oxford Handbook of Contextual Political Analysis*, Oxford: Oxford University Press.

Held, D., McGrew, A., Goldblatt, D., and Perraton, J. (1999) *Global Transformations: Politics, Economics and Culture*, Cambridge: Polity Press.

Hengehold, L. (2007) *The Body Problematic: Political Imagination in Kant and Foucault*, University Park: Pennsylvania State University Press.

Hewett, B.L., Robideaux, C., and Remley, D. (2010) "Principles for Exploring Virtual Collaborative Writing", in B.L. Hewett and C. Robideaux (eds) *Virtual Collaborative Writing in the Workplace: Computer-Mediated Communication Technologies and Processes*, Hershey: IGI Global.

Heyes, C. (2007) *Self-Transformations: Foucault, Ethics, and Normalized Bodies*, New York: Oxford University Press.

Higgin, T. (2010) "'Turn the Game Console Off Right Now': War, Subjectivity, and Control in Metal Gear Solid 2", in N. Huntemann and M. Thomas Payne (eds) *Joystick Soldiers: The Politics of Play in Military Video Games*, New York: Routledge.

Hill, M.R. (1993) *Archival Strategies and Technique*, London: SAGE Publications.

Hochschield, A.R. (1979) "Emotion Work, Feeling Rules, and Social Structure", *American Journal of Sociology*, 85(3): 551–575.

—— (1983) *The Managed Heart: The Commercialization of Human Feelings*, Berkeley: University of California Press.

Hook, D. (2005) "Genealogy, Discourse, 'Effective History': Foucault and the Work of Critique", *Qualitative Research in Psychology*, 2(1): 3–31.

Hopf, T. (2010) "The Logic of Habit in International Relations", *European Journal of International Relations*, 16(4): 539–561.

Howell, A. (2007) "Victims or Madmen? The Diagnostic Competition over "Terrorist" Detainees at Guantánamo Bay", *International Political Sociology*, 1(1): 29–47.

—— (2010) "Sovereignty, Security, Psychiatry: Liberation and the Failure of Mental Health Governance in Iraq", *Security Dialogue*, 41(4): 347–367.

—— (2011) *Madness in International Relations: Psychology, Security, and the Global Governance of Mental Health*, New York: Routledge.

Huntemann, N. (2010) "Interview with Colonel Casey Wardynski", in N. Huntemann and M.T. Payne (eds) *Joystick Soldiers: The Politics of Play in Military Video Games*, New York: Routledge.

Huynh, K. (2008) *Where the Sea Takes Us: A Vietnamese–Australian Story*, Sydney: Harper Collins.

Huysmans, J. (2006) *The Politics of Insecurity: Fear, Migration and Asylum in the EU*, New York: Routledge.

—— (2008) "The Jargon of Exception: On Schmitt, Agamben and the Absence of Political Society", *International Political Sociology*, 2(1): 165–183.

IETF Secretariat, CNRI, and Malkin, G. (1994) "The Tao of IETF: A Guide for New Attendees of the Internet Engineering Task Force", RFC 1718.

Inayatullah, N. (ed.) (2010) *Autobiographical International Relations: I, IR*, New York: Routledge.

Inayatullah, N. and Blaney, D. (2004) *International Relations and the Problem of Difference*, New York: Routledge.

Innis, R.E. (ed.) (1985) *Semiotics: An Introductory Reader*, London: Hutchinson.

Intergovernmental Panel on Climate Change (IPCC) (2011) *The Intergovernmental Panel on Climate Change Website*. Online: www.ipcc.ch/organization/organization.shtml (accessed 28 April 2011).

Irlbacher-Fox, S. (2009) *Finding Dahshaa: Self-Government, Social Suffering and Aboriginal Policy in Canada*, Vancouver: UBC Press.

Isin, E.F. (2002) *Being Political: Genealogies of Citizenship*, Minneapolis: University of Minnesota Press.

—— (2007) Personal correspondence with author (Peter Nyers). 5 April 2007.

—— (2008) "Theorizing Acts of Citizenship", in E.F. Isin and G.M. Nielsen (eds) *Acts of Citizenship*, London: Zed Books.

Isin, E.F. and Nielsen, G. (eds) (2008) *Acts of Citizenship*, London: Zed Books.

Jackson, P. (2008) "Pierre Bourdieu, the 'Cultural Turn' and the Practice of International History", *Review of International Studies*, 34(2): 155–181.

Jackson, P.T. (2008a) "Can Ethnographic Techniques Tell Us Distinctive Things About World Politics?" *International Political Sociology*, 2(1): 91–94.

—— (2008b) "Foregrounding Ontology: Dualism, Monism, and IR Theory", *Review of International Studies*, 43: 29–53.

—— (2011) *The Conduct of Inquiry in International Relations: Philosophy of Science and Its Implications for the Study of World Politics*, New York: Routledge.

Jackson, P.T. and Kaufman, S.J. (2007) "Security Scholars for a Sensible Foreign Policy: A Study in Weberian Activism", *Perspectives on Politics*, 5(1): 95–103.

Jackson, R. (2005) *Writing the War on Terrorism: Language, Politics and Counter-Terrorism*, Manchester: Manchester University Press.

Jahn, B. (2000) *The Cultural Construction of International Relations: The Invention of the State of Nature*, New York: Palgrave.

James, C. (2011) *Philosophy: An Introduction to the Art of Wondering*, Boston: Wadsworth Publishing.

Jenkins, R. (1992) *Pierre Bourdieu*, New York: Routledge.

Jerving, S. (2011) *Jeremy Scahill: How the US Strengthens Al Qaeda in Yemen*, thenation.com, Online: www.thenation.com/blog/159637/jeremy-scahill-how-us-strengthens-al-qaeda-yemen (accessed April 2, 2011).

Joint Committee on Human Rights (2010) *Counter-Terrorism Policy and Human Rights (Seventeenth Report): Bring Human Rights Back In*, London: The Stationery Office Limited.

Jutila, M., Pehkonen, S., and Väyrynen, T. (2008) "Resuscitating a Discipline: An Agenda for Critical Peace Research", *Millennium: Journal of International Studies*, 36(3): 623–640.

Kafka, F. (1973) "The City Coat of Arms", in M. Pasley (ed.) *Shorter Works, Vol. I*, London: Secker and Warburg.

Kalyvas, S. (2003) "The Ontology of 'Political Violence': Action and Identity in Civil Wars", *Perspectives on Politics*, 1(3): 475–494.

Kangas, A. (2007) *The Knight, the Beast and the Treasure: A Semiotic Inquiry into the Finnish Political Imaginary of Russia, 1918–1930s*, Tampere: Tampere University Press.

Kaplan, R.D. (1994) *Balkan Ghosts: A Journey Through History*, New York: Vintage.

Kauppi, N. (2003) "Bourdieu's Political Sociology and the Politics of European Integration", *Theory and Society*, 32(5/6): 775–789.

Keane, A. and Horner, A. (eds) (2000) *Body Matters: Feminism, Textuality, Corporeality*, Manchester: Manchester University Press.

Keohane, R.O. (1989) "International Relations Theory: Contributions of a Feminist Standpoint", *Millennium: Journal of International Studies*, 18(2): 245–253.

—— (1998) "Beyond Dichotomy: Conversations between International Relations and Feminist Theory", *International Studies Quarterly*, 42(1): 193–197.

Keohane, R.O. and Victor, D.G. (2011) "The Regime Complex for Climate Change", *Perspectives on Politics*, 9(1): 7–23.

Khandor, E., McDonald, J., Nyers, P., and Wright, C. (2004) *The Regularization of Non-Status Immigrants in Canada, 1960–2004: Past Policies, Current Perspectives, Active Campaigns*, Toronto: STATUS Campaign.

Kimmel, M.S. (2000) "Masculinity as Homophobia: Fear, Shame, and Silence in the Construction of Gender Identity", in M. Adams (ed.) *Readings for Diversity and Social Justice*, New York: Routledge.

King, C. (2001) "The Benefits of Ethnic War: Understanding Eurasia's Unrecognized States", *World Politics*, 53(4): 524–552.

Kirsch, G.E. and Rohan, L. (2008) *Beyond the Archives: Research as a Lived Process*, Chicago: Southern Illinois University Press.

Kittle, P. and Hicks, T. (2009) "Transforming the Group Paper with Collaborative Online Writing", *Pedagogy*, 9(3): 525–538.

Kleinman, S. and Copp, M.A. (1993) *Emotions and Fieldwork*, Newbury: SAGE Publications.

Klotz, A. and Prakash, D. (eds) (2008) *Qualitative Methods in International Relations: A Pluralist Guide*, New York: Palgrave Macmillan.

Kobrin, S.J. (2002) "Economic Governance in an Electronically Networked Global Economy", in

R.B. Hall and T.J. Biersteker (eds) *The Emergence of Private Authority in Global Governance*, Cambridge: Cambridge University Press.

Komesaroff, P. (1995) *Troubled Bodies: Critical Perspectives on Postmodernism, Medical Ethics, and the Body*, Durham: Duke University Press.

Kondo, D.K. (1990) *Crafting Selves: Power, Gender, and Discourses of Identity in a Japanese Workplace*, Chicago: University of Chicago Press.

Kovach, M. (2009) *Indigenous Methodologies: Characteristics, Conversations, and Contexts*, Toronto: University of Toronto Press.

Kraska, P.B. (1998) "Enjoying Militarism: Political/Personal Dilemmas in Studying U.S. Police Paramilitary Units", in J. Ferrell and M.S. Hamm (eds) *Ethnography at the Edge: Crime, Deviance, and Field Research*, Boston: Northeastern University Press.

Kratochwil, F. (2011) *The Puzzles of Politics: Inquiries into the Genesis and Transformation of International Relations*, New York: Routledge.

Krause, K. and Williams, M. (eds) (1997) *Critical Security Studies: Concepts and Cases*, Minneapolis: University of Minnesota Press.

Kunz, R. (2011) *The Political Economy of Global Remittances: Gender, Governmentality and Neoliberalism*, New York: Routledge.

Lakoff, A. and Collier, S. (2010) "Infrastructure and Event: The Political Technology of Preparedness," in B. Braun and S. Whatmore (eds) *Political Matter: Technoscience, Democracy and Public*, Minnesota: University of Minnesota Press.

Lapid, Y. (1989) "The Third Debate: On the Prospects of International Theory in a Post-Positivist Era", *International Studies Quarterly*, 33(3): 235–254.

Larner, W. (2000) "Neo-Liberalism: Policy, Ideology, Governmentality", *Studies in Political Economy*, 63(1): 5–26.

Lash, S. and Lury, C. (2007) *Global Culture Industry: The Mediation of Things*, Cambridge: Polity.

Lather, P. (2001) "Postbook: Working the Ruins of Feminist Ethnography", *Signs: Journal of Women in Culture and Society*, 27(1): 199–227.

Latour, B. (1987) *Science in Action*, Cambridge: Harvard University Press.

—— (1996) *Aramis or the Love of Technology*, Cambridge: Harvard University Press.

—— (1999) *Pandora's Hope*, Cambridge: Harvard University Press.

—— (2004) *Politics of Nature: How to Bring the Sciences into Democracy*, Cambridge: Harvard University Press.

—— (2005) *Reassembling the Social: an Introduction to Actor-Network-Theory*, New York: Oxford University Press.

Latour, B. and Woolgar, S. (1979) *Laboratory Life: The Social Construction of Scientific Facts*, Princeton: Princeton University Press.

Law, J. (2002) "Objects and Spaces", *Theory, Culture and Society*, 19(5/6): 91–105.

—— (2004) *After Method: Mess in Social Science Method*, New York: Routledge.

Law J. and Hassard J. (eds) (1999) *Actor Network Theory and After*, Oxford: Blackwell.

Law, J. and Mol, A. (2011) "Veterinary Realities: What is Foot and Mouth Disease?", *Sociologia Ruralis*, 51(1): 1–19.

Law, J. and Singleton, V. (2005) "Object Lessons", *Organization*, 12(3): 331–355.

Law, J. and Urry, J. (2004) "Enacting the Social", *Economy and Society,* 33(3): 390–410.

Leander, A. (2005) "The Power to Construct International Security: On the Significance of Private Military Companies", *Millennium: Journal of International Studies*, 33(4): 803–826.

—— (2008) "Thinking Tools", in A. Klotz and D. Prakash (eds) *Qualitative Methods in International Relations: A Pluralist Guide*, New York: Palgrave.

—— (2011) "The Promises, Problems, and Potentials of a Bourdieu-inspired Staging of International Relations", *International Political Sociology*, 5(3): 294–313.

Leech, B.L. (2002) "Asking Questions: Techniques for Semistructured Interviews", *PS: Political Science and Politics*, 35(4): 665–668.

Lefebvre, H. (1996) *The Production of Space*, trans. D. Nicholson-Smith. Oxford: Blackwell Publishers.

LeGreco, M. and Tracy, S.J. (2009) "Discourse Tracing as Qualitative Practice", *Qualitative Inquiry*, 15(9): 1516–1543.

Lentzos, F. and Rose, N. (2009) "Governing Insecurity", *Economy and Society*, 38(2): 230–254.

Lerum, K. (2001) "Subjects of Desire: Intimate Ethnography, and the Production of Critical Knowledge", *Qualitative Inquiry*, 7(4): 466–483.

Lessig, L. (1999) *Code and Other Laws of Cyberspace*, New York: Basic Books.

Leys, R. (2011) "The Turn to Affect: A Critique", *Critical Inquiry*, 37(2): 434–472.

Li, T.M. (2007) *The Will to Improve: Governmentality, Development, and the Practice of Politics*, Durham: Duke University Press.

Lincoln, Y.S. and Cannella, G.S. (2004) "Dangerous Discourses: Methodological Conservatism and Governmental Regimes of Truth", *Qualitative Inquiry*, 10(5): 5–13.

Lippert, R. (2005) *Sanctuary Sovereignty Sacrifice: Canadian Sanctuary Incidents, Power and Law*, Vancouver: UBC Press.

Lippert, R. and O'Connor, D. (2003) "Security Assemblages: Airport Security, Flexible Work and Liberal Governance", *Alternatives: Global, Local, Political*, 28(1): 331–358.

Lipschutz, R.D. (2001) *Cold War Fantasies: Film, Fiction, and Foreign Policy*, Lanham: Rowman and Littlefield.

Lipson, E. (1934) *The Economic History of England, Vol. III: The Age of Mercantilism*, London: Adam and Charles Black.

Lloyd, M. (2007) *Judith Butler*, Cambridge: Polity.

Lobo-Guerrero, L. (2010) *Insuring Security: Biopolitics, Security and Risk*, New York: Routledge.

—— (2012) *Insurance and War: Political Economy of Marine Security and Risk*, New York: Routledge.

Lopez, L. (2003) "Placement Report: Political Science Ph.D.s and ABDs on the Job Market in 2001–2002", *PS: Political Science and Politics*, 36(4): 835–841.

Lowry, M. and Nyers, P. (2003) "Roundtable Report: 'No One is Illegal': The Fight for Refugee and Migrant Rights in Canada", *Refuge: Canada's Periodical on Refugees*, 21(3): 66–72.

Lundborg, T. and Vaughan-Williams, N. (2011) "Resilience, Critical Infrastructure, and Molecular Security: The Excess of 'Life' in Biopolitics", *International Political Sociology*, 5(4): 367–383.

Lunde, L. (1991) *Science or Politics in the Global Greenhouse: The Development Towards Scientific Consensus on Climate Change*, Oslo: Fridtjof Nansen Institute.

Lutz, C. and White, G.M. (1986) "The Anthropology of Emotion", *Annual Review of Anthropology*, 15: 405–436.

Lyon, D. (2003) "Airports as Data Filters: Converging Surveillance Systems after September 11th", *Journal of Information, Communication and Ethics in Society*, 1(1): 13–20.

Mackenzie, C. and Stoljar, N. (2000) "Autonomy Refigured" in C. Mackenzie and N. Stoljar (eds) *Relational Autonomy: Feminist Perspectives on Autonomy, Agency, and the Social Self*, Oxford: Oxford University Press.

Madden, R. (2010) *Being Ethnographic: A Guide to the Theory and Practice of Ethnography*, London: SAGE Publications.

Madison, D.S. (2005) *Critical Ethnography: Method, Ethics and Performance*, London: SAGE Publications.

Madra, M.Y. and Özselcuk, C. (2010) "Jouissance and Antagonism in the Forms of the Commune: A Critique of Biopolitical Subjectivity", *Rethinking Marxism*, 22(3): 481–497.

Malkki, L. (1995) "Refugees and Exile: From 'Refugee Studies' to the National Order of Things", *Annual Review of Anthropology*, 11(3): 495–523.

Managhan, T. (2012) *Gender, Agency, War: The Maternalized Body in U.S. Foreign Policy*, New York: Routledge.

Manning, E. (2007) *Politics of Touch: Sense, Movement, Sovereignty*, Minneapolis: University of Minnesota Press.

—— (2009) *Relationscapes: Movement, Art, Philosophy*, Cambridge, Mass.: The MIT Press.

Marcus, G. (1994) "On Ideologies of Reflexivity in Contemporary Efforts to Remake the Human Sciences", *Poetics Today*, 15(3): 383–404.

—— (1995) "Ethnography In/of the World System: the Emergency of Multi Sited Ethnography", *Annual Review of Anthropology*, 24: 95–117.

—— (1998) *Ethnography through Thick and Thin*, Princeton: Princeton University Press.

Marlin-Bennett, R., Wilson, M., and Walton, J. (2010) "Commodified Cadavers and the Political Economy of the Spectacle", *International Political Sociology*, 4(2): 159–177.

Martin, F. (1876) *The History of Lloyd's and of the Marine Insurance in Great Britain*, London: Macmillan and Co.

Martin, M.J. and Sasser, C.W. (2010) *Predator: The Remote-Control Air War over Iraq and Afghanistan: A Pilot's Story*, Minneapolis: Zenith Press.

Massey, D. (1994) *Space, Place and Gender*, Cambridge: Polity.

Massumi, B. (1995) "The Autonomy of Affect", *Cultural Critique*, 31: 83–109.

—— (1996) "The Autonomy of Affect", in P. Patton (ed) *Deleuze: A Critical Reader*, Oxford: Blackwell.

—— (2002) *Parables for the Virtual: Movement, Affect, Sensation*, Durham: Duke University Press.

—— (2005) "Fear (The Spectrum Said)", *Positions*, 13(1): 31–48.

Masters, C. (2008) "Bodies of Technology and the Politics of the Flesh", in J. Parpart and M. Zalewski (eds) *Rethinking the Man Question: Sex, Gender and Violence in International Relations*, New York: Zed Books.

McDonald, M. (2008) "Securitization and the Construction of Security", *European Journal of International Relations*, 14(4): 563–587.

McLaren, M. (2002) *Feminism, Foucault, and Embodied Subjectivity*, Albany: SUNY Press.

McLuhan, M. (1962) *The Gutenberg Galaxy*, Toronto: University of Toronto Press.

—— (1964) *Understanding Media: The Extensions of Man*, 2nd edn, New York: Penguin.

McNabb, D. (2010) *Research Methods for Political Science: Quantitative and Qualitiative Approaches*, 2nd edn, New York: M.E. Sharpe.

McNay, L. (2000) *Gender and Agency: Reconfiguring the Subject in Feminist and Social Theory*, Cambridge: Polity.

McWhorter, L. (1989) "Culture or Nature? The Function of the Term 'Body' in the Work of Michel Foucault", *The Journal of Philosophy*, 86(11): 608–614.

Meijer, I. and Prins, B. (1998) "How Bodies Come to Matter: An Interview with Judith Butler", *Signs: A Journal of Women in Culture and Society*, 23(2): 275–286.

Melzer, N. (2008) *Targeted Killing in International Law*, Oxford: Oxford University Press.

Menand, L. (2010) *The Marketplace of Ideas: Reform and Resistance in the American University*, New York: W.W. Norton.

Mérand, F. (2008) *European Defence Policy: Beyond the Nation State*, Oxford: Oxford University Press.

Mérand, F. and Pouliot, V. (2008) "The World of Pierre Bourdieu: Elements for a Social Theory of International Relations", *Canadian Journal of Political Science*, 41(4): 603–625.

Meyer, M. (1986) *De la problématologie. Philosophie, science et langage*, Paris: Pierre Mardaga.

Miller, D. (2005) "Materiality: An Introduction", in D. Miller (ed.) *Materiality*, Durham: Duke University Press.

MindFreedom International. Online: www.mindfreedom.org (accessed 14 March 2012).

Mitchell, T. (2002) *Rule of Experts: Egypt, Techno-Politics, Modernity*, Berkeley: University of California Press.

—— (2009) "Carbon Democracy", *Economy and Society*, 38(3): 399–432.

Mitchell, W.J.T. (1986) *Iconology: Image, Text, Ideology*, Chicago: University of Chicago Press.

—— (1994) *Picture Theory: Essays on Verbal and Visual Representation*, Chicago: Chicago University Press.

—— (2011) *Cloning Terror: The War of Images, 9/11 to the Present*, Chicago: The University of Chicago Press.

Mol, A. (1998) "Missing Links, Making Links: the Performance of Some Artheroscleroses", in A. Mol and M. Berg (eds) *Differences in Medicine: Unravelling Practices, Techniques and Bodies*, Durham: Duke University Press.

—— (2002) *The Body Multiple: Ontology in Medical Practice*, Durham: Duke University Press.

Möller, F. (2007) "Photographic interventions in Post–9/11 security policy", *Security Dialogue*, 38(2): 179–196.

Montag, W. (1995) "'The Soul is the Prison of the Body': Althusser and Foucault, 1970–1975", *Yale French Studies*, 88: 53–77.

Montsion, J-M. (2010) "Research (Im)Possibilities: Reflections from Everyday International Relations", *Alterités*, 7(2): 72–94.

Moore, L. and Kosut, M. (2010) *The Body Reader: Essential Social and Cultural Readings*, New York: New York University Press.

Morgan, K. (2002) "Mercantilism and the British Empire 1688–1815", in D. Winch and P.K. O'Brien (eds) *The Political Economy of British Historical Experience, 1688–1914*, Oxford: Oxford University Press.

Moses, J.W. and Knutsen, T.L. (2007) *Ways of Knowing: Competing Methodologies in Social and Political Research*, New York: Palgrave Macmillan.

Moulin, C. and Nyers, P. (2007) "'We Live in a Country of UNHCR': Refugee Protests and Global Political Society", *International Political Sociology*, 1(4): 356–372.

Mueller, J. (2000) "The Banality of "Ethnic War", *International Security*, 25(1): 42–70.

Muller, B.J. (2009) *Security, Risk, and the Biometric State: Governing Borders and Bodies*, New York: Routledge.

Mullings, B. (1999) "Insider or Outsider, Both or Neither: Some Dilemmas of Interviewing in a Cross-Cultural Setting", *Geoforum*, 30(4): 337–350.

Muppidi, H. (2010) *The Colonial Signs of International Relations*, New York: Columbia University Press.

Nancy, J-L. (2000) *Being Singular Plural*, trans. R.D. Richardson and A.E. O'Byrne. Stanford: Stanford University Press.

—— (2008) *Corpus*, trans. R.A. Rand. New York: Fordham University Press.

Native Women's Association of Canada (NWAC) (2009) *Sisters in Spirit Research Strategy: Reflecting on Method and Process*, Ottawa: NWAC-SIS Initiative.

Neal, A.W. (2010) *Exceptionalism and the Politics of Counter-Terrorism: Liberty, Security and the War on Terror*, New York: Routledge.

—— (2012) "Normalisation and Legislative Exceptionalism: Counter-Terrorist Lawmaking and the Changing Times of Security Emergencies", *International Political Sociology*, 6(3).

Nelson, G.S. (2009) *Sovereignty and the Limits of the Liberal Imagination*, New York: Routledge.

Nencel, Lorraine (2005) "Feeling Gender Speak: Intersubjectivity and Fieldwork Practice with Women who Prostitute in Lima, Peru", *European Journal of Women's Studies*, 12(3): 345–361.

Network of Concerned Anthropologists (2009) *The Counter-Counterinsurgency Manual, or Notes on Demilitarizing American Society*, Chicago: Prickly Paradigm Press.

Neufeld, M. (1993) "Reflexivity and International Relations Theory", *Millennium: Journal of International Studies*, 22(1): 53–76.

Neumann, I.B. (1999) *Uses of the Other: "The East" in European Identity Formation*, Minneapolis: University of Minnesota Press.

—— (2005) "To be a Diplomat", *International Studies Perspectives*, 6(1): 72–93.

—— (2008a) "The Body of the Diplomat", *European Journal of International Relations*, 14(4): 671–695.

—— (2008b) "Discourse Analysis", in A. Klotz and D. Prakash (eds) *Qualitative Methods in International Relations: A Pluralist Guide*, New York: Palgrave.

Neumann, I.B. and Wæver, O. (eds) (1997) *The Future of International Relations: Masters in the Making?* New York: Routledge.

Newell, P. (2000) *Climate for Change: Non-state Actors and the Global Politics of the Greenhouse*, Cambridge: Cambridge University Press.

Nietzsche, F. (1980) *On the Advantage and Disadvantage of History for Life*, Indianapolis: Hacket Publishing Company.

—— (1990) *Twilight of the Idols: And the Anti-Christ*, New York: Penguin.

—— (2000) "Beyond Good and Evil, Part I: 9" in W. Kaufmann (ed.) *Basic Writings of Nietzsche*, New York: The Modern Library.

Noël, S. and Robert, J.–M. (2003) "How the Web is used to Support Collaborative Writing", *Behaviour and Information Technology*, 22(4): 245–262.

Noland, C. (2009) *Agency and Embodiment: Performing Gestures/Producing Culture*, Cambridge: Harvard University Press.

Nordstrom, C. (1995) "War on Front Lines" in C. Nordstrom and A.C.G.M. Robben (eds) *Fieldwork under Fire: Contemporary Studies of Violence and Survival*, Berkeley: University of California Press.

—— (1997) *A Different Kind of War Story*, Philadelphia: University of Pennsylvania Press.

—— (2004) *The Shadows of War: Violence, Power and International Profiteering in the Twenty First-Century*, Berkeley: University of California Press.

Nordstrom, C. and Martin, J. (1992) "The Culture of Conflict: Field Reality and Theory", in C. Nordstrom and J. Martin (eds) *The Paths to Domination, Resistance, and Terror*, Berkeley: University California Press.

Nordstrom, C. and Robben, A.C.G.M. (1995) "The Anthropology and Ethnography of Violence and Sociopolitical Conflict" in C. Nordstrom and A.C.G.M. Robben (eds) *Fieldwork under Fire: Contemporary Studies of Violence and Survival*, Berkeley: University of California Press.

Norris, A. (2000) "Giorgio Agamben and the Politics of Living Dead", *Diacritics*, 30(4): 38–58.

Norton, P. (2005) *Parliament in British Politics*, New York: Palgrave Macmillan.

Nussbaum, M.C. (2010) *Not for Profit: Why Democracy Needs the Humanities*, Princeton, NJ: Princeton University Press.

Nye, J.S. (2004) *Power in a Global Information Age*, New York: Routledge.

—— (2011) *The Future of Power*, New York: PublicAffairs.

Nyers, P. (1999) "Emergency or Emerging Identities: Refugees and Transformations in World Order", *Millennium: Journal of International Studies*, 28(1): 1–26.

—— (2003) "Abject Cosmopolitanism: The Politics of Protection in the Anti-Deportation Movement", *Third World Quarterly*, 24(6): 1069–1093.

—— (2005) "The Regularization of Non-Status Immigrants in Canada: Limits and Prospects", *Canadian Review of Social Policy*, 55: 109–114.

—— (2006a) "The Accidental Citizen: Acts of Sovereignty and (Un)Making Citizenship", *Economy and Society*, 34(1): 22–41.

—— (2006b) "Taking Rights, Mediating Wrongs: Disagreements over the Political Agency of Non-Status Refugees", in J. Huysmans, A. Dobson, and R. Prokhovnik (eds) *The Politics of Protection: Sites of Insecurity and Political Agency*, New York: Routledge.

—— (2006c) *Rethinking Refugees: Beyond States of Emergency*, New York: Routledge.

—— (2008) "Community without Status: Non-Status Migrants and Cities of Refuge", in D. Brydon and W. Coleman (eds) *Renegotiating Community: Interdisciplinary Perspectives, Global Contexts*, Vancouver: University of British Columbia Press.

—— (ed.) (2009) *Securitizations of Citizenship*, New York: Routledge.

—— (2011a) "Forms of Irregular Citizenship", in V. Squire (ed.) *The Contested Politics of Mobility: Borderzones and Irregularity*, New York: Routledge.

—— (2011b) "Alien Equality", *Issues in Legal Scholarship*, 9(1): 1–13.

—— (forthcoming 2012) "Liberating Irregularity: No Borders, Temporality, Citizenship", in X. Guillaume and J. Huysmans (eds) *Citizenship and Security: The Constitution of Political Being*, New York: Routledge.

O'Brien, P.K. (2002) "Fiscal Exceptionalism: Great Britain and its European Rivals from Civil War to Triumph at Trafalgar and Waterloo" in D. Winch and P.K. O'Brien (eds) *The Political Economy of British Historical Experience, 1688–1914*, Oxford: Oxford University Press.

O'Malley, P., Weir, L., and Shearing, C. (1997) "Governmentality, Criticism, Politics", *Economy and Society*, 26(4): 501–517.

Ohmae, K. (1996) *The End of the Nation State*, New York: Free Press.

Onuf, N. (1989) *World of Our Making: Rules and Rule in Social Theory and International Relations*, Columbia: University of South Carolina Press.

Orsini, M. (2007) "Discourses in Distress: From 'Health Promotion' to 'Population Health' to 'You Are Responsible for Your Own Health'", in M. Orsini and M. Smith (eds) *Critical Policy Studies*, Vancouver: UBC Press.

Orsini, M. and Smith, M. (eds) (2007) *Critical Policy Studies*, Vancouver: UBC Press.

Orsini, M. and Wiebe, S. (forthcoming) "Between Hope and Fear: Comparing the Emotional Landscapes of Autism and Autistic Activism in Canada and the U.S.", in L. Turgeon, J. Wallner, S. White, and M. Papillon (eds) *Canada Compared: People, Politics, and Policy*, Vancouver: UBC Press.

Ortiz, S.M. (2005) "The Ethnographic Process of Gender Management: Doing the "Right" Masculinity with Wives of Professional Athletes", *Qualitative Inquiry*, 11(2): 265–290.

Ó Tuathail, G. (1996) *Critical Geopolitics: The Politics of Writing Global Space*, Minneapolis: University of Minnesota Press.

Paglen, T. (2010) *Blank Spots on the Map: The Dark Geography of the Pentagon's Secret World*, London: Penguin.

Paglen, T. and A.C. Thompson (2008) *Torture Taxi: On the Trail of the CIA's Rendition Flights*, Hoboken: Melville House.

Palmié, S. (2006) "Creolization and its Discontents", *Annual Review of Anthropology*, 35: 433–456.

Paltemaa, L. and Vuori, J.A. (2006) "How Cheap is Identity Talk? A Framework of Identity Frames and Security Discourse for the Analysis of Repression and Legitimization of Social Movements in Mainland China", *Issues and Studies*, 42(3): 47–86.

Pascoe, C.J. (2007) *Dude, You're a Fag: Masculinity and Sexuality in High School*, Berkeley: University of California Press.

Pascoe, D. (2001) *Airspaces*, London: Reaktion.

Paterson, M. (1996) *Global Warming and Global Politics*, New York: Routledge.

—— (2007) *Automobile Politics: Ecology and Cultural Political Economy*, Cambridge: Cambridge University Press.

Peirce, C.S. (1985) "Logic as Semiotic: The Theory of Signs", in R.E. Innis (ed.) *Semiotics: An Introductory Reader*, London: Hutchinson.

Peoples, C. and Vaughan-Williams, N. (2010) *Critical Security Studies: An Introduction*, New York: Routledge.

Philo, Chris (2007) "Review Essay: Michel Foucault, Psychiatric Power: Lectures at the Collège de France 1973–74", *Foucault Studies*, 4: 149–163.

Pond, E. and Waltz, K.N. (1994) "International Politics, Viewed from the Ground", *International Security*, 19(1): 195–199.

Pouliot, V. (2010) *International Security in Practice: The Politics of NATO–Russia Diplomacy*, Cambridge: Cambridge University Press.

Protevi, J. (2009) *Political Affect: Connecting the Social and the Somatic*, Minneapolis: University of Minnesota Press.

Pugliese, J. (2004) "Subcutaneous Law: Embodying the Migration Amendment Act 1992", *The Australian Feminist Law Journal*, 21: 23–34.

Punday, D. (2000) "Foucault's Body Tropes", *New Literary History*, 31: 509–528.

Pupavac, V. (2002) "Pathologizing Populations and Colonizing Minds: International Psychosocial Programs in Kosovo", *Alternatives: Global, Local, Political*, 27(4): 489–511.

Puumala, E. and Pehkonen, S. (2010) "Corporeal Choreographies: Failed Asylum-Seekers Moving from Body Politics to Bodyspaces", *International Political Sociology*, 4(1): 50–65.

Puumala, E., Väyrynen, T., Kynsilehto, A., and Pehkonen, S. (2011) "Events of the Body Politic: A Nancian Reading of Asylum-seekers, Bodily Choreographies and Resistance", *Body and Society* 17(4): 83–104.

Rabinow, P. (1977) *Reflections on Fieldwork in Morocco*, Berkeley: University of California Press.

Rabinow P. and Dreyfus, H. (1982) *Michel Foucault. Beyond Structuralism and Hermeneutics*, Chicago: The University of Chicago Press.

Rabinow, P. and Rose, N. (eds) (1994) *The Essential Foucault*, New York: The New Press.

Rabinowitch, E. (1947) "Editorial: Let's Have Clear Thinking", *Bulletin of the Atomic Scientists*, 3(6): 137–138.

Rajaram, P.K. and Grundy-Warr, C. (2004) "The Irregular Migrant as Homo Sacer: Migration and Detention in Australia, Malaysia, and Thailand", *International Migration*, 42(1): 33–64.

—— (eds) (2007) *Borderscapes: Hidden Geographies and Politics at Territory's Edge*, Minneapolis: University of Minnesota Press.

Rancatore, J. (2010) "It Is Strange: A Reply to Vrasti", *Millennium: Journal of International Studies*, 39(1): 65–77.

Rancière, J. (1999) *Disagreement: Politics and Philosophy*, trans. J. Rose, Minneapolis: University of Minnesota Press.

—— (2009) "A Few Remarks on the Method of Jacques Rancière", *Parallax*, 15(3): 114–123.

—— (2011) *The Emancipated Spectator*, trans. G. Elliot, London: Verso.

Rappert, B. (2001) "Toward an Understanding of Nonlethality", *Peace and Change*, 26: 31–54.

—— (2003) "Less-lethal Options", *Police Review*, 22–23.

—— (2004) "A Framework for the Assessment of Non-Lethal Weapons", *Medicine, Conflict and Survival*, 20: 35–54.

Regional Thematic Working Group on International Migration including Human Trafficking (2008) *Situation Report on International Migration in East and South-East Asia*, Bangkok: International Organization for Migration.

Ridge, T. (2004) *Transcript of the Secretary of Homeland Security Tom Ridge at the Center for Transatlantic Relations at Johns Hopkins University*. Online: www.dhs.gov/xnews/speeches/speech_0206.shtm (accessed 28 January 2009).

Riley, D. (1999) "Bodies, Identities, Feminisms", in J. Price and M. Shildrick (ed.) *Feminist Theory and the Body: A Reader*, New York: Routledge.

Ritchie, S.M. and Rigano, D.L. (2007) "Writing Together Metaphorically and Bodily Side-by-Side: an Inquiry into Collaborative Academic Writing", *Reflective Practice*, 8(1): 123–135.

Robson, C. (2002) *Real World Research: A Resource for Social Scientists and Practitioner-Researchers*, London: John Wiley and Sons.

Rogers, P. (2006) *The World as a Battlefield*, openDemocracy, Online: www.opendemocracy.net/conflict/battlefield_3251.jsp (accessed 25 March 2011).

Rorty R. (1982) *Consequences of Pragmatism (Essays 1972–1980)*, Minneapolis: University of Minnesota Press.

—— (1989) *Contingency, Irony and Solidarity*, Cambridge: Cambridge University Press.

Rose, G. (1997) "Situating Knowledges: Positionality, Reflectivities, and Other Tactics", *Progress in Human Geography*, 21(3): 305–320.

Rose, N. (1989) *Governing the Soul: The Shaping of the Private Self*, 2nd edn, New York: Free Association Books.

—— (1999) *Powers of Freedom: Reframing Political Thought*, Cambridge: Cambridge University Press.

Rosenau, J.N. and Singh, J.P. (2002) *Information Technologies and Global Politics: The Changing Scope of Power and Governance*, Albany: SUNY.

Rubenstein, M.J. (2009) *Strange Wonder: The Closure of Metaphysics and the Opening of Awe,* New York: Columbia University Press.

Ruggie, J.G. (1998) *Constructing the World Polity: Essays on International Institutionalization*, New York: Routledge.

Russell, J. (2007) *Russia-Chechnya's "War on Terror"*, New York: Routledge.

Said, E. (2000) *Reflections on Exile and Other Essays*, Cambridge: Harvard University Press.

Salter, M.B. (2004) "Passports, Mobility, Security: How Smart Can the Border Be?", *International Studies Perspectives*, 5(1): 71–91.

—— (2006) "The Global Visa Regime and the Political Technologies of the International Self: Borders, Bodies, Biopolitics", *Alternatives: Global, Local, Political*, 31(2): 167–189.

—— (2007a) "Governmentalities of an Airport: Heterotopia and Confession", *International Political Sociology*, 1(1): 49–66.

—— (2007b) "SeMS and Sensibility: Security Management Systems and the Management of Risk in the Canadian Air Transport Security Authority", *Journal of Air Transportation Management*, 13(6): 389–398.

—— (2008a) "The Global Airport: Managing Space, Speed, and Security", in M.B. Salter (ed.) *Politics at the Airport*, Minneapolis: University of Minnesota Press.

—— (ed.) (2008b) *Politics at the Airport*, Minneapolis: University of Minnesota Press.

—— (2008c) "Securitization and Desecuritization: Dramaturgical Analysis and the Canadian Aviation Transport Security Authority", *Journal of International Relations and Development*, 11(4): 321–349.

—— (2008d) "Imagining Numbers: Risk, Quantification, and Aviation Security", *Security Dialogue*, 39(2/3): 243–266.

—— (2010) "When Securitization Fails: The Hard Case of Counter–Terrorism Programs", in T. Balzacq (ed.) *Securitization Theory: How Security Problems Emerge and Dissolve*, New York: Routledge.

Salter, M.B. and Mutlu, C.E. (2012) "Psychoanalytic Theory and Border Security", *European Journal of Social Theory*, 15(2): 179–195.

Sassen, S. (2006) *Territory, Authority, Rights: From Medieval to Global Assemblages*, Princeton: Princeton University Press.

Sasson-Levy, O. (2007) "Individual Bodies, Collective State Interests: The Case of Israeli Combat Soldiers", *Men and Masculinities* 10(3): 296–321.

Saurette, P. (2006) "'You Dissin Me?' Humiliation and Post 9/11 Global Politics", *Review of International Studies*, 32(3): 495–522.

Sbisà, M. (2002) "Speech Acts in Context", *Language and Communication*, 22(4): 421–436.

Scarry, E. (1985) *The Body in Pain: The Making and Unmaking of the World*, Oxford: Oxford University Press.

Schaffer, F.C. (2006) "Ordinary Language Interviewing", in D. Yanow and P. Schwartz-Shea (eds) *Interpretation and Methods: Empirical Research Methods and the Interpretative Turn*, London: M.E. Sharpe.

Schatz, E. (2009a) "Ethnographic Immersion and the Study of Politics", in E. Schatz (ed) *Political Ethnography: What Immersion Contributes to the Study of Power*, Chicago: Chicago University Press.

—— (2009b) "What Kind(s) of Ethnography Does Political Science Need?", in E. Schatz (ed) *Political Ethnography: What Immersion Contributes to the Study of Power*, Chicago: Chicago University Press.

Scheurich, J. and Bell McKenzie, K. (2005) "Foucault's Methodologies: Archaeology and Genealogy", in N.K. Dezin and Y.S. Lincoln (eds) *The SAGE Handbook of Qualitative Research*, London: SAGE Publications.

Schoenhals, M. (1992) *Doing Things with Words in Chinese Politics – Five Studies*, Berkeley: Institute of East Asian Studies.

Schonhardt-Bailey, C. (2006) *From the Corn Laws to Free Trade: Interests, Ideas and Institutions in Historical Perspectives*, Boston: MIT Press.

Schwartz-Shea, P. (2006) "Judging Quality: Evaluative Criteria and Epistemic Communities", in D. Yanow and P. Schwartz-Shea (eds) *Interpretation and Methods: Empirical Research Methods and the Interpretative Turn*, London: M.E. Sharpe.

Schwartz-Shea, P. and Yanow, D. (2012) *Interpretive Research Design: Concepts and Processes*, New York: Routledge.

Scott, J.C. (1998) *Seeing Like a State: How Certain Schemes to Improve the Human Condition Have Failed*, New Haven: Yale University Press.

—— (2009) *The Art of Not Being Governed: An Anarchist History of Upland Southeast Asia*, New Haven: Yale University Press.

Scott, J.W. (1992) "Experience", in J. Butler and J.W. Scott (eds) *Feminists Theorize the Political*, New York: Routledge.

Searle, J.R. (1969) *Speech Acts*, Cambridge: Cambridge University Press.

—— (1995) *Construction of Social Reality*, New York: Free Press.

—— (2011) *Making the Social World: The Structure of Human Civilization*, Oxford: Oxford University Press.

Searle J.R. and Vanderveken, D. (1985) *Foundations of Illocutionary Logic*, Cambridge: Cambridge University Press.

Segall, D. (2011) "Is Law a Losing Game?" *New York Times*, 8 January 2011. Online: www.nytimes.com (accessed 16 June 2011).

Selzer, J. and Crowley, S. (eds) (1999) *Rhetorical Bodies*, Madison: University of Wisconsin Press.

Shah, N. (2010) "Terra Infirma", *Political Geography*, 29(6): 352–355.

Shakespeare, W. (1937) *The Tragedy of King Lear*, New York: Penguin Books.

Shapiro, M. (1981) *Language and Political Understanding: The Politics of Discursive Practices*, New Haven: Yale University Press.

—— (ed.) (1984) *Language and Politics*, New York: New York University Press.

—— (1989) "Textualising Global Politics", in J. Der Derian and M. Shapiro (eds) *International/ Intertextual Relations: Postmodern Readings of World Politics*, Lexington: Lexington Books.

—— (1990) "The Ethics of Encounter", in D. Campbell and M. Shapiro (eds) *Moral Spaces: Rethinking Ethics and World Politics*, Minneapolis: University of Minnesota Press.

—— (1997) *Violent Cartographies: Mapping Cultures of War*, Minneapolis: University of Minnesota Press.

Sheehan, C. (2006) *Peace Mom: A Mother's Journey through Heartache and Activism*, New York: Atria Books.

Shepherd, L.J. (ed.) (forthcoming) *Critical Approaches to Security: An Introduction to Theory and Methods*, New York: Routledge.

Sherif, B. (2001) "The Ambiguity of Boundaries in the Fieldwork Experience: Establishing Rapport and Negotiating Insider/Outsider Status", *Qualitative Inquiry*, 7(4): 436–447.

Shildrick, M. and Price, J. (1999) *Feminist Theory and the Body*, Edinburgh: Edinburgh University Press.

Shilling, C. (1993) *The Body and Social Theory*, London: SAGE Publications.

—— (2007) *Embodying Sociology: Retrospect, Progress and Prospects*, Oxford: Blackwell.

Shinko, R. (2010) "Ethics after Liberalism: Why (Autonomous) Bodies Matter", *Millennium: Journal of International Studies*, 38(3): 723–745.

—— (2011) "This is not a Mannequin: Enfashioning Bodies of Resistance", presented at the International Studies Association Conference, Montreal, 16–19 March.

Shore, C. and Wright, S. (2011) "Conceptualising Policy: Technologies of Governance and the Politics of Visibility", in C. Shore and S. Wright (eds) *Anthropology of Policy: Critical Perspectives on Governance and Power*, New York: Routledge.

Shotter, J. (2008) *Conversational Realities Revisited: Life, Language, Body and World*, Chagrin Falls, Ohio: The Taos Institute.

Sil, R. and Katzenstein, P.J. (2010) *Beyond Paradigms: Analytic Eclecticism in the Study of World Politics*, New York: Palgrave Macmillan.

Singer, P.W. (2009a) *Wired for War: The Robotics Revolution and Conflict in the 21st Century*, New York: Penguin.

—— (2009b) "Military Robots and the Laws of War", *New Atlantis*, 23: 25–45.

Skinner, Q. (2002) *Visions of Politics. Volume I: Regarding Method*, Cambridge: Cambridge University Press.

Skodvin, T. (2000) *Structure and Agent in the Scientific Diplomacy of Climate Change: An Empirical Case Study of Science-Policy Interaction in the Intergovernmental Panel on Climate Change. Advances in Global Climate Change Research*, London: Kluwer Academic.

Smith, D.E. (1987) *The Everyday World as Problematic: A Feminist Sociology*, Toronto: University of Toronto Press.

—— (1999) *Writing the Social: Critique, Theory, and Investigations*, Toronto: University of Toronto Press.

—— (2005) *Institutional Ethnography: A Sociology for People*, Walnut Creek: Alta Mira Press.

Smith, S. (2004) "Singing Our World into Existence: International Relations Theory and September 11", *International Studies Quarterly*, 48(3): 499–515.

Snow, D.A., and Benford R.D. (1992) "Master Frames and Cycles of Protest", in A.D. Morris and C. McClurg Mueller (eds) *Frontiers in Social Movement Theory*, New Haven: Yale University Press.

Soguk, N. (1999) *States and Strangers: Refugees and Displacements of Statecraft*, Minneapolis: University of Minnesota Press.

Soldz, S. (undated) *Psyche, Science and Society*, Online: http://psychoanalystsopposewar.org/blog

Soreanu, R. and Hudson, D. (2008) "Feminist Scholarship in International Relations and the Politics of Disciplinary Emotion", *Millennium: Journal of International Studies*, 37(1): 123–151.

Squire, V. (2009) *The Exclusionary Politics of Asylum*, New York: Palgrave Macmillan.

—— (ed.) (2010) *The Contested Politics of Mobility: Borderzones and Irregularity*, New York: Routledge.

Sriram, C.L., King, J.C., Mertus, J.A., Martin-Ortega, O., and Herman, J. (eds) (2009) *Surviving Field Research: Working in Violent and Difficult Situations,* New York: Routledge.

Stanley, L. (2004) "The Epistolarium: On Theorizing Letters and Correspondences", *Auto/Biography*, 12(3): 201–235.

Star, S.L. (2002) "Infrastructure and Ethnographic Practice: Working on the Fringes", *Scandinavian Journal of Information Systems*, 14(2): 107–122.

Star, S.L. and Bowker, G. (2006) "How to Infrastructure", in L.A. Lievrouw and S. Livingstone (eds) *Handbook of New Media*, London: SAGE Publications.

Steger, M. (2005) "From Market Globalism to Imperial Globalism: Ideology and American Power after 9/11", *Globalizations*, 2: 31–46.

Stoller, P. (1995) *Embodying Colonial Memories: Spirit Possession, Power, and the Hauka in West Africa*, New York: Routledge.

Stone, A. (2005) "Towards a Genealogical Feminism: A Reading of Judith Butler's Political Thought", *Contemporary Political Theory*, 4(1): 4–24.

Strange, S. (1988) *States and Markets*, London: Continuum.

Stritzel, H. (2007) "Towards a Theory of Securitization: Copenhagen and Beyond", *European Journal of International Relations*, 13(3): 357–383.

Stump, J. (2011) "Weakness Leaving my Body: An Essay on the Interpersonal Relations of International Politics", in N. Inayatullah (ed.) *Autobiographical International Relations: I, IR*, New York: Routledge.

Swales, J. (1990) *Genre Analysis: English in Academic and Research Settings*, Cambridge: Cambridge University Press.

Swartz, D. (1997) *Culture and Power: The Sociology of Pierre Bourdieu*, Chicago: University Of Chicago Press.

Sylvester, C. (1994) "Empathetic Cooperation: A Feminist Method for IR", *Millennium: Journal of International Studies*, 23(2): 315–334.

—— (2006) "Bare Life as a Development/Postcolonial Problematic", *The Geographical Journal*, 172(1): 66–77.

Taussig, M. (1987) *Shamanism, Colonialism and the Wild Man: A Study in Terror and Healing*, Chicago: University of Chicago Press.

Taylor, M.C. (2010) *Crisis on Campus: A Bold Plan for Reforming our Colleges and Universities*, New York: Knopf

Taylor, T.L. (2006) *Play Between Worlds: Exploring Online Game Culture*, Cambridge: MIT Press.

Thacker, E. (2004) "Foreword: Protocol Is as Protocol Does", in A.R. Galloway (ed.) *Protocol: How Control Exists after Decentralization*, Cambridge: MIT Press.

Thrift, N. (2004) "Intensities of Feeling: Towards a Spatial Politics of Affect", *Geografiska Annaler Series B*, 86(1): 57–78.
—— (2008) *Non-Representational Theory: Space, Politics, Affect*, New York: Routledge.
Tickner, A.B. and Wæver, O. (eds) (2009) *International Relations Scholarship Around the World*, New York: Routledge.
Tickner, J.A. (1997) "You Just Don't Understand: Troubled Engagements between Feminists and IR Theorists", *International Studies Quarterly*, 41(4): 611–631.
—— (1998) "Continuing the Conversation. . .", *International Studies Quarterly*, 42(1): 205–210.
Tonkiss, F. (2004) "Analysing Text and Speech: Content and Critical Discourse Analysis", in S. Seale (ed.) *Researching Society and Culture*, London: SAGE Publications.
Tripp, A.M. (2002) "Combining Intercontinental Parenting and Research: Dilemmas and Strategies", *Signs: A Journal of Women in Culture and Society*, 27(3): 794–811.
—— (2006) "Why So Slow? The Challenges of Gendering Comparative Politics", *Politics and Gender*, 2(2): 249–263.
Tsing, A. (2005) *Friction: An Ethnography of Global Connection*, Princeton: Princeton University Press.
Tuhiwai Smith, L. (1999) *Decolonizing Methodologies: Research and Indigenous Peoples*, London: Zed Books.
Turkle, S. (2005) "Computer Games as Evocative Objects: From Projective Screens to Relational Artifacts", in J. Raessens and J. Goldstein (eds), *Handbook of Computer Game Studies*, Cambridge: MIT Press.
—— (2010) *Evocative Objects: Things We Think With*, Cambridge: MIT Press.
Turner, F. (2006) *From Counterculture to Cyberculture: Steward Brand, The Whole Earth Network, and the Rise of Digital Utopianism*, Chicago: University of Chicago Press.
United Kingdom Home Office (2009) *Pursue Prevent Protect Prepare: The United Kingdom's Strategy for Countering International Terrorism*, Online: www.homeoffice.gov.uk/counter-terrorism/uk-counter-terrorism-strat
United Nations Development Project (UNDP) (1994) *Human Development Report 1994*, Oxford: Oxford University Press.
United Nations High Commissioner for Refugees (1996 [1951]) *Convention and Protocol Related to the Status of Refugees*, Online: www.unhcr.org (accessed 16 March 2011).
United States Senate Committee on Homeland Security and Governmental Affairs (2008) *Violent Islamist Extremism, the Internet and the Homegrown Terrorist Threat*, Online: http://hsgac.senate.gov/public/_files/IslamistReport.pdf
Valentin, J-M. (2005) *Hollywood, the Pentagon and Washington: The Movies and National Security from World War II to the Present Day*, London: Anthem Press.
de Vaus, D. (2001) *Research Design in Social Research*, London: SAGE Publications.
Veyne, P. (2010) *Foucault: His Thought, His Character*, Cambridge: Polity.
Voelkner, N. (2011) "Governing Pathogenic Circulation: Human Security and the Migrant Health Assemblage in Thailand", *Security Dialogue*, 42(3): 239–259.
Vrasti, W. (2008) "The Strange Case of Ethnography and International Relations", *Millennium: Journal of International Studies*, 37(2): 279–301.
—— (2010) "Dr. Strangelove or How I Stopped Worrying about Methodology and Love Writing", *Millennium: Journal of International Studies*, 39(1): 79–88.
—— (2011) "In Memory of a Country that Has Never Existed as Such", in N. Inayatullah (ed.) *Autobiographical International Relations: I, IR*, New York: Routledge.
—— (2012) *Volunteer Tourism: Giving Back in Neoliberal Times*, New York: Routledge.
Vucetic, S. (2011) "Genealogy as a Research Tool in International Relations", *Review of International Studies*, 37(3): 1295–1312.
Vuori, J.A. (2003) "Security as Justification: An Analysis of Deng Xiaoping's Speech to the Martial Law Troops in Beijing on the Ninth of June 1989", *Politologiske Studier*, 6(2): 105–118.
—— (2007) "Securitization in a Totalitarian Regime – Combining Micro-level Analysis with a Macro-

level Model", in J.A. Vuori *Chinese Securitisation – Broadening the Scope of Securitisation Studies with Three Case Studies in the Context of the People's Republic of China*, Turku: Department of Political Science, University of Turku.

—— (2008) "Illocutionary Logic and Strands of Securitisation: Applying the Theory of Securitisation to the Study of Non-Democratic Political Orders", *European Journal of International Relations*, 14(1): 65–99.

—— (2010a) "A Timely Prophet? The Doomsday Clock as a Visualization of Securitization Moves with a Global Referent Object", *Security Dialogue*, 41(3): 255–277.

—— (2010b) "Religion Bites: Falungong, Securitization/Desecuritization in the People's Republic of China", in T. Balzacq (ed.) *Securitization Theory: How Security Problems Emerge and Dissolve*, New York: Routledge.

—— (2011a) "Three Takes on the Counter-Revolutionary: Studying Asymmetrical Political Concepts in the People's Republic of China", in K. Postoutenko and K. Junge (eds) *35 Years after Koselleck: Asymmetrical Concepts in Politics, Language and Society*, Bielefeld: Transcript Verlag.

—— (2011b) "Towards a Methodology for Studying the Semiotics of Securitization", presented at the International Studies Association Conference, Montreal, 16–19 March.

—— (2011c) *How to Do Security with Words. A Grammar of Securitisation in the People's Republic of China*, Turku: University of Turku Press.

Wacquant, L. (1989) "Towards a Reflexive Sociology: an Interview with Pierre Bourdieu", *Sociological Theory*, 7(1): 26–63.

—— (2002) "The Sociological Life of Pierre Bourdieu", *International Sociology*, 17(4): 549–556.

—— (2007) "Pierre Bourdieu", in R. Stones (ed.) *Key Sociological Thinkers*, 2nd edn, New York: Palgrave Macmillan.

Wæver, O. (1995) "Securitization and Desecuritization", in R.D. Lipschutz (ed.) *On Security*, New York: Columbia University Press.

—— (1998) "The Sociology of a Not So International Discipline: American and European Developments in International Relations", *International Organization*, 52(4): 687–727.

—— (1999) "Securitizing Sectors?: Reply to Eriksson", *Cooperation and Conflict*, 34(3): 334–340.

—— (2002) "Identity, Communities and Foreign Policy: Discourse Analysis as Foreign Policy Theory", in L. Hansen and O. Wæver (eds) *European Identity and National Identity: The Challenge of the Nordic States*, New York: Routledge.

—— (2004) "Aberystwyth, Paris, Copenhagen: New 'Schools' in Security Theory and their Origins Between Core and Periphery", presented at the International Studies Association Conference, Montreal.

—— (2008) "Peace and Security: Two Evolving Concepts and their Changing Relationship", in H.G. Brauch, Ú.O. Spring, C. Mesjasz, J. Grin, P. Dunay, N.C. Behera, B. Chorou, P. Kameri-Mbote and P.H. Liotta (eds) *Globalization and Environmental Challenges: Reconceptualizing Security in the 21st Century*, New York: Springer.

—— (2009) "Waltz's Theory of Theory", *International Relations*, 23(2): 201–222.

Wahab, S. (2003) "Creating Knowledge Collaboratively with Female Sex Workers: Insights from a Qualitative, Feminist, and Participatory Study", *Qualitative Inquiry*, 9(4): 625–642.

Walker, R.B.J. (1993) *Inside/Outside: International Relations as Political Theory*, Cambridge: Cambridge University Press.

Walkerdine, V. et al. (2010) *Reflections on the Researching Affect and Affective Communication Network and Seminar Series*. Online: www.cardiff.ac.uk/socsi/newsandevents/events/innovation/seminar6/combined.document.doc (accessed 15 February 2012).

Walt, S. (1991) "The Renaissance of Security Studies", *International Studies Quarterly*, 35(2): 211–239.

Walters, W. (2002) "The Power of Inscription: Beyond Social Construction and Deconstruction in European Integration Studies", *Millennium: Journal of International Studies*, 3(1): 83–108.

—— (2006) "Border/Control", *European Journal of Social Theory*, 9(2): 187–203.

—— (2008) "Putting the Migration–Security Complex in its Place", in L. Amoore and M. de Goede (eds) *Risk and the War on Terror*, New York: Routledge.

—— (2010) "Migration and Security", in J.P. Burgess (ed.) *The Routledge Handbook of New Security Studies*, New York: Routledge.

—— (2011) "Rezoning the Global: Technological Zones, Technological Work and the (Un-)making of Biometric Borders" in V. Squire (ed.) *The Contested Politics of Mobility: Borderzones and Irregularity*. New York: Routledge.

Waltz, K.N. (1979) *Theory of International Politics*, London: McGraw-Hill.

Webb, J., Schirato, T., and Danaher, G. (2002) *Understanding Bourdieu*, London: SAGE Publications.

Weber, C. (1994) "Good Girls, Little Girls, and Bad Girls: Male Paranoia in Robert Keohane's Critique of Feminist International Relations", *Millennium: Journal of International Studies*, 23(2): 337–349.

—— (2001) "The Highs and Lows of Teaching IR Theory: Using Popular Films for Theoretical Critique", *International Studies Perspectives*, 2(3): 281–287.

—— (2005) *International Relations Theory: A Critical Introduction*, New York: Routledge.

—— (2006) *Imagining America at War – Morality, Politics, and Film*, New York: Routledge.

Wedeen, L. (2009) "Ethnography as Interpretative Enterprise", in E. Schatz (ed.) *Political Ethnography: What Immersion Contributes to the Study of Power*, Chicago: Chicago University Press.

—— (2010) "Reflections of Ethnographic Work in Political Science", *Annual Review of Politics*, 13: 255–272.

Weeks, G. (2006) "Facing Failure: The Use (and Abuse) of Rejection in Political Science", *PS: Political Science and Politics*, 39(4): 879–882.

Weldes, J. (1999) "Going Cultural: Star Trek, State Action, and Popular Culture", *Millennium: Journal of International Studies*, 28(1): 117–134.

—— (2003) *To Seek Out New Worlds: Science Fiction and World Politics*, New York: Palgrave.

Wendt, A. (1999) *Social Theory of International Politics*, Cambridge: Cambridge University Press.

White, Josh (2005) *You're (Virtually) in the Army Now: And Recruiters Hope the Real Thing Is Next*, Chicago Tribune. Online: http://articles.chicagotribune.com/2005-06-01/news/0506010360_1_potential-recruits-game-web-site-multiplayer (accessed 14 June 2011).

Widdowfield, R. (2000) "The Place of Emotions in Academic Research", *Area*, 32(2): 199–208.

Wierzbicka, A. (1991) *Cross-Cultural Pragmatics: The Semantics of Human Interaction*, New York: Mouton de Gruyter.

Wight, C. (2002) "The Philosophy of Social Science and International Relations", in W. Carlsnaes, T. Risse, and B. Simmonds (eds), *Handbook of International Relations*, 2nd edn, London: SAGE Publications.

Wilkinson, P., and Jenkins, B.M. (eds) (1999) *Aviation Terrorism and Security*, New York: Frank Cass.

Williams, M.C. (1999) "The Practices of Security: Critical Contributions: Reply to Eriksson", *Cooperation and Conflict*, 34(3): 341–344.

—— (2003) "Words, Images, Enemies: Securitization and International Relations", *International Studies Quarterly*, 47(4): 511–531.

—— (2007) *Culture and Security: Symbolic Power and the Politics of International Security*, New York: Routledge.

Wintour, P. and MacAskill, E. (2011) "Is Muammar Gaddafi a Target? PM and Military Split over War Aims". *The Guardian Online*, 22 March 2011, www.guardian.co.uk/world/2011/mar/21/muammar-gaddafi-david-cameron-libya (accessed 4 July 2012).

Woliver, L.R. (2002) "Ethical Dilemmas in Personal Interviewing", *PS: Political Science and Politics*, 35(4): 677–678.

Wong, Leonard, Kolditz, Col. Thomas A., Millen, Lt. Col. Raymond A., and Potter, Col. Terrence M. (2003) *Why They Fight: Combat Motivation in War*. U.S. Army. Online: www.strategicstudies institute.army.mil/pdffiles/PUB179.pdf (accessed 5 April 2006).

Wood, E.J. (2006) "The Ethical Challenges of Field Research in Conflict Zones", *Qualitative Sociology,* 29(3): 307–341.

Wright, C. (2003) "Moments of Emergence: Organizing by and with Undocumented and Non-citizen People in Canada after September 11", *Refuge: Canada's Periodical on Refugees*, 21(3): 5–15.

Wright, C. and Fayle, C.E. (1928) *A History of Lloyd's, From the Founding of Lloyd's Coffee House to the Present Day*, London: Macmillan and Company Ltd.

Yamineva, Y. (2010) *The Assessment Process of the Intergovernmental Panel on Climate Change: A Post-Normal Approach*, Cambridge: Centre of International Studies, Cambridge University.

Yanow, D. (2000) *Conducting Interpretive Policy Analysis*, London: SAGE Publications.

—— (2003) "Assessing Local Knowledge", in H.M.A. Wagenar (ed.) *Deliberative Policy Analysis: Understanding Governance in the Network Society*, Cambridge: Cambridge University Press.

—— (2006) "Philosophical Presuppositions and the Human Sciences", in D. Yanow, and P. Schwartz-Shea (eds) *Interpretation and Method*, Armok: M.E. Sharpe.

—— (2009) "Dear Author, Dear Reader: The Third Hermeneutic in Writing and Reviewing Ethnography", in E. Schatz (ed.) *Political Ethnography: What Immersion Contributes to the Study of Power*, Chicago: University of Chicago Press.

Young, I.M. (1990) *Throwing Like a Girl and Other Essays in Feminist Philosophy and Social Theory*, Bloomington: Indiana University Press.

—— (2005) *On Female Body Experience*, New York: Oxford University Press.

Zalewski, M. (1996) "'All These Theories yet the Bodies Keep Piling Up': Theory, Theorists, Theorizing", in K. Booth, S. Smith, and M. Zalewski (eds) *International Relations: Positivism and Beyond*, Cambridge: Cambridge University Press.

—— (2000) *Feminism after Postmodernism: Theorising through Practice*, New York: Routledge.

Zillman, J. (2007) "Some Observations on the IPCC Assessment Process 1988–2007", *Energy and Environment*, 18(7/8): 869–892.

Zito, A., and Barlow, T. (1994) *Body, Subject and Power in China*, Chicago: University of Chicago Press.

Index

access 4, 13, 21, 22, 31, 33, 44, 55, 74–75,
107–108, 122, 134; to information 20, 47,
76–77, 115, 116, 121, 125, 126, 131, 143,
163, 193, 196–197; to subjects 11, 17, 18, 35,
64–65, 67–68, 105–106, 175, 193
actor 3, 16, 30, 31,63, 67, 70, 76, 77, 79, 85, 88,
93, 95, 103, 106, 107, 116, 124, 125–126,
130, 132, 141, 151, 156, 174, 186–188, 192,
197
actant 1, 8–9, 12, 20, 151, 173–176, 178–179;
non-human 170, 174, 178, 182, 204
actor network theory 8–9, 173–175, 192
advocacy 38, 40, 65, 88, 89, 99,
aesthetic 163, 200
affect 3, 7, 12, 16, 20, 60, 81, 139–142, 143,
145, 150–153, 163–164, 169, 172; definitions
of 141, 150, 156, 159; see also emotions
agency 2, 9, 16, 42, 65, 70, 97–98, 142, 146,
163, 170, 171–172, 176, 182, 197; of
non-human objects see actant
anthropology 13, 17, 34, 51, 53, 56, 59–60
archive 10, 11, 13, 16, 18–19, 20, 26–27, 51, 81,
86, 98, 102–103, 115–116, 118, 121–125,
126–127, 131, 142, 145, 159, 196, 197, 199
artifact 17, 61, 126, 129, 134, 135, 160, 178,
191, 195
assemblage 8, 12, 16, 20, 130, 149, 151,
173–176, 178, 183, 192, 203–206
asylum see mobility

Barad, K. 174, 182, 183–184
belief 2, 21, 64, 85, 86–87, 98, 100, 101–102,
105, 129, 131, 137, 158, 179; see also doxa
Bennett, J. 8, 139, 164, 172–175, 178–179, 183,
184, 204,
Bigo, D. 4, 17, 76–77, 86, 88–90, 191,
biopolitics 170, 183; biometrics 103, 170, 176,
184, 195,
body 4, 6, 7, 20, 35, 73, 74, 75, 140–144, 146,
149, 159, 165–168, 169–172; in IR 12, 139,
162–164, 166, 171

border 67–70, 98, 103, 105, 110–112, 129, 132,
150–151, 184, 187
Bourdieu, P. 3, 4–5, 9, 11, 13, 16, 20, 22, 77,
85–89, 93–96, 105, 128, 150–151
Butler, J. 7–8, 139, 141, 163, 176,

Campbell, D. 6, 113, 114, 157, 162, 165
Citizenship 6, 12, 97–100; see also mobility
Clarity 1, 11, 13, 15, 16, 37, 38, 105, 145, 176
Clifford, J. 60, 82
Collaboration 10, 46–49, 86–87, 98–99,
158–160, 171
colonialism 7, 22, 53, 82, 139; post-colonialism
8, 12, 63
Connolly, W. 3, 7, 139, 140, 151 see also
emergent causality
Copenhagen School see Securitization Theory
corporeal 1, 7, 12, 13, 16, 17, 20, 139–140,
142–146, 152, 156–157, 169–170, 172, 174,
176
criticality 1–4, 9, 10, 15, 18, 25, 29–31, 40, 48,
52–54, 87, 90, 100, 108, 110, 111, 130, 133,
158, 170, 181, 196–198, ; critical security
studies 1, 34, 42–5, 52, 55, 127, 141, 143,
192
culture 3, 13, 15, 18, 51–52, 56, 73, 85, 134,
204

deconstruction 17, 77, 109, 113, 130,
177–178
Deleuze, G. 102, 104, 151
Der Derian, J. 4, 53, 54–55, 57, 111, 113, 114
development 12, 26, 28, 54, 64–65; of
knowledge 29–30, 63
disciplinarity 10, 13, 17, 26, 27, 34, 36, 37, 42,
51, 86, 94, 113, 165, 171
discourse 3, 9, 18, 20–21, 39, 43, 51, 85, 87, 89,
98, 101, 113–118, 126–128, 130, 134, 140,
142, 146, 152, 171, 174, 178, 184, 187, 188,
196, 198–200
dispositif 11, 17, 102–104, 128, 175, 182, 183

document 11, 17, 43, 48, 89, 98, 101, 103,
106–107, 113–118, 123, 126, 130–132, 144,
145, 150, 163, 171, 178, 182–184, 188, 193,
196–198; *see also* discourse
doxa 4, 19, 85; *see also* culture

emergence 5, 26, 38, 47–48, 103, 114, 151, 162,
167–168, 173, 175–176, 178, 183
emergent causality 2, 3, 16–17, 23,149; *see also*
Connolly W.
emotion 1, 7, 10, 16, 20, 34–36, 53, 61, 68, 74,
81, 139, 141, 143, 145–146, 149, 152,
154–157, 159–160, 174, 176, 200; *see also*
affect
empirics 2–4, 10, 15, 17, 20, 25, 28, 38–40,
42–45, 55–56, 59, 62–63, 87–90, 94–95, 101,
103, 108, 126, 129–130, 133–134, 136,
145–146, 150, 167, 169, 171, 182, 191, 199,
201–202
Enloc, C. 52, 55, 61, 72, 79, 142, 165, 166
ethics 12, 17, 20–22, 35, 47, 53–54, 56–57,
59–60, 65–66, 74, 79, 82, 129, 132, 142,
144–145, 163, 171–172, 196, 198, 204
ethnography 10–13, 15–17, 18–22, 34–35, 40,
51–57, 59–62, 63–66, 67–71, 72–75, 76–79,
80–83, 115–116; 158–160, 171, 174, 176,
178, 190; auto-ethnography 107–108, 140,
141, 146
everyday 4, 8, 31, 52, 54–55, 60, 62, 68, 70, 72,
75, 88, 100, 106–107, 114–115, 125, 135,
149, 158–159, 167, 171, 173, 176, 178–179,
190, 203
exceptionalism 8, 11, 16, 25, 34, 52, 113–115,
117–118, 125–127, 140, 145, 156, 178,
expert 11, 22, 42, 56, 63, 77, 94, 101, 106, 108,
109–112, 130–132, 145, 150, 159, 181, 182;
expertise 105, 107, 129, 161, 189–190, 204

failure 9, 10, 13, 22, 23, 36, 52, 65, 73, 77–78,
108–111, 118, 131, 134, 144, 154
field 4, 5, 7, 9, 11, 15, 51, 57, 86–90, 93–95,
105–108, 110–111, 115, 117, 134, 144, 150,
156; empirical field 2, 10, 15, 17, 56
field analysis 3, 10, 16, 17, 18, 20, 22, 55, 85,
98, 106, 116, 176
fieldwork 33, 34, 35, 54, 59–61, 63–64, 67, 69,
72–75, 76–79, 80–83, 105, 142, 158–161,
169–172, 204
Foucault, M. 5–6, 7, 17, 18, 21–23, 25, 38, 44,
59–60, 63, 77, 101–103, 113–114, 123, 125,
128, 130, 159, 163–164, 167, 182, 183, 187,
198, 203–205
framing 2, 13, 36, 39, 57, 96, 110, 111, 118, 152,
160, 191, 201

gender 7, 12, 20, 21, 29, 35, 55, 63–64, 67, 73,
75, 80, 83, 85, 135, 142, 150–152, 163, 166

genealogy 2, 5, 6, 8, 13, 15, 17, 101, 105, 113,
114, 130, 176, 181, 183, 192, 196, 198
geography 34, 113, 139, 183, 194
governmentality 6, 63, 64, 149, 171

habitus 3, 4, 11, 16, 55, 77, 85–90, 94, 98,
105–106, 108, 149–151, 159
hermeneutics 33–35, 79, 114

identity 7, 17, 22, 23, 30, 31, 35, 42, 51, 55, 64,
70, 73, 74, 114, 118, 134, 139, 151, 155,
159, 165, 166, 170, 174, 176
immigration *see mobility*
international political sociology 12, 86, 90,
179
intersubjectivity 150, 151, 152, 155, 156,
interview 10, 17, 18, 33, 35, 36, 39–40, 51, 54,
60, 63–66, 67–70, 78, 81–82, 85–86, 88–89,
95–96, 98, 106, 109, 110, 113, 117, 118, 122,
131, 140, 142, 144, 159, 160, 163, 169,
171–172, 177–178, 188, 190, 205

Jackson, P.T. 36, 74, 86

Kant, I. 43, 101, 104, 141

Latour, B. 8–9, 13, 151, 173–175, 178–179, 182,
186–188, 192
Law, J. 8, 16, 173, 174, 188, 198
legislation 10, 11, 16, 107–108, 116, 187, 189;
counter-terror 16, 20, 125–128

Massumi, B. 17, 139–141, 149–151
materiality 3, 8–9, 12–13, 17, 19–20, 149, 164,
173–179, 181–185, 186–190, 191–194,
195–198 203–205; *see also* new materialism
metaphor 12, 18, 79, 114, 116, 118, 167, 168,
187, 189, 202
mess 2, 13, 16, 17, 38, 39, 40, 102, 130, 136,
165, 198, 204; *see also* Law, J.
migration *see* mobility
military 4, 21, 22, 53, 54, 57, 60, 73–75, 77, 101,
103, 114, 114, 130, 139, 149, 166, 168, 188,
191–196, 200; base 11, 55, 56
mobility 11, 12, 68, 70, 103, 176, 178, 179,
205; (anti-)deportation 12, 35, 69, 97–99,
asylum 22, 67–70, 118, 169–171; control 20,
67–68, 70, 74, 76–78, 170–171, 184; refugee
12, 20, 67–70, 97–100, 131–132, 162,
169–170

narrative 5, 11, 16, 17, 27, 36, 53, 55, 61, 67–70,
73, 82, 101–103, 114–116, 123–124, 158,
160, 167, 171
Neumann, I. 20, 51, 52, 74, 114, 116, 119
new materialism 3, 8, 12; *see also* actor network
theory; materialism

norm 1, 4, 6, 16, 18, 19, 34, 85, 86, 106, 117, 133, 140, 167, 170, 176, 197; gender norms 7, 12, 163

object *see* actant
observation 9, 20, 40, 70, 89, 183, 205

Paris School 76; *see also* field analysis, international political sociology
participant observation 9, 15, 18, 19, 39, 40, 51, 54, 60, 68, 73, 75, 76, 78, 85–86, 88–89, 98, 140–142, 144, 160, 171, 173, 175, 177–178
performativity 7, 8, 113, 163–164, 175, 179; *see also* Butler J.
policy 4, 11, 17, 53, 59, 68, 87–89, 94–95, 98, 105–108, 109–111, 113–115, 126–127, 130–131, 142, 144, 150, 156, 158, 160, 161, 165, 171–172, 176, 178, 182, 188, 191, 198, 201; *see also* legislation
population 6, 21, 66–67, 69–70, 81, 99, 130–132, 170, 181, 204
popular culture 7, 11, 19, 56, 194, 196
positivism 10, 13, 44, 88, 126, 181, 182; post-positivism 165, 196
postcolonialism *see* colonialism
power 1, 2, 5, 6, 12, 17, 20, 52, 64, 70, 77, 90, 104, 127, 133, 142, 159, 167, 170, 171, 192, 196, 203, 205; power relations 28, 34, 38, 43, 59, 61, 63, 69, 82, 109, 124, 126, 156, 165; sovereign power 3, 99, 102, 123
practice 1, 4, 6, 11, 13, 31, 37, 43, 60, 62, 68, 94, 105–108, 195; political practice 3, 30, 75; practice-turn 5, 86–91, 113, 115–116, 134, 140, 162, 174, 176, 179, 188; research practice 2, 8, 9, 10, 42, 55; security practice 3, 78, 118, 132, 149, 150, 152, 158
publication 10, 13, 21, 33, 49, 52, 59, 65, 86, 115, 130, 142, 155

Rancière, J. 100, 182, 202
Reflexivity 1, 3, 5, 15, 20–21, 23, 29–31, 34, 51, 52, 54, 56, 65, 74, 82, 116, 118, 142–143, 146, 152, 158, 162, 172, 176; self-reflexivity 4, 13, 16, 64, 78, 100, 102
refugee *see* mobility
representation 17, 18, 53, 60, 61, 68, 82, 94, 113,

118, 130, 140, 152, 155, 162, 166, 168, 181–182, 199, 201
research design 1, 3, 4, 5, 7, 9, 10, 13, 15–17, 20, 22, 25, 29, 30, 31, 33, 37, 39–40, 44, 46, 48, 54, 56, 63, 67, 77–78, 81–82, 101, 108, 110, 115, 140–142, 149, 154–155, 158–159, 169–172
rigor 1, 13, 18, 46, 101, 113, 143
risk 6, 27,43, 65, 69, 78, 81, 89, 90, 105–108, 111, 122, 127, 144, 149, 18–184, 193, 195, 204–205

Scarry, E. 17, 139, 143, 145
securitization theory 12, 20, 42, 57, 76, 97, 99, 108, 114, 115, 133–137, 141, 154–157, 177, 181, 182–184, 199–202
Shapiro, M. 104, 113, 114, 162
Sociology 4,8, 13, 17, 42, 44, 61, 106, 174, 179, 183, 196, 198
somatic 2, 3, 7, 12, 15, 18–20, 139–146, 151, 153, 163, 169, 172–173, 176
space 3, 30, 40, 47, 48, 65, 67–70, 73, 81, 86, 94, 99, 101, 103, 105, 106, 115, 121, 152, 161, 163, 171, 174, 184, 188, 192
subjectivity 7, 18, 30, 60, 67, 73, 80, 85, 99, 126, 142, 146, 156, 158, 176, 196, 198; intersubjectivity 7, 8, 30, 152, 155, 158, 161, 163, 203–205; subjectivization 6, 44, 61

technology 9, 26, 28, 48, 106, 130, 144, 150, 173–174, 176–177, 186, 190, 193–195, 200, 204

visuality 39, 47, 56, 113, 115, 116, 140, 141, 154, 156–157, 163, 172, 194, 199, 200–202
vulnerability 17, 18, 53, 67, 69, 74, 135, 145, 181

Walters, W. 176, 187, 192, 196
Wæver, O. 42, 43, 52, 57, 105, 114, 119, 133–135, 137, 171, 191
Williams, M.C. 5, 14, 17, 57, 88, 105
Writing 2, 3, 9, 10, 11, 16, 17, 33, 36, 47–49, 52–55, 59–62, 75, 82, 89, 93–96, 104, 197

Yanow, D. 33, 36, 158, 159, 160, 161